What Does the Minimum Wage Do?

Dale Belman
Paul J. Wolfson

2014

W.E. Upjohn Institute for Employment Research
Kalamazoo, Michigan

Library of Congress Cataloging-in-Publication Data

Belman, Dale.
  What does the minimum wage do? / Dale Belman, Paul J. Wolfson.
    pages cm
  ISBN 978-0-88099-456-9 (pbk. : alk. paper) — ISBN 0-88099-456-8 (pbk. : alk.
paper) — ISBN 978-0-88099-457-6 (hardcover : alk. paper) — ISBN 0-88099-457-6
(hardcover : alk. paper)
    1. Minimum wage—United States. 2. Working poor—United States. 3. Poverty—
United States. 4. Minimum wage. 5. Working poor. 6. Poverty I. Wolfson, Paul J.
II. Title.
  HD4918.B45 2014
  331.2'30973—dc23
                                    2014012215

The facts presented in this study and the observations and viewpoints expressed are
the sole responsibility of the authors. They do not necessarily represent positions of
the W.E. Upjohn Institute for Employment Research.

Cover design by Alcorn Publication Design.
Indexes prepared by Diane Worden.
Printed in the United States of America.
Printed on recycled paper.

What Does the Minimum Wage Do?

To my family, Sarah, Jesse, and Margie, for whom
my minimum wage has been love and devotion.

–PJW

Thanks to Amy, Livia, and Aaron for their patience
with the demands of the book and occasional lectures
during dinner. Love to each of you.

–DLB

Contents

Acknowledgments   xiii

Abbreviations   xv

1 Introduction   1
Minimum Wage and the Distribution of Hourly Earnings   3
Three Labor Market Models Used in New Minimum Wage Research   10
An Overview of the Book   15

Part 1: Micro

2 Employment   21
Early New Minimum Wage Research   21
The New Minimum Wage Research Since 2000   31
U.S. Studies   32
Other Developed Countries   77
The Timing of the Employment Response   102
Conclusion   107

3 Hours of Employment   119
U.S. Studies   120
Other Developed Countries   131
Summing Up   141

4 Meta-Analysis   147
A Brief Survey of Recent Prior Work   149
The Data   151
Metaregressions—Part 1   159
Metaregressions—Part 2   165
Conclusion   176

5 Wages and Earnings   183
Measuring the Effects of the Minimum Wage   184
Wage Distribution   186
Sectoral and Industry Studies   211
Workers Who Are Bound by the New Minimum Wage   223
Spillover Effects   236
Conclusion   249

6 Human Capital   259
The Logic of Individual and Firm Investment in Human Capital   260
Human Capital and the Minimum Wage   262
The Effect of the Minimum Wage on School Enrollment: Theory   263
and Findings
The Minimum Wage and Employer-Supplied Training: Theory   280
and Findings
The Minimum Wage and Employer-Provided Benefits: Health Care   288
and Pensions
Summary   294

7 Poverty and Inequality   301
Inequality and the Distribution of Wages   301
The Effect of the Minimum Wage on Poverty and   308
Economic Inequality
How Long Do Minimum Wage Earners Continue to Earn the   326
Minimum Wage?
Conclusion   336

Part 2: Macro

8 Gross Flows in the Labor Market   343
Data Issues   345
Studies of Gross Flows That Lean Heavily on Specific Labor   348
Market Models
Studies of Gross Flows That Are Agnostic about Labor Market   355
Models
Discussions of Findings on Separations and Accessions   356

9 Labor Force Participation Rate, Unemployment, and Vacancies   365
Labor Force Participation   368
The Unemployment Rate   370
Unemployment Duration   375
Vacancies   377
Conclusion   379

10 The Product Market   383
Prices   384
Output   392
Profitability   392

11 Conclusion   401
   A Summary of Our Findings   401
   What We Know with Confidence   405
   Big Ideas   406
   Issues of Innovation and Craftsmanship   410
   Intended Consequences   411

Appendix A: Data Sources and Variables   413

References   425

Authors   447

Author Index   449

Subject Index   457

About the Institute   471

Figures

1.1   Competitive Labor Market with a Minimum Wage   10
1.2   Monopsony Labor Market with No Minimum Wage   13
1.3   Monopsony Labor Market with a Minimum Wage   13

4.1   Employment and Hours Elasticities vs. Precision   154
4.2   Distinguishing between Reliable and Unreliable Standard Errors: 155
         Employment and Hours Elasticities vs. Precision
4.3   Eating and Drinking Places and Youth: Employment and Hours   156
         Elasticities vs. Precision
4.4   Distinguishing between Quasi-Experiments and (Other)   157
         Regressions: Employment and Hours Elasticities vs. Precision

5.1   Kernel Density Estimate of Hourly Wages   193
5.2   Kernel Density Estimates of the Ratio of Hourly Earnings to the   195
         Applicable Minimum Wage
5.3   Kernel Density Estimate of Average Hourly Earnings, 1981   197
5.4   Distribution of Hourly Wages in the United Kingdom, 1998–2004   228
5.5   Increase in Percentile Gross Hourly Earnings Excluding   230
         Overtime Minus Increase in the Median, Male Employees
         (Aged 22 and Over), 1992–2003

5.6	Increase in Percentile Gross Hourly Earnings Excluding Overtime Minus Increase in the Median, Female Employees (Aged 22 and Over), 1992–2003	230
5.7	Increase in Percentile Gross Hourly Earnings Excluding Overtime Minus Increase in the Median, Full-Time Employees (Aged 22 and Over), 1992–2003	231
5.8	Increase in Percentile Gross Hourly Earnings Excluding Overtime Minus Increase in the Median, Part-Time Employees (Aged 22 and Over), 1992–2003	231

Tables

1.1	The Distribution of Hourly Wages and Hourly Earnings in 2010 for Individuals Not Enrolled in High School or College	5
1.2	How the Minimum Wage Relates to Measures of Income Adequacy	8
2.1	Youth (Panels, U.S. Data)	34
2.2	Youth (Individual-Level Data, U.S. Data)	40
2.3	Youth (Simpler Data Structures, U.S. Data)	48
2.4	Other Groups (U.S. Data)	52
2.5	Restaurants and Hotels (U.S. Data)	62
2.6	Other Low-Wage Sectors (U.S. Data)	73
2.7	Youth (Other Developed Countries)	80
2.8	Other Low-Wage Groups (Other Developed Countries)	94
2.9	Studies of Industries (Other Developed Countries)	100
3.1	Youth (U.S. Data)	121
3.2	Other Groups (U.S. Data)	125
3.3	Studies of Industries (U.S. Data)	126
3.4	Youth (Foreign Data)	132
3.5	Other Groups (Foreign Data)	135
3.6	Studies of Industries (Foreign Data)	140
4.1	Studies Included in the Metaregression	152
4.2	Percentage of Observations in the Left and Right Tails	158
4.3	Preliminary Meta-Estimates of the Minimum Wage Elasticity, b_1	161
4.4	Meta-Estimates of the Minimum Wage Elasticity of Employment, b_1, When a Correction for Publication Bias Is Included	164
4.5	Meta-Estimates of the Minimum Wage Elasticity of Employment and Hours	168

4.6 Meta-Estimates of the Minimum Wage Elasticity of Employment 173
and Hours for Models with Controls for Youth and Eating and
Drinking Places

4.7 Meta-Estimates of the Minimum Wage Elasticity of Employment 174
and Hours for Models with Controls for Youth and Eating and
Drinking Places

5.1 The Distribution of Hourly Wages and Hourly Earnings by Dollar 187
Amount, 2010

5.2 The Distribution of Hourly Wages and Hourly Earnings by 189
Percentile, 2010

5.3 The Distribution of Hourly Wages and Earnings Relative to the 190
Minimum Wage, 2010

5.4 The Effect of the Minimum Wage on Average Wages, Vulnerable 202
Groups: Teens

5.5 The Effect of the Minimum Wage on Average Wages, Vulnerable 206
Groups: Other

5.6 The Effect of the Minimum Wage on Average Wages 209

5.7 The Effect of the Minimum Wage on Average Wages: Restaurants 214

5.8 The Effect of the Minimum Wage on Average Wages: Service 218
Industries

5.9 The Effect of the Minimum Wage on Average Wages: Studies of 221
the United Kingdom

5.10 The Effect of the Minimum Wage on Those Bound by the 224
New Minimum Wage

5.11 The Effects of Minimum Wage Increases in California, 1994–1999 226

5.12 The Effect of the Minimum Wage on Those Bound by the New 233
Minimum Longitudinal Studies

5.13 Spillover Effects: The Effect of the Minimum Wage on Those 240
Earning More but Close to the New Minimum Wage

6.1 Schooling and Human Capital 264

6.2 Firm-Provided Training 284

6.3 The Minimum Wage and Benefits 292

7.1 The Effect of the Minimum Wage on the Distribution of Wages 304

7.2 Poverty Thresholds for 2010 by Size of Family and Number of 311
Related Children under 18 Years ($, 2010)

7.3 Labor Force Status in 2006 by Family Income in 2005 314

7.4 Statistical Studies of the Minimum Wage and Poverty 318

7.5 Simulation Studies of the Minimum Wage and Poverty 322

7.6   Studies of the Minimum Wage and Antipoverty Policies   324
7.7   The Dynamics of Minimum Wage Earners: How Long Do Those   328
      Earning the Minimum Wage Remain Close to the Minimum?
7.8   Share of Population in Minimum Wage or Near-Minimum Wage   330
      Jobs by Years into Career
7.9   The Dynamics of the Minimum Wage   332
7.10 The Dynamics of Minimum Wage Earners: How Is Wage Growth   335
      Affected by Receiving the Minimum Wage?

8.1   Gross Labor Flows   346
8.2   Changes in Teen Shares in Gross Flows in Portugal Following   352
      the 1987 Minimum Wage Increase
8.3   Gross Flows for Teens and Adults in Portugal Following the   353
      1987 Minimum Wage Increase (%)
8.4   Estimated Elasticities   354

9.1   Labor Force Definitions   366
9.2   Labor Force Measures   367
9.3   Labor Force Participation Response   369
9.4   Unemployment Rate/Duration   372
9.5   Vacancies   378

10.1 Prices   384
10.2 Profitability and Failure Rates   394

Acknowledgments

We wish to express our sincere thanks to Tim Bartik and Kevin Hollenbeck of the Upjohn Institute for Employment Research for their guidance and patience with this long effort. We are particularly indebted to Tim Butcher, chief economist at the UK Low Pay Commission, and Felix Ritchie, professor at the University of the West England, for providing the data needed to reproduce graphics in their reports. Also, thanks to the participants in the Upjohn Institute seminar in March 2010 on the minimum wage and the Meta-Analysis of Economic Research Network Colloquium in September 2013 for comments and insights. Particular thanks are owed to Kritkorn Nawakitphaitoon, a former gradate student in the School of Human Resources and Labor Relations at Michigan State University, now a professor at Renmin University in Beijing, for assembling the data on the overwhelming number of articles reviewed in this book, and for an almost equal amount that was dropped from the review. And, of course, deepest thanks to Allison Colosky not only for her help in thinking through the book and for working with us on the rewriting and editing of the manuscript, but also for her boundless patience and good humor.

Abbreviations

ACS: American Community Survey
ASHE: Annual Survey of Hours and Earnings
BHPS: British Household Panel Survey
BLS: Bureau of Labor Statistics
BLS-CES: Bureau of Labor Statistics-Current Establishment Survey
CPS: Current Population Survey
CSE: Confederation of Swedish Enterprise
CRSP: Center for Research in Security Prices
EE: Enrolled and employed
EITC: Earned Income Tax Credit
ENE: Enrolled in school but not employed
EOPP: Employment Opportunities Pilot Projects
EPAS: Economically Active Population Survey
EPI: Economic Policy Institute
FAME: Financial Analysis Made Easy
FSI: French Statistical Institute
FTE: Full-time equivalent
GPEU: Geographic Profile of Employment and Unemployment
HLFS: Household Labour Force Survey
IRSs: Impulse response functions
IRG: Investment Research Group
IRS: Internal Revenue Service
IS: Income Survey
LFPR: Labor Force Participation Rate
LFS: Labour Force Survey
MCL: Marginal cost of labor
MPL: Marginal product of labor
MSA: Metropolitan statistical area
NAIRU: Nonaccelerating inflation rate of unemployment
NEE: Not enrolled but employed
NENE: Neither enrolled nor employed
NES: New Earnings Survey

(continued)

Abbreviations (*continued*)

NLSY: National Longitudinal Survey of Youth
NMW: National Minimum Wage
NMWR: New minimum wage research
OECD: Organisation for Economic Co-Operation and Development
OLS: Ordinary least squares
ORG: Outgoing Rotation Groups
PCC: Partial correlation coefficients
PCSE-PSAR: Panel-corrected standard errors, panel-specific AR1
    autocorrelation structure
REIS: Regional Economic Information System
SIPP: Survey of Income and Program Participation
SLID: Survey of Labour and Income Dynamics
QCEW: Quarterly Census of Employment and Wages
QE: Quasi experiment
QP: Quadros de Pessoal
QWI: Quarterly Workforce Indicators
VARs: Vector autoregressions
WERS: Workplace Employment Relations Survey

1
Introduction

The birth of the new minimum wage research (NMWR) can be dated to a conference at Cornell University held in late 1991 and the subsequent symposium that appeared in *Industrial and Labor Relations Review* (see Ehrenberg [1992] for a description of the conference and its attendees). The first period of this research came to a close nine years later. Prior to the conference, empirical research on the minimum wage had been dominated by studies that considered only the effect of the federal minimum wage on teenage employment, using aggregate time-series data. These earlier studies generally concluded that a 10 percent increase in the minimum wage is associated with a 1–3 percent decrease in teenage employment (Brown 1999). Energized by increases in the federal minimum wage in 1990, 1991, 1996, and 1997, researchers approached minimum wage issues through a variety of statistical frameworks, techniques, and data sources; explanatory economic models proliferated, as did the number of articles.

By the end of the first period in 2000, it was no longer possible to identify a dominant line of research. In this review, which primarily focuses on articles published from 2000 forward, we have considered more than 200 scholarly and policy papers relating to the minimum wage that have appeared in English since the conference. While a few are surveys, most are original analyses, and most of these are statistical in nature rather than presentations of theoretical models or survey results. This book is our attempt to make sense of the research.[1] We look at which observable, measurable variables (e.g., wages, employment, school enrollment) the minimum wage influences; how long it takes for the variables to respond to the minimum wage and the size and desirability of the effect; why the minimum wage has the results it does (and not others); and the workers most likely to be affected by changes to the minimum wage. Our emphasis is on studies that analyze data from the United States, but we also touch on studies of data from other countries: Canada, Australia, New Zealand, and the United Kingdom and other countries in Western Europe.

One set of issues revolves around who is affected by changes in the minimum wage. It is almost a given that those living in poverty are less likely to be affected than low-wage employees, since those below the poverty line, to a great extent, are not involved in the labor market (Freeman 1996). There remains an issue of who, among those who are employed and those who want to be employed, is affected when the minimum wage is increased. Among the employed, does the minimum wage affect only those who would be earning less than the minimum without it, or does it also affect those higher up the wage scale? Older minimum wage studies have generally focused on teenage workers—with their low skills and limited attachment to the labor market, it was thought that teenagers were most sensitive to the minimum wage and therefore any effect would be clearest here. While much of the NMWR examines what happens to teenagers when the minimum wage rises, many studies focus on other demographic groups with limited skills and labor market attachment, as well as workers identified specifically by their low wages, by membership in a specific demographic group (such as single mothers, young women, or immigrants), or by the industry in which they work (primarily hospitality and home care/nursing home).

Another issue relates to identifying the outcomes of minimum wage increases. As with earlier research, most NMWR focuses on the number of jobs or the probability of employment. However, there has been considerable expansion of issues, even within the realm of employment broadly defined. We review studies of the consequences for hours worked, turnover, unemployment, and labor force participation, along with studies of the effects on wages and their distribution, fringe benefits and training, prices and profitability, and the effect of the minimum wage on school enrollment.

The timing of effects of the minimum wage has become a recognized and challenging issue. How long it takes for the response to the minimum wage to play itself out is central to the effectiveness of policy. Before the NMWR, response to the minimum wage was thought to be nearly immediate. Most recent research also assumes that the response is rapid and examines only a short period immediately following an increase. Baker, Benjamin, and Stanger (1999), in a look at the Canadian experience with a minimum wage, argue that such assumptions result in missing much of the response, which can take up to six years. Studies of timing require careful attention to dynamics, which is generally absent in the NMWR. The few analyses of this issue (including some of our own work, such as Belman and Wolfson [2010]) suggest that the response is not entirely immediate but ends well before six years.

Assessing the size of effects is also important to understanding the minimum wage. By and large, the size of the impact of an increase in a minimum wage is related only to the issue of job loss, and the observations are all over the map. For over a decade, the minimum wage elasticity of employment was widely believed to be between -0.3 and -0.1, with greater faith in values closer to zero.[2] This accord no longer exists, with the range of estimates for U.S. teenagers extending "from well below -1.0 to well above zero" (Neumark and Wascher 2007, p. 107). In addition, the issue of the magnitude of the impact is composed of at least two distinct parts: 1) does the wide range of results apply to all outcomes or only to employment, and 2) are patterns in the magnitude of the response related to who is under study, the methods used in the study, measurement issues, or other factors?

Researchers have spent a great deal of effort developing models to explain the results just mentioned, but no agreement yet exists on which, if any, should replace the simple supply and demand model of the labor market that Stigler (1946) expounded. Card and Krueger (1995) devote a chapter to various theoretical models before leaning toward one in which employers have market power in the labor market, enabling them, up to a point, to set wages rather than take them as given by the market. They conclude that "this . . . is inconsistent with the proposition that the *standard* model is always correct" (p. 383). We take no stand on which model is most useful, much less settle the question. Rather, we present three general models discussed in the literature—the competitive labor market, the monopsony labor market, and search models of the labor market—and show how they relate to the issues at hand.

MINIMUM WAGE AND THE DISTRIBUTION OF HOURLY EARNINGS

As much as the minimum wage is an issue of importance in policy circles, few of those involved in the analysis or debate have had recent experience with the minimum wage. Many may have earned the minimum wage or close to the minimum wage when in high school or college, but that was typically many years ago. To many of those involved in this issue, the minimum wage would seem very low and unlikely to affect many in the labor force.

Contrary to this view, the minimum wage and jobs that pay close to the minimum wage play an important role in the U.S. labor force. Research reviewed in this monograph indicates that changes in the minimum wage affect 20–30 percent of the labor force. As such, considering minimum wage policies and their effect is more than a scholastic exercise—they may affect a large portion of the labor force. We consider in detail the place in the earnings distribution of the minimum wage itself and near minimum wage earnings in the chapter on wages and earnings, but we briefly discuss this now.

Table 1.1 provides three views on the importance of the minimum wage in the distribution of wages and hourly earnings. The first, panel A, considers the wages associated with points in the distribution of individual wages in 2010. Panel B displays the percentiles of the wage distribution associated with specific hourly wages. Panel C considers the proportion of the employed earning no more than a percentage of the minimum wage in their state. In each panel, the left-hand column of data is for individuals who are paid by the hour, and the right-hand column adds employed salaried workers. The distributions are limited to those who report that they are not enrolled in school. Individuals who report being enrolled in school are fairly evenly distributed across family incomes. By removing this group from our data, we improve the association between being employed near the minimum wage and being from a lower-income household, and thereby improve the association between the minimum wage and economic need.

Panel A displays the association between individuals' place in the national distribution of wages and the wage they earn. Those at the 5th percentile for wages or hourly earnings are very close to the federal minimum of $7.25 and below the minimum wage for some states. At the 10th percentile, those paid by the hour earn $8.00, 110 percent of the federal minimum wage; for all employees the 10th percentile is $8.50. Twenty percent of wage earners earn $9.25 or less; 20 percent of all employees earn $10.00 or less. Thirty percent of wage earners earn no more than $10.25, $3.00 per hour more than the federal minimum; the 30th percentile for all employees is $12.00. Considering the distribu-

Table 1.1 The Distribution of Hourly Wages and Hourly Earnings in 2010 for Individuals Not Enrolled in High School or College

	Panel A: Earnings by percentiles		Panel B: Percentiles by wage or hourly earnings		
Percentile	Wage of those paid hourly at this percentile ($)	Wage at this percentile including salaried workers ($)	Wage ($) or hourly earnings	Percent of those paid by the hour below	Percent below including salaried workers
5th	7.50	7.50	< 7.00	1.2	1.8
10th	8.00	8.50	< 7.51 (minimum wage)	4.7	4.1
20th	9.25	10.00	< 8.00 (1.10% of federal min.)	7.3	6.0
30th	10.25	12.00	< 9.00 (1.25% of federal min.)	16.7	12.5
40th	12.00	14.00	< 10.00	24.7	17.8
50th (median)	13.50	16.34	< 11.00 (150% of federal min.)	34.9	24.9

Panel C: The distribution of hourly wages and earnings relative to the effective minimum wage in 2010

	Percent of those paid by the hour below minimum wage	Percent below minimum wage including salaried workers
Less than the minimum wage	2.9	3.0
At the minimum wage	5.9	4.8
Less than 110% of the minimum wage	10.7	8.1
Less than 125% of the minimum wage	21.9	15.7
No more than 150% of the minimum wage	36.4	26.0

NOTE: Calculations of average hourly earnings (inclusive of salaried workers) does not include those who report variable hours.
SOURCE: Authors' calculations from the 2010 Outgoing Rotation File of the Current Population Survey.

tion for all employees, the more complete of the two distributions, only 1 in 20 employees works at or very close to the minimum wage, but 1 out of 10 employees who are not also students earn within $1.25 of the minimum wage, and 1 out of 5 employees who are not also students earn within $2.75 of the minimum wage.

Panel B provides a different view of the same data. Here we calculate the percentage of our sample who work at or below particular wage levels. For example, 4 percent of all employees (the right-hand data column) work at or below the federal minimum wage (allowing for rounding). Six percent earn no more than 1.1 times the federal minimum, 13 percent earn no more than 1.25 times the federal minimum wage, and 1 out of 4 employees work for no more than $11.00 per hour, 1.5 times the federal minimum wage. Research reviewed in this volume suggests that increases in the minimum wage affect the earnings of those in the lower quarter of the earnings distribution; and we might then expect that those earning up to $11 per hour would see their wages rise in response to the minimum wage.

A limitation of Panels A and B is that we compared wages to the federal minimum in a period when many states have minimum wages above the federal minimum wage. In Panel C we calculate the ratio of individuals' wages and hourly earnings with respect to the higher of the federal or state minimum wage, often called the *effective* minimum wage, and then create a distribution from this ratio. Again, focusing on the more complete distribution, that for all employees (right-hand column), 8 percent of the nonstudent workforce are employed in jobs paying no more than the minimum wage, 8 percent are in jobs paying no more than 1.1 times the minimum wage, 16 percent are paid no more than 1.25 times the effective minimum, and 25 percent are paid no more than 1.5 times the effective minimum. The proportion earning no more than each of the levels above the effective minimum is, of course, substantially higher for those on hourly pay. Again, although the proportion of employees earning exactly the minimum wage is modest, the proportion earning close to the minimum wage comprises a substantial proportion of the labor force. Given evidence that increases in the minimum wage extend to some of those whose earnings are above the new minimum wage, and that the minimum wage is a benchmark for those earning above the minimum, the minimum wage can affect a substantial proportion of the employed labor force.[3]

Another view to consider is the ability of those earning the minimum wage to meet their basic needs. To do this, we consider a household with either one or two individuals working full time at the minimum wage, and compare its total earnings to three standards of income adequacy: 1) the poverty line, 2) the income limit for qualifying for food stamps, and 3) a basic family budget provided by the Economic Policy Institute (EPI) (Bernstein and Lin 2008). The latter measure updates a budget developed by the Bureau of Labor Statistics, which compiled the costs of essentials such as housing, transportation, food, and like items. We also consider a household with one or two members earning 150 percent of the minimum wage, a point near the upper limit at which wages respond to changes in the minimum wage.

The upper panel of Table 1.2 provides calculations of family income with one and two earners who earn either the minimum wage or 150 percent of the minimum wage. In the first row, the household has either one or two earners working full time, 2000 hours, at the current federal minimum wage. If there is only one earner, the annual earnings for a 2,000-hour work year are $14,500; if two, $29,000. The second row provides annual household income if a household has one or two individuals working full time in positions that pay 150 percent of the minimum wage. In this case, household earnings are $21,750 and $43,500, respectively.

The second, middle panel, considers two common measures of income adequacy, the poverty line and food stamp eligibility, for families of between one and four members.[4] Poverty thresholds are used to evaluate the extent of serious economic deprivation in our society and determine eligibility for income maintenance programs. To establish the adequacy of the minimum wage in providing an income that moves households beyond this threshold, we can compare our annual earnings estimates from the upper panel to the poverty threshold for households of various sizes. For example, comparing the 2012 federal poverty threshold to our annual income calculations for households earning exactly the minimum wage, we find that a single-earner household is above the poverty line for a single-person household, at the poverty line for a two-person household with no other income, and below the poverty line for a three- or four-person household. With two minimum wage earners, the household income is well above the poverty line for even a four-person family. A household with one member employed

**Table 1.2 How the Minimum Wage Relates to Measures of Income
Adequacy**

Family earnings if family members work 2,000 hours		
	One earner ($)	Two earners ($)
Earners employed full time at minimum wage	14,500	29,000
Earners employed at 150% of the federal minimum wage	21,750	43,500

Measures of income adequacy				
Number of family members	1	2	3	4
Federal poverty threshold ($, 2011)	10,890	14,710	18,530	22,350
Food Stamp eligibility ($)	14,157	19,123	24,089	29,055

Low family budget (2007)				
	1 adult, 1 child	1 adult, 2 children	2 adults, 1 child	2 adults, 2 children
Utah (rural) ($)	26,089	32,961	33,358	39,125
Utah (Salt Lake City) ($)	31,898	38.769	37,933	43,499

SOURCE: Bernstein and Lin (2008). Food Stamp eligibility guidelines: http://www
.fns.usda.gov/snap/eligibility#income (accessed March 18, 2014). Health and Human
Services poverty guidelines: http://aspe.hhs.gov/poverty/11poverty.shtml (accessed
March 18, 2014).

full time at 150 percent of the minimum wage comes close to exceeding
the poverty line for a family of four, and, with two earners, household
income is well in excess of the poverty line for even a family of four.

Food stamp eligibility is a second measure of whether a family is
earning enough to avoid serious economic deprivation.[5] A one-member
household whose member earns the minimum wage is only $343 above
the income limit for food stamps. Larger households without additional
earners are between $4,623 and $14,555 below the limit on food stamp
eligibility. Households with the income from two people earning just
the minimum wage are slightly below the limit (that is, eligible for food
stamps) if they have four members, and above the limit with only three.
A household with a single earner who earns 150 percent of the minimum wage (at 40 hours per week or 2,000 hours per year) is below the
food stamp limit for a household of three or more. The household of

four is not eligible for food stamps if it has two full-time earners with wages equal to 150 percent of the minimum wage. Just as in the case of the poverty line, full-time earnings at the minimum wage help move a household above the threshold, and earnings of 150 percent of the minimum wage on an annual basis substantially improves the likelihood that a household would be above the threshold for food stamps.

An alternative measure is a basic family budget, the income a family needs to secure safe and decent-yet-modest living standards. The Bureau of Labor Statistics developed the basic family budget as part of a broader set of standard-of-living measures, which were published annually from 1966 to 1979 (the program was discontinued after 1979; see Johnson, Rogers, and Tan [2001]). The basic family budget is the income that a household needs for a nutritionally adequate diet, shelter, clothing, and transportation. The EPI updated this basic budget in 2007. It includes the cost of health insurance, renting shelter at the 40th percentile of the rental housing distribution in the area, child care, limited necessities, and taxes, but it does not include savings of any type, restaurant meals, emergency funds, or insurance to cover emergencies. EPI calculates this budget for rural areas and for the metropolitan statistical areas of each state. We use basic family budgets for Utah, the state that has a median income closest to the U.S. median family income. Table 1.2 provides the 2007 basic budgets for rural areas and for Salt Lake City. The budgets are calculated for one- and two-adult households; all households include at least one child.

Households in which the earners only make the minimum wage do not net enough for the basic family budget, even when there are two working adults. The maximum income earned by two adults employed at the minimum wage is $29,000. The minimum income required for the modest but decent basic budget in Utah is $33,358; in Salt Lake City it is $37,933. The result is substantially better if the adults are earning 150 percent of the minimum wage. A single earner is still not able to earn a sufficient income to meet any of the basic family budgets, even in rural areas. A two-earner household earns somewhat more than the rural basic family income, and just at the level of a basic family income in Salt Lake City.

In summary, a large proportion of the labor force works at or relatively close to the minimum wage. While only about 1 in 20 nonstudent employees work at no more than 110 percent of the minimum wage, almost 1 in 6 earn no more than 125 percent of the effective minimum wage, and better than 1 in 4 earn no more than 150 percent of the effective minimum. Having a single minimum wage earner does not assure any but the smallest households of incomes above the thresholds for economic deprivation, but having two full-time minimum wage earners moves households above this mark. With two individuals earning 150 percent of the minimum wage, the representative family of four moves into the ranks of those living at a safe and decent standard of living.

THREE LABOR MARKET MODELS USED IN NMWR

Competitive

Relying on the simplest and most widely used economic model to analyze the labor market leads to the conclusion that whenever the minimum wage results in higher wages, someone who would have been employed, in the absence of the minimum wage at a wage less than the minimum wage, must instead now be out of work. This is easily seen in

Figure 1.1 Competitive Labor Market with a Minimum Wage

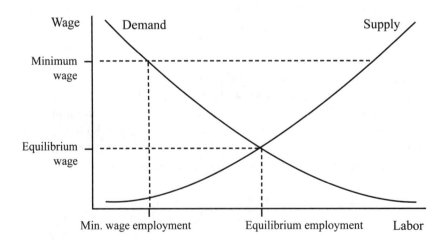

Figure 1.1, which shows the demand for labor increasing as the wage decreases, and the supply of labor increasing as the wage increases. In the absence of a minimum wage, their intersection indicates how many people will be working, indicated by *equilibrium employment*, and the wage that they will receive, the *equilibrium wage*. In this analysis there are many firms, none large enough to have a detectible effect on the labor market by itself, and there are many prospective employees, none of whom individually have any effect on the wage or employment. Each firm hires just to the point where if it employed one worker more or fewer, profits would be lower. If there is a minimum wage that exceeds the equilibrium wage, more people will want jobs, but firms will not want to employ as many. Both of these facts can be seen where the dashed line indicating the minimum wage intersects the supply and demand curves. Because there is no compulsion to hire but there is to pay at least the minimum wage, the wage will be higher, but there will be fewer jobs than in the absence of a minimum wage.

Before moving on to the next model, an explanation is required to explain the derivation of these demand and supply curves and to make the two analyses comparable. The marginal product of labor (MPL) for each firm is defined as the increase in total output that is associated with employment of the last, or marginal, worker: $MPL(N) = Q(N) - Q(N-1)$, where $Q(N)$ is the amount of output the firm produces when employing N workers. The marginal cost of labor (MCL) is the increase in total payroll from employing the marginal worker: $MCL = W(N) - W(N-1)$, where W is the total payroll when N workers are employed. Both must be measured in the same units if they are to be compared, so let both be measured in money terms (dollars), and let $R(N)$ be the firm's revenue when it employs N workers, net of all costs of production other than labor (materials, energy, and so forth).

Deriving the industry or aggregate demand curve requires working backward. Each firm can calculate its MPL for each level of employment, each value of N. The labor demand curve is the horizontal sum of the individual firm MPL curves. That is, for each value of the wage, we find the level of employment for each firm that equates the MPL to the wage, and add all those values of employment. Doing this for all values of the wage gives the demand curve. The equilibrium wage is the value that equates this sum, total labor demanded, to the corresponding value of the supply curve. The way the market is considered to work is that it is already functioning when each firm enters the market. There is already an equilibrium wage that the entering firm can see, and the firm knows it must pay that wage if it is to hire any employees. It will hire employees to the point where the MPL equals the equilibrium wage.[6] Because each firm is small, and because each firm's impact on the market is not detectible, its decisions have no effect on the equilibrium wage, and the firm can hire as many or as few workers as it wants at this wage. The equilibrium wage is its MCL; it hires to the point that MPL = MCL = equilibrium wage. A competitive market is at one logical extreme.

Monopsony

Another labor market model is *monopsony*, in which only one firm is in the labor market, appropriately defined: only one firm that hires teenagers, for instance. Here, the competitive assumption is replaced by the assumption that the single firm recognizes its effect on wages, and that if it wants to hire an additional worker, it must not only pay a higher wage to attract that one, it must also raise wages for all current employees.

Like the competitive firm, the monopsonist hires until MPL = MCL, but unlike the competitive firm, the wage necessary to attract the desired amount of labor is less than the MCL (because in raising the wage to attract an additional worker it must also raise wages to that level for all current employees), so it pays a lower wage. This is graphed in Figure 1.2. Equilibrium employment here is less than it would be if the monopsonist did not recognize its effect on wages; if the monopsonist did not recognize this effect, the equilibrium level of employment would be the same as in the competitive model, where MPL = supply.

Figure 1.3 shows what may happen when a minimum wage is imposed on a monopsony labor market. Because the employer must pay at least the minimum wage to all its employees, its MCL equals the minimum wage for all levels of employment less than some value (labeled minimum wage employment). The MCL exceeds the minimum wage only at employment levels higher than this, where a higher wage is necessary to attract that much labor. In Figure 1.3, the relevant MCL schedule is indicated with a solid line, and the one that is relevant only in the absence of a minimum wage is indicated with a dotted line. The

Figure 1.2 Monopsony Labor Market with No Minimum Wage

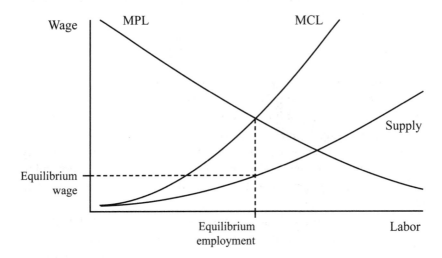

Figure 1.3 Monopsony Labor Market with a Minimum Wage

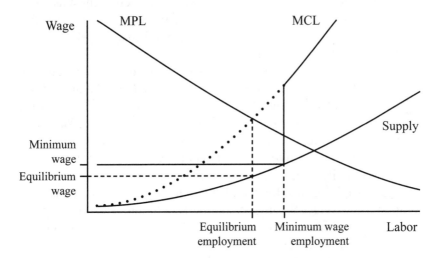

monopsony firm once again hires until the further hiring would raise the MCL above the MPL, and this is a higher level of employment than without the minimum wage.

Search Models

While the minimum wage can raise both employment and wages in the case of monopsony, the monopsony model has one important drawback. Evidence that it is relevant to low-wage labor markets where the minimum wage is relevant is scarce on the ground. Except for those living in the most isolated areas, teenagers in the United States typically have more than one fast food establishment in a small neighborhood to canvas for employment opportunities, and often possibilities exist in other sectors as well.

A more plausible but more complicated class of models that generate analytic results similar to those of monopsony is that of search models. The fundamental distinguishing feature is that prospective workers and employers cannot find each other without some cost, so that not all individuals willing to work at wages that firms are willing to pay can find employment. This is based on the observation that information is neither free nor perfect, and that individuals must use time and resources to determine who is hiring. Individuals recognize this and must decide on the basis of incomplete information whether it is worthwhile even to engage in search.[7]

Two key variables in search models are 1) the contact rate, the probability that someone who is searching for a job will be offered one in any period of time; and 2) the distribution of wage offers. In the competitive model, the contact rate equals one and the offer distribution implies that all offers equal the equilibrium wage. In search models, the contact rate is positive but less than one, and the wage distribution is not necessarily degenerate. Other important parameters include an individual's cost of searching, typically positive; the rate at which jobs disappear due to layoffs, firings, and quits; and the value of not being employed, for instance, the value of additional schooling, leisure, or unpaid work in the home.

Along with other details of model specification, it is possible to use these models to analyze not only employment but also unemployment, participation in the labor force, job vacancies, and wage distributions within and among firms. While it is not necessarily the case that search models of the labor market generate results similar to that seen in Figure 1.3—that is, both higher wages and employment—it is a possibility when the model is appropriately specified. In Flinn (2006) and Ahn, Arcidiacono, and Wessels (2011), this is largely because the participation rate responds to the minimum wage, and within a certain range, the greater ease of hiring dominates the greater cost of employment in the response of firms to the minimum wage.

AN OVERVIEW OF THE BOOK

This review includes more than 200 articles on the minimum wage. Most date from 2000 forward but some, on topics that have not received much attention, date back to the 1980s and 1970s. Chapters are organized around narrowly defined topics. We focus on micro and market-specific outcomes in the earlier chapters and then turn to broader, macro issues toward the end of the review.

Chapter 2, the first chapter in the Micro section of the book, considers the research on employment, or more precisely, on the effect of the minimum wage on the number of employees or jobs. Chapter 3 broadens the measures of employment in considering research on the effect of the minimum wage on hours of work. Here we find strong evidence that the implementation of a minimum wage in the United Kingdom reduced hours of work, but that the evidence for the United States is inconclusive. Chapter 4 presents a meta-analysis of the employment and hours research, providing estimates of the effect of the minimum wage corrected for publication bias and article-specific effects, including specific estimates for young workers and the restaurant industry. Although estimates of the elasticity of employment/hours with respect to the minimum wage vary across estimates, most are either statistically nonsignificant or are too small in magnitude to be economically meaningful.

Starting with Chapter 5, the review considers a broader set of the labor market outcomes. Chapter 5 addresses the effect of the minimum wage on the level and distribution of wages and the provision of fringe benefits. We find almost universal agreement that increasing the minimum wage raises the wages of bound and near-bound workers, and that the effect of the minimum wage is far stronger for women than for men. Chapter 6 considers the effects on human capital formation, including education and employer-provided training. Results on education are sufficiently varied, and sufficiently problematic, to preclude a simple conclusion; the evidence on training is likewise too varied to support a straightforward summary. Chapter 7 looks at the evidence about the impact of the minimum wage on wage inequality, poverty, and the length of time individuals remain at low wages. Although the magnitude of the effect remains in play, there is universal agreement that the minimum wage reduces wage inequality, particularly among women. In contrast, the minimum wage appears to have no effect on the poverty status of individuals, possibly because so few of those below the poverty line are employed. Finally, although most employees who earn a wage at or close to the minimum rapidly move to wages considerably above the minimum, a substantial number remain at wages no more than 150 percent of the minimum wage in the initial decade of employment.

Chapters 8 and 9 return to employment-related issues, with Chapter 8 looking at gross flows in the labor market and Chapter 9 considering the effect of the minimum wage on firms' hiring and layoff behavior and unemployment. Current research finds that increases in the minimum wage reduce both hiring and layoffs almost equally; both labor force participation rates and unemployment appear to increase slightly with increases in the minimum wage. The minimum wage has a differential effect on unemployment duration, with duration declining for better-educated and rising for less-educated workers. The effect of the minimum wage on product markets is addressed in Chapter 10. Although there is too little research to reach any conclusions about the effects of the minimum wage on firm performance in the United States, research using data from the United Kingdom suggests that profitability declines with increases in the minimum wage, but this does not lead to an increase in firms leaving the market or a decrease in share prices.

Rounding things off, the conclusion attempts the yeoman's work of summarizing our review, suggesting issues that are in need of further research, and providing some thoughts on improving the quality of research on the minimum wage. The conclusion is followed by an appendix, which discusses data sources and variables and their construction.

Finally, a brief discussion on our statistical approach is in order. According to one well-known opinion, the function of cavalry in modern warfare is "to give tone to what would otherwise be a mere vulgar brawl!" (Hammerton 2011). It is our hope that this is not the role of statistics in the minimum wage debate. Our approach has been to hold the articles we discuss to reasonable standards. We typically apply a 5 percent p-value in determining whether there is an effect. Given typical sample sizes used in this research, this standard is a low hurdle. We also require that specifications be reasonably complete—that there are no grounds to be skeptical about estimated standard errors. This may lead to an apparent fetish about p-values, but with the large number of studies we consider, setting a minimum standard is a necessary screening device.

Different standards and criteria may appeal to readers. Our meta-analysis of the employment and hours studies remedies this otherwise arbitrary, discontinuous, either/or cutoff with a continuous method of weighting estimates based on their estimated standard error. The summary tables in each chapter provide fairly complete information about the studies included in this review. The reader is invited to use these to reach their own conclusions.

Notes

1. More than 600 scholarly and policy papers that mention the minimum wage have been published since 2000. The 200 that we review were selected because they included empirical research on developed countries.
2. An elasticity between −0.3 and −0.1 indicates that a 10 percent increase in the minimum wage will reduce employment by 1–3 percent.
3. We use *benchmark* to mean a guideline for assessing how satisfactory a wage or wage offer is.
4. The column for a one-person household reports only the annual income from having a single person employed at the minimum wage because it is difficult to have more than one earner in a one-person household. The balance of the columns report household earnings with both one and two individuals receiving the minimum wage.
5. Although based on both income and assets, we attend only to the income requirement since that is the only one that the minimum wage directly affects.
6. In the standard analysis, it is assumed both that the MPL is positive in the range of employment considered, and that it gets progressively smaller as N increases.

7. This is most often modeled from the perspective of the individual looking for work. Depending on the issue of interest, it can also be viewed from the perspective of the firm, so that all firms willing to pay wages that individuals are willing to accept can find people to hire only with some cost. In this case, firms must devote resources to identifying individuals appropriate to hire and the suitable wage. Finally, both perspectives can be combined, so that firms and individuals encounter difficulty finding suitable partners for an employment relationship.

Part 1

Micro

2
Employment

Employment—specifically, the number of jobs—is square one for disputes about the minimum wage and its effects. Support for the minimum wage is premised on its improving the lives of those most vulnerable in the labor market. If a minimum wage leads to job loss for many of those same people, serious questions arise with respect to its relative benefits and costs, especially if third parties, such as employers, also bear some of the costs. The disagreement here is not so much whether the minimum wage ever leads to some loss of jobs but whether it always or usually does. If it does not, then legislation setting a minimum wage is not necessarily a bad idea. The NMWR has yet to come to any widely accepted resolution on this issue, and we will not presume that we can settle the matter here. This chapter presents a comprehensive review of research on the effects of a minimum wage on employment, describing the contributions and mutual criticisms of the best-known early protagonists in the NMWR, followed by a detailed look at more recent research.

EARLY NEW MINIMUM WAGE RESEARCH

The employment effect of the minimum wage is the topic of four of the five (revised) papers from the conference that appeared the following year in the *Industrial and Labor Relations Review*. Among them, they contained many of the features that were to become common in the NMWR: state-level panels and establishment data rather than national aggregates, quasi experiments in addition to regressions, and ways of gauging minimum wage changes other than the Kaitz index (or similar measures).[1] Neumark and Wascher (1992) draw on the framework of the earlier aggregate time-series research on teenagers to study a panel of state-year observations. Card (1992a) performs a differences analysis of state-level data to examine the response of teenage employment to the federal minimum wage increase in 1990; the minimum wage variable is the fraction affected, the percentage of a state's teenage employees who were earning less than the higher minimum wage in the three quarters before the increase.[2] Katz and Krueger (1992) perform a differences analysis of establishment data to examine the employment response of Texas's fast food industry to the federal minimum wage increase in 1991; the minimum wage variable is a wage gap measure, how much an establishment's starting wage would have to rise from its value five months before the increase in order to comply with the new minimum wage. Card (1992b) uses the 1988 increase in California's minimum wage as an opportunity for a (proto-) difference-in-differences analysis of several employment responses: of teenagers, of the retail sector as a whole, and of one specific part of the retail sector, eating and drinking establishments.[3] Only Neumark and Wascher (1992) find a negative employment response, consistent with the earlier literature.

A year and a half later, an exchange between Card, Katz, and Krueger (1994) and Neumark and Wascher (1994) appeared. Card, Katz, and Krueger (1994) criticized aspects of Neumark and Wascher's (1992) analysis, including the reconciliation with Card (1992a,b) that Neumark and Wascher believe shows that Card's (1992b) specification was unable to detect much of the employment response. Card and Krueger (1994), the most well-known and controversial analysis in the NMWR, appeared almost immediately following this exchange. Building on Katz and Krueger (1992) and Card (1992b), Card and Krueger (1994) use the 1992 increase in New Jersey's minimum wage to construct a quasi experiment. The treatment group consists of fast food establishments in New Jersey, and the control group consists of similar establishments in nearby Pennsylvania counties. This generated a final exchange of criticism (Neumark and Wascher 2000) and response (Card and Krueger 2000). In describing this work in detail, the focus will be on what has turned out to be most influential: Neumark and Wascher (1992), Card and Krueger (1994), and the exchange that each generated.

The Conference: Staking Out Positions

Prior to NMWR, studies of the minimum wage and teenage employment in the United States relied on aggregate time-series data or, much less frequently, a cross section of states. Neumark and Wascher (1992) introduce to this literature state-by-year panels based on the CPS

Outgoing Rotation Groups. Analysis of data sets like this became possible because of both advances in computer technology and the availability of data at this level of aggregation, and it was useful because of the increasing variation in the minimum wage across states.[4] The basic version of Neumark and Wascher's (1992) empirical model resembles that of the older time-series work. Their outcome variable is the teenage employment ratio, their minimum wage variable is the Kaitz index, and their control variables, reflecting fluctuations in supply and demand, are drawn from the same short list as in the older literature.[5] The panel structure allows for an obvious extension, two-way fixed effects (i.e., dummy variables for each state and year) to account for factors that are roughly constant within each state over time or within each year across states. They present several versions of the basic model to verify robustness of results, and the one that became the most prominent included not only a contemporaneous term of the minimum wage but also a single (i.e., one-year) lagged term. For this version they report an employment elasticity (with respect to the minimum wage) of −0.19.

The importance of the lagged minimum wage term becomes apparent when Neumark and Wascher (1992) reconcile their results with Card's (1992a,b) report of a "positive contemporaneous correlation between changes (that is, short first differences) in the minimum wage and changes in the employment of teenagers" (p. 67). When Neumark and Wascher estimate their model in first differences, they too find no employment response to the minimum wage (or a small positive response). The difference between the two specifications, one in first differences and one in levels with both contemporaneous and lagged minimum wage terms, is that the former can capture only short-term effects of the minimum wage, while the latter can capture longer ones as well. That is, it takes time for the minimum wage to influence teenagers' employment, and specifications that do not allow for this possibility will be unable to detect it.

Card, Katz, and Krueger (1994) make serious criticisms of Neumark and Wascher (1992), the most important of which concerns the variant of the Kaitz index that Neumark and Wascher use.[6] A major part of the index is a ratio, of which the numerator is the nominal value of the minimum wage and the denominator is the average nominal adult wage. Card, Katz, and Krueger object that this way of measuring the minimum wage leads to the mistaken attribution of effects to the minimum wage when they are actually due to other factors.[7] Card, Katz, and Krueger conclude by reconsidering Card's (1992a) examination of the 1990 increase in the federal minimum wage, modifying the analysis in two ways. First, they include a measure of teenage school enrollment. Second, they measure employment change over two years rather than one to capture the same phenomena that the lagged minimum wage term does in Neumark and Wascher's specification. The minimum wage variable remains the fraction affected. With only the minimum wage variable on the right-hand side of the equation, its effect on teenage employment is positive and statistically significant. However, once they include a variable to control for the business cycle, the estimated minimum wage coefficient remains positive but is no longer statistically significant.

Neumark and Wascher (1994) disagree with each criticism that Card, Katz, and Krueger (1994) level at their work and argue that the two-year window that Card, Katz, and Krueger consider in their re-analysis is not equivalent to the lagged term in their own specification. We are left neither with agreement between the two parties nor with an obvious way to determine independently who is correct. The dispute has no clear winner. In addition to the question, "Does the minimum wage always reduce employment if it leads to higher wages?" other issues that are left unresolved include the appropriate way to measure the minimum wage in addressing this question and the time frame in which employment responds (if indeed it does).

Card and Krueger (1994) and After

Card and Krueger (1994), the best-known article in the NMWR, is the coming-of-age of the quasi experiment in this literature. Like Katz and Krueger (1992), they survey several hundred fast food restaurants, but they do so in two states rather than one: in New Jersey and in several counties of eastern Pennsylvania that are close to New Jersey. Like Katz and Krueger (1992), they perform a differences analysis using a measure of the wage gap, but the best-known part of their study is a difference-in-differences analysis using a treatment dummy. In April 1992, the minimum wage in New Jersey rose from $4.25 to $5.05, while that in Pennsylvania remained constant at $4.25. This allows Card and Krueger to define their treatment group as fast food establishments in New Jersey and their comparison group as the fast food establishments in eastern

Pennsylvania. They also consider a secondary comparison group of New Jersey fast food establishments that were paying at least $5 per hour at the time of their first survey, before the law went into effect. With neither comparison group are they able to detect a loss of employment in response to the minimum wage increase. Nor could they detect any effect when they considered the opening of new McDonald's establishments rather than employment. Card and Kreuger find that prices did rise in New Jersey more than in Pennsylvania following the increase, but not more in lower-wage New Jersey establishments than in the higher-wage ones that constituted the secondary comparison group (p. 792).

Neumark and Wascher (2000) begin their response to Card and Krueger's (1994) analysis with a long, detailed critique of the data set that Card and Kreuger constructed. At the center of their argument is an alternative data set that they constructed from historical payroll records for fast food establishments in the same areas and the same chains as Card and Kreuger examined, and that they believe is superior to Card and Krueger's. It consists of two parts, one of establishments for which they compiled the data, and one of other establishments whose data were given to them independently of their own efforts. Neumark and Wascher assert that a comparison of their data set with Card and Kreuger's brings to light problems in the latter that cast doubt on the results. Further, when they replicate Card and Krueger's analysis on their data, they find employment losses in the New Jersey fast food establishments relative to those in Pennsylvania that are about the size one would expect from their earlier analyses of teenage employment. To bolster their case, they next turn to two government data sets for employment in the entire restaurant industry (since neither allows them to examine the fast food sector alone). Based on both a quick examination along quasi experimental lines and a more careful regression analysis over a longer period, Neumark and Wascher conclude, "Taken as a whole, it is our view that the BLS data on employment at eating and drinking places neither confirm nor reject our findings from the payroll data that the New Jersey minimum-wage increase appears to have reduced fast-food employment in that state. The BLS data do, however, provide complementary evidence that minimum-wage increases reduce employment in the restaurant industry" (pp. 1389–1390).

Neumark and Wascher (2000) explain the differences between their results and Card and Krueger's (1994):

> We think that there is simply considerable measurement error in
> [Card and Krueger's] data, attributable to the design of their sur-
> vey. In contrast, our data should accurately reflect the actual
> quantity of labor employed at each restaurant in each survey pe-
> riod. . . . Because the Pennsylvania sample in both data sources
> is rather small, and much of the difference between the two data
> sources arises for Pennsylvania, it is entirely possible that random
> measurement error in Card and Krueger's data is the culprit. . . .
> The second possibility is that the measurement error is not random.
> (p. 1387)

Card and Krueger (2000) respond in several steps. First, addressing
the criticisms of the data set that they had constructed themselves, they
follow Neumark and Wascher's (2000) lead and turn to the same BLS
data that are gathered to administer the unemployment insurance program.[8] Using the same type of analysis as in Card and Krueger (1994),
they generate similar results about the employment effects. New Jersey's 1992 minimum wage increase.[9] Second, having constructed a
sample through the middle of 1997 from the government data, they perform the same analysis for the 1996 increase in the federal minimum
wage, which increased the minimum wage for Pennsylvania but not
New Jersey.[10] Once again, Card and Krueger (2000) find no evidence of
employment responding to the minimum wage.

Finally, they turn their attention to the data set at the heart of Neumark and Wascher's (2000) critique. Neumark and Wascher clearly feel
vulnerable to questions about the two different sources for their data,
devoting several pages to showing that, despite concerns about its provenance, it is in important ways similar to unquestionably reliable data.
Card and Krueger have elsewhere labeled the two parts of the sample as
the NW sample and the Berman sample, BNW when combined (Card
and Krueger 1999). They detail numerous problems with the samples,
the most serious being that the Berman sample, more than 40 percent
of the whole, was constructed in part through personal contacts in the
industry. As a result, it is not at all a random sample and has all the
problems that that entails for statistical analysis. All 23 observations for
Pennsylvania in the Berman sample came from a single Burger King
franchisee. Neither subsample contains any establishments in Pennsylvania affiliated with KFC, one of the slower-growing chains in Card
and Krueger's (1994) original sample. In comparing these data with

their own, Card and Krueger (2000) find a strong resemblance in the New Jersey portions, but not in those for Pennsylvania until they remove the 23 Pennsylvania observations of the Berman sample. They conclude, "*The increase in New Jersey's minimum wage probably had no effect on total employment in New Jersey's fast-food industry, and possibly had a small positive effect . . .*" [italics in the original].

> The only data set that indicates a significant decline in employment in New Jersey relative to Pennsylvania is the small set of restaurants collected by [Berman]. Results of this data set stand in contrast to our survey data, to the BLS's payroll data, and to the supplemental data collected by Neumark and Wascher. . . . We suspect the common denominator is that representative samples show statistically insignificant and small differences in employment growth between New Jersey and eastern Pennsylvania, while the nonrepresentative sample informally collected for Berman produces anomalous results.

> An alternative interpretation of the full spectrum of results is that the New Jersey minimum wage increase did not reduce total employment, but it did slightly reduce the average number of hours worked per employee. Neumark and Wascher (1995b) reject this interpretation. Although we are less quick to rule out this possibility, we are skeptical about any conclusion concerning average hours worked per employee that relies so heavily on the informally collected Berman/EPI sample, and the exclusion of controls for the length of the reporting interval. Moreover, within New Jersey the BNW data indicate that hours grew more at restaurants in the lowest wage areas of the state, where the minimum-wage increase was more likely to be a binding constraint. This finding runs counter to the view that total hours declined in response to the New Jersey minimum wage increase. (Card and Krueger 2000, pp. 1419–1420)

In contrast with the exchange following the conference (Card, Katz, and Krueger 1994; Neumark and Wascher 1994), this one leaves the reader feeling confident about the appropriate resolution of the disagreements between the two contending parties. Card and Krueger (1994, 2000) demonstrate that the minimum wage is not necessarily bad for employment, contra Neumark and Wascher (1992, 1994, 2000). Rather than directly defend their original data set, they analyze an alternative one drawn from government data about which no serious concerns have been raised; the results are similar to their original results.

Finally, they examine Neumark and Wascher's (2000) BNW data set thoroughly and show that once questionable observations are deleted, it too gives similar results.

The 1990s Studies in Retrospect

The next important developments for this literature (but not actually of or by it) were several methodological pieces that brought to light statistical issues sufficiently severe to destroy confidence in most inferences from both lines of research, both the state-year panels of Neumark and Wascher and the simple quasi experiments of Card and Krueger. Rather than explain this in media res, it will be better to start at the beginning. Kloek (1981) and Moulton (1986, 1990) examine situations in which ordinary least squares (OLS) is used on data that can be grouped, and within each group either some regressors have a constant value or it is plausible that the error term is correlated (as with a random effect) or both. Not only are the coefficients inefficiently estimated but the estimated standard errors are biased downward. A common solution is to estimate the coefficients with OLS and to cluster observations by group when estimating the standard errors.

Bertrand, Duflo, and Mullainathan (2004) demonstrate that even where the Moulton problem as conventionally understood is appropriately addressed, serial correlation remains and results in estimated standard errors that have a large downward bias.[11] They begin with a 50×20 (50 states by 20 years) repeat cross section in a difference-in-differences framework, soon switching over to a 50×20 panel of aggregated data to make clear that the symptoms they are examining are related to serial correlation. Hansen (2007a,b) explores this further in the context of panels and more conventional serial correlation than is typical of the treatment dummy of difference-in-differences analyses. Hansen (2007a,b) and Bertrand, Duflo, and Mullainathan demonstrate that in the presence of positive serial correlation, the estimated standard errors of key variables are biased downward substantially, leading to fantastically high rates of false positive results. This is true not only for estimates based on conventional formula that take no account of serial correlation but also for several commonly used parametric and nonparametric treatments of serial correlation (Wolfson 2011). Only clustering and several bootstrap procedures that account for unspecified serial correlation do not exhibit this problem.[12]

Donald and Lang (2007) examine (what has become known as) the Moulton problem, specifically in the difference-in-differences framework. In the two-by-two framework of Card and Krueger (1994, 2000)—two states and two periods—if all restaurants within each state are subject to common factors each year (other than the minimum wage) that affect their employment, and these are not included on the right-hand side of the regression equation, the dummy variable for each cell will reflect those factors. Calculated as the difference-in-differences from these dummy variables, the estimate of the employment effect absorbs these common non–minimum wage factors. With a mean of zero, they do not cause the estimate of the employment effect to be biased. However, its estimated variance reflects only the contribution from the sample of restaurants within each state-year cell and nothing from the sample of the common non–minimum wage factors across the state-year cells. With additional time periods or states in either the comparison or control group, it is possible to estimate this part of the variance, but not in the two-by-two framework. Consequently, the standard errors are biased downward.

Where does this leave us? First, it is worth noting that both of the problems identified raise more serious questions for studies that report a statistically significant employment effect, whether negative or positive, than for those that do not. Second, Donald and Lang (2007) show that those results of Card and Krueger's (1994, 2000) that are based on a statistically significant treatment dummy are questionable. However, Donald and Lang's point does not undermine those results based on a treatment variable that varies across treated units, as (for example) a wage gap variable that relates the ex ante wage or wage bill to ex post employment. Since both of their analyses include a differences analysis using a wage gap, Donald and Lang's point also does not undermine the statistically significant positive employment effect that they report. Third, the problem of serial correlation that Bertrand, Duflo, and Mullainathan (2004) highlight is an issue not only for Neumark and Wascher's (1992, 1994, 2000) analyses of panels during the 1990s but also for much of the work into the first decade of the new millennium.

In what follows, rather than repeating these concerns with each analysis, we take up only results for which we believe the problems are not too serious. This is (almost completely) straightforward with respect to quasi experiments and the bias problem that Donald and Lang

(2007) describe. Several factors come into play, however, with regard to serial correlation in panels: the degree of bias in the standard errors depends not only on the amount of serial correlation in the error term but also on the minimum wage variable and the number of time periods in the data. Further, when the number of groups is too small, neither clustering nor the simplest bootstrap procedure that accounts for serial correlation (known variously as the cluster-robust or block bootstrap) turns out to be ineffective. What number of groups is "too small"? The Monte Carlo results of Hansen (2007b) suggest that clustering works reasonably well with as few as 10 groups, while those of Bertrand, Duflo, and Mullainathan (2004) and Cameron, Gelbach, and Miller (2008) indicate a figure closer to 20. Cameron, Gelbach, and Miller examine several alternative techniques when there are very few groups, three of which appear to work reasonably well with as few as five groups.

This leads us to some rules of thumb in evaluating analyses that rely on panels or longitudinal data. The first is that analyses based on more than seven periods must account for serial correlation. Second, if there are fewer than 10 groups, clustering is ineffective. A third is that the degrees of freedom depend on the number of groups: while a consensus about the precise value does not currently exist, there is some agreement that it should be no more than the number of groups (Angrist and Pischke 2009; Cameron, Gelbach, and Miller 2008); t-statistics should be evaluated accordingly.

We respond to these problems by discussing entire articles in some cases, while discussing only parts of others. Where we entirely neglect a study, we nevertheless include it in our tabulations of papers and articles toward the bottom and indicate with a footnote that the standard errors are suspect. This set includes nearly all panel-based analyses that appeared before 2008. It also includes all difference-in-differences analyses that use a two-by-two framework and an at-risk or treatment dummy, as well as those that have more comparison groups or periods but do not take advantage of that fact to correct the estimated standard error of the employment effect so that it is not biased. With multiple comparison and treatment groups, as in Allegretto, Dube, and Reich (2009, 2011) and Dube, Lester, and Reich (2010), the estimated standard error automatically reflects this contribution to the variance, so this source of bias is not a problem. Because clustering is ineffective with fewer than 20 groups, several otherwise attractive analyses of Canadian provincial data are not discussed.[13]

THE NEW MINIMUM WAGE RESEARCH SINCE 2000

To provide an understanding of the current state of research on the minimum wage and employment, we review 50 articles published or written between 2001 and early 2013 that address this issue (and include more than 20 additional analyses with suspect standard errors or other serious problems toward the bottom of the tables). The primary focus will be studies of U.S. data, but English-language studies of data from other advanced (that is, OECD) economies are also included. Analyses are organized in two broad classifications. The first concerns the employment response of a demographic group; the list of groups studied includes not only teenagers but also young adults, women who satisfy various criteria, immigrants, and a small assortment of others. The second concerns the employment response of selected industries, most often fast food or restaurants more broadly, but also hotels and motels, retail, broader sets of low-wage industries, and, in the United Kingdom, nursing homes. In the first category, the dependent variable is most often the employment rate of the target demographic group when aggregate data are being studied and the employment status of members of the target demographic group when individual data are used. In the second category, the dependent variable is the number of jobs, whether in the entire industry or particular establishments. In both categories, several consider either group members who were employed prior to a minimum wage increase or industry employees prior to an increase, to examine the effect of the minimum wage on their likelihood of continued employment. The discussion below makes no attempt at complete descriptions of any studies, focusing only on what is directly germane to employment and the minimum wage in each, and largely ignores those that exhibit the econometric problems described above. The tables, however, will include them at the bottom.[14] Finally, fewer studies than one would wish report elasticities, and those that do too rarely report the relevant standard errors. Unless an elasticity is reported, the focus in the discussion of an article will be qualitative, not quantitative.

Since the end of the first decade of the NMWR, the study of the teenage and youth employment response remains the most common, both in studies that examine U.S. data and in those that use data from other countries. Less than a handful of these analyses use one-dimensional data structures, aggregate time-series, and cross sections, to which they apply much more sophisticated econometric techniques than typical in this literature. Panels are the most common data structure early in the period, giving way to repeat cross sections in the second half of this period. The most common analytic approach in this group of papers is similar to that of Neumark and Wascher (1992) and the older time-series literature, although several studies, of both youth and other groups, rely on economic search models. Individual-level data are more common much earlier in studies of other countries than of the United States, especially longitudinal data. Quasi experiments are relatively infrequent in studies of both U.S. demographic groups and industries but quite common in foreign studies. Rather than rely solely on a broadly defined demographic group, a handful try to identify those affected, whether employed or not, based on traits typically found in a wage equation. Several pay careful attention to the choice of the implicit or explicit comparison group against which the employment effect of the minimum wage is measured. Below, studies of U.S. data are discussed first, then of foreign data. Within the discussion of U.S. studies, the order is youth employment, other low-wage groups, other demographic groups, the hospitality sector, and other low-wage sectors. The discussion of other countries has no section on other demographic groups and combines all low-wage sectors into one section.

U.S. STUDIES

Demographic Groups

Youth

Studies that use aggregate panels. Table 2.1 lists the 12 studies that analyze panel data for the United States; all but one rely on data from the Current Population Survey (CPS). The typical or canonical framework is that of Neumark and Wascher (1992): estimation of a single equation in which the dependent variable is the employment ratio and the list of independent variables includes both one that reflects the value of the minimum wage and others that reflect supply and demand characteristics of the labor market: for example, the unemployment rate for all workers in a state, and teenagers' share of the population in a state. It is common to include two-way fixed effects, though those for time are not universal, and occasionally a trend term is included. A lagged term of the minimum wage variable is not uncommon, either instead of or in addition to the contemporaneous value of the variable. Neumark and Wascher (2004) include separate trends for each country in some specifications, while Keil, Robertson, and Symons (2009) include no regressors other than the two-way fixed effects and separate trends for each state.

Neumark (2001) was to be part of an intended symposium for which he turned out to be the only participant.[15] It was organized out of concern that the protagonists in the minimum wage debates of the 1990s were able, consciously or not, to adjust their analyses to provide "satisfactory" results. Neumark locked in his specification before the data to be used, the CPS for the last three months of each year in 1995–1998, were available. The specific question examined is the response of teenage (and young adult) employment to the federal minimum wage increases of 1996 and 1997. In contrast with all the rest of the minimum wage work that Neumark published before Neumark and Wascher (2011), the evidence presented in support of the hypothesis that the minimum wage reduces teenage employment is quite sparse. The only statistically significant results are for those who are both not currently enrolled in school and have no education beyond high school. Neumark states that it is in this group, the youngest and least skilled part of the labor force, where one would expect the strongest disemployment effects; he suspects that one reason for the lack of definite results is that with such a short sample, imposed by the need to lock in the specification in advance of the data, the standard errors are larger than they likely would be in a longer sample. However, it is also in just such a short sample that serial correlation is least likely to lead to biased standard errors; that is, the results may be more, not less, reliable than in analyses of longer samples that contain no correction for serial correlation.

To reconcile the first-round NMWR results of Neumark and Wascher (1992, 2000) with those of Card and Krueger (1994, 2000), Bazen and Le Gallo (2009) suggest that changes in the federal minimum wage influence teen employment differently than changes in state minimum wages. They examine several recent intervals: the mid- to late 1980s,

Table 2.1 Youth (Panels, U.S. Data)

Study	Effect	Novelty	Target group[a]	Sample period	Analytic approach	Unit of observation	Type of standard error	Data set[b]
Addison, Blackburn, and Cotti (2013)	Mixed	Amplifying effect of recessions?	Teenagers	2005–2010 2006–2009	Regression	State-month State-year	Clustered	CPS ACS
Bazen and Le Gallo (2009)	Mixed	Reconciling results of Neumark and Wascher and Card and Krueger	Teenagers	Various	Regression	State-year	Block bootstrap	CPS
Neumark (2001)	None	Prespecified research design	Teenagers, young adults	1995–1998	Regression	State-year	Conventional	CPS
Neumark and Nizalova (2007)	None	Long-term consequences	Teenagers, young adults	1979–2001	Regression	State-cohort-year	Clustered (state)	CPS
Orrenius and Zavodny (2008)	Mixed	Immigrants	Teenagers	1995–2005	Regression	State-year	Clustered (state)	CPS
Sabia (2009a)	Negative	Using CPS to study the retail sector	Teens in retail	1979–2004	Regression	State-month	Clustered (state)	CPS
Sabia (2009b)	Negative	Annual vs. business cycle effects	Teenagers	1979–2004	Regression	State-month	Clustered (state)	CPS
Thompson (2009)	Negative	County-level data	Teenagers	1996–2000	Quasi experiment	County-quarter	Clustered (state)	QWI
Keil, Robertson, and Symons (2009)[c]	None	Rise in precision from post-2000 data	Youth	1977–1995	Regression	State-year	Various, none clustered	CPS, QCEW, GPEU
Neumark and Wascher (2002)[c]	Negative	Disequilibrium methods	Youth	1977–1989 1973–1976	Regression	State-year	Conventional	CPS
Neumark and Wascher (2003)[c]	Negative	Extending work on enrollment-employment	Teenagers	1977–1998	Regression	State-year	Conventional, PCSE-PSAR[d]	May CPS

| Wessels (2007)[c] | Mixed | Redoing C&K's teenager study | Teenagers | 1989–1997 | Regression | State-year | Conventional | CPS |

[a] Teenagers refers to those aged 16–19. Young adults refers to those aged 20–24. Youth combines the two groups together.

[b] CPS = Current Population Survey. ACS = American Community Survey. GPEU = Geographic Profile of Employment and Unemployment. QCEW = Quarterly Census of Employment and Wages. QWI = Quarterly Workforce Indicators (based on Unemployment Insurance records).

[c] This study has standard errors that are suspect for reasons identified by Bertrand, Duflo, and Mullainathan (2004).

[d] PCSE-PSAR = Panel-corrected standard errors, allowing for different serial correlation coefficients for the residuals of each state.

when the only increases in the minimum wage were at the state level; the increases in the federal minimum wage of the early 1990s; and the mid-1990s, when there were only a few increases in state minimum wages and most but not all of the action was at the federal level. Bazen and Le Gallo conclude that, on the whole, increases in state minimum wages have no impact on employment but that increases in the federal minimum wage do. Why? In the 1980s, few states increased the minimum wage, and most of the increases were both regionally localized (in New England, the upper midwest, and the Pacific Coast states) and individually small, even if their cumulative total over time was large. This suggests some selection bias to Bazen and Le Gallo; states that increased their minimum wages did so knowing from experience that the employment effect would be small. Over the same period, firms in those states acquired experience in preparing for and responding to binding minimum wages, further reducing the employment effects of increases in the state minimum wages. In the 1990s, when increases in the federal minimum wage played a more important role, the changes were both relatively larger and more widespread, and firms in many affected states lacked this expertise. These conditions were reflected in teen employment. Because Neumark and Wascher (1992, 2000) consider both state and federal minimum wage increases over an extended period of time, and the increases at the federal level had effects on teenage employment, while Card and Krueger (1994, 2000) study only a single state minimum wage increase, which did not affect employment, it should be no surprise that their conclusions disagree, according to Bazen and Le Gallo.[16]

Analyzing a five-year-long quarterly panel of county-level data, Thompson (2009) starts with the assumption that a county's sensitivity to the minimum wage is negatively related to the mean quarterly earnings of its employed teenagers. Employment will be more sensitive to the minimum wage in a county where mean quarterly earnings of employed teenagers is low than in a county where that figure is high.[17] With this, he constructs a quasi experiment to examine the effect of the federal minimum wage increases of the late 1990s on the teen share of employment. The treatment group consists of counties with low values for teens' earnings, while the comparison group is another set of counties with high values for teens' earnings. In addition to the quasi experiment, which entails excluding a large fraction of counties with intermediate values of mean teens' earnings, he also performs a regression analysis on a full sample, using teens' earnings in the first quarter of 1996 as the measure of sensitivity to the minimum wage. Following the increase in October 1996, the teenage employment share fell in the treatment counties by three percentage points relative to that in the comparison group, using a broad definition of high- and low-earnings counties, and by six percentage points using a narrower one. The regression results show that the teen share of employment fell by about one percentage point for each $100 decline in prior per capita teens' earnings.

Different cuts at the data are illuminating. Teenage employment can be split into roughly equal halves: stable jobs, which last the full quarter in which the minimum wage rose, and transitory jobs (all others). This dichotomy indicates that the minimum wage had no impact on stable employment but a substantial effect on transitory employment. Further analysis shows that employment of young adults (age 19–22) is not measurably affected, and that much of the decline in the teen employment share, at least in 1997, can be attributed to a drop in the hiring of teens.[18]

Addison, Blackburn, and Cotti (2013) ask, "What accounts for the difficulty in uncovering adverse minimum wage effects in recent studies?" (p. 1). They examine the possibility that relatively tight labor markets in the U.S. data may explain this. That is, the employment response to moderate minimum wage increases is muted when labor is scarce, only to be amplified during recessions. To study this, they use two data sets and several equation specifications to study the impact on teenagers in a period that straddles the beginning of the 2007–2009 recession, a period when both the federal minimum wage and the average of state minimum wages rose from one-third of the average manufacturing wage or less to about three-eighths or more. The key variable is an interaction between the minimum wage, on the one hand, and on the other, the difference between the state unemployment rate and the mean national unemployment rate in the three years before the onset of the recession. In the absence of the interaction term, three of four point estimates of the effect on teenagers' employment are positive, and none are statistically significant.[19] The point estimate on the interaction term is negative, statistically significant, and quite small. It appears that teenagers' hold on their jobs may be unusually tenuous during recessions, and the authors believe that the previously tighter labor market is the answer to the question posed at the beginning of this paragraph.

Full discussions of four analyses, Neumark and Nizalova (2007), Orrenius and Zavodny (2008), and Sabia (2009a,b), appear later because they each consider minimum wage effects on youth employment only as by-products of their main concern. Neumark and Nizalova examine the long-term effects of the minimum wage experienced as a teenager and young adult. For Orrenius and Zavodny the focus is the effect of the minimum wage on immigrants who lack a high school diploma, while for Sabia (2009a) it is the effect on employment in retail.[20] Sabia (2009b) is more methodological, primarily concerned with the best way to account for the business cycle in minimum wage studies. In both of his articles, Sabia uses similar but not identical models to analyze the same data. He reports point estimates of the elasticity of employment with respect to the minimum wage, ranging from a low of about −0.20 in specifications without annual dummies to a high of about −0.30 in specifications that include them, but he makes no mention of standard errors.[21] The lack of standard errors nevertheless makes it difficult to determine whether the differences between his elasticity estimates are statistically significant. None of the elasticity estimates that Orrenius and Zavodny (2008) report for all teenagers or for teenage girls is statistically significant. For teenage boys, the elasticity estimate from a regression equation that includes business cycle controls is statistically significant, and at about −0.20, in the middle of what was previously the consensus range. For teenagers, Neumark and Nizalova report no statistically significant employment response to the average minimum wage that has prevailed since one turned 16 in the current state of residence. Substituting 20 for 16, they report the same for young adults (20–24), even those with no more than a high school education.

Studies that use individual-level data. Table 2.2 lists eight studies that examine individual-level data. Three—Ahn, Arcidiacono, and Wessels (2011); Eckstein, Ge, and Petrongolo (2011); and Flinn (2006)— start with fairly sophisticated search models of the labor market, which they put to quite different uses. The remainder broadly resemble earlier work, though each has its own novelty or twist. Allegretto, Dube, and Reich (2009, 2011) emphasize the importance of controlling for regional heterogeneity and show that neglecting it can result in holding the minimum wage responsible for effects that are due to factors with which it is correlated. Neumark and Wascher (2011) present results for teenage girls in the course of examining the employment response of single mothers to both the minimum wage and the Earned Income Tax Credit (EITC). Sabia, Burkhauser, and Hansen (2012) study the minimum wage increases in New York in 2005 and 2006 from several different quasi experiment perspectives and conclude that it reduced employment of young people who had not graduated from high school. These six studies all rely on repeated cross sections, where individuals are not followed over time.

Flinn (2006) develops and analyzes a search model in which the minimum wage can affect both the probability of finding a job and the wage offer. Only unemployed individuals engage in search; once employed, workers remain at that job until it disappears, an event that happens with a constant probability. Individuals are identical except for factors that influence their decisions about labor participation, especially the opportunity cost of participation. Similarly, firms are identical. These assumptions imply that no firm or individual is consistently more or less productive than any others. Productivity depends only on the specific match of individual and firm. The value of a match is its productivity and is immediately known to both parties when they begin to consider the possibility of joining forces; it is the basis of the wage negotiation, the outcome of which depends on the relative bargaining power of labor and management. Because employed workers do not engage in search, an individual will turn down a wage offer that is too low, since accepting it would preclude further search.

A minimum wage creates a distinction between jobs that would have been offered in its absence. Those for which the value is less than the minimum wage will not be offered, and matches that would have been made because the low offered wage would nevertheless have been acceptable to the searcher will not be made. In this way, the minimum wage reduces the value of search. Firms will continue to make job offers where the value of the match exceeds the minimum wage, but the wage offered will now always be at least the minimum wage. The minimum wage imposes a wage floor for these matches since, previously, workers' low bargaining power would have otherwise allowed firms to make some of these offers for a lower wage. In this way, the minimum wage increases the value of search. Flinn (2006) describes this latter

Table 2.2 Youth (Individual-Level Data, U.S. Data)

Study	Effect	Novelty	Target group[a]	Sample period	Analytic approach	Unit of observation	Data structure	Type of standard error	Data set[b]
Eckstein, Ge, and Petrongolo (2011)	Negative	Enforcement of MW in a search model	White male high school graduates	1979–1996	Regression	Individual-month	Longitudinal	General method of moments	NLSY
Ahn, Arcidiacono, and Wessels (2011)	Mixed	Search model of the labor market	White teenage boys	1989–2000	Regression	Individual-year	Repeated cross section	Conventional	CPS
Allegretto, Dube, and Reich (2009)	None	Addressing regional heterogeneity, commuting zones	Teenagers	Various	Regression and quasi experiment	Individual-quarter	Repeated cross section	Clustered (state)	Census, ACS
Allegretto, Dube, and Reich (2011)	None	Addressing regional heterogeneity	Teenagers	1990–2009	Regression and quasi experiment	Individual-year	Repeated cross section	Clustered (state)	CPS
Flinn (2006)	Mixed	Search model of the labor market	Youth	1996–1998	Regression	Individual	Repeated cross section	Conventional	CPS
Neumark and Wascher (2011)	Mixed	MW-EITC interaction	Single mothers	1977–2006	Regression	Individual-month	Repeated cross section	Clustered (state)	Various, CPS
Sabia, Burkhauser, and Hansen (2012)	Negative	New York State minimum wage increase	Youth, 16–29, not high school graduates	2004, 2006	Quasi experiment	Individual	Repeated cross section	Clustered SE bootstrap	CPS
Turner and Demiralp[c] (2001)	Mixed	Minority and inner-city teens	Teenagers	1991	Regression	Individual	Longitudinal	FO Taylor Expansion	SIPP

[a] Teenagers refers to those aged 16–19.

[b] ACS = American Community Survey. NLSY = National Longitudinal Survey of Youth. SIPP = Survey of Income and Program Participation.

[c] This study has standard errors that are suspect for reasons identified by Bertrand, Duflo, and Mullainathan (2004).

effect as the equivalent of an increase in labor's bargaining power. Both of these effects increase total unemployment, the first because some workers who would have willingly accepted a low wage cannot now find a match, the second because individuals with higher reservation wages now enter the labor market in response to the wage floor. If the second dominates, both labor force participation and total employment may increase.[22]

Flinn (2006) derives a likelihood function and estimates it using data from CPS outgoing rotation groups for four nonconsecutive months that together span each of the two federal minimum wage increases of the mid-1990s. To measure the effects of the minimum wage, he plugs different values of the minimum wage into two versions of the estimated model. The second model, which Flinn believes to be more reliable, indicates that employment of young workers rises until the minimum wage equals about $7.50 per hour.[23] It further implies that the youth employment rate rose slightly in response to the 1990s increases in the federal minimum wage, from a bit more than 57 percent to a bit more than 58 percent. As with more than one analysis previously discussed, the lack of confidence bands for these results (equivalent to standard errors) makes it impossible to determine whether this difference is statistically significant or the equivalent of noise.

Ahn, Arcidiacono, and Wessels (2011) elaborate on Flinn's (2006) model to study the compositional effect of the minimum wage on the employment and labor force participation of white teenage boys. They distinguish these boys according to traits of the head of the household in which they live: marital and employment status, and especially educational achievement. The intuition is that the opportunity cost of working is greater for boys living in households that are more affluent and more stable, so drawing these boys into the labor market requires a higher expected wage. Once in the market, however, they are better at navigating the process of finding a job because of skills associated with their background. Because the expected wage is a product of the probability of finding a job and the wage paid once a job is found, the effect of the minimum wage on their decision is ambiguous. If they decide to enter the market, they likely outcompete others already in the market, taking jobs that would otherwise have gone to boys from less favored backgrounds.

Ahn, Arcidiacono, and Wessels (2011) estimate the model with data from 12 years (1989–2000) of CPS outgoing rotation groups (excluding summer months), which leads to problems. Their theoretical and econometric work is ambitious and impressive, but they overlook the issue of serial correlation and standard errors already mentioned. They report statistically significant results for the expected compositional effects (i.e., higher employment and labor force participation of boys from advantaged backgrounds, lower values of these variables for boys from disadvantaged backgrounds). With standard errors that are almost certainly biased downward, it is not possible to ascertain whether the estimates are statistically significant.

Eckstein, Ge, and Petrongolo (2011) analyze the importance of non-compliance with federal minimum wage laws, along the way generating estimates from which it is possible to calculate employment elasticities (but not their standard errors) for white males who completed high school between the ages of 17 and 19 and were never in either college or the armed forces. Their search model specifies two types of workers and assumes that the wage distribution depends on the distribution of productivity across firms. Increases in the minimum wage affect both sides of the labor market. On the demand side, an increase reduces employment by driving low-productivity firms out of business, resulting in a lower rate at which job seekers receive job offers. On the supply side, it raises both the reservation wage and the expected wage of job offers. The first two effects both lead to lower employment, but the last one leads to higher employment, so what happens to the employment rate following a minimum wage increase is not evident a priori.

For the population Eckstein, Ge, and Petrongolo (2011) study, the minimum wage elasticity of employment during the first year after graduation and in the labor force is −0.061, and it is −0.035 during the next three years, two to four years after graduation and in the labor force.[24] These values correspond roughly to those for teenagers and young adults, respectively. It is difficult to evaluate them both because they are for groups that do not closely match those examined elsewhere, and no standard errors are reported. In any event, both point values are very small. Eckstein, Ge, and Petrongolo write,

> Increases in the minimum wage and/or compliance deliver small effects on the wage distribution and the nonemployment rate. (p. 580)

According to our model, the employment effect of the minimum wage comes from a combination of lower job offer arrival rates and (ambiguous) changes in the reservation wage. However, empirically we find that [the minimum wage] has a negligible impact on [the reservation wage]. Thus the increase in nonemployment driven by the increase in the minimum wage is almost entirely driven by the fact that [most but not all low productivity firms choose not to evade the new minimum but instead] leave the market. (p. 604)

The vein of research that rests on data aggregated or grouped by state has from the start addressed the possibility of geographic heterogeneity with state fixed effects. Using two different approaches, Allegretto, Dube, and Reich (2009, 2011) show that this is insufficient because the problem is not just one of heterogeneity but one of local or regional correlation. Both analyses measure the correlation between employment and the minimum wage only within well-defined regions in order to reduce the likelihood of mistakenly attributing to the minimum wage employment effects that are instead due to other factors with which the minimum wage is correlated. Allegretto, Dube, and Reich (2011) argue that regions of the country have different economic cultures that result in regional differences in both the level of the minimum wage and the functioning of labor markets.[25] Distinguishing the specific effect of the minimum wage from that of the broader economic culture requires comparing states only with close neighbors rather than, say, Maine to Texas or California to North Dakota. Allegretto, Dube, and Reich (2009) approach this issue from a different angle, drawing on other work that relies on the Bureau of Labor Statistics' definition of commuting zones to treat them as local labor markets. In their data, 74 of these commuting zones straddle state boundaries and comprise counties with different contemporaneous minimum wages at some time in their sample.

Allegretto, Dube, and Reich (2011) account for geographic correlation with a set of dummy variables for census division by quarter combinations. This reduces the point estimate of the employment elasticity by two-thirds, from statistical significance to insignificance. The effect of these controls on the response of teenagers' wages to the minimum wage is just the opposite, increasing the elasticity by about one-third (more than one standard error) with no discernible effect on the estimated standard error.[26] Their treatment group consists of those counties whose minimum wage is contemporaneously higher than that of other counties in the same commuting zone, and they are matched to specific counties in the comparison group, those in the same commuting zone with a lower contemporaneous minimum wage. To show the importance of the commuting zone to their results, Allegretto, Dube, and Reich begin with a conventional regression framework that they apply to all 741 commuting zones. Then, in two steps, they move to a difference-in-differences framework by changing the regressors until the estimated coefficient of the minimum wage comes entirely from the difference that exists within each of the 74 cross-state commuting zones.[27]

After the obligatory demonstration of a wage response in each of their specifications, Allegretto, Dube, and Reich (2009) turn to the employment response. In the version that corresponds to the conventional model, they get a conventional result: an elasticity of −0.16. The result from their difference-in-differences analysis is an employment elasticity that is positive and almost as large in magnitude, 0.13. An intermediate specification that controls for regional heterogeneity at a grosser level, census divisions, generates an intermediate elasticity of 0.01. None of these are statistically significant at a 0.05 level, although using their preferred specification, they state that "we can rule out at the 5 percent level an employment elasticity more negative than −1.5 percent. Tests of coefficient equality between [the conventional model and the difference-in-differences analysis] can be rejected at the 1 percent level" (p. 17).

The central concern of Neumark and Wascher (2011) is interactions between the minimum wage and the EITC, but they also briefly consider the side effect of what happens to teen employment.[28] In equations that include only the minimum wage variable, the employment impact for boys who are black or Hispanic is negative and significant but insignificant for other boys.[29] For both groups of boys, the results appear not to be statistically significant when the EITC is considered.[30] The pattern is different for girls: by itself, the minimum wage reduces employment for girls who are neither black nor Hispanic but not for those who are either black or Hispanic. However, once interactions with the EITC are accounted for, the only statistically significant effect is on girls who are either black or Hispanic, for whom "the additional increase in labor supply among adult women in response to the combination of a high minimum wage and generous EITC [leads] to noticeable reductions in both the employment rates and wages of female teenagers, thereby reducing their earnings sharply." This effect is not found to apply to teenage boys.

Sabia, Burkhauser, and Hansen (2012) construct a quasi experiment to study the combined effect of New York's 2005 and 2006 minimum wage increases on the employment of those aged 16–29 who do not have a high school diploma.[31] Their primary analysis is a 4 × 2 difference-in-differences, with a comparison group consisting of three nearby states, New Hampshire, Pennsylvania, and Ohio. The availability of several comparison states makes it possible to avoid the problems of biased standard errors produced in the simpler 2 × 2 model (Donald and Lang 2007), but they do not take advantage of this; however, they present two other analyses that sidestep the problem. The first uses the technique of difference-in-differences-in-differences (D3), and the second uses the synthetic comparison group technique of Abadie, Diamond, and Hainmueller (2010).

The additional dimension for comparison in the analysis based on the D3 approach is people in their twenties who have completed high school. To the extent that this group and the less-educated one experience the same state-year shock to employment, the three-way differencing removes it from both the treatment and comparison groups, and Donald and Lang's (2007) concern is no longer an issue. While more-educated individuals in their twenties do not make an ideal comparison group for teenagers who have not completed high school, the use of this group in both the treatment and comparison states means that, at worst, the only likely consequence is additional noise in the estimates. The point estimates are negative for both the whole target group (aged 16–29) and for each of three subgroups: teenagers, those aged 20–24, and those aged 25–29. The only statistically significant point estimate, however, is for teenagers, and the point estimate of the corresponding elasticity, −0.95, is more than three times the size of the largest value in the older consensus range.

In the second analysis, a synthetic New York is constructed from the 25 states that had a minimum wage that both remained constant from 2002 through 2006 and was equal to New York's ex ante minimum wage of $5.15. This approach relies on calculating, from the 25 nontreatment states, a weighted average that very closely matches employment of the target group in New York for several years before the minimum wage increase, and then comparing the two ex post values of employment, for New York and synthetic New York. Sabia, Burkhauser, and Hansen (2012) instead perform a difference-in-differences analysis, likely because in the synthetic New York, the employment ratio of those aged 16–29 who did not possess a high school diploma was consistently 0.05 to 0.10 higher than in actual New York, something that was also true of the original comparison group of neighboring states. It appears that the synthetic control technique is not a substantial improvement over the original analysis, but this is not quite right. Inference is based on a quasi t-distribution that is derived from pretending that each of the 25 nontreatment states, one by one, raises its minimum wage in 2005 and 2006, and applying to it the same technique of synthetic comparison groups.[32] Because Donald and Lang's (2007) concern is equally an issue for all combinations of states, the quasi t-distribution incorporates it and the problem disappears. All point estimates of the employment effect using the synthetic control technique are negative, for the target group as a whole and for each of the three age subgroups listed above, but when the test statistics are compared to those of the quasi t-distributions, none are statistically significant.[33]

Studies that use simpler data structures. Table 2.3 lists three remaining analyses of youth employment and the minimum wage, each distinguished by the use of sophisticated statistical techniques in an attempt to extract all the information from data sets with simpler internal structures than panels and repeat cross sections. Two, Williams and Mills (2001) and Bazen and Marimoutou (2002), analyze aggregate data on teenage employment typical of the older literature but use newer, more powerful techniques of time-series analysis. The third, Kalenkoski and Lacombe (2008), applies techniques of spatial econometrics to a cross section of counties using data drawn from the 2000 census.

Williams and Mills (2001) use techniques of time-series analysis that have become part of the standard tool kit since the older literature on the minimum wage, testing for unit roots and correcting as appropriate, and estimating vector autoregressions (VARs) in order to calculate impulse response functions (IRFs) that are estimates of the dynamic response to a shock. This allows them to examine how employment

Table 2.3 Youth (Simpler Data Structures, U.S. Data)

Study	Effect	Novelty	Target group[a]	Sample period	Analytic approach	Unit of observation	Data structure	Data set[b]
Bazen and Marimoutou (2002)	Negative	Structural time-series models	Teenagers	1954–1999	Regression	Year	Time series	Old time-series data
Kalenkoski and Lacombe (2008)	Negative	Addressing geographic correlation	Teenagers	2000	Regression	County	Cross section	Census
Williams and Mills (2001)	Mixed	Time-series issues: unit roots, VARs	Teenagers	1954–1993	Regression	Quarter	Time series	Old time-series data

[a] Teenagers refers to those aged 16–19.

[b] The Current Population Survey is the source for most of this data, but the authors received the data sets from earlier workers in the literature, which facilitates comparison with prior work.

changes over time following a minimum wage increase, something more interesting than a typical coefficient estimate. A drawback of IRFs is that the results can be sensitive to necessary but arbitrary choices. To address this problem, Williams and Mills report results from several IRFs, examining in each the employment response to a 10 percent increase in the minimum wage. The results are quite similar, with the teen employment ratio decreasing for eight quarters, until it is four to eight percentage points lower than it would otherwise be. It remains roughly flat for the next four quarters, after which it returns to normal by the 16th quarter after the increase. Williams and Mills place more faith in the smaller estimates of the response, the intermediate drop of four rather than eight percentage points. Even according to the generous 90 percent confidence intervals (corresponding to a test size of 0.10) that they report, the decline is significant only in quarters 8 and 12 following the increase; this pattern suggests that the apparent statistically significant response to the minimum wage may well be due to inadequate treatment of seasonality.

Bazen and Marimoutou (2002) use structural time-series modeling techniques based on the Kalman filter, which allows for unusually flexible treatment of trend, seasonality, and business cycles. This approach generates estimates of the employment response to the minimum wage that are much more stable than was apparent from the accumulated results of the older literature. They find a statistically significant short-term elasticity of -0.10 and a long-term elasticity of -0.30, the two extremes of the range commonly reported in the older literature. The contrast with the results of Williams and Mills (2001), who found a large short-term response that, rather than getting larger, disappeared over time is worth noting.

Kalenkoski and Lacombe (2008) apply techniques from spatial econometrics that correct for correlation between observations made at locations near each other, similar to statistical techniques that correct for correlation over time. These tools, which are not in widespread use in economics, allow for much finer correction of spatial correlation than dummy variables of the sort used to control for state and census-division effects. The authors estimate three models of geographic correlation on county-level teenage employment ratios. The simplest, analogous to a one-period moving average, allows for correlation between adjacent counties but not those farther apart. In the intermediate model, analogous to a first-order serial correlation process, correlations attenuate more gradually as the number of counties in between grows. The most general version allows for both kinds of correlation. Specification tests support the second model. The corresponding minimum wage elasticity of teenage employment equals −0.3, at the high end of the range of the old consensus range.

The techniques used in these three pieces efficiently extract information from the data to which they are applied, but the one-dimensional nature of the data limit the information that they contain. The time-series data obscure much regional variation that is quite important and illuminating, as the analyses of Allegretto, Dube, and Reich (2009, 2011) have shown. Because the cross section that Kalenkoski and Lacombe (2008) analyze consists of only a single period, going beyond a very careful study of the correlation between the minimum wage and employment is not possible. To draw reliable inferences about causal relationships, it is necessary to distinguish carefully what is due to the minimum wage and what is due to other, correlated factors, something that is exceedingly difficult or impossible with these data.

Summary of the effect on youth employment. What do studies since the last exchange between Neumark and Wascher (2000) and Card and Krueger (2000) tell us about the response of youth employment to the minimum wage? Of the seven discussed based on aggregate panels, only Neumark (2001) finds no detectable effect. Three, Sabia (2009a,b) and Thompson (2009) find unambiguous negative effects. Two others, Bazen and Le Gallo (2009) and Addison, Blackburn, and Cotti (2013), find an occasional negative effect that each attributes to the timing of increases in the minimum wage. Orrenius and Zavodny (2008) report mixed results, negative for teenage boys, but no detectable effect on either teenage girls or teenagers as a whole.

Of the seven studies that use individual-level data, four build on the approach that Neumark and Wascher (1992) introduced, which itself built on the older time-series approach. Three of these four, Allegretto, Dube, and Reich (2009, 2011) and Sabia, Burkhauser, and Hansen (2012), pay careful attention to the comparison group, essentially the counterfactual of what would have happened in the absence of a minimum wage increase. They give different answers: Allegretto, Dube, and Reich (2009, 2011) report no impact on teenage employment while

Sabia, Burkhauser, and Hansen (2012) detect a much stronger one for teenagers than is typically reported in this literature. The fourth of these studies, Neumark and Wascher (2011), reports a negative employment response for teenage girls who are black or Hispanic but not for other teenagers. The other three studies—Ahn, Arcidiacono, and Wessels (2011), Eckstein, Ge, and Petrongolo (2001), and Flinn (2006)—ground their analysis in a search model that allows for examination of a variety of effects on the minimum wage, but because none reports reliable standard errors, it is not at all clear how much faith we should place on the point estimates of their most interesting results.

We are left with some interesting hints but nothing definite. It is unlikely that increases in the minimum wage that raise wages always or even often have negative consequences for youth employment. They may, however, perhaps because of poor timing, as Bazen and Le Gallo (2009) and Addison, Blackburn, and Cotti (2013) suggest, perhaps for other reasons such as low education, as is implied by Sabia, Burkhauser, and Hansen's (2012) definition of their target. Or it may be that the apparent, occasional negative impact is due to inadequate controls for other factors, as Allegretto, Dube, and Reich (2009, 2011) argue.

Other groups

Table 2.4 lists several studies that consider the effect of minimum wage legislation on groups other than young workers. Four of these appeared in the sections on young workers, including three that glanced at the response of youth employment response along the way to examining the effect on other groups, and which are presented in more detail below: Orrenius and Zavodny (2008), Neumark and Wascher (2011), and Neumark and Nizalova (2007). The fourth, already discussed in some detail, is Eckstein, Ge, and Petrongolo (2011). Two other studies are introduced here: Sabia (2008) examines the effect of the minimum wage on single mothers, including their employment; and Luttmer (2007) uses the rotation structure of the CPS estimate to examine how the minimum wage affects the wage and skill structure of the low end of the labor market, and the consequent effect on the employment of unskilled and low-skilled individuals.

As poorly educated immigrant populations grow in the United States, Orrenius and Zavodny (2008) believe that it is increasingly im-

Table 2.4 Other Groups (U.S. Data)

Study	Effect	Novelty	Target group	Sample period	Analytic approach	Unit of observation	Data structure	Type of standard error	Data set[a]
Eckstein, Ge, and Petrongolo (2011)	Negative	Enforcement of MW in a search model	White male high school graduates	1979–1996	Regression	Individual-month	Longitudinal	GMM	NLSY
Luttmer (2007)	Mixed	Focus on job rationing	Unskilled, low-skilled workers	1989–1992	Regression (differences)	State	Cross section	Huber-White	CPS
Neumark and Nizalova (2007)	Negative	Long-term consequences	Adults, 25–29	1979–2001	Regression	State-cohort-year	Panel	Clustered (state)	CPS
Neumark and Wascher (2011)	Mixed	MW-EITC interaction	Low-income, single mothers	1997–2006	Regression	Individual-month	Repeated cross section	Clustered (state)	CPS
Orrenius and Zavodny (2008)	Mixed	Immigrants	Immigrants	1995–2005	Regression	State-year	Panel	Clustered (state)	CPS
Sabia (2008)	Mixed	Focus on poverty	Low-income, single mothers	1992–2005	Regression	Individual-year	Repeated cross section	Clustered (state)	CPS
Grogger (2003)[b,c]	None	Effect on welfare rolls	Female heads of families	1979–2000	Regression	Individual	Repeated cross section	Clustered (state-year)	March CPS
Hoffman and Ke (2012)[b]	None	National quasi experiment, DIDID	Low-skill workers	2009	Quasi experiment	Individual-month	Repeated cross section	Conventional	CPS

Study	Effect	Law/Policy	Group	Years	Method	Unit of observation	Type of data	Standard errors	Data source
Hoffman and Trace (2009)[b]	Negative	NJ-PA (1996 increase)	Youth and those w/low education	1996	Quasi experiment	Inidividual-month	Repeated cross section	Conventional	CPS
Mastracci and Persky (2008)[b]	None (Emp.)	IN-IL (2004, 2005 increases in IL)	Low-wage workers	2003–2005	Quasi experiment	Individual-year	Repeated cross section	Conventional	CPS
Neumark, Schweitzer, and Wascher (2004)[b]	Negative	Those earning (much) higher than minimum wage	Wage earners	1979–1997	Regression	Individual-month	Longitudinal	Robust	CPS

[a] NLSY = National Longitudinal Survey of Youths. CPS = Current Population Survey.

[b] For repeat cross-section data, clustering within each state and year rather than within each state (over all years) does not resolve serial correlation; much too frequent rejection of the null hypothesis (of no effect) remains a problem (Bertrand, Duflo, and Mullainathan [2004]).

[c] This study has standard errors that are suspect for reasons identified by Bertrand, Duflo, and Mullainathan (2004) or Donald and Lang (2007).

portant to understand the effect of various policies on this group. To this end, they construct a state-year panel from the CPS for the years 1994–2005 to study the minimum wage, focusing on immigrants who have not completed high school. They report that the overall response of these immigrants' wages is nearly as large as that of teenagers' wages, with elasticities in the range of 0.15 to more than 0.20. Wages of low-educated immigrant women respond more strongly than those of teenage girls. However, Orrenius and Zavodny detect no employment effect on these immigrants, neither overall nor for either men or women separately. They question whether the absence of an employment effect may be due to immigrants' choosing to avoid or leave states with higher minimum wages in the expectation that employment there is harder to come by. To explore this, they calculate simple regressions of several variables on the minimum wage, including the population shares of both native born and immigrants without a high school diploma, the average years of education of both these groups, and the fraction of each group that lacks a high school diploma. They find that states with higher minimum wages have lower proportions of immigrants in their populations and suspect that immigrants pay attention not specifically to the minimum wage but to the location of appropriate jobs, and that firms with such jobs relocate in response to the minimum wage. This suggests issues similar to those that Allegretto, Dube, and Reich (2009, 2011) raise concerning correlation between economic growth rates and the minimum wage across regions of the country, and the need for appropriate controls to disentangle minimum wage effects successfully.

Using CPS data to construct a state-year panel for 1991–2004, Sabia (2008) studies the effect of the minimum wage on single mothers. After concluding that it does not affect whether their income is less than the poverty line, he turns to consideration of other outcomes, including their employment status. He finds no employment response for either the entire sample of single mothers or for those who have high school diplomas but does find a substantial employment effect when he narrows his focus to the 20 percent of the sample that have not completed high school; the point estimate of the employment elasticity with respect to the minimum wage is −0.9 (he reports no standard error). This is quite large, comparable to the elasticity that Sabia, Burkhauser, and Hansen (2012) report for youth without a high school diploma. Orrenius and Zavodny (2008) report statistically insignificant estimates of the employment elasticity that range between −0.1 and −0.2 for female immigrants who lacked high school diplomas. An explanation for these divergent effects on different groups of low-educated women is that employers do not view single mothers as desirable employees; when child care arrangements fall apart or a child is sick, a single mother is likely to miss work on short notice. If the minimum wage draws into the labor force women who do not have these problems, it is likely that employers will substitute toward them (even if there are legal issues related to this). It would be useful to know if this is indeed the explanation, or at least to know who replaces less-educated single mothers among the employed when the minimum wage rises.

As previously discussed, Neumark and Wascher (2011) use individual-level data from the CPS to examine whether and how the minimum wage interacts with the EITC.[34] The EITC subsidizes the earnings of low-income families, primarily those with children. With regard to the minimum wage and employment, their analysis considers two issues:

1) Intended effects. If the EITC encourages employment by increasing returns from working, does the minimum wage amplify this effect or attenuate it by reducing employment opportunities?

2) Unintended consequences. If the EITC harms others who are already in the labor market but ineligible for the EITC by increasing competition for jobs, does the minimum wage amplify this by reducing employment opportunities?

To examine these issues, Neumark and Wascher (2011) run two similar sets of regressions, one set for intended effects and one for unintended consequences or side effects; within each set, the estimation sample is what distinguishes the results. The first regression for examining intended effects uses a sample of all single women aged 21–44; the next two use two overlapping subsamples: single women with no education beyond high school, and black and Hispanic single women. The first regression for examining side effects begins with a sample of childless individuals, 21–34, "who are not eligible for the much more generous EITC available to families with children" (Neumark and Wascher 2011, Note 5). The sample is then reduced once by deleting those who did not go past high school and are neither black nor Hispanic; the treatment group is childless blacks and Hispanics who did not go past high school, and the comparison group is childless individuals who completed high school. It is reduced a second time by deleting all black and Hispanics who did not go past high school and were not single males; the treatment group is now childless, single black and Hispanic men, aged 21–34, who did not go past high school, while the comparison group remains childless individuals who completed high school.

For both sets of equations, the dependent variable is a dummy that indicates employment status, and the ancillary variables are the state-year unemployment rate and dummies for a variety of demographic traits and state and year effects. The focal variables are the two policy variables that measure the minimum wage and EITC, their interaction, and interactions of these three variables with a treatment dummy that indicates the group of interest in the regression. In the regressions that examine intended effects on different groups of single women, the treatment dummy indicates whether the household includes children. Consequently, in each sample considered (all single women, single women whose education went no further than completion of high school, or black or Hispanic single women), the treatment group is single mothers in the sample and the comparison group is single women in the sample who are not mothers. In the regressions examining the unintended consequences on ineligible individuals, the treatment dummy indicates whether education proceeded no further than high school. Consequently, the comparison group in each sample considered is the same: all childless men and women aged 21–34 whose education continued past high school. In the first sample, the treatment group is all childless men and women in this age group whose education went no further than high school (designated low-skilled). In the second, the treatment group is childless black or Hispanic men and women whose education went no further than high school, and the final treatment group is childless black or Hispanic single men whose education went no further than high school. Neither type of regression includes the treatment dummy by itself, without interactions with other policy variables.

This absence begs the question, "With regard to the interaction terms between the policy variables and the treatment dummies, do the coefficient estimates partly reflect the effect of the dummy alone?" If the answer is "Yes," then the estimates do not accurately measure the effects of the policies. As specified, each equation is based on an assumption that without the two policies, labor market outcomes of otherwise identical individuals distinguished only by the dummy variable would be identical; whether or not they have children, single women would be expected to have the same employment status but for the EITC and the minimum wage; similarly, were it not for the EITC and the minimum wage, otherwise identical ineligible individuals would be expected to have the same employment status whether or not their education continued past high school graduation. The statement about single women seems doubtful as soon as it is stated, and the one about ineligible individuals seems so after a moment's thought, since many who continue in school past high school are out of the labor market in their early twenties until they leave school.[35]

Finally, of interest from the perspective of this survey is the coefficient of the stand-alone minimum wage term in each equation and some of the sums of this coefficient and that of the interaction term. While point estimates of the sums are easily calculated, standard errors are not, in the absence of the relevant covariance terms.[36]

Turning first to the regressions that examine the intended effects of the policies, of those on samples of single women, nearly all reported coefficients on the terms of interest (both policy variables, their interaction, and all three of these interacted with the treatment dummy) are positive, and the three that are not are dwarfed by their standard errors. The only terms that are statistically significant are the minimum wage by itself in the regression on those whose education did not go beyond high school, and those that include the EITC interacted with the treatment dummy (with and without the minimum wage).[37] These results suggest that, at worst, the minimum wage does not reduce employment of single women, whether or not they have children, and, at best, it slightly increases employment of single women who have no more education than high school. Further, the minimum wage and the EITC appear to work quite powerfully together to draw single mothers into employment. If the equation included a stand-alone dummy for children, it is plausible that its coefficient would be negative (single mothers are less likely to be employed than childless single women), in which case the positive effect of these two policies on the employment of single mothers is even larger.

In the regressions that examine the unintended consequences of these policies, those on samples of childless individuals aged 21–34, the overall effect of the minimum wage on employment (to the extent that we can tell) appears to be positive. In the largest sample, considering all childless individuals in this age group, the only statistically significant estimate of the six coefficients is the one where the minimum wage stands alone, and it is positive. When the sample is reduced so that the only people in the sample with no more than a high school education are either childless single blacks and Hispanics or childless single black and Hispanic men, the story is more complicated. The results clearly indicate that the EITC reduces the employment of these groups and the minimum wage amplifies this effect, but without the EITC, the minimum wage increases their employment. For the two samples restricted to blacks and Hispanics, the statistically significant coefficients are precisely the interactions that include the treatment dummy. Unlike the previous set of regressions where the absence of the treatment indicator may well have reduced the size of the estimated effects, here it is less clear, which makes it harder to feel confident in these results and what they mean. It does not appear that the minimum wage reduced employment of low-skilled individuals, certainly not in the absence of the EITC, but we cannot be certain.

Luttmer's (2007) central concern is whether minimum wage increases disorganize the labor market so much that some individuals who are employed have higher reservation wages than some otherwise identical people who are not employed; he deems this situation allocatively inefficient. Estimation of reservation wages requires some ingenuity, especially with respect to the CPS's rotation structure in a way that may be a step too far. As part of this, he classifies employed individuals into skill categories according to their wage decile and considers the effect of the minimum wage on the employment of the unskilled and low-skilled, those who are in the bottom two deciles (or would be if employed). Luttmer

> find[s] suggestive evidence that the 1990/91 increase in the federal minimum wage reduced employment among unskilled workers. However, their employment reduction seems to be largely compensated for by increased employment among the next skill group, which is likely to be a close substitute. Hence, for a more broadly

defined group of less skilled workers, [he does] not find evidence of a large negative employment impact. (p. 31)[38]

Neumark and Nizalova (2007) raise the possibility of scarring, long-term effects on individuals' employment prospects; if the minimum wage reduces employment among teenagers, they will have less opportunity to develop skills and behaviors that will lead to labor market success in the long run. Neumark and Nizalova (2007) construct an aggregate panel that is similar to those often used to study the minimum wage with CPS data, but instead of a single observation for each state-year combination constructed from the corresponding information for teenagers aged 16–19, they construct a separate observation for each state-year-age, where age runs from 16 to 29: 15 observations for each state and year rather than one. For the equation in which they are most interested, they use the observations for ages 25–29. The dependent variable of interest here is the employment ratio. They regress this on three minimum wage variables and fixed effects for state, year, and each age (16, 17, 18, and 19 for teens; 20, 21, 22, 23, and 24 for young adults; and 25, 26, 27, 28, and 29 for adults in their late twenties). The minimum wage variables are the mean value of the minimum wage in the current state of residence when individuals of this age were 1) in their teens, aged 16–19; 2) young adults, aged 20–24; and 3) aged 25–29. The estimated effect on employment for those in their late twenties of the mean minimum wage at the time when they were teenagers is negative and statistically significant. The corresponding employment effect on the same age group of the minimum wage when they were in their early twenties is negative, statistically significant, and twice as large.[39]

One serious problem is that the channel through which this is supposed to work is reduced employment at an early age, which leads to less human capital, which in turn reduces employment at a later age. As discussed in the earlier brief mention of this article in the section on youth, none of the estimated employment effects for teenagers or young adults are statistically significant; the contemporaneous minimum wage reduces the employment of neither teenagers nor those in their early twenties. It is not evident how the minimum wage could then have any effect on human capital formation that would have consequences later in life, undercutting their explanation for their primary result.

More important is that the data used are poorly suited to this analysis. With Current Population Survey Outgoing Rotation Group (CPS

ORG) data, it is possible to track individuals for no more than a year, but the analysis is based on relations between variables over periods of more than a decade. As a result, very strong assumptions are necessary about what happens during periods in which data are not observed.

In their analysis of the importance of noncompliance with federal minimum wage laws, Eckstein, Ge, and Petrongolo (2011) present estimates from which it is possible to calculate employment elasticities with respect to the minimum wage (but not their standard errors) for white male high school graduates. Having already considered those for men in the first four years of their work history, roughly older teenagers and younger young adults, we now turn to those for somewhat older men. For those who graduated between five and nine years ago, the elasticity is −0.040 and for those 10–18 years out, it is 0.034. These elasticities are both very small and roughly constant after the first year in the labor force.

Of the six studies that have examined the effect of the minimum wage on the employment of groups other than the young, Orrenius and Zavodny (2008) find no effect on the employment of immigrants who have not completed high school. The results of Neumark and Wascher (2011) suggest that the minimum wage by itself has a small positive effect on the employment of single women, aged 21–44, with no more than a high school education; of childless individuals, aged 21–34; and of adults who have gone beyond high school, whether single women or blacks and Hispanics. Further it amplifies the measured effects of the EITC on employment, both positive and negative. Luttmer (2007) can find no net employment effect on the lowest skilled workers (as defined by position in the wage distribution), although there may be some compositional effect. Elasticities for male high school graduates in, roughly, their early twenties through mid-thirties can be calculated from the numbers that Eckstein, Ge, and Petrongolo (2007) report. They are negative and quite small. Whether they rise above background noise is something that we cannot tell since no standard errors are available. Neumark and Nizalova (2007) report a long-term scarring effect on employment prospects from the minimum wage experienced when a teenager and young adult, but there are several problems with these results, including both the alleged transmission mechanism and the appropriateness of the data for this analysis. Ultimately, only Sabia (2008) finds any adverse effect on employment, a very large one for single mothers who have not completed high school.[40] This is not precisely the same group that Neumark and Wascher (2011) denote "low-skilled," since their group includes high school graduates, but their results do not seem to be consistent with Sabia's (2008). Further work is necessary to determine the source of the differences, whether they are due to the varying definitions of "low-skilled" or the specification issues raised in this section and elsewhere by Allegretto, Dube, and Reich (2009, 2011).

Sectoral Studies

Restaurants (and hotels)

Table 2.5 lists 11 analyses of the restaurant industry or restaurant and hotel industries. Six are regression-based analyses, 5 supplement that technique with difference-in-differences analyses, and 1 relies primarily on the response of prices to the minimum wage in the United States to infer the employment response. The 3 that rely on the QCEW, derived from data collected as part of the unemployment insurance system, use county-quarter panels, and the fourth uses a state-quarter panel. The 4 based on private surveys have before-and-after observations (or occasionally only before) on each establishment. The other data sources provide monthly or annual time series at the state-industry level.

Dube, Naidu, and Reich (2007) follow the approach pioneered by Card and Krueger (1994), collecting data and performing a difference-in-differences analysis of the effect on restaurants: primarily their wages and employment. They study the establishment of a citywide minimum wage in San Francisco that went into effect in early 2004 for firms with at least 10 employees. They divide restaurants into three size categories: small (4–8 employees ex ante), midsize (14–35 workers ex ante), and larger ones. The treatment group is midsize restaurants in San Francisco with at least one employee whose ex ante wage would have to rise in response to the new law. Midsize restaurants in nearby communities are the primary comparison group, and results from this analysis are subject to the problem that Donald and Lang (2007) identify. However, Dube, Naidu, and Reich (2007) also report results for two other comparison groups of restaurants in San Francisco: small restaurants, which were initially excused from the minimum wage, and similar-sized restaurants that prior to the law had no employees whose wages would have to be raised. In addition, they report regression results where the minimum

Table 2.5 Restaurants and Hotels (U.S. Data)

Study	Effect	Novelty	Target	Sample period	Analytic approach	Unit of observation	Data structure	Type of standard error	Data set[a]
Aaronson and French (2007)	Negative	Test output price implications of monopsony model	Restaurant industry	—	Calibration	Labor market	—	—	—
Addison, Blackburn, and Cotti (2012)	None	New data source	Eating and drinking establishments	1990–2005	Regression	County-quarter	Panel	Clustered (state)	QCEW
Addison, Blackburn, and Cotti (2013)	Mixed	Amplifying effect of recessions?	Eating and drinking establishments	2006–2009 2005–2010	Regression	State-year county-qtr. state-month	Panel	Clustered (state)	ACS QCEW CPS
Dube, Lester, and Reich (2010)	None	Addressing regional heterogeneity	Eating and drinking establishments	1990–2006	Quasi experiment	County-quarter	Panel	Clustered (state)	QCEW
Dube, Naidu, and Reich (2007)	None	Replicate Card and Krueger (1994) for SF	San Francisco restaurants	2003–2004	Quasi experiment and regression	Firm-year	Longitudinal	Robust	Private survey
Even and Macpherson (2014)	Negative	Tip credit	Full-service restaurants	1990–2011	Regression	State-quarter	Panel	Clustered (state)	QCEW, CPS
Hirsch, Kaufman, and Zelenska (2011)	None	Studying other dimensions of adjustment	Fast food restaurants in GA and AL	2007–2009	Regression	Establishment-month	Longitudinal	Clustered (establishment)	Private survey

Persky and Baiman (2010)	Mixed	IL minimum wage increases	IL fast food establishments	2003–2005	Quasi experiment (2x2)	Firm-year	Longitudinal	Conventional	Private survey
Singell and Terborg (2007)	Mixed	Loosely modeled on C&K (1994)	SIC 58, 70 OR, WA	1994–2001	Regression	State-industry month	Multiple time series	Conventional	BLS-CES
Powers (2009)[b]	Negative	IL minimum wage increases	IL fast food establishments	2003–2005	Quasi experiment (2x2)	Firm-year	Longitudinal	Conventional	Private survey
Ropponen (2011)[b]	Mixed	Change-in-changes analysis of C&K (1994) and N&W (2000) data	NJ fast food establishments	1991–1992	Quasi-experiment (2x2)	Firm-year	Longitudinal	—	Private surveys

[a] QCEW = Quarterly Census of Employment and Wages. ACS = American Community Survey. CPS = Current Population Survey. BLS-CES = Bureau of Labor Statistics-Current Establishment Survey.

[b] This study has standard errors that are suspect for reasons identified by Donald and Lang (2007).

wage variable is the fraction affected (à la Katz and Krueger [1992]), and the estimation samples are the union of the treatment group and variously defined comparison groups. The discussion below is limited to these results, which should be robust to this statistical issue.

Dube, Naidu, and Reich (2007) detect a wage effect from regression results except in models that exclude fast food restaurants from the treatment group. In the difference-in-differences analysis that neglects restaurant closings, three of the four point estimates of the employment effect are positive and none are statistically significant. When they take account of establishments that closed between the two surveys, which occurred at higher rates in both comparison groups, the positive point estimates of the employment effect become larger, the negative estimate becomes positive, and all remain statistically not significant. Regression estimates also indicate only employment elasticities that are positive and not statistically significant. Dube, Naidu, and Reich conclude that there is no evidence of a disemployment effect, and that their confidence intervals are sufficiently tight as to rule out relatively large effects, both the positive ones of Card and Krueger (1994) and the negative ones of Neumark and Wascher (2000).

Addison, Blackburn, and Cotti (2012) perform a regression analysis on a national data set of employment and payroll in eating and drinking establishments for each county in the United States that they created from Quarterly Census of Employment and Wages (QCEW) data for 1990–2005. They loosely derive their regression equations from simple specifications of labor supply and demand and then present results from a variety of specifications in order to examine their sensitivity to different modeling choices. Only the sparest specification (the one with the fewest controls) indicates a negative employment response. Once they begin adding additional controls, in particular allowing for county-specific trends, they report a statistically significant elasticity of earnings with respect to the minimum wage of about 0.17, but no discernible employment response.

Powers, Persky, and Baiman (2007) collect data from about 200 fast food outlets in eastern Illinois and western Indiana to analyze the effects of the minimum wage increases in Illinois that occurred at the beginning of 2004 and 2005, à la Card and Krueger (1994). Not reaching agreement on the interpretation of the analysis of the data, they published two separate reports, Powers (2009) and Persky and Baiman (2010). As with Card and Krueger, the central analysis in each uses a difference-in-differences framework, but both also present alternative analyses of the employment effect. Persky and Baiman (2010) present results from a regression based on a wage gap to measure the incidence of the minimum wage that avoids the problems that Donald and Lang (2007) identify, and Powers (2009) presents results from a D3 analysis that does not avoid these problems. The D3 analysis splits the sample period into two parts, comparing the differences from after and in between the minimum wage increase with those from in between and before. Each of these difference-in-differences is subject to distinct, independent shocks of the type that Donald and Lang (2007) identified; the point estimate of the D3 value is unbiased and its standard error is inconsistently estimated.

The definition of the wage gap that Persky and Baiman (2010) use is the percentage increase in an Illinois establishment's 2003 starting wage that is necessary to bring it up to the 2005 value of the Illinois minimum wage. As dependent variables, they consider both the change in the number of positions in each establishment and the size-weighted growth rate (Note 11, p. 135). In different specifications and samples (the differences are mostly attempts to control for potential data problems), while most estimated coefficients of the minimum wage are negative, all are not statistically significant.

Dube, Lester, and Reich (2010) present a very rich analysis of QCEW data that uses several distinct but closely related frameworks to address the most serious criticisms of earlier studies. These frameworks allow for close comparison of conflicting findings, which they believe are due to several overlooked statistical problems. All of their results derive from regressions in which the dependent variable is restaurant employment for 1990–2006, and the right-hand-side variables include total employment and population in each county, and the effective minimum wage.[41] What distinguishes the analyses from one another is the sample of counties, dummy variables, and trends. Two important features of their work relate to their concern with unobserved heterogeneity, and the careful way that they sequentially structure their analyses so that the reader can understand the source of differences in results.

Dube, Lester, and Reich (2010) do not identify a particular source of unobserved heterogeneity, instead listing a variety of traits that are similar across states within the same region but differ between states that are farther apart. Among these are the cost of living, regulation, growth rates, and business cycle behavior and how the local economy responds. They observe that

> as recently as 2004, no state in the South had a state minimum wage. Yet the South has been growing faster than the rest of the nation, for reasons entirely unrelated to the absence of state-based minimum wages. . . . By itself, heterogeneity in overall employment growth may not appear to be a problem, since most estimates control for overall unemployment trends. Nonetheless, using states with very different overall employment growth as controls is problematic. The presence of such heterogeneity in overall employment suggests that controls for low-wage employment using extrapolation, as is the case using traditional fixed effects estimates, may be inadequate. (pp. 6–7)

To address this problem, their regression equations include separate dummy variables for each quarter by census division rather than a single national dummy for each quarter. As a result, the effect of the minimum wage in New York in the first quarter of 2005, when it rose from $5.15 per hour to $6.00 per hour, is calculated in comparison with only New Jersey and Pennsylvania, where it remained at $5.15 per hour, rather than all states across the country.

To make the source of their results transparent, Dube, Lester, and Reich (2010) begin with an analysis designed to resemble Neumark and Wascher's (1992, 1994) regression-based studies of teenage employment.[42] They then proceed, step-by-step, to an analysis designed to resemble the difference-in-differences studies of Card and Krueger (1994, 2000). Along the way, they demonstrate the importance of the unobserved heterogeneity described above. The key analyses are the first and last pairs.[43]

In the first pair of analyses, the sample consists of quarterly observations of all counties in the continental (contiguous) United States from 1990 through the first half of 2006. The first analysis includes fixed effects for each county and quarter so that the analysis is similar in form to studies of teenage employment based on state-year panels. The point estimate of the employment response to the minimum wage is in the range of those often reported for teenagers, -0.18, and statistically significant. The second specification replaces the aggregate time effects with controls for unobserved regional factors, quarterly effects that differ across each of the nine census divisions. The consequence is a reduction in the employment response by nearly five-sixths, to −0.03, and it is now, at about half the size of its standard error, statistically insignificant. Dube, Lester, and Reich (2010) infer from this pair of analyses that the results of studies of the minimum wage and teenage employment based on the canonical framework of Neumark and Wascher (e.g., 1992) are due to neglect of unobserved regional heterogeneity.

In the last pair of analyses, which culminates in a difference-in-differences analysis, Dube, Lester, and Reich (2010) reduce their sample to counties that are within metropolitan statistical areas (MSAs) that have more than one minimum wage for at least one quarter during the sample period; by and large, the MSAs straddle a state border, and these counties are adjacent to each other on opposite sides of the border. The first analysis of this pair resembles the first analysis of the previous pair, with a set of aggregate quarterly dummies; it indicates a minimum wage effect of −0.11, about two-thirds as large as that for the complete national sample (−0.18) and statistically significant only at the 0.10 level. The second analysis in this pair replaces the aggregate quarterly dummies with quarterly dummies for each pair of adjacent counties. As a consequence, the minimum wage effect is estimated from only minimum wage differences within MSAs, exhibiting a familial resemblance to Card and Krueger (1994, 2000). The estimated employment response is positive and about half the size of its standard error.

Following an extensive sensitivity analysis in which they vary the specification and industry examined, Dube, Lester, and Reich (2010) offer some suggestions about why the results of studies that examine national data on teenage employment differ from those that use local data on low-wage sectors. They disagree with the view that it is due to the short duration of the samples used in the local studies, which arbitrarily cut off the data before the minimum wage has had time to reduce employment. Rather, the differences

> result from insufficient controls for unobserved heterogeneity in employment growth in the national-level studies using a traditional fixed-effects specification. The differences do not arise from other possible factors, such as using short before-after windows in local case studies. . . . The large negative elasticities in the traditional specification are generated primarily by regional and local differences in employment trends that are unrelated to minimum wage policies. (p. 962)

Singell and Terborg (2007) analyze the experiences of Washington and Oregon, adjacent states with similar economies and largely complementary histories of minimum wage increases for several years beginning in the mid 1990s. The heart of the analysis consists of two multiple regression analyses, one of monthly employment data for eating and drinking establishments, and another for hotels and lodging that makes little use of time-series techniques. They estimate several slightly different equations for monthly employment growth rates in two industries in each state. Their results are statistically significant and largely consistent within each industry. For restaurants, the elasticity of employment growth with respect to minimum wage growth ranges from −0.07, when no lag of the minimum wage is in the equation, to −0.20 percent when it is. For hotels, the figures are 0.15 and 0.19, which Singell and Terborg explain on the grounds that the minimum wage was not binding in this industry and that employment was instead responding to other factors, especially the health of the economy. This, of course, raises questions about the quality of their control variables, since if the minimum wage is not binding, positive estimates are possible but ought not be (highly) statistically significant. In addition, residual serial correlation is the norm with time-series data, and if present and not addressed, undercuts statistical inference. The authors mention serial correlation and refer somewhat vaguely to a test that indicates it is not a problem.[44]

The focus of Even and Macpherson's (2014) study is the tip credit, which allows employers in full-service restaurants to pay certain employers a much lower minimum wage under the assumption that tips that these individuals receive make up at least the difference between the typical minimum wage and this lower one. The two minimum wages do not move together, with no increase in the federal level of the tipped minimum since April 1991, but they report that more than 30 states have higher tipped minimums. Except for the presence of two contemporaneous minimum wage terms, one for the regular minimum wage (hereafter called "the minimum wage") and one for the tipped minimum, their log-log regression equation resembles the canonical model that Neumark and Wascher (1992) developed to study youth employment. Although uncomfortable with the use of state-specific trends, they estimate equations that include them. However, their more interesting method for controlling for state-specific time-varying confounding factors is to perform an analysis analogous to the "triple-difference" approach. With data from the QCEW, the dependent variable is not the change in employment in the full-service sector but the difference between the change in employment in the two sectors—the full-service sector minus the limited-service sector—where they judge the tipped minimum wage to be almost entirely irrelevant.[45] With data from the CPS, which has occupational information, they can distinguish between workers who are likely tipped and others who most likely are not; here, the dependent variable is the difference between change in employment of the two types of workers.

Even and Macpherson (2014) follow a two-step process, first confirming that the minimum wage affects eating and drinking places, then studying the effect on employment. They find that the QCEW's average weekly earnings in the full-service sector respond to both the tipped minimum wage and the minimum wage, but those in the limited-service sector respond only to the latter. The tipped minimum wage reduces employment in the full-service sector in three of the four sets of estimates, the exception being that from the full sample when state-specific trends are included. The statistically significant elasticities lie in the interval [−0.102, −0.029]. They conclude that using QCEW data, their models indicate an elasticity of employment with respect to the tipped minimum wage of less than 0.1 in the full-service sector. When they apply their analysis to CPS data, they detect no effect of either the minimum wage or of the tipped minimum wage to either group of workers.[46]

A limitation of these four regression-based studies is that, despite the length of their data sets—64 quarters in Addison, Blackburn, and Cotti (2012), 66 quarters for Dube, Lester, and Reich (2010), 88 quarters for Even and Macpherson (2014), and 96 months for Singell and Terborg (2007), long enough to model the dynamics of employment using techniques common in time-series analysis—they neglect the time-series nature of their data. The econometric model underlying their equations includes the explicit assumption that, but for the minimum wage (and random noise), the labor market is at equilibrium in every period. The location of that equilibrium responds to supply and demand factors, but wherever it is, the market always finds itself there (with the same proviso concerning the minimum wage). The substantial inertial component of employment means that this assumption is unlikely to be satisfied, but this need not interfere with estimation of the response of employment to the minimum wage if it is appropriately modeled. Including lagged employment terms among the regressors or, if necessary, removing unit roots should address the problem adequately. The reporting of standard errors and *t*-statistics based on clustering at the state level goes some way toward mitigating skepticism about statistical inference in three of these studies. This solution would not be appropriate for the two-state data set of Singell and Terborg (2007), but they present no other solution and appear to be unaware of any possible problems.

We have already encountered Addison, Blackburn, and Cotti (2013) in the section on youth, where they study whether recessions amplify the effect of the minimum wage on teenagers' employment. They perform a similar analysis for the restaurant industry using county-level data from the QCEW, as well as state-level data from the CPS and the ACS, which they examine in their consideration of teenagers. In the basic model, which lacks the key variable, the interaction between the minimum wage and the unemployment rate, they do not detect any employment result either for the sector as a whole nor for its constituents, full-service restaurants, and limited-service restaurants.[47] When they include the interaction term, the QCEW data provide clear evidence of a small effect in the sector as a whole. Once they look at the two subsectors separately, it is clear that the effect is only in the limited-service sector. Although there appears to be a basic effect (one not dependent on recessions to amplify it) for the full-service sector in this specification, a joint test that the minimum wage terms as a group do not belong in this equation is resoundingly not rejected. The CPS data tell a clearer story, providing no support for the hypothesis that recessions amplify the employment effect of the minimum wage. Addison, Blackburn, and Cotti conclude that even for the restaurant sector, recessions do not appear to amplify any negative employment effects of the minimum wage.

Aaronson and French (2007) take an ingenious approach, constructing a model of the restaurant industry that includes both a labor market and an output market. They use this to determine whether the restaurant labor market is better described by the competitive or monopsonistic model. Drawing on a variety of estimates for values of the model's parameters, especially on the response of restaurant prices to minimum wage increases (Aaronson 2001; Aaronson, French, and MacDonald 2008), this analysis works back from the product market to the labor market in order to infer the implied response of employment to the minimum wage. Two key assumptions are that the price and quantity of output vary inversely with each other, and the quantities of employment and output vary positively with each other. The logical consequence of these assumptions is that a rise in employment following a minimum wage increase leads to a rise in output and a decline in prices. Because prices in fact rise, both output and employment must fall. In each market, they examine the implications of different degrees of deviation from perfect competition. After calculations based on a range of parameter values, they conclude that the elasticity for total employment in the industry is about −0.2, and about −0.3 for the employment of low-skilled labor.

Hirsch, Kaufman, and Zelenska (2011) begin with a statistical analysis of the employment response to the three increases in the federal minimum wage of 2007–2009 using electronic payroll data for 81 fast food establishments in Alabama and Georgia, all in the same national chain and owned by three franchising corporations. Although their use of a wage gap variable rather than a treatment dummy allows them to avoid the problems that Donald and Lang (2007) had, the nonrandom nature of their sample, similar in some regard to that of Neumark and Wascher (2000), leads to other problems of inference. However, this analysis is merely the stepping off point for a careful consideration of how establishments in this industry respond to the minimum wage, based on an extensive survey of managers and employees. The authors' implicit position is that "the minimum wage increases raised operating costs, yet employment has not decreased to match. The restaurants must have adjusted in other ways. What are they?" The answer, according to Hirsch, Kaufman, and Zelenska, is higher prices, lower profit margins, reduced turnover, higher performance standards, and, in the short to medium term, wage compression. This study trades off generality and rigor for detail and the possibility of generating useful hypotheses for further work, something rarely seen in this literature.

Beyond the hospitality sector: other low-wage sectors

Table 2.6 shows nine analyses that examine the employment response in various parts of the retail sector. Addison, Blackburn, and Cotti (2009) study several low-wage parts of the sector in an analysis that parallels their study of the restaurant industry (Addison, Blackburn, and Cotti 2012). Sabia (2009a) studies the whole retail sector using a state-quarter panel. Orazem and Mattila (2002) report on a two-part analysis of the retail and nonprofessional service sectors in Iowa from 1989 to 1992, the beginning of a period when the Iowa minimum wage exceeded the federal minimum wage. Giuliano (2013) analyzes very detailed data from a single company with more than 700 stores throughout the United States. Finally, the pieces by Belman and Wolfson (2010) and Wolfson and Belman (2001, 2004) use current time-series techniques to study employment in a collection of low-wage industries.

Using quarterly, county-level data from the QCEW, Addison, Blackburn, and Cotti (2009) study the effect of the minimum wage on both earnings and employment in each of five low-wage retail sectors: 1) food and beverage stores, 2) supermarkets and other grocery stores, 3) convenience stores, 4) specialty food stores, and 5) beer, wine, and liquor stores. They consider a variety of specifications in order to examine the sensitivity of their results to their modeling choices. The most basic specification suggests that earnings respond to the minimum wage in only one industry (beer, wine, and liquor stores), and even here there is no indication of an employment response. Once they include county-specific trends, they also detect earnings responses in convenience stores and in specialty food stores, and find positive employment responses in convenience stores and in beer, wine, and liquor stores; that is, in two of the three industries in which they detect a positive wage response, they also detect a positive employment response. A Hausman specification test strongly favors the model with county-specific trends in two of these industries (not beer, wine, and liquor stores), and its estimates are more precise than those of the basic model, without the trends. A conservative interpretation is that these results indicate positive wage responses in all three of the industries mentioned, a positive employment response in convenience stores, and no employment response in any of the remaining industries.[48]

Sabia (2009a) constructs a state-month panel from CPS data to study the effect of the minimum wage on employment in the retail sector. As part of a robustness check, he presents a variety of estimates based on differences in the sample, estimation technique, way of measuring the minimum wage, and model specification. The last involves whether to include a lagged minimum wage term, a correction for serial correlation, and/or state-specific trends (à la Dube, Lester, and Reich [2010]). The elasticities range from a statistically insignificant 0.07 at

Table 2.6 Other Low-Wage Sectors (U.S. Data)

Study	Effect	Target sector	Sample period	Analytic approach	Unit of observation	Data structure	Type of standard error	Data set[a]
Addison, Blackburn, and Cotti (2009)	None	Low-wage retail food	1990–2005	Regression	County-quarter	Panel	Clustered (state)	QCEW
Belman and Wolfson (2010)	None	Low-wage	1972–2003	Regression	Industry-month	Multiple time series	Conventional	BLS-CES
Giuliano (2013)	Positive	Retail	1996–1998	Regression	Establishment-month	Longitudinal	Huber-White Robust	Private + Census
Orazem and Mattila (2002)	Negative	Retail, service not professional	1989–1992	Regression	County-industry-quarter	Panel	Conventional	Various
Sabia (2009a)	Negative	Retail workers	1979–2004	Regression	State-month	Panel	Clustered (state)	CPS
Wolfson and Belman (2001)	None	Low-wage industries	1961–1997	Regression	Industry-month	multiple time series	Conventional	BLS-CES
Wolfson and Belman (2004)	None	Low-wage	1947–1997	Regression	Industry-month	multiple time series	Conventional	BLS-CES
Potter (2006)[b]	None	All, some low-wage	2003–2005	Quasi experiment (2x2)	Firm-year	Longitudinal	Conventional	ES-202
Dodson (2002)[b]	Negative	All jobs	1988–1995	Regression	County-year	Panel	Robust	REIS, Census

NOTE: The column for Novelty does not appear because in this table it would largely echo the information in Target sector.

[a] QCEW = Quarterly Census of Employment and Wages. BLS-CES = Bureau of Labor Statistics-Current Establishment Survey. REIS = Regional Economic Information System.

[b] This study has standard errors that are suspect for reasons identified by Bertrand, Duflo, and Mullainathan (2004) or Donald and Lang (2007).

one end, when state-specific trends are included, to a statistically significant −0.11 at the other. Most are right around −0.10, the low end of the previous consensus (for teenagers, not retail). He gently dismisses the positive point estimate on the grounds that "state trends may, in fact, be capturing retail employment variation that the model seeks to explain" (Sabia 2009a, p. 88). The question, then, is how to account for the type of regional factors that Dube, Lester, and Reich (2010) and Allegretto, Dube, and Reich (2010) show to be of great importance. Either trends or annual effects specific to each census division would go far to addressing this issue without raising his concerns (and an F-test would indicate whether they belong in the regression). The neglect of time-series issues, already discussed with reference to studies of the restaurant and hotel industries, is also problematic in both Addison, Blackburn, and Cotti (2009) and this study.

Iowa established its own minimum wage above the federal minimum wage at the beginning of 1990, and it remained higher until late 1996. Orazem and Mattila (2002) present two analyses for 1989–1992, one based on quarterly data for Iowa counties, the other on data for about 170,000 employees that they generated from their own survey of retail firms. Both analyses consider retail and nonprofessional services. For the county-level analysis, they detect no employment response after either one quarter or one year. In the second part of their analysis, Orazem and Mattila estimate a wage equation as a function of characteristics of the employee, employer, and county of employment, which they then use to examine whether, in quarters immediately following increases, the minimum wage is higher than an employee's wage would otherwise have been. With this information, they examine the consequent compositional change in firms' workforces, and consider, cui bono, who benefits and who suffers from the minimum wage. For those who would otherwise have earned less than the minimum wage, they report elasticities of their share in firms' labor forces of between −0.03 and −0.10. That is, if 50 percent of a firm's labor force after a 10 percent increase in the minimum wage consists of workers whose wages would otherwise have been less than the new minimum, then without the increase, such workers would have instead made up between 50.15 percent and 50.5 percent of the labor force.

In what is essentially a statistically oriented case study, Giuliano (2013) examines a single retail company that provided 30 months of sales and personnel records (February 1996–July 1998) and descriptive information for each of its more than 700 stores located throughout the United States. The data are sufficiently rich that she is able to verify compliance with the law both before and after the increases that she studies—those of the federal minimum wage in 1996 and 1997. Combining these data with information from the 1990 census, she identifies whether each employee lived in a high- or low-income zip code and then examines some of the same compositional consequences of the minimum wage as Ahn, Arcidiacono, and Wessels (2011).

Using the wage gap to measure the sensitivity of each establishment to the minimum wage, Giuliano (2013) compares the first and last six months of her sample, two periods that bracket the minimum wage increases. The effect of the increases on wages is very clear. Although the mean effect on overall employment is negative, the variance is high—enough so that one would be (or should be) unwilling to accept a bet at odds of 95 to 5 that for a store selected at random from this sample, the employment response is negative (but one should accept the same bet that the effect is positive for the share of teenagers in that store's labor force).[49] The flip side of these employment results is a decline in adult employment.[50] An in-depth examination shows that the employment share of teenagers from zip codes of all income levels rises, but only the increase of those who live in affluent zip codes is worth betting on.

To make sense of her results, Giuliano (2013) begins by distinguishing between models of dynamic monopsony (Burdett and Mortensen 1998) and monopsonistic competition (Bhaskar and To 1999) on the one hand, and models of search (Flinn 2006) and of adverse selection (Akerlof 1970; Drazen 1986) on the other. Models of either type can rationalize the rise in teenage employment. That the share of teenagers in new hires rose following the minimum wage increase suggests the greater appropriateness, she believes, of the second sort of model, with its emphasis on induced changes to labor supply. The second group of models gains further support from another result: teenagers from affluent zip codes, who likely had higher opportunity cost of employment, increased their share of both teenager hiring and employment. This suggests an increase in their labor force participation at the same time that other teens experienced no decline in their share of either overall hiring or employment.

Wolfson and Belman's three articles (2001, 2004; Belman and Wolfson 2010) all study a variety of low-wage industries in the United States, applying techniques of time-series analysis to national monthly employment data. In each case, out of concern that the set of industries is too broad and may include some that are not sensitive to the minimum wage, the first step is to identify industries that exhibit a wage response to the minimum wage.

Using monthly data from the BLS Current Employment Statistics, Wolfson and Belman (2001) take Milton Friedman's methodology of positive economics to heart by examining whether including information about minimum wage increases in forecasting equations reduces the forecast error. Looking separately at each increase in the federal minimum wage between 1961 and 1996, and at data for as many as 33 industries, they find that even in situations where the minimum wage improves wage forecasts, it leads to an improvement in the employment forecast only half as often as not. They conclude that any link between low-wage employment and the minimum wage as historically experienced is tenuous.

Wolfson and Belman (2004) and Belman and Wolfson (2010) are more conventional statistical analyses of the same data that pay careful attention to the time-series properties of the data. Examining the impact of the federal minimum wage on 23 low-wage industries between the mid-1970s and early 2003, they detect a wage response in 17 of the industries, but an employment response to increases in only 6, 1 of which is positive: and an employment response to declines in the real value of the minimum wage in only 7, 2 of which are negative. A simulation of a 10 percent increase in the minimum wage shows that the wage response is complete by 24 months, and that no trace of any employment is detectable in the four years following the increase.

Direct estimates of the restaurant sector with reliable standard errors do not indicate that minimum wage increases lead to a decline in employment that is different from zero, certainly not substantively different and typically not significantly different statistically. Indirect estimates that work back from the behavior of restaurant prices imply a demand elasticity for low-skilled labor of −0.3 (Aaronson and French 2007). While the former should be more reliable, a question remains until these differences can be explained. Studies of other sectors give results that are all over the map. Paying careful attention to the time-series dynamics that confound many studies of this topic, Belman and Wolfson (2010) and Wolfson and Belman (2001, 2004) analyze several low-wage industries and find no systematic employment response. Unfortunately, the nature of their data permits them to study only the federal minimum wage, not any of the state minimum wages that are important in the later part of the period that they study. Studies of a single state, like Orazem and Mattila's (2002), are even more vulnerable to the common criticism of Card and Krueger's (1994) study that it was excessively narrow in space and time, focusing on a single episode. Sabia (2009a) also reports a negative employment response but does not address issues of either regional heterogeneity or time-series dynamics. Giuliano's (2013) analysis is ingenious, and the results are both very interesting and strongly suggestive, but in the end it remains a case study and it is not obvious that these results hold generally. Finally, in their examination of low-wage retail sectors, Addison, Blackburn, and Cotti (2009) do not find a negative employment response, but this may reflect inadequate treatment of dynamics.

OTHER DEVELOPED COUNTRIES

More than a few studies of the minimum wage and employment that use data from developed countries other than the United States have appeared in English during this period. Two differences from studies of American data most stand out. One is the much heavier reliance on individual-level data, especially longitudinal data (rather than repeated cross sections). The other is the frequency with which the focus is on bound workers, that is, workers who were employed and earning less ex ante than the ex post minimum wage, rather than all members of a demographic group or the number of jobs in an industry.

Yuen (2003) and Campolieti, Fang, and Gunderson (2005a) use longitudinal Canadian data to explore the sensitivity of results in quasi experiments to the definitions of both the comparison group and the policy variable.[51] Although both report standard errors that are almost certainly biased downward (Moulton 1990), the methodological points that they examine are important. Stewart (2002, 2004a) analyzes the employment response of bound workers to the imposition of the

National Minimum Wage (NMW) in the United Kingdom, after several years with no minimum wage, and Stewart (2004b) repeats part of the latter study for the first two subsequent increases in the NMW. Mulheirn (2008) continues this with a look at the effect of the 2006 increase. Dolton, Rosazza-Bondibene, and Wadsworth (2012) study the entire period of the NMW, 1999–2007, using an approach similar to Stewart's (2002). Pereira (2003) and Portugal and Cardoso (2006) examine very detailed data that the Portuguese tax agency collects on every firm in the country to assess the response of employment to the large minimum wage increases in the late 1980s. Pinoli (2010) uses Spanish data to study an implication of the rational expectations hypothesis, that the timing of the employment response may depend on whether a minimum wage increase is anticipated or not. Using quarterly time-series data from several Australian states, Lee and Suardi (2011) test employment equations for parameter instability if minimum wage increases are not explicitly modeled, something that would be expected if the minimum wage were relevant for employment. Hyslop and Stillman's (2007) analysis of New Zealand's minimum wage increases early in the new millennium is the closest approach to the canonical framework of Neumark and Wascher among this group. Pacheco's (2011) study of New Zealand over a longer period adds an ingenuous twist in an attempt to focus more carefully on those whom the minimum wage directly affects.[52]

Kramarz and Philippon (2001) consider a variety of costs that French employers incur, including the minimum wage, in their study of the employment of low-wage workers. Laroque and Salanie (2002) consider a variety of social welfare policies in France, including the minimum wage, in their study of employment of married women. For Machin and Wilson (2004) and Machin, Manning, and Rahman (2003), the UK care home industry (similar to the U.S. nursing home industry) plays much the same role as the restaurant industry does in analyses of U.S. minimum wage policy, a very low-wage industry where employment should respond to the minimum wage if employment does in any industry. Galindo-Rueda and Pereira (2004) is an ambitious examination of the NMW throughout the entire United Kingdom economy that ultimately founders on the inadequacy of the data to the task.[53]

Young Workers

Table 2.7 lists 15 analyses of data from countries other than the United States to examine the response of youth employment to the minimum wage.[54] Although both Yuen (2003) and Campolieti, Fang, and Gunderson (2005a) fall prey to problems with standard errors discussed earlier in the chapter (and for this reason appear in the lower part of the table), they both raise and address other issues of interest, and the latter piece makes itself part of a careful and thoughtful discussion between the two. It is therefore worthwhile to start here.

Canada

Using 12 quarters of data on each of 9,000 Canadian youth aged 16–24 at the beginning of the sample, Yuen (2003) shows that the definition of the comparison group can greatly influence the perception of the employment response to the minimum wage. After defining his treatment group as those who were employed in a province in the quarter before a provincial minimum wage increase and were earning less than the ex post minimum wage, he considers two different comparison groups. One of the groups, which he describes as similar to those used in much prior work, includes all those who are not in the treatment group but are employed at the same time as members of the treatment group. This comparison group consists of two sets of employed individuals: 1) those in a province-quarter cell that does not include members of the treatment group (because the province quarter did not experience a minimum wage increase), and 2) those in province-quarter cells that did experience a minimum wage increase but whose wage is too high for them to be in the treatment group. The other comparison group is smaller and includes only low-wage workers who are contemporaneously employed in other provinces, where low-wage means a wage no more than Can$0.25 above the minimum wage in their own province.[55] Using an at-risk dummy to identify members of the treatment group, he reports an estimated effect that is negative and statistically significant with the larger comparison group, similar to that in prior work, but negative and not statistically significant with the smaller comparison group of similarly paid workers. En route to the smaller comparison group, he presents another result using the larger, conventional com-

Table 2.7 Youth (Other Developed Countries)

Study	Effect novelty	Novelty	Target group[a]	Country	Sample period	Analytic approach	Unit of observation	Data structure	Type of SE	Data set[b]
Hyslop and Stillman (2007)	Mixed	New Zealand	Teenagers	New Zealand	1997–2003	Quasi experiment	Individual-year	Repeated cross section	Clustered (age-quarter)	HLFS
Lee and Suardi (2011)	None	Structural breaks in time series	Teenagers	Australia	1992–2008	Regression	State-quarter	Time series	Conventional	LFS
Pacheco (2011)	Negative	Identify, focus on minimum wage youth, aged 16–29	Minimum wage youth	New Zealand	1986–2004	Regression	Individual-quarter	Repeated cross section	Conventional	HLFS
Pereira (2003)	Negative	Portugal	Teenage workers	Portugal	1986–1989	Quasi experiment	Firm-year	Longitudinal	Conventional	QP
Pinoli (2010)	Mixed	Rational expectations	Youth	Spain	2004, 2006	Quasi experiment	Individual-quarter	Longitudinal	Conventional	EPAS
Portugal and Cardoso (2006)	Positive	Response to Pereira (2003)	Teenage workers	Portugal	1986–1989	Regression	Firm-worker-year	Longitudinal	Conventional	QP
Stewart (2002)	None	The United Kingdom's NMW	Bound youth	United Kingdom	1998–1999	Regression	Local area-year	Panel	Clustered (region)	LFS, NES
Stewart (2004a)	None	The United Kingdom's NMW	Bound youth	United Kingdom	Various	Quasi experiment	Individual-year	Longitudinal	Conventional	LFS, BHPS, NES
Stewart (2004b)	None	The United Kingdom's NMW	Bound youth	United Kingdom	1999–2002	Quasi experiment	Individual-year	Longitudinal	Robust	LFS

Study										
Böckerman and Uusitalo (2009)[c]	Mixed	Changes in youth subminimum	Youth in retail	Finland	1991–1996	Quasi experiment	Firm year	Longitudinal	Conventional	Payroll records
Campolieti, Fang, and Gunderson (2005a)[c]	Negative	Response to Yuen (2003)	Bound youth	Canada	1993–1999	Quasi experiment	Individual-year	Longitudinal	White robust and clustered (individual)	SLID
Campolieti, Fang, and Gunderson (2005b)[c]	Negative	N&W 1990s study using Canadian data	Teenagers	Canada	1993–1999	Regression	Individual-year	Longitudinal	Conventional	SLID
Neumark and Wascher (2004)[c]	Negative	Cross-national analysis	Youth	17 OECD countries	1975–2000	Regression	Country-year	Panel	Conventional, GMM	OECD
Shannon (2011)[c]	None/negative	Abolishing youth subminimums	Aged 15–16	Canada	1976–2003	Quasi experiment	Individual-year	Repeated cross section	Conventional	LFS
Yuen (2003)[c]	Mixed	Importance of comparison group definition	Bound youth	Canada	1988–1990	Quasi experiment	Individual-quarter	Longitudinal	Conventional	LMAS

[a]Teenagers refers to those aged 16–19 in Canada, 17–19 in Portugal, and 15–19 in Australia. Young adults refers to those aged 20–24. Youth refers to 18–21-year-olds in the United Kingdom, teenagers and young adults in Canada, workers younger than 25 years in Finland, individuals aged 16–24 in Spain, and 16–29 in New Zealand. In Neumark and Wascher's (2004) cross-country analysis, the definitions vary from country to country, "but generally cover some subset of workers between the ages of 15 and 24" (Neumark and Wascher 2004, Note 1, p. 225).

[b]HLFS = (New Zealand) Household Labor Force Survey (quarterly CPS counterpart). LFS = Labor Force Survey. IS = (New Zealand) Income Survey. QP = (Portugal) *Quadros de Pessoal* (Personnel Records, Portuguese Ministry of Qualification and Employment). NES = (United Kingdom) New Earnings Survey. BHPS = British Household Panel Survey. EPAS = (Spain) Economically Active Population Survey (quarterly household survey). LMAS = (Canadian) Labour Market Activity Survey. SLID = (Canadian) Survey of Labour and Income Dynamics. Finland's payroll records come from the Finnish employers' association.

[c]This study has standard errors that are suspect for reasons identified by Bertrand, Duflo, and Mullainathan (2004) or Donald and Lang (2007) or have other data problems.

parison group to motivate the switch to the smaller one. For the at-risk dummy he substitutes a low-wage dummy that identifies not only those in the treatment group but also those in both of the comparison groups described above. For both teens and young adults, the estimate for the coefficient on the low-wage dummy is negative (though smaller than that of the at-risk dummy in the initial regression) and statistically significant; low-wage workers have a lower probability of continued employment whether or not they are subject to a minimum wage increase. This is likely part of what the at-risk dummy measures when the sample contains the larger comparison group.[56]

Analyzing seven years of annual data from the successor to the survey that Yuen (2003) uses, Campolieti, Fang, and Gunderson (2005a) begin by replicating Yuen's results. They next introduce nine intermediate comparison groups defined by steps in the wage ceiling that start from the ceiling of Yuen's original narrow comparison group and culminate in his original broad comparison group. Starting from the narrow one with the lowest wage ceiling, as the ceiling rises, so too do both the point estimate and t-statistic of the employment effect. Both soon stabilize within a narrow range about half way through the set of comparison groups. The t-statistic (apparently) indicates statistical significance of the point estimate. While of interest, this supports rather than contradicts Yuen's emphasis on the definition of the comparison group.

To capture the intuition that the likelihood of being laid off rises with the difference between the ex post minimum wage and the ex ante wage, Campolieti, Fang, and Gunderson's (2005a) next step is to replace the at-risk dummy with a more sensitive measure: the wage gap. For individuals in the comparison group, this is zero; for individuals in the treatment group, it is the difference between the ex post minimum wage and the individual's ex ante wage. With even with the narrowest definition of the comparison group, the specification with the wage gap indicates that minimum wage increases reduce the probability of continued employment, and the size of the employment response is in the middle of the range at which it stabilizes when using the at-risk dummy. The point estimates remain statistically significant for all broader definitions of the comparison group. For the broader half of groups, the response is about 15 percent larger than for the narrowest one.

Finally, allowing that the wage gap variable may be picking up some purely low-wage effects, they introduce the wage gap variant model. Their approach is problematic; understanding why requires a detailed explanation. Their narrowest comparison group is composed of individuals who satisfy two conditions. First, they were employed in a year after which there was no minimum wage increase in their own province but there was in at least one other province. Second, they were earning at least the minimum wage in their own province and less than that minimum wage plus Can$0.25. The next larger comparison group has a $0.50 ceiling instead of a $0.25 ceiling, and so on up to a ceiling of $1, then increments of $0.50 rather than $0.25, up to $4 more than the minimum wage. For the wage-gap variant model, they introduce a new variable (let us call it the low-wage worker variable) to capture the effect of all purely low-wage effects on the probability of continued employment. For those in the treatment group, the low-wage worker variable equals the wage gap. For those who are in the same province or provinces as members of the treatment group, but whose wage puts them in the comparison group, it is zero. Finally, for members of the comparison group who are not in the same provinces as members of the treatment group, it is a quasi-wage gap using the ceiling that defines the comparison group rather than the minimum wage; it equals the difference between that ceiling and the individual's ex ante wage.

This definition of the low-wage worker variable is sensitive not only to the wage ceiling that defines the comparison group but also to which group (i.e., province) a worker is in. It would work well if all minimum wage increases were roughly the same size. Most of the year-over-year increases that Campolieti, Fang, and Gunderson (2005a) consider are no more than $0.25. However, several are larger, with the largest being $1.00. Based on this, Campolieti, Fang, and Gunderson argue that a ceiling of $0.25 is too restrictive and prefer one of $0.50, $0.75, or $1.00. Consider the situation where the treatment group is defined by a $0.25 increase in the minimum wage, and the comparison group is defined by a $0.75 wage ceiling. The low-wage worker variable treats the following two individuals equivalently: a member of the treatment group who had been earning the ex ante minimum wage plus $0.20, $0.05 less than the ex post minimum, and a member of the comparison group in another province who had been earning $0.70 more than that province's minimum wage, $0.05 less than the wage ceiling used to define the comparison group. If distinct traits common to low-wage workers do exist, the low-wage worker variable is likely to conflate two (or more) types of worker when the comparison group has a ceiling higher than the ex ante minimum wage of the treatment group.

The results presented suggest that this is indeed happening. When the wage-gap variant model is estimated with the narrow comparison group, the estimated minimum wage effect is small and not statistically significant. As ever broader definitions of the comparison group (and of the low-wage worker variable) are used, the estimated size of the effect grows almost monotonically until it peaks at the second-most broad comparison group (each is statistically significant except when the narrowest definition is used). Furthermore, except when using the narrowest comparison group, the estimated employment effect of the minimum wage from this model is almost as large or larger than the estimate from the simple wage-gap model, typically exceeding it by 20–30 percent. This is the opposite of what would be expected if, absent the low-wage worker variable, the wage gap alone were reflecting low-wage worker traits. It suggests that the low-wage worker variable is assigning to members of the treatment group traits that belong to higher-paid workers, and that the estimated effect of the minimum wage increase is having to grow to offset this.

Neither of these analyses corrects for the source of bias in the standard errors that Moulton (1990) identified, undercutting both their methodological and substantive results. It is nevertheless worth listing the former, keeping in mind what might have been. Yuen (2003) demonstrates the sensitivity of results to the choice of the comparison group. Campolieti, Fang, and Gunderson (2005a) show with their wage-gap model that the use of a more sensitive measure of the treatment can offset these problems. Finally, Campolieti, Fang, and Gunderson's (2005a) attempt to control for low-wage characteristics is ingenious but is not successful and causes more problems than it solves. Alternative approaches that might well better address the situation include using a variable that identifies the provincial wage quantile in which an individual is located, or performing a difference-in-differences-in-differences analysis to control for unsatisfactory fit between treatment and comparison groups, à la Sabia, Burkhauser, and Hansen (2012). It would be worth revisiting these issues while simultaneously addressing the Moulton problem and, depending on the data used, any other statistical issues, for example, serial correlation.

The United Kingdom

Starting early in the twentieth century, the United Kingdom had a system of administratively set minimum wages that differed by industry.[57] The Conservative government weakened the system in 1986, effectively making minimum wage law one of the issues separating the Labour and Conservative parties in the 1992 election. The Conservatives won and abolished the minimum wage altogether in 1993. This situation was replayed in 1997, when Labour won and established a NMW of £3.60 per hour starting in April 1999. The level has increased several times since then.

As part of his study of the NMW, Stewart (2002, 2004a) looks specifically at the employment effect on bound workers, aged 18–21. Although the NMW imposed a uniform minimum wage in the United Kingdom, local wage distributions varied considerably across the country just prior to it, especially in the location of the bottom of the distribution relative to the NMW. Across the 140 administrative regions of the United Kingdom, the percentage of bound workers varied between 1 and 12 percent. After confirming that establishment of the NMW raised wages of young bound workers, Stewart (2002) presents a variety of results on employment effects, using regional variation in percent of bound workers to measure vulnerability to the NMW.[58] Looking at a variety of data sources and specifications (e.g., employment ratio, probability of continued employment), he reports both positive and negative employment effects for bound youth, none statistically significant. In the later article, Stewart (2004a) examines the same episode with data from three different surveys, each with its own relative strengths and weaknesses. The New Earnings Survey (NES) collects data from the electronic payroll records of 1 percent of all employees every April, leading to great confidence in its accuracy. Although quite large, the breadth of information it collects leaves something to be desired, as does its coverage of very low-paid workers, many of whom are women working part time. The British Household Panel Survey (BHPS) is a considerably smaller survey that collects more detailed information on individuals over many years. Finally, the Labour Force Survey, which follows individuals for five consecutive quarters, is smaller than the NES but has better coverage of low-paid workers and is larger than the BHPS but has less detail.

Stewart (2004a) focuses on the probability of continued employment of young men and women who previously had been earning less than the £3 hourly wage set as the youth minimum wage (the adult minimum wage was set to £3.60 per hour). In addition to the different surveys, he also tries different approaches, including both difference-in-differences using a comparison group of slightly higher paid workers, and regression analysis where the minimum wage measure is the wage gap. He reports effects for young men that are positive but nearly all are not statistically significant, and for young women that are generally positive and never statistically significant.

Stewart (2004b) extends the analysis of Stewart (2004a) using the Labour Force Survey to examine the effects of the increase in 2000. The study is fairly elaborate, using pseudo-treatment and pseudo-comparison groups to correct for the comparison group's being a less than ideal match for the treatment group; this requires finding two additional groups that respond similarly to the NMW but whose differences otherwise parallel those of the original treatment and comparison groups. That is, the pseudo groups are otherwise equally less than ideal matches as the original groups. Then the difference between the pseudo-treatment and pseudo-comparison group can be subtracted from the difference between the actual treatment and comparison group, thus correcting for the original mismatch. Because the pseudo-groups respond similarly to the minimum wage (presumably, not at all), this entire operation will not mask the estimated minimum wage effect based on the original groups. The results resemble those of the two other studies (Stewart 2002, 2004a): mostly positive point estimates for young workers and for adult men, slightly more negative than positive ones for adult women, and none at all that are statistically significant.

Portugal and Spain

Pereira (2003) and Portugal and Cardoso (2006) study the increase in the teenage minimum wage due to repeal of the subminimum wage for teenagers in Portugal at the beginning of 1987. This led to an overnight increase of 50 percent in the effective minimum wage for teenagers, and a year-over-year real increase of more than one-third. The dependent variable in both studies is the teenage share of firms' labor forces. Both analyses rely on detailed employment data that the government requires firms to report each March. Because the change in policy was first broached in August 1986, data from March 1986 should be free of any taint if used as the ex ante period for a quasi experiment.

Pereira (2003) asks, "On average, did Portuguese firms change the age structure of their workforce in response to the increase in the relative cost of young workers?" She answers the question using a sample of 30 percent of the firms in the data set. Her treatment group is 18- and 19-year-olds, and her primary comparison group is young adults, 20–24-year-olds. Recognizing that older workers are not the best comparison group for teenagers, she performs a difference-in-difference-in-differences analysis, using much older workers, 30–34 years old, as controls on the controls. Pereira finds that the answer to her question is affirmative: employment shares of both teenagers and young adults grew, but growth in the share of young adult employment was much larger, and statistically significant, while employment growth of teenagers was not statistically significant.

Portugal and Cardoso (2006) begin with the same data set but construct their sample differently because

> The overall employment trends reported for teenagers in the affected age group—both by the Ministry of Labor, covering the population of firms employing wage earners in the private sector, and by the National Statistical Office, in its Labor Force Survey— are at odds with the ones offered in the study by Pereira. . . . Her data set is a nonrandom sample from the Ministry of Labor data; this sample is not representative of the population of firms (that we use) and, in particular, is severely biased with respect to the actual trend in employment for the affected group of workers. (pp. 994–995)

They also ask different questions, examining differences in gross employment flows of teenagers and adults less than 35, rather than in the net change of each group's employment.

To understand gross flows into and out of employment, it is necessary to consider each of the following three categories separately:

1) Entry: new firms that only came into being in the period after the minimum wage rose.

2) Exit: previously existing firms that disappeared in the period after the minimum wage rose.

3) Survival: previously existing firms that continued following the increase.

Entering firms contribute only to gains in employment and exiting ones only to losses, while surviving firms contribute to both gains and losses. Portugal and Cardoso (2006) note three responses to the rise in the minimum wage for teenagers that separately and together contributed to a decrease in the employment share of teenagers. First, new firms, those that came into existence following the increase, had lower shares of teen employees than did new firms before the increase. Second, firms that went out of existence following the increase had larger shares of teen employees than did exiting firms before the increase. Third, at continuing (or surviving) firms, the teen share of hiring declined. However, outweighing all these effects put together was a sharp decline in the teen share of separations at continuing firms. As a result, teen employment rose both absolutely and relative to adults. That is, when the minimum wage increased, those teenagers who were already employed hung onto their jobs so tenaciously (or perhaps the firms hung onto these employees so tenaciously, or both) as to outweigh the other consequences of the minimum wage increases. Among the several reasons that Portugal and Cardoso offer for the sharp decline in separations of teens is the possibility that having hired and trained them, firms were reluctant to lay them off because they were at least as productive as older workers who would have to be hired, trained, and paid as much. They also offer several caveats that limit how much these results can reasonably be generalized.

Pinoli's (2010) central insight is that those studying the minimum wage may be missing its impact because they are looking in the wrong place or, rather, at the wrong time. Many minimum wage changes are anticipated well in advance, and cost-minimizing firms may well begin preparing for them in advance, likely by not replacing employees following separations. Most studies look for the consequences only after the increase in the minimum wage, by which time much of the response will have already occurred. She uses the search model of Mortensen and Pissarides (1994) to place this idea on a firm theoretical footing and then turns to the data to distinguish anticipated from unanticipated increases in the minimum wage. Anticipated increases are either announced well in advance or occur on a regular schedule, while unanticipated ones satisfy neither of these conditions. The minimum wage increase in New Jersey that Card and Krueger (1994) studied, which was widely expected about two years before it went into effect, was an anticipated increase. So too were the Spanish minimum wage increases that went into effect on the first day of each year between 1997 and 2004. The Spanish minimum wage increase of mid-2004 was an unanticipated increase; it was passed and implemented by a government that unexpectedly won an election in March 2004, three days after a major terrorist action in Madrid.

Using individual-level (quarterly) data, Pinoli's (2010) dependent variable is employment status. Her central variables are the percentage increase in the minimum wage interacted with dummy variables that identify whether the increase is anticipated or unanticipated; the equation also includes both leads and lags of these variables and control variables. She sets up the analysis as a quasi experiment, using various demographic groups aged 16–24 in the role of the treatment group, and various parts of the adult population aged 25 years and older in the role of the comparison group. For all young workers, the unanticipated increase had an effect only following the increase, while the anticipated one had an equally large effect only in the period before the increase. For young women, the estimates are inconclusive, and for low-educated young women, both increases had an effect only following the increase. The section late in this chapter on the timing of effects discusses this issue further.

Australia and New Zealand

At first glance, the approach that Lee and Suardi (2011) take in their study of the Australian minimum wage resembles those of both the older literature and the aggregate state-year panel framework that Neumark and Wascher introduced to this literature, with controls for supply and demand factors in the labor market. The important way in which Lee and Suardi's approach differs is that they do not include a minimum wage term in their equation, examining instead whether point estimates of other coefficients in the equation change coincident with increases in the minimum wage. In April 1997, a federal government agency in Australia established a minimum wage that was legally (though not necessarily economically) binding on all or nearly all employees in three states. Lee and Suardi analyze teen employment from each state as a separate time series. In no states does the minimum wage affect employment or, rather, as they say, employment dynamics (since the nature of the data requires that they consider employment growth rather than employment itself). They engage in some careful sensitivity analysis to ensure that their statistical test is reasonably able to find no effect when there is none and to detect one when one indeed exists.[59] How well their results generalize is not clear, not only because the institutional structure of the minimum wage they study is unusually complicated but also because wages well above the minimum wage are pegged to the minimum, rising along with it. As a result, firms are less likely to substitute higher paid, more-skilled workers for lower-paid, less-skilled ones, than in countries such as the United States, the United Kingdom, and Canada, where the minimum wage directly affects only low-paid workers.

Hyslop and Stillman (2007) perform a difference-in-differences analysis of the minimum wage response of teenage employment in New Zealand.[60] Following an election in late 1999, the new government made large changes in the youth subminimum wage. Starting in March 2001 and continuing through March 2003, in steps well announced in advance, the minimum wage was increased by 87 percent between 2000 and 2003 for 18–19-year-olds and by 49 percent for 16–17-year-olds. Over the same interval, that for older adults increased only 13 percent. In their analysis, the two treatment groups are 16–17-year-olds and 18–19-year-olds, and their main comparison group is 20–25-year-olds, though they also look at 20–21-year-olds. They compare employment in the five quarters following the last of these increases (2002Q2–2003Q3) with the last five quarters before the election in 1999 (1998Q2–1999Q3). Relative to the main comparison group of 20–25-year-olds, employment increased by a statistically insignificant amount following the policy reform.

Pacheco (2011) proposes a solution for a widely perceived issue in the minimum wage literature. Although the minimum wage may reduce the employment of teenagers as a whole more than that of any other easily identified group, defining the treatment group to be all teenagers may nevertheless result in estimates of the effect that are so imprecise as to be statistically insignificant not because there is no effect but because many teenagers may not be so affected (recall the compositional effects that Flinn [2006]; Ahn, Arcidiaco, and Wessels [2011]; and Giuliano [2013] report). Relying on the same primary data source as Hyslop and Stillman (2007), Pacheco (2011) combines it with an annual supplement to identify those aged 16–29 most likely to be earning at or near the minimum wage and to weight the effect of the minimum wage on an individual accordingly. This leads not only to a much larger (negative) estimate of the employment effect in comparison to the estimate from a regression without the weights but also one that is statistically significant; however, the employment elasticity when considering all teenagers only changes from −0.045 to −0.089.[61]

Pacheco's (2011) approach is ingenious but problematic, so it is worth considering it in some detail. Rather than consider a few increases in the minimum wage around the turn of the century, as Hyslop and Stillman (2007) do, Pacheco (2011) uses data from the beginning of the Household Labor Force Survey (HLFS) in the period 1986–2004. It contains a wealth of demographic detail but little or nothing with which to identify an earned wage level. For that, Pacheco turns to the Income Survey, an annual supplement begun in 1997 that collects information on pretax income from a variety of sources for individuals in the HLFS. For the years 1997–2004, Pacheco (2011) uses the Income Survey to create a dummy variable equal to 1 "if the individual is deemed to be affected by increases in the minimum wage. This is the case if they are either a sub–minimum or a minimum wage worker" (p. 596). The dummy variable is the dependent variable in a probit equation that otherwise resembles a wage equation conditional on employment, and the estimated equation is used to generate fitted values for all observations in the bigger HLFS sample, for all years and whether or not the individual is then employed. The fitted values are the weights used to mediate the effect of the minimum wage on the probability of employment in the estimated employment equation. To distinguish these two probit equations, we will designate the first as the minimum wage worker equation and the second as the employment equation.

Pacheco (2011) alludes to two problems with her technique. The first is the classic problem of sample selection bias, often referred to as the Heckman problem. She writes,

> Assuming no sample selection bias (i.e., that nonworkers and workers with the same X_i characteristics face the same probability of working at the minimum wage), the coefficients from Equation

(2) are used to create a probability of the individual earning the minimum wage for all individuals in the 1986–2004 HLFS data set (i.e., no longer restricting analysis to only those employed). (p. 597)

If they have done nothing else, years of research in labor economics have demonstrated the existence of systematic differences in the expected wages of those not employed and the actual wages of otherwise observationally equivalent individuals who are employed. Turning the wage equation into a binary variable does not persuasively get around this issue. At the very least, test results for sample selection bias would be helpful. This problem raises serious questions about the usefulness of the calculated weights.[62]

The second issue concerns identification of the probability measure. Pacheco (2011) uses the same demographic variables in both probit equations, the one used to calculate the probability of being affected by the minimum wage and the one estimating the employment effect. About this she writes,

> One potential issue with the use of this adjusted policy variable is collinearity, because of the similar nature of the variables used to construct $\hat{P}_{it}$ and those used as explanatory variables along with $\ln RMW_{i,t-k}\hat{P}_{it}$ in Equation (4). However, this issue is minimised by the method of constructing $\hat{P}_{it}$, in that the specified characteristics it depends on enter Equation (3) in a nonlinear and multiplicative fashion, and therefore does not result in perfect collinearity in Equation (4). (p. 598)

That there are no variables in the minimum wage worker equation that are excluded from the employment equation raises serious issues of identification. In his survey of sample selection bias, Vella (1998) discusses this issue, concluding that "these two-step procedures should be treated cautiously when the models are not identified through exclusion restrictions" (p. 135). It is hardly an exaggeration to say that without any exclusion restrictions, Pacheco's (2011) approach is not a new way of measuring the effect of the minimum wage that allows it to vary across individuals but an employment equation that includes interactions between the minimum wage and all the demographic dummy variables.

In Canada, Campolieti, Fang, and Gunderson (2005a) detected a negative net employment response of young workers to the minimum wage. The studies of the NMW in the United Kingdom find no effect on youth employment, and the more reliable of the studies of Portugal reports a net positive effect on employment because previously employed teenagers are much more likely to continue in their current employment when the minimum wage rises. Pinoli's (2010) analysis of anticipated and unanticipated increases in Spain finds negative effects where she expected to when looking at all young workers but was not able to detect any for either young women or for young women with little education. The two studies of data from Down Under also found no effects on the employment of young workers. That is, except for Pinoli (2010), to which we will return in the final section of this chapter, and Campolieti, Fang, and Gunderson (2005a), these studies do not contain evidence of a negative effect on the employment of the young. Recent work from both the United States and from other countries are similar in providing no clear consensus about the employment response of youth workers, but the trend, certainly in the United States, as various statistical issues are recognized and addressed, seems to be fewer and fewer reports of statistically significant negative employment responses.

Other Low-Wage Workers

Table 2.8 displays information about nine studies of the employment response of other low-wage groups to the minimum wage in countries other than the United States (although the multinational data set of Addison and Ozturk [2012] includes U.S. data).

Canada

Fang and Gunderson (2009) use the same data and approach as Campolieti, Fang, and Gunderson (2005a) to study the employment response of older workers (those at least 50 years old) whose ex ante wage was less than the ex post minimum wage. Because of the close similarities, it is not necessary to repeat a description of their framework. Unlike the earlier piece, they report standard errors clustered by province, although with only seven years of data, it is not certain that this correction is necessary, and with exactly 10 provinces, there is some reason for doubting its effectiveness.[63] Fang and Gunderson report nearly four dozen probit estimates based on three different specifications and many definitions of the comparison group, where the dependent variable indi-

Table 2.8 Other Low-Wage Groups (Other Developed Countries)

Study	Effect	Novelty	Target group	Country	Sample period	Analytic approach	Unit of observation	Data structure	Type of standard error	Data set[a]
Dolton, Rosazza-Bondibene, and Wadsworth (2012)	Mixed, mostly Positive	The United Kingdom's NMW	Bound workers	United Kingdom	1999–2007	Regression	Region-year	Panel	Clustered (by region)	NES, ASHE
Kramarz and Philippon (2001)	Negative	Total employment cost	Low-wage workers	France	1990–1998	Quasi experiment	Individual	Repeated cross section	Conventional	LFS
Laroque and Salanie (2002)	Negative	Formal model of participation, employment	Married women	France	1997	Regression	Individual	Cross section	Conventional	LFS
Mulheirn (2008)	None	The United Kingdom's NMW	Bound workers, aged 22–59	United Kingdom	2005–2007	Quasi experiment	Individual-year	Longitudinal	Conventional	LFS
Stewart (2002)	None	The United Kingdom's NMW	Bound workers	United Kingdom	1998–1999	Quasi experiment	Local area-year	Panel	Clustered (by region)	NES
Stewart (2004a)	None	The United Kingdom's NMW	Bound workers, aged > 21	United Kingdom	Various	Quasi experiment	Individual-year	Longitudinal	Conventional	LFS BHPS NES
Stewart (2004b)	None	The United Kingdom's NMW	Bound workers, aged 22–59	United Kingdom	1999–2002	Quasi experiment	Individual-year	Longitudinal	Robust	LFS
Fang and Gunderson (2009)[b]	Positive	Older workers (at least aged 50)	Bound older workers	Canada	1993–1999	Quasi experiment	Individual-year	Longitudinal	Clustered (province)	SLID

Addison and Oturk (2012)[b]	Negative	Cross-national analysis	Women	OECD	1980s–2000s	Regression	Country-year	Panel	Huber-White robust	OECD

[a] ASHE = (United Kingdom) Annual Survey of Hours and Earning. NES = (United Kingdom) New Earnings Survey. LFS = Labor Force Survey. BHPS = British Household Panel Survey. SLID = (Canadian) Survey of Labour and Income Dynamics.

[b] This study has standard errors that are suspect for reasons identified by Bertrand, Duflo, and Mullainathan (2004) or Donald and Lang (2007).

cates whether or not an individual who was employed ex ante remains employed ex post. All the point estimates are positive, but few are statistically significant: 3 of the 11 results for the wage-gap variable and 11 results for the wage-gap variant variable. They suspect that employers are substituting away from young workers toward older ones, but the Scotch verdict, not proven, seems most in order.

The United Kingdom: Bound Workers

Stewart (2002, 2004a) considers not only bound young workers (18–21) but also bound older workers.[64] In both studies, Stewart confirms that wages of the treatment group rose after the NMW was established in April 1999. In neither does he report any adverse effect on the employment of bound older workers. Stewart (2002) finds negative effects on the employment of various high-risk groups (women, those with less than a whole year of tenure, the unskilled, the hotel and restaurant industries, and those in industries with a large fraction of bound workers). To study the effect of the first two increases in the NMW subsequent to its implementation (3 percent in 2000 and 11 percent in 2001), Stewart (2004b) uses the Labour Force Survey, one of the three data sets he analyzed earlier (Stewart 2004a). He concludes that these increases also had no effect on the employment of bound workers.

Mulheirn (2008) repeats Stewart's (2004b) analysis to examine the effect of the 6 percent increase in 2006. He reports results that vary by specification, either a simple difference-in-differences framework with an at-risk dummy or one that incorporates a wage-gap variable, and for men and women combined and for each separately. The only statistically significant results—several of those for men—strike him as implausible; the probability of separating from a job following the increase falls by about four percentage points. Mulheirn warns against making too much of this because of the small sample size but is struck that the only evidence of an employment effect is that the higher minimum wage leads low-wage men to become more attached to their jobs.[65] Noting that by design this study cannot detect any reduction in hiring due to the NMW, Mulheirn (2008) concludes that this increase in the NMW did not increase the likelihood of those already employed losing their jobs.

Dolton, Rosazza-Bondibene, and Wadsworth (2012) expand on Stewart's (2002) analysis in three dimensions. They use three different measures of the minimum wage, including the fraction affected. They use three different definitions of regions, including the local administrative regions that Stewart (2002) examines. They extend the time period to include all the increases in the NMW through 2006; this last involves concatenating data from the NES, which Stewart (2002) used, to data from the Annual Survey of Hours and Employment, its successor. In addition to the fraction affected, they also consider the Kaitz index, despite its problems, so that their results are comparable with other work, and the *spike*, the fraction earning exactly the minimum wage ex post. In addition to the local administrative region, they consider both a less aggregated and a more aggregated definition of geographic area.[66] The longer sample and the annual increases in the NMW that began 18 months after the NMW went into effect allow them to do something that Stewart (2002) could not: consider the possibility of time-varying impacts. However, they first report results that allow only for a constant impact; once they include two-way fixed effects and a set of controls, the estimated effects are predominantly positive, tiny, and not statistically significant.[67] Estimates from the equation with time-varying employment effects show a few statistically significant negative point estimates in the early and middle years for the spike measure; however, for this measure in the late years (after 2003), for the fraction affected in the middle to late years (after 2002), and for the Kaitz index throughout, the only statistically significant point estimates are positive.

France

Laroque and Salanie (2002), like Neumark and Wascher (2011), worry that social welfare policies, among them the minimum wage, may have unintended consequences in the labor market. Instead of single mothers, the demographic group that concerns them is married women. They use 1997 data from an annual survey of French households to examine this issue. The econometric model is itself fairly simple, but its derivation is informed by a sophisticated theoretical model. The first part of their model is a wage equation for women aged 25–49 who live with a partner (i.e., are considered married). This relates the wage that they earn (or would if employed) to personal characteristics. The second equation relates their reservation wage to the wage that the first equation predicts, and to a number of household characteristics, including the number of children, their husband's employment status, and the total value of income derived from social welfare benefits.

Laroque and Salanie (2002) distinguish four possible states for each woman based on her employment status and the sign of the difference between her actual or prospective wage and reservation wage:

1) *employed*, in which case her wage exceeds her reservation wage;

2) *voluntarily unemployed* if her reservation wage exceeds what she could earn;

3) *classically unemployed* (one way to be involuntarity unemployed) if the minimum wage exceeds her prospective wage and that in turn exceeds her reservation wage, then the minimum wage prices her out of the market; and

4) *otherwise unemployed* (all other ways to be involuntarily unemployed): if her prospective wage exceeds both her reservation wage and the minimum wage, she is unemployed for other reasons, e.g., due to the business cycle or to being between jobs while searching for one.

Between 50 and 60 percent of the married women in Laroque and Salanie's (2002) sample are not employed. Based on their model, they estimate that 38 percent of the sample chooses not to be employed, and that slightly more than one-half of the remaining unemployed—about one-tenth of all married women—are in a situation of classical unemployment, which they attribute to the minimum wage. They estimate an elasticity of employment with respect to the minimum wage of −0.7, quite large and comparable to Sabia's (2008) result for a group of single mothers in the United States. This is much bigger than other estimates for American women or for American teenagers, which is likely due to institutional differences between France and the United States. They present standard errors of their parameter estimates but not of the derived elasticity estimates.

Kramarz and Philippon (2001) inform us that in France, the true cost of the minimum wage to employers is much higher than its nominal value because payroll taxes finance mandatory employee benefits. Offsetting this are tax exemptions, which differ across the wage distribution and have changed over time. Using data primarily from the French Labor Force Survey for the years 1990–1998, they define their treatment group to be workers whose wages fall between the contemporaneous value of the minimum wage and its value in the following year (bound workers). The comparison group consists of individuals whose wages in the first year are at least as high as the greater of these two values of the minimum wage, and no more than 110 percent of this value.[68] They report a substantial employment effect: a 1 percent increase in employment costs due to a minimum wage increase leads to a 1.5 percent decrease in the probability of being employed.[69]

Taken together, analyses of demographic groups other than youth indicate that the minimum wage can have unintended consequences. No evidence has come to light that the NMW has reduced the employment of previously bound workers, young or old. In France, however, the effect of the minimum wage appears to generate classical unemployment, which employment subsidies reduce to some extent. This contrasts with the United States, where the direct effects of the EITC and minimum wage complement rather than counteract each other (although the increased competition for jobs that results has adverse spillover effects for individuals who are not eligible for the EITC).

Industry Studies

Table 2.9 presents information for four studies that consider the effect of the minimum wage on industry employment—three use data from the United Kingdom and one uses data from Sweden.

The United Kingdom

Machin, Manning, and Rahman (2003) and Machin and Wilson (2004) examine the effect of the 1999 introduction of the NMW on the British care home industry, a particularly low-wage sector, using establishment data collected in surveys in the 1990s and early 2000s. Machin and Wilson perform several differences analyses that vary along several dimensions: the presence or absence of control variables, the geographic range of the sample, and whether the fraction affected or the wage gap is used to measure the NMW. Machin, Manning, and Rahman perform a difference-in-differences analysis by combining the data mentioned above with that from an earlier survey that allows them

100

Table 2.9 Studies of Industries (Other Developed Countries)

Study	Effect	Target sector	Country	Sample period	Analytic approach	Unit of observation	Data structure	Type of SE	Data set[a]
Machin and Wilson (2004)	Negative	Home care	United Kingdom	1998–1999	Regression	Firm-survey wave	Longitudinal	Conventional	Private survey
Machin, Manning, and Rahman (2003)	Negative	Home care	United Kingdom	1992–1999	Quasi experiment	Firm-survey wave	Longitudinal	Conventional	Private survey
Skedinger (2006)	Negative	Hospitality sector	Sweden	1979–1999	Quasi experiment	Individual-year	Longitudinal	Conventional	CSE
Galindo-Rueda and Pereira (2004)	Negative	All firms	United Kingdom	1997–2001	Regression	Firm-year	Panel	Clustered (firm)	Various

NOTE: Galindo-Rueda & Pereira (2004) is included for completeness but not discussed in the text because of severe data problems.
[a] CSE = Confederation of Swedish Enterprise.

to construct a comparison group with a pseudo–minimum wage at the same point of the earlier wage distribution as the NMW falls in the later survey and a corresponding pseudo impact.[70] Both studies report statistically significant, positive wage responses.

Machin, Manning, and Rahman (2003) try several minimum wage measures and report negative but statistically insignificant employment responses. However, they present average employment elasticities based only on a differences analysis of the period in which the NMW was instituted. These range between −0.14 and −0.38. The larger ones are derived from statistically significant point estimates, so it is unclear how to reconcile these with the results of the quasi experiment. Although in the middle to high end of (what is considered) the consensus range of employment elasticities for American teenagers, Machin, Manning, and Rahman believe them to be small relative to the wage impact. Because this is one of the lowest-paid industries in the United Kingdom, they caution against generalizing these results to the whole labor market.

Machin and Wilson (2004) report statistically significant, negative employment responses to the introduction of the NMW for two minimum wage measures (fraction affected and wage gap) in their most complete model when they use a sample that covers the entire country. However, when they restrict the sample to the South Coast, the wage gap (their more sensitive measure of vulnerability to the minimum wage) does not generate this effect.[71] This result reminds us of the pattern that Allegretto, Dube, and Reich (2009, 2011) and Dube, Lester, and Reich (2010) report in their explorations of geographic correlation, and more broadly the issues that Yuen (2003) and Campolieti, Fang, and Gunderson (2005a) examine: that when large differences between the treatment group and the implicit comparison group make the entire sample too heterogeneous, effects of other factors may be attributed to the minimum wage. Extending their analysis to the effects of the 2001 increase in the NMW on the South Coast, Machin and Wilson (2004) report a negative but not statistically significant employment effect, which is broadly consistent with their results for the introduction of the NMW in that area.

Reconciliation of these two analyses is difficult, one finding a statistically significant employment effect that the authors judge to be small, the other finding none. This contrasts with studies of low-wage sectors in the United States, some of the most careful analysis of U.S. data, which has, with a few exceptions, reported no effect on employment.[72]

THE TIMING OF THE EMPLOYMENT RESPONSE

Several studies have explored the timing of the employment response to minimum wage increases.[73] Before the NMWR, the most common specification included lags of the minimum wage variable in the regression equation, which was estimated on quarterly data (Brown, Gilroy, and Kohen 1982, p. 507, Note 25). When compared, however, the dynamic implications of estimates of this specification with those from specifications that included only the contemporaneous term indicated little difference, suggesting that the minimum wage had its entire impact in the quarter of the increase. In the first decade of the NMWR, concern with the presence or absence of a lagged minimum wage term was a by-product of attempts to reconcile results from examination of aggregate panels with those based on other data structures (cross sections in which the dependent variable was the change in employment before and after a change in the minimum wage, and the two-period panels used in quasi experiments). Pinoli (2010) raises the issue from the perspective of the rational expectations approach, suggesting that much of the response to anticipated increases precedes the increase itself, and several analyses tested her claim as part of their robustness check. Two studies relied on time-series techniques, which allow for dynamic simulations to study the response over time.

Whether the chosen regression models provide dependable estimates of the dynamic response to the minimum wage is an important issue. The body of statistical technique most concerned with estimation of dynamics, especially with the problems that arise in estimation, is time-series analysis, and it is most thoroughly developed for time-series data. Panel data have the potential for more complete examination of dynamics, but it presents difficulties of estimation that were until recently considerably less tractable. Perhaps as a result, attempts to study dynamics with panel data have rarely relied on time-series techniques and more on ad hoc approaches. Because the former are rare in the NMWR and ad hoc approaches that use panel data are more numerous, we begin with a discussion of the latter. With one exception, Baker, Benjamin, and Stanger (1999), all the studies below have already been discussed, and it is the only one that will be examined in detail (except as necessary).

The Early Debate: Panel Studies That Include a Lagged Term of the Minimum Wage

Neumark and Wascher (1992) pay a fair amount of attention to explaining why they detected a statistically significant, negative response of employment to the minimum wage, whereas Card (1992a) does not. They repeat and extend this effort (Neumark and Wascher 1994) with regard to Card, Katz, and Krueger's (1994) response. They make two related points in this discussion that shape later analyses of the timing of the employment response: 2) omitted variable bias, and 2) a lengthy period for adjusting employment in response to changes in the minimum wage.[74]

The omitted variable bias was due to the absence of a lagged minimum wage term in the regressions of Card (1992a) and Card, Katz, and Krueger (1994). Although the primary results in Neumark and Wascher's (1991) conference paper are based on regressions that include only a contemporaneous (same year) minimum wage term, they present results from several regressions that include a lagged term, variously as a robustness check or to reconcile different results. In the revised version published a year later (Neumark and Wascher 1992), they rely more heavily on specifications with the lagged term, referring to them as "correctly specified models" and writing "that the failure to consider lagged effects of minimum wages . . . results in substantial upward bias in the estimated effects of minimum wages on employment, leading to elasticities that are too close to zero, and frequently positive" (p. 78).[75] Under certain conditions for which they present evidence, the consequence of omitting a lagged minimum wage term is a finding of no effect.[76]

Their second, closely related observation is the qualitative difference in results between those based on a first difference of consecutive observations, say 1990 and 1989 (similar to Card [1992a]), and those from a first difference of observations further apart, 1998 and 1990, for example. Relative to the shorter period, differences over the longer period are shifted to the left, that is, smaller if both are positive or negative and farther from zero.

Baker, Benjamin, and Stanger (1999) substantially clarify matters when they apply theoretical techniques of time-series analysis to a province-by-year panel of Canadian data. Decomposing the minimum wage into short-term and long-term components, they demonstrate that the lagged term is a rough-and-ready approximation of the long-term component. Refining their analysis to identify long-term and short-term components more precisely, they conclude that in Canada, it takes at least six years for the full effects of the minimum wage to be apparent in the teen employment figures. They speculate that this is because of interplay between lags in adjusting capital and the long-run expectations about labor costs that are relevant when making investment decisions.

Unfortunately, the serial correlation that Bertrand, Duflo, and Mullainathan (2004) identified as a problem for statistical inference in panels is almost certainly a problem for the analysis of Baker, Benjamin, and Stanger (1999). They examine the Canadian counterpart to the U.S. data of Neumark and Wascher, and both the outcome and policy variable exhibit serial correlation similar to that in the U.S. data. For the initial regression, with only the contemporaneous minimum wage, they report standard errors corrected for second-order serial correlation, but it is not clear that this solves the problem of exaggerated t-statistics (Wolfson 2011). Furthermore, for the regressions based on their time-series analysis, Baker, Benjamin, and Stanger report only conventional standard errors. It is well known that the moving average transformation that underlies their long-term component creates serial correlation where none previously existed and increases it in variables that already exhibit positive serial correlation.[77] In their more complete decomposition, Baker, Benjamin, and Stanger distinguish the components more finely into five terms ranging from shortest term to longest term. This concentrates the serial correlation in the longer-term components more completely than the simpler distinction does, causing a greater amount of bias in its standard error than in that of the moving average term of the simpler decomposition.

Does the Response Ever Precede the Increase?

Pinoli (2010) argues that firms will begin responding to minimum wage increases well in advance of their occurrence if they anticipate them, because gradual adjustment will minimize the cost of this adjustment. She reports a response to expected increases before they take effect.

Allegretto, Dube, and Reich (2011) examine this possibility in several different ways in their study of teenage employment. Their regression equations include both leads of four and eight quarters of the minimum wage, and lags of 4, 8, 12, and 16 quarters. In addition, they reestimate their equations both on a sample that excludes automatic increases that respond to inflation because they believe that these are likely to be well anticipated, and on a sample that excludes states that ever indexed their minimum wage, reasoning that this sample should further heighten the contrast between anticipated and unanticipated minimum wages. They detect no response of employment or hours in advance of a minimum wage increase, and neither of their restricted samples provides any evidence of a response to unanticipated increases after the increase.

Dube, Lester, and Reich (2010), in their border discontinuity study of teenage and restaurant employment, allow for not only a contemporaneous response to minimum wage increases but also responses up to two years before and up to four years after an increase. They find only contemporaneous effects: a decline in separations of both teenagers and restaurant workers, an increase in earnings, and a decrease in the overall turnover rate.

Time-Series Studies

Williams and Mills (2001) rely on time-series techniques to study the response to the federal minimum wage of the teenage employment ratio, and Belman and Wolfson (2010) do the same for employment growth in low-wage industries. Williams and Mills simulate the response of the teen employment ratio to a 10 percent increase in the minimum wage, based on regressions using different minimum wage measures. Simulations based on relative minimum wage measures indicate a decrease in the employment ratio that first becomes statistically significant between one and one and a half years after the increase in the minimum wage.[78] It moves in and out of statistical significance for the following two years and disappears altogether after about three years. The maximum decline in employment during this interval, relative to the initial period just before the increase, is between 4 and 5 percent (not percentage points). Simulation results based on the real minimum wage are similar; the only statistically significant response is a 5 percent decrease (relative to employment in the initial period) 11 quarters after the minimum wage increase, and this disappears shortly thereafter.

In their analysis of 23 low-wage industries, Belman and Wolfson (2010) perform a simulation to examine the question, "What would have happened to the average wage, the total number of jobs and total hours if the federal minimum wage had increased by 10 percent in September 1998?" For the next 42 months, the simulation tracks the difference in outcomes between the hypothesized situation of a 10 percent increase and one of no change.[79] The average hourly wage is immediately higher than it would have been by about 1.25 percent, and the size of the difference fluctuates in a narrow range, mostly less than 1.25 percent, until about two years after the increase; at that point it begins a slow, steady increase to between about 1.3 percent and 1.4 percent, three and a half years after the increase. After about six months, the point estimate of the number of jobs is about one-half percent less than it would otherwise have been, the difference slowly growing to −0.75 percent two years after the minimum wage increase, and fluctuating around that value for the remaining year and a half of the simulation. At no point is the difference statistically significant. The response of total hours worked is initially much noisier, and while the difference stabilizes after a year at −0.1 percent, it too is not statistically significant at any point.

Summary

During what interval of time, relative to a change in the minimum wage, do the data for employment contain evidence of it? The little work that addresses this issue is mixed. Baker, Benjamin, and Stanger (1999) is the earliest and by far the most cited study to examine this issue; however, their use of conventional standard errors in the canonical panel framework of Neumark and Wascher leaves it vulnerable to the critique of Bertrand, Duflo, and Mullainathan (2004), raising serious questions about the statistical significance of their results. More recently, Pinoli (2010) reports that Spanish firms begin preparing or responding to minimum wage increases at the earliest moment that it is cost effective to do so, once they can reasonably anticipate them. Allegretto, Dube, and Reich (2011) and Dube, Lester, and Reich (2010) find no evidence of this phenomenon in U.S. data. While time-series analysis of U.S. data picks up an immediate increase in teenagers' wages that eventually leads to further wage growth after two years, the employment data suggest at most a decrease in youth employment after one year or more, perhaps not until nearly three years. In any case, this decrease has disappeared altogether after three years. In low-wage industries, it is not possible to reliably detect an employment response at any point in the three and a half years following an increase. Finally, it is worth observing that not much work considers the timing of the response to minimum wage increases. Not only is additional examination of this point necessary, but it is likely that until the disagreement about the existence of a response is settled, questions about its timing will also remain unsettled.

CONCLUSION

At the end of the first round of the NMWR, nothing was resolved. Although parts of Card and Krueger's (2000) analysis contain statistical problems identified by Moulton (1990) and Donald and Lang (2007), other parts remain. Their message is that in the months following the 1992 increase in New Jersey's minimum wage, employment at fast food establishments there did not suffer in comparison with employment at those just across the state border in Pennsylvania. There were criticisms of this work: the time period following the increase was too short to correct and account for long-term employment trends that differed between the two states; the time period was too short to capture the employment response, much of which occurred after the end of the period; and because information about the increase was available well in advance, much of the adjustment occurred before the beginning of the sample period.

A further decade of debate has not resolved the disagreements, but there has been progress, much based on improvements in technique. A significant amount of the earlier work was seen to suffer from mistakenly small estimates of standard errors, which implied effects that it is now understood were not reliably detected. More recent work is better at avoiding this problem. Yuen (2003) and Campolieti, Fang, and Gunderson (2005a) explore the importance of both accurate measures of the treatment's impact and of control groups that are well matched for the treatment group under study. With more recently developed awareness of econometric pitfalls, Allegretto, Dube, and Reich (2009, 2011) and Dube, Lester, and Reich (2010) demonstrate (rather than explore) the importance of appropriate control variables to avoid misattribution of effects, and show through step-by-step changes in sample and specification the connection between a conventional regression framework and a quasi experiment. The result is convergence, not yet complete, between results from best practice in both frameworks.

What is necessary for the employment response of the minimum wage to be better understood? First is more careful technique. The longitudinal data sets in increasing use allow more careful attention to time-series dynamics, something not previously the case. One consequence would be standard errors that are not only robust to serial correlation but also reliably smaller so that minimum wage impacts can be measured more precisely. Similarly important are spatial correlation and geographic heterogeneity, not only as in the articles mentioned just above, but also using spatial econometric techniques introduced by Kalenkoski and Lacombe (2008).

Second, we need to recognize that studies can come to apparently different results without contradicting each other. If employment in a demographic group moves in response to the minimum wage, that reveals nothing about total employment absent further information; it is certainly possible that employers substitute workers from other demographics who are perhaps more skilled than those displaced. Ahn, Arcidiacono, and Wessels (2010); Neumark and Wascher (2011); and Giuliano (2013) all provide evidence for this sort of offset. Similarly, if employment in an industry does not move in response to the minimum wage, that reveals nothing about employment elsewhere in the economy. Although it is certainly possible that employment falls elsewhere, the typical choice of researchers is to examine industries in which employment is thought to be especially sensitive to the minimum wage.

Third, the focus on employment, or rather on the number of jobs, is perhaps misplaced. It may be that the effect is felt not in employment but in hours of work. That is the topic of the next chapter. Another possibility is that there are changes in the gross flows, in accessions and separations that combine to determine changes in employment. If these change but in such a way that the net result is zero, that would not show up in an employment response as measured in these studies. That, too, is the topic of another chapter.

Finally, some way of summarizing the results would be beneficial. The formal body of statistical technique that does this, combining many studies into a single result, is known as meta-analysis. One particular technique that is especially useful is metaregression. After looking at studies that consider hours of employment, we will present results of a formal meta-analysis.

Notes

1. Brown, Gilroy, and Kohen (1982, p. 499) define the Kaitz index as "the ratio of the nominal legal minimum wage to average hourly earnings weighted by coverage."
2. An older term for individuals who make up the fraction affected is *bound workers*.
3. "Proto-" because the article contains none of the formal statistical analysis or hypothesis testing currently characteristic of difference-in-differences analysis. Instead, it consists of a very detailed descriptive analysis of a treatment group (California) and a control group, states chosen to be similar to California in important ways but that did not experience a minimum wage increase during the period in question.
4. At the beginning of 1982, only Alaska and Connecticut had minimum wages higher than the federal minimum wage (and Connecticut's was $0.02 higher). By the beginning of 1990, 16 states, including all of New England and all the states that border the Pacific, had a minimum wage that was higher than the federal minimum wage.
5. In the older time-series literature, the demand side of the list is a business cycle indicator; for example, an adult unemployment rate. The variables on the supply side were the teenage share of the population, and the fractions of teenagers who are enrolled in school, in the armed forces, and in government employment and training programs (Brown, Gilroy, and Kohen 1982, p. 501). Neumark and Wascher (1992) include the first three of these variables, the importance of the last two having declined considerably since the 1970s.

6. Another criticism concerns the definition chosen for school enrollment, a variable meant to control for teenage labor supply, and whether it is reasonable to treat any measure of school enrollment as exogenous to teenage employment. While this generated a flurry of work shortly thereafter, the effect of enrollment on employment is no longer relevant in this literature. We discuss school enrollment and the minimum wage in the chapter on human capital.

7. Over the business cycle, wages and employment of both adults and teenagers move up and down together. During a business cycle expansion, employment of both groups rises; so too (in particular) do wages of adults. Because the Kaitz index includes the adult wage in its denominator, it falls as teenage employment is rising, and this employment growth is credited to the Kaitz index. The unemployment rate is used to control for business cycle effects, but since the Kaitz index, by construction, fluctuates with the business cycle, it will inevitably capture some of this variation. Aggravating this phenomenon is that the unemployment rate is a lagging indicator of the business cycle.

8. Known then as the ES-202 file, it is the basis for the currently available Quarterly Census of Employment and Wages.

9. One difference between Card and Krueger's (2000) use of this data and Neumark and Wascher's (2000) is worth noting: Card and Krueger (2000) use establishment-level data for the four chains that they had previously studied. Neumark and Wascher (2000) aggregate up to the level of each state.

10. In this way, Card and Krueger (2000) respond to concerns that the unusual results in Card and Krueger (1994) were due to employment trends in New Jersey (but not Pennsylvania) for which they had not explicitly accounted. The 1996 federal minimum increase raised the minimum wage in Pennsylvania but not New Jersey, where the minimum wage was already 6 percent higher than the new federal minimum.

11. The examples that Bertrand, Duflo, and Mullainathan (2004) consider may suggest that their concern is a particular instance of the Moulton problem, one in which a group consists of observations of a state over time and the variable that is constant within each group is the at-risk dummy, the treatment variable. However, as Hansen (2007b) shows, the problem they address persists when the variable of interest is not constant but merely exhibits positive serial correlation.

12. For more detailed discussions of these issues, see Imbens and Wooldridge (2009, section 6.5, "Difference-in-Differences Methods") and Angrist and Pischke (2009, section 8.2, "Clustering and Serial Correlation in Panels").

13. Cameron, Gelbach, and Miller (2008) present numerous possible solutions, at least two of which should be effective for Canadian provincial data.

14. Several of these studies (for example, Mastracci and Persky [2008]) use data that would allow them to address the issue that Donald and Lang (2007) raise, with multiple states in the comparison group, but do not take advantage of this.

15. Neumark (2001) makes no correction for serial correction, but the panel he uses is short enough that serial correlation is unlikely to be a problem.

16. Allegretto, Dube, and Reich (2010) agree with Bazen and Le Gallo (2009) about selection bias but disagree about its direction. They report that states that raised

their minimum wages had low and declining teenage employment rates in the eight quarters before increases.

17. Thompson (2009) defines teenagers to be those aged 14–18 years old.

18. Unlike Portugal and Cardoso (2006) and Dube, Lester, and Reich (2010), Thompson (2009) does not report the response of the teen share of separations.

19. Of the four, the only one that is negative is one that includes the state trends, which Sabia (2009a, p. 88) objects to (below) in Dube, Lester, and Reich (2010).

20. Both of these analyses will be described more fully in later sections, where the prime focus of each paper is discussed.

21. In replicating earlier work, Sabia (2009a,b) also reports one very much smaller elasticity estimate, which he refers to as statistically insignificant. Except for three point estimates of long-run elasticities, all derived from equations estimated with a serial correlation correction and for which Sabia (2009b) reports very high levels of statistical significance, the standard errors and significance results that he reports are all for the coefficient point estimates rather than the elasticities themselves.

22. Recall that to be considered unemployed, an individual must have previously decided to participate in the labor market, that is, to engage in search.

23. Flinn (2006) warns against placing too much weight on implications based on minimum wage values well outside the observed range ($4.25 per hour to $5.15 per hour), pp. 1059–1060.

24. Calculated from the top panel of Table V in Eckstein, Ge, and Petrongolo (2011), these are the averages of elasticities from increases and decreases to the minimum wage.

25. Dube, Lester, and Reich (2010) had previously relied on this hypothesis in their analysis of employment in restaurants. The discussion of their work includes a fuller explanation of sources of geographic correlation.

26. The wage response is statistically significant whether or not these dummy variables are included.

27. For the bulk of their analysis, Allegretto, Dube, and Reich (2011) use individual data, combining 5 percent samples from the 1990 and 2000 U.S. censuses, with 1 percent samples from the American Community Surveys of 2005 and 2006. They supplement this with a similar analysis of quarterly cross sections of individuals from the CPS. It is not possible to apply the commuting zone framework to the CPS data, so they cannot run exactly the same regressions, but this allows them to compare their results more closely with previous work and demonstrate that they are not due to the use of different data.

Following an earlier version of Neumark and Wascher (2011), Allegretto, Dube, and Reich (2009) include trends that vary geographically. The issue of their use has become increasingly important in recent years. We will see it again in Addison, Blackburn, and Cotti (2009, 2012); Dube, Lester, and Reich (2010); Neumark and Wascher (2004, 2011); and Sabia (2009b).

28. The EITC subsidizes earnings for low-income households with the goal of encouraging labor force participation and employment. The response of teen employment is of interest because if the interaction of the minimum wage and the EITC encourages individuals with few skills to enter the labor force, the greater

competition may reduce teen employment. This study is discussed in greater detail on pp. 55–58.

29. Neumark and Wascher (2011) are not clear about their tripartite division that mixes ethnic and racial categories, in particular which category includes individuals who are both black and Hispanic; this is most likely Hispanic.

30. Neumark and Wascher (2011) do not present the total minimum wage effect, so the numbers here are calculated from their tables. As is conventional, they do not display covariances, so the statements here about statistical significance assume small or negative covariances between the coefficients that are added to form the total effect.

31. Warren and Halpern-Manners (2007) raise serious questions about the accuracy of CPS measures of the educational attainment of teenagers.

32. This pretense is referred to as a placebo policy.

33. The synthetic control group was constructed to match New York employment trends for everyone without a high school diploma between the ages of 16 and 29; it is not obvious that use of the same synthetic control group for hypothesis tests concerning age subgroups is appropriate. That is, just because a weighted average of some states is a good match for the aggregate employment experience of 16–29-year-olds without a diploma in New York in the years 2002–2004, it is not obvious that the same weighted average of states is a good match for the aggregate employment experience of 16–19-year-olds without a high school diploma in New York in the years 2002–2004.

34. Neumark and Wascher (2011) mention that they had also considered other social welfare policies that may influence labor market outcomes, but preliminary work persuaded them to focus on the EITC. The minimum wage and the EITC are often discussed together because both are policies intended to ameliorate poverty, and proponents see the minimum wage as a tool for ensuring that all benefits of the EITC go to workers rather than act as employment subsidies.

35. This also hints at another issue, which Allegretto, Dube, and Reich (2009, 2011); Campolieti, Fang, and Gunderson (2005a); Dube, Lester, and Reich (2010); and Yuen (2003) examine, the choice of the comparison group and how this can affect the point estimates.

36. In the absence of elasticity estimates and their standard errors, it is often difficult to make comparisons with other results in a way that is both precise and meaningful; for instance, specification differences prevent a direct comparison with Sabia's (2008) coefficient estimates for single mothers that could be circumvented with employment elasticities with respect to the minimum wage.

37. In the equation for black and Hispanic single women, the coefficient on the EITC variable interacted with the treatment dummy is not statistically significant, only the coefficient of the three interaction terms for the EITC variable, treatment dummy, and minimum wage variable.

38. Luttmer (2007) continues, "My findings do not suggest that the minimum wage increase led to a more inefficient rationing of jobs among unskilled workers. If anything, the allocation of jobs seems to have become relatively more efficient in states where the impact of the federal minimum wage increase was larger" (p. 31).

39. An issue with the use of the CPS to study the effects of past periods on the present is that the CPS provides, at most, one year of retrospective data. As a result, Neumark and Nizalova (2007) argue that a large proportion of young workers continue working in the state in which they grew up and that the history of that state's minimum wages can be used as the history of the individuals' minimum wages. While this assumption tends toward the heroic, it is possible that labor market scarring occurs within states, that higher minimum wages do long-term damage to the reputation of certain cohorts of young workers, and low-wage employers become permanently reluctant to hire individuals from those cohorts.

40. It may seem peculiar that although Sabia (2008) reports a strong negative effect on the employment of single mothers who have not completed high school, he finds no effect on their poverty status. This has at least as much to do with peculiarities of the formal definition of poverty as anything else. We address this issue in Chapter 7.

41. Total employment serves as the control for demand factors, i.e., the business cycle, and total population as the control for labor supply factors. Because the results that they report for both the restaurant industry and the entire private sector are qualitatively similar in each specification, only those for the restaurant sector are discussed. The calculation of the reported standard errors clusters observations by county to allow for both unspecified forms of serial correlation in the residuals and unspecified, arbitrary heteroscedasticity.

42. Although they are studying employment in restaurants, not of teenagers, Dube, Lester, and Reich (2010) believe that sensitivity to the minimum wage should be similar because the proportion of workers near the minimum wage is similar in the two groups (employed teenagers and employees in the restaurant industry), and the two groups overlap substantially.

43. This discussion elides some intermediate specifications for clarity. For example, Dube, Lester, and Reich (2010) highlight the use of state-specific trends in combination with the time effects specific to each census division. We neglect these results because they are not statistically significant (although positive), and because of Sabia's (2009b) concern that this specification begs the question, "Are state-specific trends due at least in part to minimum wage policy?"

44. The reference, to Durbin's test, is unsettling because Durbin's name is associated with more than one test for serial correlation, none of which is known specifically as Durbin's test, and they neither elaborate further nor include values of the test statistic in their results.

45. In a different context, Even and Macpherson (2014) mention that "it is possible that a higher tipped minimum wage could increase employment at limited-service restaurants as customers and/or employers switch from full-service to limited-service restaurants in response to an increase in the relative cost at full-service restaurants" (p. 12). If this does indeed happen, the differencing would overstate the impact of the tipped-minimum wage.

46. Although they did not consider the tipped minimum wage, Addison, Blackburn, and Cotti (2012) and Dube, Lester, and Reich (2010), both using QCEW data, and Dube, Naidu, and Reich (2007) consider full-service and limited-service sectors

separately in some of their analysis and report rather different effects of the minimum wage in both sectors than Even and Macpherson (2014). Recognition and discussion of this would have enriched this analysis.

47. One interesting result is that the point estimates from the CPS data are several times as large as those from the QCEW, but so are the standard errors.

48. We ignore the positive, statistically significant employment response in food and beverage stores because the lack of a wage response makes it difficult to understand the mechanism through which the minimum wage would influence employment.

49. Because it is difficult to treat this data set as a sample from an underlying population or process, much less a random sample, conventional interpretation of the standard errors is not reasonable: thus, this focus on betting.

50. This result agrees with Yuen's (2003) findings for teenagers and young adults, discussed below.

51. Recall that Allegretto, Dube, and Reich (2009, 2011) and Dube, Lester, and Reich (2010) have also addressed this general problem in a very different situation, that of geographic correlation. Fang and Gunderson (2009) use the same data and analytic framework as Campolieti, Fang, and Gunderson (2005a) to study the employment response of older workers.

52. Campolieti, Fang, and Gunderson (2005b), in another analysis of longitudinal data from Canada, examine the effect of the minimum wage jointly on employment and enrollment of teenagers. The key result, the minimum wage elasticity of the probability of being employed, is incorrectly calculated from the elasticities of the probabilities of being "employed and enrolled" and "employed and not enrolled." Instead of reporting the average weighted by the relative size of each group, they sum the two elasticities.

53. Skedinger (2006) is a very elegant and thorough analysis of the minimum wage experience in the Swedish hospitality industry. However, the institutional framework resembles not so much a minimum wage, at least to someone in an English-speaking country, as an industrywide collective bargaining agreement, with wage floors that vary by job classification, the age and experience or job tenure of the individual, and, before 1985, region. Consequently, we will pass it by, other than to quote briefly from the conclusion:

> Using data from hotels and restaurants over the period 1979–1999, we find that job separations tend to increase with rising minimum wages (except for teenagers during 1993–1998). The evidence regarding accessions is less conclusive . . . there is some evidence of supply effects, i.e., increasing accessions as minimum wages rise. This is contrary to the assumptions of the underlying model of demand-determined employment and may be consistent with a monopsony model. (p. 287)

The result for separations is quite different from what others found, e.g., Portugal and Cardoso (2006) or Dube, Lester, and Reich (2010).

54. Böckerman and Uusitalo's (2009) study of Finland is problematic. They report decreases in the youth share of employment from both the decline and the increase

in the minimum wages, a result they attribute largely to differential trends in labor force participation or employment that they cannot control for in their short sample.

55. Yuen (2003) justifies the Can$0.25 definition because nearly two-thirds of minimum wage increases in his sample period were for precisely this amount.

56. One explanation for the negative relation between turnover and pay is that employers can identify and reward desirable characteristics of individuals that are invisible in the data available to the econometrician. For more on this relation, see Ehrenberg and Smith (2012, especially pages 385–387).

57. Dolton, Rosazza-Bondibene, and Wadsworth (2012) is discussed in the section "Other Workers," but they report that "when the analysis is repeated for youths, aged 16 to 24, arguably the age group most likely to be at the margin of adjustment, the point estimates are similar to those for all workers, but are generally insignificant, no matter which measure of the bite of the NMW is used" (p. 89).

58. Stewart (2002) presents results not only from regressions where the percent of bound workers measures a region's sensitivity to the minimum wage but also quasi experiments where the control and treatment groups are determined by the percent bound measure. Although less likely to suffer from the Moulton problem than analyses based on states and provinces in North America, if only because treatment and control regions experience the same minimum wage, this discussion takes a conservative approach and considers only results of the quasi experiment framework.

59. Lee and Suardi's (2011) examination of the power of their approach requires some arbitrary choices, specifically about the particular alternative hypothesis that they use, which, unfortunately, they neither explain nor justify.

60. Hyslop and Stillman (2007) also perform several regression analyses that are not discussed here because of their vulnerability to the critique of Bertrand, Duflo, and Mullainathan (2004), unlike the quasi experiment.

61. Pacheco (2011) does not report these elasticities; however, information that is presented in the text for calculating elasticities from the estimated contemporaneous affect, in combination with other estimates, is sufficient for the reader to calculate these values. As is too often usual, no standard errors are available.

62. A straightforward approach is to estimate a linear wage equation that is corrected for selection bias between the employed and the nonemployed. This equation (along with estimates of the inverse Mills ratio) can then generate a wage estimate for each individual, whether or not employed, and the estimates in turn allow for the classification of individuals as minimum wage or above minimum wage.

63. With 10 clusters, the t-statistics that Fang and Gunderson (2009) report should be compared to critical values from the t-distribution with 10 degrees of freedom: the critical values for a two-sided 0.05 test are $\pm t_{10}(0.975) = 2.23$.

64. Both analyses have been described in some detail above, in the section on non-U.S. studies of youth employment.

65. Recall that Portugal and Cardoso (2006) found the same effect for teenagers in Portugal.

66. Data at the more aggregated level are not available throughout their sample period, so they relegate those results to the appendix. Point estimates based on the less aggregated definition of regions are generally closer to zero and less often of statistical significance, something that the authors attribute to greater measurement error.

67. The controls, listed not in this article but in Dolton, Rosazza-Bondibene, and Wadsworth (2010), are average age, and the gender and graduate shares.

68. Recognizing that this comparison group may not be ideal, Kramarz and Philippon (2001) develop conditions based on demand and supply elasticities for the two groups in which the comparison group as defined is well suited to this role, and they state that the conditions are satisfied.

69. Kramarz and Philippon (2001) report no standard error for this value, although they do for the ones on which it is based, and these are statistically significant.

70. Machin and Manning had conducted an initial pair of surveys in 1992–1993 to prepare for the possibility of a Labour electoral victory.

71. The reason for considering the South Coast separately is that it was the area covered by the survey of 1992–1993 that was previously mentioned.

72. Galindo-Rueda and Pereira (2004) present an analysis of the economy-wide impact of the introduction of the NMW, but their data are ill suited to their purposes, and construction of key variables depends on numerous assumptions and approximations. Trying hard, and failing, to match individuals across data sets, they find that they must impute local industry averages of the fraction affected to individual firms. Their conclusion is "that firms thought to be most affected by the introduction of pay floors (by region and industry) responded to the introduction of a NMW by reducing the speed at which they hired new workers" (p. 8, point 18).

73. As discussed previously, Neumark and Nizalova (2007) examine the long-run impact on individuals' employment histories, but the phenomenon that they examine, scarring, is quite different from that discussed here, a slow response to a policy change.

74. Card, Katz, and Krueger (1994) and Card and Krueger (1995) respond to these points, reinterpreting them in a way that they clearly thought appropriate for the specification and minimum wage variable that they used. Neither their response nor their specification had much influence in the subsequent discussion of the timing of the response, so we skip over it here.

75. Neumark and Wascher repeat this point in their later discussion (1994; Card, Katz, and Krueger 1994), writing that "there is evidence of lagged minimum wage effects in the data, and . . . the omission of these lagged effects leads to substantial upward bias in short first-difference estimates" (p. 508).

76. The lagged term implies that it takes more than a year for the full impact of the minimum wage on teenage employment to play out, due to "hiring and training costs, or because of an inability to adjust other inputs quickly" (Neumark and Wascher 1992, Note 19).

77. Sargent (1987) discusses this in section XI.9, crediting Slutsky with the first recognition of this in economics.

78. Recall that Card, Katz, and Krueger (1994) identify problems with minimum wage measures of this type. During a business cycle upturn, both employment and the

average wage increase, and the increase in the average wage mechanically causes a decrease in the relative wage. In this way, this minimum wage measure automatically has a negative correlation with employment, correlated not through any causal relation but through a third variable.

79. The data sample ends 42 months after September 1998, March 2002, so the simulation comes to a halt there. It is not necessarily the last month in which the minimum wage has an effect.

3
Hours of Employment

Perhaps evidence for the employment response is weak because of the way that employment is being measured—as the number of jobs or percent of people with jobs.[1] Employees in minimum wage jobs are paid by the hour. Unless the number of hours worked is the same in all minimum wage jobs, jobs and hours worked are not equivalent measures of employment. Measuring employment by the number of jobs is like measuring the total amount of water in different-sized pitchers by counting the number of pitchers. Instead, the volume of water should be measured directly by adding the amount in each pitcher to get the total. If the number of hours that individual employees work varies, then measure the number of hours. Perhaps rather than reduce staffing in response to the minimum wage, employers should reduce hours of some or all employees.

Underlying this hypothesis is another: that up to a point, hiring and firing workers is more difficult or costly than raising and lowering the hours that current employees work. Hiring involves some or all of the following actions: get the word out about openings, review applications to decide whom to interview, interview, check references, evaluate the information acquired from the interview, and make a decision. Further, even if no training is necessary, new hires in many jobs will initially be less productive until they become familiar with the particular workplace and its routines. If employers lay off people when the minimum wage rises, they will lose the value in these implicit training costs as well as any skills developed on the job. Given this, it seems likely that raising and lowering the number of hours individuals work is an easier, less expensive way to adjust the amount of paid labor that is employed (again, up to a point).

In the NMWR, Zavodny (2000) was the first to examine whether these two measures of employment (jobs and hours) give different answers to the question, "Does the minimum wage (necessarily) reduce employment?"[2] Coming several years prior to Bertrand, Duflo, and Mullainathan (2004), this study does not report a clustered standard, so we do not include it in the discussion below, but a number of studies followed her lead, including several already discussed in Chapter 2.[3]

U.S. STUDIES

Demographic Groups

Youth

Table 3.1 shows the five studies that examine the effect of the minimum wage on teenagers' hours of employment: Orrenius and Zavodny (2008) and Sabia (2009a,b), which use state-level panels; and Allegretto, Dube, and Reich (2009, 2011), which use repeated cross sections of individual-level data. We will consider first the studies of aggregate data. Both Orrenius and Zavodny and Sabia aggregate CPS ORG data to the level of the state; the first use annual data and the second monthly, and both report results for unconditional average usual hours.[4] Sabia also reports estimates for conditional usual hours.[5] Because a main theme of Sabia's analysis is the resolution of disagreement about the best way to control for business cycle effects, he reports several results.

Orrenius and Zavodny (2008) estimate a conventional equation, with two-way fixed effects (for state and year), the adult male unemployment rate and the teenage share of the population as the control variables for demand and supply conditions, and one or the other of two different minimum wage variables. The first is constructed using a deflator that is common to all states in the same year, and the second uses the average adult wage in each state and year, which therefore has the same endogeneity problems as the Kaitz index (see Chapter 2). On the basis of the common deflator, they report a negative response of the hours of teenage girls to the minimum wage.[6] The elasticity of total hours with respect to the minimum wage is -0.31, with a standard error of -0.12.[7]

Sabia (2009b) presents results for different log-log specifications where the list of regressors always includes state and month dummies, the adult male unemployment rate, the fraction of 16–64-year-olds who are teenagers, and nominal values of the minimum wage and the mean

Table 3.1 Youth (U.S. Data)

Study	Effect: elasticity	Target group	Sample period	Analytic approach	Unit of observation	Data structure	Variable
Allegretto, Dube, and Reich (2009)	−0.03 (0.03)	Teenagers	1990, 2000, 2005, 2006	Regression, QE[a]	Individual-year	Repeated cross section	Usual weekly hours
Allegretto, Dube, and Reich (2011)	−0.03 (0.04)	Teenagers	1990–2009	Regression	Individual-year	Repeated cross section	Usual weekly hours
Orrenius and Zavodny (2008)	−0.31 (0.12) −0.23 (0.12)	Teen girls	1994–2005	Regression	State-year	Panel	Usual weekly hours
Sabia (2009a)	−0.51, −0.37, −0.29	Teen girls	1979–2004	Regression	State-month	Panel	Usual weekly hours
Sabia (2009b)	−0.42	Teenagers in retail	1979–2004	Regression	State-month	Panel	Usual weekly hours
Couch and Wittenburg (2001)[b]	−0.44– −0.77	Teenagers	1979–1992	Regression	State-month	Panel	Usual weekly hours in primary job
Zavodny (2000)[b]	0.24 (0.12) −0.11 (0.08)	Teenagers	1979–1993	Regression, QE	State-year and individual-year	Panel	Usual weekly hours (calcs cond avg)

NOTE: Youth refers to those younger than 25; teenagers are 16–19. Standard errors are in parentheses.
[a] Quasi experiment.
[b] This study has standard errors that are suspect for reasons identified by Bertrand, Duflo, and Mullainathan (2004).

adult wage. His specifications differ according to whether they include in addition a one-year lag of the minimum wage, and either a set of annual dummy variables or a dummy to indicate whether the economy was in recession that month. A hazard of using monthly CPS aggregates is the tiny sample sizes underlying some of that state-month observations, and Sabia reports results in which he weights each observation by the number of respondents on which it is based. His sample is 1979–2004.[8]

In all of his specifications for unconditional hours, either the current minimum wage or the lagged minimum wage is statistically significant (but not both). Sabia (2009b) reports elasticities' p-values only for the two specifications that include the lagged term, and both are statistically significant: −0.51 when the equation includes the recession dummy rather than the annual dummies, and −0.37 with the annual dummies rather than the recession dummy. The effect on conditional hours is somewhat less pronounced; in one specification, the minimum wage has no effect, and in the others the effect of either the contemporaneous or lagged term is much smaller, although one or both remain statistically significant. The one significant elasticity is much smaller, −0.28 (with the recession dummy).

Recall that the focus in both analyses of Allegretto, Dube, and Reich (2009, 2011) is that the employment response to the minimum wage reported in analyses that rely on the approach introduced by Neumark and Wascher (1992) disappears in specifications that include controls for factors correlated with but not caused by the minimum wage. Teenagers' hours of employment is one of the variables that they examine in each study. An important difference between the two studies is the data used, which requires different control variables: Allegretto, Dube, and Reich (2011) use CPS data that allow for sensitivity at a relatively high frequency, but not for the fine-grain geographic distinctions that Allegretto, Dube, and Reich (2009) can make using census and related data. Neither finds a statistically significant reduction in hours.

Recall that the focus in Allegretto, Dube, and Reich (2011) is on economic factors that vary not only over time, which conventional fixed time effects would control for, but also regionally over time, so that the New England states have their own set of time effects distinct from those of the mid-Atlantic states, and so forth. Their hypothesis is the existence of important regional differences in cultural traits and institutions that are both important for economic outcomes and correlated with regional differences in average minimum wages. Controlling for these regional differences leaves the minimum wage to account only for differences among states in the same region rather than these regional differences across the whole country.

Point estimates from a model designed to resemble the canonical one of Neumark and Wascher's extensive oeuvre indicate a negative response for all teens and especially for teenage girls of usual hours worked. However, once the regional controls are included, this effect disappears; the hours elasticity is −0.03, with a standard error of 0.04. While Allegretto, Dube, and Reich's (2011) specification addresses only the effect on (usual weekly) conditional hours, lack of any detectable effect on the number of jobs implies that their result also holds for unconditional hours. In response to concerns that the effect of well anticipated increases will be largely complete by the time of the increase (recall Pinoli [2010]), they also distinguish between increases that occur as a result of automatic indexing for inflation, which are likely to be anticipated, and other increases that are less likely to be anticipated. When Allegretto, Dube, and Reich consider only nonindexed increases in the minimum wage, they detect a "modest" and statistically insignificant negative hours response, with an elasticity of −0.07 (standard error equals 0.04). When estimates are allowed to differ among white, black, and Hispanic teenagers, they indicate no effect on hours for members of the first two groups, but the effect is large and negative for Hispanics (with an elasticity of −0.33, and standard error of 0.14). This is puzzling since they find no evidence that the minimum wage affects the wages of Hispanic teenagers.

Allegretto, Dube, and Reich (2009) take a different tack. Figuring that a commuting zone is a (reasonably) unified labor market, they compare the experience of teenagers who live in different parts of commuting zones, where the different parts simultaneously have more than one minimum wage because the zone straddles a state boundary. They find a small, negative, and statistically insignificant effect on usual hours (an estimated elasticity of −0.031, with a standard error of −0.032). Combining this with the absence of any negative jobs effect (the response of the number of jobs is positive and statistically insignificant), there appears to be, at worst, no effect on total hours worked.

Sabia's (2009a) study of the retail sector includes results for hours of teenagers in the retail sector. The most credible point estimate of the elasticity, because it is based on a regression with an autocorrelation correction, is a long-run elasticity of −0.42, in the middle of the range that Sabia (2009b) reported for all teenagers. The absence of any standard errors for the elasticity makes it difficult to judge the precision of the estimate.

Other groups

Table 3.2 lists five studies that present results for the hours of employment of other demographic groups in the United States. Two of these have questionable standard errors, and problems with a third, Neumark and Nizalova (2007), are discussed in Chapter 2; two studies remain.[9] The primary concern of Orrenius and Zavodny (2008) is the effect of the minimum wage on immigrants who lack a high school diploma.[10] They detect no effect on immigrants' hours of work and speculate that immigrants may take local labor market conditions into account in their location decisions, generating a pattern of location choice that obscures the effect of the minimum wage on hours and employment. Sabia (2008) uses the annual March supplement to the CPS to study the effect of the minimum wage on the poverty status of single mothers to find very large negative effects on hours worked: −0.92 for usual weekly hours, and −0.012 percent for annual hours. While he reports (state-clustered) standard errors for the regression coefficients on which these elasticities are based, and they indicate statistical significance at a 1 percent level, he does not report them for the elasticities, nor does he explain precisely how they are calculated. Although these coefficients are statistically significant, the precision of the elasticities themselves is not clear.

Sectoral Studies

What ties the studies in this section together is that they examine the effect of the minimum wage on industries or sectors, rather than on demographic groups or groups of employees (see Table 3.3).[11] Three use the two-by-two quasi experiment framework of Card and Krueger (1994) to examine the effect of a local increase in the minimum wage on employment in affected restaurants: Dube, Naidu, and Reich (2007); Persky and Baiman (2010); and Powers (2009). Of course, Donald and

Table 3.2 Other Groups (U.S. Data)

Study	Effect: elasticity	Target group	Sample period	Analytic approach	Unit of observation	Data structure	Variable
Neumark and Nizalova (2007)	−0.09 −1.2 (3.8)	Adults, 25–29	1979–2001	Regression	State-year cohort	Panel	Weekly hours (avg. over all)
Orrenius and Zavodny (2008)	−0.11 (0.08)	Immigrants	1994–2005	Regression	State-year	Panel	Usual weekly hours
Sabia (2008)	−0.92 −1.18	Single mothers with less than high school degree	1991–2004	Regression	Individual-year	Repeated cross section	Hours worked last year
Mastracci and Persky (2008)[b]	None (Emp.)	Low-wage workers	2003–2005	QE[a]	Individual-year	Repeated cross section	Hours usually worked
Neumark, Schweitzer, and Wascher (2004)[b]	Negative	Many wage earners	1979–1997	Regression	Individual-month	Longitudinal	Usual weekly hours

NOTE: Standard errors are in parentheses.

[a] Quasi experiment.

[b] This study has standard errors that are suspect for reasons identified by Bertrand, Duflo, and Mullainathan (2004).

Table 3.3 Studies of Industries (U.S. Data)

Study	Effect: elasticity	Target group or sector	Sample period	Analytic approach	Unit of observation	Data structure	Variable
Belman and Wolfson (2010)	−0.01 (0.05)	Low-wage industries	1972–2003	Regression	Industry-month	Multiple time series	Avg. monthly hours (calcs. total)
Dube, Naidu, and Reich (2007)	None	San Francisco restaurants	2003–2004	QE[a] and regression	Firm-year	Longitudinal	FTE based on avg. weekly hours
Even and Macpherson (2014)	None	Full-service restaurants	1990–2011	Regression	State-quarter	Panel	Aggregate usual hours
Orazem and Mattila (2002)	−1.10 −1.50	Retail, service not professional	1989–1992	Regression	County-qtr.-industry	Panel	—
Persky and Baiman (2010)	None	IL fast food establishments	2003–2005	QE (2×2) and regression	Firm-year	Longitudinal	FTE hours in last pay period
Powers (2009)	None	IL fast food establishments	2003–2005	QE (2×2) and regression	Firm-year	Longitudinal	FTE hours in last pay period
Sabia (2009b)	−0.1	Retail workers	1979–2004	Regression	State-month	Panel	Weekly hours (avg. of all and employed)
Vedder and Gallaway (2002)	Negative	All workers	1959–1999	Regression	Country-year, region-year	Aggregate time series	Total hours

NOTE: Standard errors are in parentheses.
[a] Quasi experiment.

Lang (2007) identify serious problems with this framework, but each study also contains regression results that are based on either a measure of the fraction affected or the wage gap, and these do not suffer from these problems. Even and Macpherson (2014) use the canonical framework of Neumark and Wascher (1992) to study the effect of the tipped minimum wage on tipped workers in the restaurant sector; they also present estimates of the effect of the nontipped minimum wage on this group, as well as the effect of both types of minimum wage on nontipped restaurant workers. Vedder and Gallaway (2002) and Belman and Wolfson (2010) use U.S. data from the BLS-EEH survey. They differ in their sample period, in the degree of aggregation used to define both the industry and the time period for each observation, and in their statistical approaches. Sabia (2009a), which we have already seen in this chapter, uses the CPS to construct a state-year panel of retail workers. Machin, Manning, and Rahman (2003) and Orazem and Mattila (2002) both rely on data from privately commissioned surveys of a group of business firms.[12]

As part of their survey of restaurants in the San Francisco Bay area, Dube, Naidu, and Reich (2007) asked about the number of full- and part-time employees, and the average for each group of the number of weekly hours worked. From these values, they calculate the total number of hours for each establishment before and after the minimum wage increase and divide by 40 to get "full-time equivalent employment." To capture the effect of the minimum wage, what they call "treatment intensity," they calculate the fraction affected, which was zero for both restaurants outside San Francisco and small restaurants in San Francisco. They then regress full-time employment-employment on treatment intensity. Over a variety of samples (differing primarily in the restaurants for which treatment intensity is zero, but also considering full-service and fast food restaurants separately), the estimated effect is always positive and never statistically significant (indeed, rarely as large as the standard error).

Both Powers (2009) and Persky and Baiman (2010) use data on fast food establishments in Indiana and Illinois that they jointly collected (Powers, Persky, and Baiman 2007) to study the effects of the Illinois increases in the minimum wage of 2004 and 2005. Powers writes, "The raison d'être of this project is to collect hours data at the establishment level" (p. 377). Both explore this with a wage gap measure, calculated as the percentage increase in ex ante starting wages needed to comply with the ex post minimum wage, and Powers also considers the fraction affected. Persky and Baiman (2010) consider both the change in full-time equivalent hours and its establishment size-weighted growth rate as dependent variables.[13] Powers reports estimates from several closely related specifications; the signs on each of the minimum wage measures are positive slightly more often than they are negative, and none are statistically significant. Persky and Baiman report results for each of their dependent variables, with and without Indiana in the sample (where the establishments were not affected by the minimum wage increases). With Indiana in the sample, the coefficients on the minimum wage are negative and statistically insignificant for each dependent variable. With it removed from the equation, the estimated effect on each dependent variable is positive, and in the equation with the growth rate of hours as the dependent variable, the coefficient is statistically significant.

Even and Macpherson (2014) use information in the CPS to identify individuals employed in the restaurant industry, distinguishing between those likely to be subject to the tipped minimum wage and those subject to the regular minimum wage (hereafter, "the minimum wage"). Similar to Neumark and Wascher's approach, they aggregate the data within each state and quarter into a single observation and estimate an equation that resembles those of Neumark and Wascher (1992), with a similar list of controls, except that it includes not one but two contemporaneous minimum wage variables, one for each type of minimum wage. Their dependent variable is total (usual) hours. To control for time-varying state-specific factors, one of their sets of estimates comes from using the log-difference of hours between tipped and nontipped workers as the dependent variable. Each of their sets of estimates (tipped workers, nontipped workers, and the log-difference) includes a long sample (1990:1–2011:4) and a short one (1994:2–2007:3) trimmed to exclude the recession at each end of the period. For each sample, Even and Macpherson estimate a specification with state-specific time trends and another without them because of skepticism that they are appropriate. All but one of the point estimates are negative, and most are bigger than their counterparts in the employment equation, but only one out of the two dozen estimates (2 minimum wage variables × 2 samples × 2 specifications × 3 dependent variables) is statistically significant: that for the tipped minimum wage and tipped workers. This is not especially compelling evidence that the tipped minimum wage is an important influence on total hours of tipped employees, or that the minimum wage is an important influence on total hours worked in the restaurant industry.

Although we have already touched on Sabia's (2009a) analysis, its primary focus, the retail sector, puts it squarely in this section. For total hours in retail, the point estimates of the hours elasticity are roughly −0.1, and the regression coefficients on which they are based are statistically significant at the 0.01 level in more than half the specifications, and at the 0.05 level in all but one of the rest.[14]

Recall from Chapter 2 that in their study of the effect of the increases in Iowa's minimum wage in the early 1990s, Orazem and Mattila (2002) analyze two types of data: 1) county-level aggregates that the state of Iowa collects in conjunction with the Unemployment Insurance program, and 2) data that they themselves collected about firms and employees in the retail and nonprofessional services sectors. In the former, Orazem and Mattila report moderately elastic responses of hours for each part of the sample, roughly −1.1 in each case over both one quarter and one year, i.e., 10 times as large as the estimated employment elasticities.[15] With the individual-level data, they estimate a wage equation to measure workers' to the minimum wage in order to identify workers who would be earning less than the minimum wage had it not risen. The reported hours elasticities are generally even larger, ranging from about −1.1 to −1.5, about two- to three-and-a-half times as large as the corresponding employment elasticities. The implication of these estimates is that during this period, when the minimum wage in Iowa rose by nearly 40 percent, weekly hours of those who would have been earning less than $4.65 in 1992 fell by roughly 45 percent to 60 percent. According to their estimates, some of this occurred through job loss, but even for those who remained employed, hours fell (though by less than this proportion). They give no indication either in the text or the table about the precision of the estimate of hours elasticities.

Belman and Wolfson (2010) analyze the response of total hours in about two dozen low-wage industries to the national minimum wage in the United States, using monthly data for the period 1972–1998, and giving special attention to modeling the dynamic behavior of the series analyzed.[16] To summarize the impact, they perform a dynamic out-of-sample analysis over all the industries, comparing what actually did occur with what their estimates imply would have happened if the minimum wage had increased by 10 percent in September 1998 (from $5.15/hour to $5.67/hour). The maximum decline in hours occurs about nine months later, −0.5 percent in June 1999, but this rebounds sharply the following month to −0.1 percent, and fluctuates close to this value for the more than three and a half years that follow. Except for that one month, the point estimate is always less than a standard deviation from zero. That is, they report a statistically insignificant elasticity of −1 percent four and a half years after the increase and for almost every month during this period.

Vedder and Gallaway (2002) use annual aggregate hours data for 1959–1999 to gauge the effect of the minimum wage. The three series they use are total hours in the private, nonagricultural sector of the economy, and both total and overtime hours in manufacturing. These sectors are considerably broader than those typically studied in the minimum wage literature, since it is widely believed that at the historical levels of the minimum wage in the United States, effects will be detectible only in relatively homogeneous categories of low-paid workers, industries, or demographic groups. They give very little information about the time aggregation of the data used, but whether it is annual or monthly, one would expect to see testing for unit roots and cointegration and, depending on the outcomes of the tests, perhaps differencing or lagged dependent variables.[17] For all three regressions, the minimum wage coefficient is both negative and associated with large t-statistics, but the lack of information about the data and the estimates themselves makes it hard to interpret these results.

Summary of Results Based on U.S. Data

Studies of the response of hours worked to the minimum wage report results for the United States that are all over the place. For teenagers, Allegretto, Dube, and Reich (2009, 2011) report point estimates of elasticities that are both miniscule and statistically insignificant. Orrenius and Zavodny (2008) report elasticity point estimates that are 5–10 times as large, but only the largest (for teenage girls) are statistically significant, and Sabia's (2009a,b) results range in size from roughly the largest of Orrenius and Zavodny's (2008) to more than half again as large (all presumably statistically significant). Turning to groups other than teenagers, Orrenius and Zavodny (2008) do not detect a statistically significant hours elasticity for immigrants who lack a high school diploma; in his study of single mothers who lack a high school diploma, Sabia (2008) finds elasticities that are roughly twice the size as those he reported for teenagers. The sectoral studies are in nearly as much disagreement. The four that examine restaurants (Dube, Naidu, and Reich 2007; Even and Macpherson 2014; Persky and Baiman 2010; Powers 2009) find no effect on hours. Sabia (2009b) reports a small effect in the broader sector of retail, and Orazem and Mattila (2002) report very large effects on hours in the even broader sector of retail and nonprofessional services. In a collection of low-wage industries that overlaps that broader sector (but does not include it), Belman and Wolfson (2010) report a tiny negative effect on hours that is statistically insignificant. Using data for the entire macroeconomy, Vedder and Gallaway (2002) report statistically significant, negative coefficients on the minimum wage but do not appear to have addressed likely problems related to serial correlation.

OTHER DEVELOPED COUNTRIES

Types of Workers

Young workers

Table 3.4 lists five studies that report estimates of the effect of the minimum wage in countries other than the United States on the working hours of youth. We limit our discussion to two of these because each of the other three has serious problems that undercut any faith in either the point estimates or statistical inference based on them.

In their analysis of the substantial increase in the effective minimum wage for teenagers in New Zealand, Hyslop and Stillman (2007) apply both a difference-in-differences framework and a regression analysis to individual-level data similar to the CPS ORG data. The first indicates that employed 16–17-year-olds experienced a 20 percent increase in hours worked and those aged 18–19 experienced a 6 percent increase, both statistically significant. In combination with the absence of statistically significant negative employment outcomes, this indicates no

Table 3.4 Youth (Foreign Data)

Study	Effect: elasticity (SE)	Target group	Country	Sample period	Analytic approach	Unit of observation	Data structure	Variable
Hyslop and Stillman (2007)	0.49	Teenagers	New Zealand	1998–2003	QE[a], regression	Individual-year	Panel	Hours worked last week
Pacheco (2011)	Negative	Minimum wage youth	New Zealand	1986–2004	Regression	Individual-qtr.	Repeated cross section	Usual weekly hours
Böckerman and Uusitalo (2009)[b]	None	Youth workers in retail trade	Finland	1991–1996	QE	Firm-year	Panel	Regular weekly working hrs.
Pereira (2003)[c]	Negative	Teenage workers	Portugal	1986–1989	QE	Firm-year	Panel	Average monthly hours
Shannon (2011)[d]	None/ negative	15–16- year-olds	Canada	1976–2003	QE	Individual- year	Repeated cross section	Actual hours worked if employed

NOTE: Youth refers to those younger than 25; teenagers are 16–19.

[a] Quasi experiment.

[b] Böckerman and Uusitalo (2009) doubt that they have adequately controlled for trends in employment and labor force participation.

[c] Portugal and Cardoso (2006) report that Pereira (2003) is not representative of the population of firms from which it is drawn, and that employment trends of teenagers in the sample and population are quite different.

[d] Although Shannon (2011) reports standard errors clustered by province, this technique is ineffective with so few clusters.

decrease in total hours. We can put these figures together with the increases in the effective minimum wage, 41 percent for 16–17-year-olds and 69 percent for 18–19-year-olds, to derive elasticity measures for the hours responses: +0.49 for the younger age group, and +0.09 for the older age group (no standard errors available).

Results from the regression analysis are murkier. Estimates when business cycle controls are not included indicate hours effects of similar magnitude and degree of statistical significance as the difference-in-differences analysis. Inclusion of the business cycle variable, which an F-test indicates to be appropriate, turns the hours effect negative though insignificant for those aged 18–19. For those aged 16–17, the point estimates of the effect remain positive, but the only one that remains statistically significant is for the year following the second increase; those for the years following the first and third increases become much smaller, and their standard errors become much larger.[18] Combining both the absence of an initial employment effect and the eventual small negative employment effects with the effect on conditional average hours leads to the conclusion that total hours increased. Hyslop and Stillman (2007) interpret this as a "positive labour supply response by teenagers (particularly 16–17-year-olds) to the minimum wage increases that was, at best, partially accommodated by the demand side . . ." (p. 227).

Pacheco's (2011) analysis, also examined more fully in Chapter 2, briefly considers the effect of the minimum wage on hours. She reports that for teenagers aged 16–17 who find the minimum wage binding, usual weekly hours falls by 19 hours; the figure for the comparable group aged 18–19 is 17 hours; for those aged 20–24, 11 hours; and those aged 25–29, 27 hours. She does not give enough information to calculate the effect either for all teenagers or for all members of any of these groups (e.g., for all aged 16–17, not just those for whom the minimum wage was binding), and given compositional employment effects that some studies have reported (also discussed in Chapter 2), it is easily conceivable that total hours of work for any of these groups, especially those of teenagers, are not affected.[19]

Other low-wage workers

Table 3.5 lists three articles—Connolly and Gregory (2002), Stewart and Swaffield (2008), and Robinson and Wadsworth (2007)—

that consider several groups of workers in the United Kingdom who were earning wages lower than the National Minimum Wage (NMW) immediately before it went into effect on April 1, 1999. All three apply a difference-in-differences framework to individual-level data, defining the treatment group as employed individuals who fit a certain demographic profile. The comparison groups are defined to be similar to the treatment group but not affected by the NMW. All three studies rely on usual, not actual, hours of work, and because they compare hours for individuals who were employed in both periods, they examine hours conditional on employment, which, as previously mentioned, does not translate directly to total hours of employment unless there are no changes in the number of jobs.[20]

Connolly and Gregory (2002) use two annual surveys to study the effect on women's hours of the introduction of the NMW: the New Earnings Survey (NES), which, with periodic updates, has used the same large sample of workers for many years, gathering information from their employers; and the British Household Panel Survey (BHPS), a smaller survey that tracks the same households across many years. They consider data from both surveys because of their complementary strengths and weaknesses. The NES, while very broad and inclusive, is likely to miss workers who are very low-paid and part time, and those who have recently started new jobs. Though smaller, the BHPS is less likely to suffer from these particular problems. The data that Connolly and Gregory use begin in 1994 and continue through autumn 2000 for the BHPS, and through spring 2001 for the NES. They compare women who had been earning less than the NMW before its introduction with those who had previously been earning up to 10 percent more than the NMW. Once they include the various control variables available in each data set, they find statistically insignificant effects on hours worked (negative in the NHS data, positive in the BHPS data). Other studies to which they refer have analyzed these data sets and found no effect on the total number of jobs, which suggests that "there was no effect on total hours" is a reasonable conclusion.

Stewart and Swaffield (2008) examine the hours response of low-paid workers of both sexes and also use two different surveys because of complementary features, the annual NES from 1994–2000 and the quarterly Labour Force Survey (LFS) from 1997:Q1–2000:Q3. In this case, the complementary features are the greater frequency of the LFS

Table 3.5 Other Groups (Foreign Data)

Study	Effect: elasticity	Target group	Country	Sample period	Analytic approach	Unit of observation	Data structure	Variable
Connolly and Gregory (2002)	None	Women working part-time	United Kingdom	1999–2003	QE[a]	Longitudinal	Individual panel	Basic hours (NES) Normal hours (BHPS)
Robinson and Wadsworth (2007)	Negative	Low-wage earners w/two jobs	United Kingdom	1998–1999	QE	Longitudinal	Individual panel	Hours worked in main job, 2nd job
Stewart and Swaffield (2008)	Negative	Low-wage earners	United Kingdom	1997–2000	QE	Longitudinal	Individual panel	Paid hours (standard and total)

[a]Quasi experiment.

versus the much larger sample size and greater reliability of data in the NES. Each of these surveys includes many if not all of the same individuals from one period to the next. In the LFS, individuals appear for five consecutive quarters, and in each quarterly survey, 20 percent of the sample is individuals who appear for the first time, and another 20 percent is individuals who appear for the last time. This 40 percent of the sample is the only part that Stewart and Swaffield use, the first and last quarter in which an individual appears in the LFS. Their (primary) comparison group is those who were earning between the NMW and 10 percent more at the time of its introduction, and they use two treatment groups: those who were earning less than the NMW at the time of its introduction, and the subset who in addition specifically experienced wage increases.[21]

Stewart and Swaffield (2008) define an initial effect and a lagged effect of the NMW for both data sets. The initial effect is calculated from the difference between the year's worth of surveys immediately before and the year's worth immediately after the NMW went into effect. The lagged effect is based on the first and second years' worth of surveys after the NMW's effective date. Because of differences in the frequency with which the two surveys are administered, this leads to differences in the definitions of the measured effect. What are the implications of these differences in how the initial and lagged effects are measured? Unless a large part of any response occurs within the first month following the implementation of the NMW, the NES-based measure of its initial effect is more accurately characterized (and referred to) as the immediate effect. Both of the LFS-based measures, not only the LFS-based lagged effect, are better compared to the NES-lagged effect than to the NES-initial effect.[22]

For each combination of sex, type of effect, and way of measuring hours worked, where sex is male or female, type of effect is initial or lagged, and hours measure is total hours or straight time hours (i.e., with overtime and without overtime, respectively), Stewart and Swaffield (2008) present 8 difference-in-differences point estimates for the NES, and 12 for the LFS.[23] For men, all but one of the point estimates of the immediate effect (i.e., the NES-based measure of the initial effect) are positive, and none are statistically significant. For women, all point estimates of the immediate effect are negative, all those for total hours are statistically significant, and all those for straight-time hours are statistically significant when the treatment is limited to those whose wages actually rose to be in compliance with the NMW. Based strictly on the range of statistically significant point estimates, total hours fell by about 35 minutes per week for all women previously earning less than the NMW, and for those women whose wages rose to be in compliance, total hours fell by just a bit more than one hour per week while straight time fell by between 40 and 50 minutes per week.

Over the year following the increase, we can compare difference-in-differences estimates of the LFS initial effect and the NES lagged effect for both sexes. The estimated hours effect for men is predominantly negative but not statistically significant (based on the LFS) or uniformly negative (based on the NES). The NES indicates declines over the course of the year of between 80 minutes and 110 minutes per week in total hours for all men, and between 75 minutes and nearly two hours per week in straight-time hours. For men whose wages rose to be in compliance with the NMW, the point estimates of the decline range from about 110 minutes per week to 140 minutes per week in total hours and from about 100 minutes to 140 minutes per week in straight time. For women, the NES point estimates of the lagged effect are also statistically significant but smaller in size, perhaps due to the considerably larger immediate impact: for all women, declines range from about 80 to 90 minutes per week in total hours and from about 65 to 80 minutes per week in straight-time hours. For women, the point estimates from LFS data are negative more often than not, but none are statistically significant.

Finally, the LFS-based difference-in-differences lagged effect is mixed. All but two of the point estimates for men are negative (both for total hours), but none of those for total hours is statistically significant. Nearly all the point estimates of the effect on men's straight-time hours are both negative and statistically significant. These indicate a decline in straight time ranging between 2 hours 20 minutes and nearly 3 hours 40 minutes per week for all men, and between 3.5 and 4.0 hours per week for those whose wages rose to be in compliance with the NMW. For women, all the LFS-based lagged estimates are negative, but only one is statistically significant.

Stewart and Swaffield (2008) mention some measurement issues that raise questions about robustness of the LFS results. They also report estimated impacts on hours based on a wage gap that are roughly the same size, at the average value of the wage gap as those estimated by difference-in-differences when the difference-in-differences estimates are statistically significant (but are often of the opposite sign when the difference-in-differences estimates are not statistically significant). Because they believe the wage gap to be more vulnerable to measurement errors than mere sorting of individuals into treatment and control groups, they interpret the wage-gap results as merely confirming the difference-in-differences ones.

How to make sense of this plethora of results? For neither survey does the estimate of the most immediate effect indicate a reduction in men's hours, but both do indicate a decline over the half year (LFS) or year (NES) after that. For women, there is evidence of an immediate decline in their hours (NES), but little thereafter. Stewart and Swaffield (2008) conclude that "in broad terms the evidence presented in this paper suggests strongly that the introduction of the minimum wage led to a reduction in the paid working hours of both male and female low-wage workers" (p. 165).[24]

Robinson and Wadsworth (2007) use the LFS to focus on the response of second-job holding to introduction of the NMW, and along the way they also examine the hours response of those who held two jobs. Their working hypothesis is that the only reason for holding two jobs is that one cannot work as many hours (and earn as much) as desired in only one of the jobs available. When the NMW was introduced, several effects were possible. If neither hours nor employment at the primary job changed, then those who both worked at two jobs and experienced a wage increase in the primary job may well have reduced their hours at the second one. If hours at the primary job declined (and more paid hours at the secondary job were available), then hours worked in secondary jobs may have increased. Their analysis compares those who earned less than the £3.60 NMW in the year before it became law—roughly the lowest decile of wage earners—with those who earned up to £4.20—roughly the second decile.[25] Robinson and Wadsworth report that those in this treatment group worked roughly 1.3 hours less per week at the main job than before the NMW (relative to the comparison group) whether or not there was a second job. This was about a 5 percent reduction in hours (i.e., average hours before the NMW was about 26 hours/week for the treatment group) and was statistically significant at a 5 percent level.

Two of these three studies report small, statistically significant reductions in weekly hours for low-wage workers. With respect to the exception, Connolly and Gregory (2002) and Stewart and Swaffield (2008) raise the possibility that the treatment group is too broadly defined. When Stewart and Swaffield narrow their treatment group to those whose wages actually increased to be in compliance with the NMW, those point estimates that were previously statistically significant become larger, but the estimates that are not statistically significant are largely unaffected by the sample used; this appears to weaken their explanation of the difference. All three analyses focus on different demographic groups, and the one that Connolly and Gregory (2002) examine, low-paid women, is a subset of the one that Stewart and Swaffield (2008) study; a priori, it seems likely that hours of low-paid women would be more responsive than those of all low-paid workers, not less.

Sectoral Studies

Machin, Manning, and Rahman's (2003) study of the care home sector in the United Kingdom, using data for individual establishments, has been discussed in Chapter 2. The minimum wage varies only over time; to introduce variation across firms, they rely on the number of employees making less than the minimum wage in each firm. They detect a negative hours effect that is about as strong as the jobs effect, suggesting that those still employed are working the same amount and that the full adjustment in hours is due to reduction in staffing. As shown in Table 3.6, they provide several elasticity estimates (but no standard errors for them), and the more reliable ones, because derived from regressions with various control variables, range between −0.2 and −0.4, depending on the minimum wage variable used.

SUMMING UP

Where does this leave us? The clearest pattern is the negative impact on hours that three of the four studies of the introduction of the NMW in the UK report.[26] The two studies of low-wage earners find statistically significant, if small, declines in hours worked. Robinson and

Table 3.6 Studies of Industries (Foreign Data)

Study	Effect: elasticity	Target group	Country	Sample period	Analytic approach	Unit of observation	Data structure	Variable
Machin, Manning, and Rahman (2003)	Negative −0.2 to −0.4	Home care	United Kingdom	1992–1999	QE[a]	Firm-survey response	Longitudinal	Weekly hours

[a]Quasi experiment.

Wadsworth (2007) report a decline of about 1.3 hours per week (roughly 5 percent) among low-wage earners with two jobs in the year following the introduction of the NMW. Stewart and Swaffield (2008) report a similar figure among all low-wage earners in the two years following the introduction. A reasonable conclusion is that the total number of hours worked declines. Machin, Manning, and Rahman (2003) is a simple, direct study of the minimum wage that uses data constructed for precisely the purpose of studying the effects of the minimum wage, and it also finds a negative hours response, with average elasticities ranging between −0.2 and −0.4 for hours in the home care industry.

Five studies examine the effect of the minimum wage on the working hours of youth and two examine the effect on hours of other groups. Orrenius and Zavodny (2008) and Sabia (2009a,b) detect negative hours responses using the state-level panels and associated analytic framework that Neumark and Wascher (1992) introduced to this line of research. Orrenius and Zavodny report an elasticity of −0.3 for the working hours of teenage girls (but none for either teenage boys or for all teenagers), Sabia (2009b) reports somewhat larger effects for the hours of all teenagers, as does Sabia (2009a) for the hours of teenagers in the retail sector. Based on repeated cross sections of individuals, Allegretto, Dube, and Reich (2009, 2011) report that they too find a statistically significant, negative response of teenage girls' working hours when they use the same analytic framework, but that when they include controls that allow for more careful matching of treatment and control regions, the responses become not only not statistically significant but also much smaller (i.e., not practically significant). The two analyses of other demographic groups report very different results from each other. Orrenius and Zavodny (2008) find no effect on the hours of immigrants without a high school diploma. Sabia (2008) reports a very large effect on hours for single mothers without a high school diploma (estimated elasticities of roughly −1.0), an outlier so much larger than any other estimates that it needs careful reexamination to understand what underlies it. At this point, the balance of results leans slightly toward there being no detectible effect on hours of teenagers or other U.S. groups studied, weighting more heavily those studies that are both more recent and more carefully constructed.

Of the sectoral studies, Belman and Wolfson (2010) find only a brief effect on hours that quickly dissipates. Machin, Manning, and Rahman

(2003) report negative elasticities on the hours worked in home care establishments in the range of −0.2 to −0.4. Vedder and Gallaway (2002) report a negative result, but their use of very large aggregates and apparent inattention to serial correlation leaves its reliability up in the air. Standard errors do not accompany the elasticity estimates reported in Sabia's (2009a) study of the retail industry or Orazem and Mattila's (2002) study of single-establishment Iowa firms. It appears that in the United Kingdom, both employees in at least one low-wage industry and members of low-wage groups worked fewer hours following the introduction of the NMW.

In conclusion, it appears that the NMW did lead to reductions in hours of various groups in the United Kingdom. It is not evident that increases in the minimum wage in the United States have led to similar effects in recent years, but further work would be necessary before accepting this with the level of confidence one would like. A useful methodological exercise that would enable better understanding of this issue is a careful comparison of the effect of the minimum wage on usual hours and hours last week, and in conditional and unconditional hours.

Notes

1. In this chapter we refer to both of these employment measures as "jobs" to distinguish them from those measures for which some measure of hours worked is central, referred to as "hours."

2. Card and Krueger (1994, 2000) consider full-time equivalents (as does Giuliano [2013]). This is based not on an underlying measurement of hours but on a formula for aggregating full-time and part-time workers.

3. Except for Stewart and Swaffield (2008), each study reports that wages did indeed rise following the minimum wage increase(s) examined (for Couch and Wittenburg [2001]), refer to Burkhauser, Couch, and Wittenburg [2000] on this point). In what follows, the minimum wage elasticity of hours is included if either the authors reported it or it is possible to calculate a meaningful elasticity at average values of the relevant variable from reported information.

4. *Conditional hours* means average hours conditional on being employed. *Unconditional hours* is the average hours worked per teenager for all teenagers, whether or not employed.

5. Sabia (2009b) is not clear about the hours variable used, but Sabia (2009a), a companion piece that includes some of the same results, contains an explicit statement to this effect. Since 1994, the CPS has allowed respondents not to specify a value

for usual hours but to answer that they vary. In 2012 this group constituted only 4 percent of the employed labor force but a much larger fraction of the low-wage labor force: 10 percent of employees who earned no more than 125 percent of the 2012 minimum wage. Because those who report variable hours have a missing value for this variable, they are effectively excluded from analyses that rely on usual hours. This may substantially affect the estimated coefficients if they are the group whose working time is reduced in response to the change in the minimum wage. Use of the actual hours data—which, in reasonably large samples, would be an accurate measure of employee average hours, including those with variable hours—would avoid this problem.

6. This is a bit peculiar when juxtaposed to their employment results; the only negative employment effect is for teenage boys. Teenage boys lose jobs, but those who remain employed experience a (statistically insignificant) rise in hours. Teenage girls do not lose (a statistically significant number of) jobs but do experience a statistically significant decrease in hours.

7. This is the effect for all individuals. When they consider the response of average hours conditional on employment, they find that those for teenage girls decline but that those for teenage boys increase, suggesting some substitution toward teenage boys.

8. Sabia (2009b) does not mention the 1993 survey redesign that resulted in a very discontinuous hours variable. To the extent that the redesign resulted only in a discontinuity in the variable and not in any other measurement differences, this may pose no problems for the specifications.

9. "Hours" is one of the outcome variables that Neumark and Nizalova (2007) consider. Because of the problems with this analysis that are described in Chapter 2, it is not considered further here.

10. Having described their analysis in detail in Chapter 2 and briefly in the preceding section on teenagers, there is no need to repeat it here.

11. Hirsch, Kaufman, and Zelenska (2011) consider hours worked as an outcome variable, but because their analysis relies on a convenience sample, it is of questionable generality.

12. Refer to the discussion of these studies in Chapter 2 for a more detailed description of the data that they use.

13. Powers (2009) is not explicit about the dependent variable in her regressions, but it appears to be the change in full-time equivalent hours, not the growth rate (p. 368).

14. The exception is his most elaborate specification, in which he both controls for serial correlation and includes state-specific time trends, as recommended in Allegretto, Dube, and Reich (2009, 2010). Sabia (2009a) is uncomfortable with this specification, saying that "state trends may, in fact, be capturing retail employment variation that the model seeks to explain" (p. 88).

15. The estimated elasticities are statistically significant, but they do not provide the information necessary for us to test the hypothesis that elasticities are (not) larger than one in magnitude.

16. The use of aggregate hours gets more directly at the volume of employment and sidesteps issues raised by the choice of either conditional or unconditional average hours.

17. Table 4 in Vedder and Gallaway (2002), which presents the relevant results and is labeled "OLS results . . ." contains a row labeled "ARIMA." This may indicate modeling of residual serial correlation but is left unexplained; if it does, then the estimation is not OLS, contradicting its labeling. No other residual diagnostics of the type one would expect with time-series data are presented.

18. For this group, the first two minimum wage increases were each nearly 20 percent, and the third was much smaller.

19. In Chapter 2 we discussed some econometric problems with Pacheco's (2011) analysis, and that discussion applies to her estimates of the hours response; they are affected by selection bias, and the standard errors have not been adjusted for the heteroscedasticity associated with using an estimated value for the likelihood of being bound. The failure to allow for selection effects in a sample that includes both the employed and the nonemployed may account for the very large impact of hours.

20. Although the British surveys distinguish between usual and actual hours, we do not know if they have the same coding rules and issues, as discussed for the studies using CPS data.

21. Stewart and Swaffield (2008) are concerned that Connolly and Gregory (2002) may have found no hours effects because the treatment group defined to include all who were initially earning less than the NMW is too broad. Suspecting less than perfect compliance, Stewart and Swaffield restrict the treatment group to be those for whom employers' compliance is not doubted, but it turns out to make no important difference to their estimates.

22. The questions in the annual NES refer to April. The NMW went into effect on April 1, 1999. The measurement of the initial effect of the NMW using data from the NES is based on the difference between April 1999 and April 1998; i.e., whatever change happened within the first month after the NMW went into effect. The lagged effect measures any additional response in the year following. As a quarterly survey, the LFS-based measurement of the initial effect responds to changes over an entire year after the NMW went into effect: the differences between four pairs of quarters where each of the quarters within each pair are separated by a year and straddle the implementation of the NMW. The first increase in the NMW occurred on October 1, 2000. To avoid contaminating measurement of the lagged effect of the implementation of the NMW with this first increase, Stewart and Swafford (2008) use only two pairs of quarters: 1999Q2 and 2000Q2, and 1999Q3 and 2000Q3. Thus, the LFS-based initial effect is the average difference in hours in the year following the implementation of the NMW compared to hours from the year before its implementation, while the NES-based initial effect is the difference in the first month after compared to the same month a year earlier. The NES-based measure of the lagged effect is the difference in hours in the thirteenth month following implementation and the first month afterward, while the two periods used for the LFS-based measure of the lagged effect start at the same time as the cor-

responding periods in the NES measurement but continue for another five months after the NES periods end. As a result of these differences in timing, the two do not measure quite the same thing.

23. These different estimates reflect different definitions of the comparison group, the real wage deflator, and so on. The term that Stewart and Swaffield (2008) use for straight time is *basic paid hours*.

24. Had Stewart and Swaffield (2008) included basic descriptive statistics for each data set, at least for average hours and average wage (both straight time and total) by sex, it would be easy to calculate the average effect of the NMW on gross weekly pay and thus determine whether the NMW was a net benefit for low-wage workers. Stewart (2002, 2004b) reports that the introduction of the NMW had no apparent impact on employment.

25. In studying the response of hours, it is not obvious that the usual caveats about this comparison group when studying employment are appropriate, that turnover of higher-paid workers is typically less than for lower-paid ones.

26. Connolly and Gregory's (2002) study of part-time working women is the exception.

4
Meta-Analysis

Meta-analysis is a body of techniques for combining many statistical studies to determine an overall result. T. D. Stanley has written extensively on a particularly useful and straightforward technique, metaregression (Stanley 2001, 2005, 2008; Stanley and Doucouliagos 2012; Stanley and Jarrell 1989), as well as two recent applications to the minimum wage (de Linde Leonard, Stanley, and Doucouliagos 2013; Doucouliagos and Stanley 2009). This section begins with a brief description of the technique, drawing heavily on these articles, followed by a discussion of these two recent meta-analyses of minimum wage research, and concludes with our own metaregression analysis of the literature covered in Chapters 2 and 3.

When confronted with results from many studies of the same phenomenon, summarizing them or combining them altogether into a single overall result can be a challenge. The first problem is that they must all be measuring the same thing and all must present the results in the same units, or at least in a way that the metaresearcher can put them into the same units. Once past this hurdle, an obvious way to aggregate results is to calculate their average value, and with some complications, this is what metaregression does. The complications arise from recognizing that for a variety of reasons, estimates are not all created equal, and that it is therefore not appropriate to give equal weight to all results in calculating the average.

Publication bias, an issue that Card and Krueger (1995) raise in their discussion of the earlier pre-NMWR literature on the minimum wage, is one reason for not treating all results as equally important. Publication bias means that the probability of a paper's being published depends on the results it reports. It can occur for reasons that are nefarious, such as journal editors' refusing to publish papers in which results do not toe a party line, or, as is more widely suspected, for reasons that are less so, where a scarcity of journal pages leads editors to reject papers as uninteresting because their results are indeterminate (i.e., not statistically significant) or they are deemed too insufficiently novel or ingenious. For whatever reason, attempts to generalize without accounting for publication bias give rise to biased meta-estimates of an effect by overcounting certain results and excluding others.

Even absent publication bias, differences in standard errors are another reason for not treating all results as equally important. Imprecisely estimated values are of less value in understanding and evaluating an effect than those that are measured with greater precision (Stanley 2001) and should not be given equal weight in any evaluation.

Finally, estimated effects may differ systematically because of differences in statistical framework, data source, data period, unknown and unrecognized actions of particular authors in analyzing the data (Stanley 2001), and others too numerous to mention. Identifying which of these factors are important and accounting for them in the meta-analysis make it possible to understand the source of differences in the estimated values.

We can chart the progress of this argument with a series of equations, in the process of which the specific technique of metaregression will become clear.[1] We start with a simple average in Equation (4.1):

$$(4.1) \quad Effect_k = \overline{Effect} + u_k = b_1 + u_k,$$

where $Effect_k$ is a meta-estimate, an overall estimate of the size of the effect in question. In the case of publication bias for statistical significance, a correlation will exist between the size of the effect and its standard error, $standard\ error_k$ in Equation (4.2):

$$(4.2) \quad Effect_k = b_1 + b_0 SE_k + u_k.$$

This equation will remove that form of publication bias from the meta-estimate of the effect size. However, it still treats estimates equally regardless of their precision. The differences in estimates' precision shows up as heteroskesdasticity. A correction for that is to weight by the inverse of the standard error, which is equivalent to dividing the variables in Equation (4.2) by the standard error, $standard\ error_k$:

$$(4.3a) \quad \frac{Effect_k}{SE_k} = \frac{b_1}{SE_k} + b_0 + v_k.$$

Dividing the estimate by its standard error turns the variable on the left of Equation (4.2) into the t-statistic; that is, Equation (4.3a) becomes

$$(4.3b) \quad t_k = b_0 + b_1 precision_k + v_k,$$

where the precision of an estimate is defined to be the reciprocal of its standard error (since this describes how precisely the estimated value has been measured. Equation (4.3b) is the basic equation for performing a metaregression on a set of estimates to derive a meta-estimate.[2] Because of differences in data source and type, analytic framework, idiosyncracies of individual researchers, and so forth, Stanley recommends including binary categorical variables to control for these. If these variables form a vector, X_k, Equation (4.3b) then becomes

$$(4.4) \quad t_k = b_0 + X_k B_0 + (b_1 + X_k B_1) precision_k + v_k,$$

where B_0 and B_1 are the metaregression vectors of coefficients for X_k. With deviation coding of the X_k variables, b_1 remains the meta-estimate of the average effect.[3] Finally, to minimize the role of the meta-analyst's judgment in determining the results, Stanley argues for including all estimates from each analysis, with dummy variables by study or researcher to prevent a large number of estimates from a single source from unduly influencing the results.

A BRIEF SURVEY OF RECENT PRIOR WORK

Doucouliagos and Stanley (2009) present results of a meta-analysis of the literature that examines the response of teenage employment in the United States to the minimum wage.[4] They identify nearly 100 studies of U.S. employment and the minimum wage between the early 1960s and 2007, of which they exclude 31 from their analysis either because inclusion would have made the sample too heterogeneous for their purposes, or because it was not possible to gather both an elasticity and its standard error from information in the study. What remain are 64 studies with nearly 1,500 point estimates of the employment elasticity. They report results from several metaregressions that differ in specifications and estimation methods, and whether or not they include moderator variables, i.e., control variables. In the simple model, without the dummy variables to control for different factors, they find strong evidence of publication bias that is large enough, by itself, to make the average reported *t*-statistic negative and significant at a 0.1 level. Of greater interest, they find that the (appropriately weighted) average employment elasticity is −0.01, or as they put it, "A 10 percent increase in the minimum wage reduces employment by about 0.10 percent . . . but even if this adverse employment effect were true, it would be of no practical relevance. An elasticity of −0.01 has no meaningful policy implications. If correct, the minimum wage could be doubled and cause only a 1 percent decrease in teenage employment" (pp. 415–416).

Interpreting results from Doucouliagos and Stanley's (2009) more elaborate specifications requires some thought. Their control variables reflect the type of data used in each analysis as well as modeling choices of each analyst. When all of these variables are zero (a not very meaningful situation), the immediate employment response reflects a statistically significant positive elasticity of about 0.1. A discussion of what constitutes "best practice" follows to suggest which control variables should be taken into account in determining the "best estimate" of the elasticity. Varying definitions give meta-estimates of the elasticity ranging between −0.003 and 0.065, none of which, they believe, are economically meaningful.

De Linde Leonard, Stanley, and Doucouliagos (2013) perform a similar meta-analysis of 16 studies of data from the United Kingdom that appeared between 1994 and 2010. From these 16 studies, they gather 236 elasticities and standard errors. In addition, they perform a parallel analysis based on partial correlation coefficients (PCC), which can be derived from *t*-statistics calculated from OLS standard errors.[5] This allows them to triple the number of observations to 710. Because partial correlation coefficients are less familiar than elasticities, it is not obvious what is a large value; according to the authors, "Cohen's [1988] guidelines suggest that any correlation less than 0.1 is negligible." In their simplest models, incorporating a correction only for publication bias (corresponding to Equation [4.2]), they report a meta-estimated employment elasticity of −0.01 that is not statistically significant, and a meta-estimated value of the PCC that is roughly one-thirtieth to one-twentieth the minimum size to be considered of practical significance. In a more complicated specification, similar to Equation (4.4) but not weighting to correct for heteroskedasticity, they examine a variety of dimensions that may systematically affect estimates and conclude that the only detectable effect in the United Kingdom of the minimum wage on employment is in the care home sector, where it is both statistically significant and just barely large enough to pay attention to: a PCC of −0.1 in the large sample and an employment elasticity in the older consensus range for teenagers, −0.15.

Overall, these two meta-analyses of research on the minimum wage conclude that the minimum wage has a detectable but negligible effect on young workers in the United States and no detectible effect in the United Kingdom outside of the care home sector, where it is just large enough to notice.

THE DATA

We began with the 74 analyses of the employment effect published from 2001 onward that are discussed or listed in Chapter 2, and the six additional pieces in Chapter 3 that were not also in Chapter 2. From these, 23 either had estimates of elasticities and their standard errors, or it was possible to calculate them from information in the study, for a total of 439 point estimates (see Table 4.1).

Before turning to further quantitative results, it will be useful to consider some graphs to get a feel for the data. Suppose we have estimates and their standard errors from a collection of reasonably well designed and executed studies. Absent publication bias, if we were to use each estimate's standard error to standardize it around the true effect and plot this value against its degrees of freedom, the resulting graph should look like random draws from the family of central t-distributions (the specific distribution identified by the number of degrees of freedom). As the degrees of freedom increase, the estimates should cluster more tightly around the true value, and at each value the estimates should be (roughly) normally distributed, symmetric about, and more densely clustered near the true value and thinning out away from it. Of course,

Table 4.1 Studies Included in the Metaregression

Authors	Title	Number of observations
Addison, Blackburn, and Cotti (2009)	Do Minimum Wages Raise Employment? Evidence from the U.S. Retail-Trade Sector	28
Addison, Blackburn, and Cotti (2012)	The Effect of Minimum Wages on Labour Market Outcomes: County-Level Estimates from the Restaurant-and-Bar Sector	6
Addison, Blackburn, and Cotti (2013)	Minimum Wage Increases in a Recessionary Environment	24
Addison and Ozturk (2012)	Minimum Wages, Labor Market Institutions, and Female Employment: A Cross-Country Analysis	4
Allegretto, Dube, and Reich (2009)	Spatial Heterogeneity and Minimum Wages: Employment Estimates for Teens Using Cross-State Commuting Zones	14
Allegretto, Dube, and Reich (2011)	Do Minimum Wages Really Reduce Teenage Employment? Accounting for Heterogeneity and Selectivity in State Panel Data	64
Dube, Lester, and Reich (2010)	Minimum Wage Effects across State Borders: Estimates Using Contiguous Counties	27
Dube, Naidu, and Reich (2007)	The Economic Effects of a Citywide Minimum Wage	30
Bazen and Marimoutou (2002)	Looking for a Needle in a Haystack?	4
Belman and Wolfson (2010)	The Effect of Legislated Minimum Wage Increases on Employment and Hours: A Dynamic Analysis	68
Campolieti, Gunderson, and Riddell (2006)	Minimum Wage Impacts from a Prespecified Research Design: Canada 1981–1997	30
Dodson (2002)	The Impact of the Minimum Wage in West Virginia: A Test of the Low-Wage-Area Theory	6
Even and Macpherson (2014)	The Effect of Tip Credits on Earnings and Employment in the U.S. Restaurant Industry	30
Hyslop and Stillman (2007)	Youth Minimum Wage reform and the Labour Market in New Zealand	4

Table 4.1 (continued)

Authors	Title	Number of observations
Keil, Robertson, and Symons (2009)	Univariate Regressions of Employment on Minimum Wages in the Panel of U.S. States	13
Neumark, Schweitzer, and Wascher (2004)	Minimum Wage Effects throughout the Wage Distribution	1
Orazem and Mattila (2002)	Minimum Wage Effects on Hours, Employment, and Number of Firms: The Iowa Case	21
Orrenius and Zavodny (2008)	The Effect of Minimum Wages on Immigrants' Employment and Earnings	36
Zavodny (2000)	The Effect of the Minimum Wage on Employment and Hours	4
Pereira (2003)	The Impact of Minimum Wages on Youth Employment in Portugal	1
Potter (2006)	Measuring the Employment Impacts of the Living Wage Ordinance in Santa Fe, New Mexico	5
Sabia (2009b)	The Effects of Minimum Wage Increases on Retail Employment and Hours: New Evidence from the Monthly CPS Data	15
Singell and Terborg (2007)	Employment Effects of Two Northwest Minimum Wage Initiatives	4

this standardization presumes more knowledge than we have, since the true value is unknown.

In lieu of this, a commonly used graph is the funnel plot, a scatterplot in which the dimension of the x-axis is the estimated parameter value and the y-axis is the precision.[6] If there were no publication bias, the estimates should be distributed symmetrically about the true value of the measured effect, and the mean should be a good measure of the true effect. Because the standard error generates a loose bound on the distance an estimate falls from the true effect, more precise estimates should be more densely clustered around the mean. The plot should roughly resemble an inverted funnel, one resting on its top. In particular, asymmetry indicates publication bias toward a desired result, while thick tails and a thinly populated central section are indicative of a tendency toward rejection of statistically insignificant results.

Figure 4.1 Employment and Hours Elasticities vs. Precision

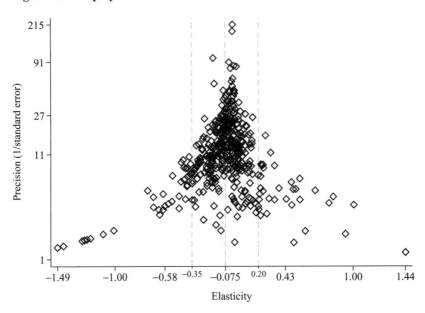

Figure 4.1 is a simple funnel plot displaying all the estimates used in the meta-analysis, using a logarithmic scale on the vertical axis. The ticks on the x-axis indicate the raw mean, −0.075, and the minimum and maximum elasticities, −1.49 and 1.44, respectively. Vertical dashed lines indicate the mean and the location of +/−1 standard deviation around the mean.[7] The ticks on the y-axis indicate the minimum precision, 1, the median precision, 11, the values at the 90th and 99th percentiles, 27 and 91, respectively, and the maximum precision, 215. The raw mean is slightly negative, and with 55 percent of the estimates lying to the right of the mean, the median (−0.052) is slightly larger than the mean. With only one-sixth of the estimates (74) lying farther than one standard deviation from the mean (39 to the left, 35 to the right), the distribution is densely populated near its mean. The mean lies slightly to the left of the median, indicating a slight asymmetry, a slight left skew that reflects not only that more points are far away from the mean to the left than to the right but also that these distant points to the left are on average somewhat farther from the mean than their counterparts to the right. Looking along the y-axis, the minimum precision is 1,

and half of the estimates have precision less than 11. Only 10 percent have precision greater than 27. The most precisely estimated elasticities are (with one exception) just to the right of the mean, suggesting that the precision-weighted mean is likely to be closer to zero than the raw mean.

The remaining figures use modified funnel plots to display different aspects of the data. Figure 4.2 separately identifies estimates with and without reliable standard errors, where "unreliable" is taken to mean that the critiques of Bertrand, Duflo, and Mullainathan (2004) and Donald and Lang (2007) are likely to be pertinent.[8] Most of the estimates lacking reliable standard errors are less than the mean, and several are a standard deviation or more less than the mean. The bulk of the exceptions to this statement are a group of very low precision estimates less than a standard deviation more than the mean. A handful of the unreliable estimates are apparently precisely estimated. Controlling for reliability in the metaregression is likely to reduce the magnitude of the average elasticity.

Figure 4.2 Distinguishing between Reliable and Unreliable Standard Errors: Employment and Hours Elasticities vs. Precision

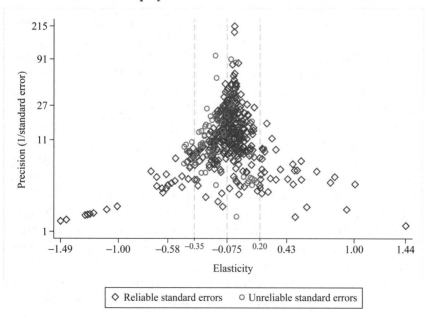

Figure 4.3 Eating and Drinking Places and Youth: Employment and Hours Elasticities vs. Precision

Figure 4.3 compares results from studies of the restaurant industry with those of youth employment (studies belonging to neither group appear in the background). With 278 observations, these two groups make up more than five-eighths of the sample: 165 (three-eighths) youth and 113 (one-quarter) eating and drinking establishments. The two distributions are somewhat shifted horizontally relative to each other, with the distribution of youth estimates to the left of that for estimates of eating and drinking establishments. One hundred of the youth estimates are less than the overall unadjusted mean, and only 65 are larger than it; 13 are more than 1 standard deviation less, and only 2 are more than 1 standard deviation more than the mean. The most precisely estimated elasticities belong to the youth group. Eighty-two of the eating and drinking estimates are larger than the mean, but only 2 are more than one standard deviation above the mean, and none are more than one standard deviation below the mean.

Figure 4.4 compares estimates from quasi experiments, which have a clearly defined comparison group with those from regressions,

Figure 4.4 Distinguishing between Quasi Experiments and (Other) Regressions: Employment and Hours Elasticities vs. Precision

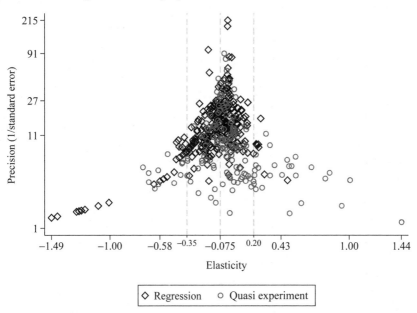

which do not. At the extreme, the most precisely estimated elasticities are from regressions, and moving away from the extreme, very precise estimates are more likely to be from regressions. The most extreme negative elasticity estimates are entirely from regressions, and the most extreme positive elasticity estimates are from quasi experiments.

Finally, there is some evidence of publication bias due not to a preferred result but to a preference for statistically significant results (what Stanley [2005] designates type II selection). Standardizing the estimates around the true value should result in a t-distribution, symmetric and with roughly 5 percent of values greater in absolute value than 1.96. Of course, the true value is not known, but we can select some plausible values: zero, the raw mean, the raw median, the precision-weighted mean, and the precision-weighted median. Table 4.2 shows the percentage of observations in each tail for each centering value and for each way of counting (unweighted and precision-weighted). When zero is the centering value, more than 20 percent of the observations are less than −1.96, and nearly 6 percent are greater than 1.96; the correspond-

Table 4.2 Percentage of Observations in the Left and Right Tails

Value used to center the elasticities	% less than −1.96	% greater than 1.96	Precision-weighted less than −1.96 (%)	Precision-weighted greater than 1.96 (%)
Zero	22.8	5.9	34.8	4.8
Raw mean −0.075	10.0	16.2	8.6	32.5
Raw median −0.054	12.3	12.1	10.8	24.8
Precision-weighted mean −0.053	12.3	11.4	10.8	23.7
Precision-weighted median −0.031	15.7	9.3	15.4	18.4

NOTE: Elasticities have been standardized by centering around the values in the second column and dividing by the estimated standard errors. Absent publication selection for statistically significant results, we should expect to see roughly 2.5 percent in at least two adjacent cells on one side or the other of the vertical lines.
SOURCE: Authors' calculations.

ing precision-weighted counts are about 35 percent and nearly 5 percent. Of course, this may well be because the true value of the elasticity is not zero. However, the other possibilities are little better. With the raw mean, more than 25 percent of observations are out beyond these two borders (more than 40 percent for precision-weighted counts), and at just under 25 percent, the number is little improved for the median (the precision-weighted count drops to about 35 percent). Using the precision-weighted mean or median generates similar percentages in the tails. In no case are roughly 5 percent of observations in any of these definitions of the tails, and with a few exceptions, symmetry is not apparent. This suggests either that many (not all) editors put a thumb on the scale in favor of statistically significant results or at least that authors believe this to be the case.

METAREGRESSIONS—PART 1

Ensuring the Quality of the Metaregression Estimates

The actions required to correct the raw sample mean in order to derive a meaningful meta-estimate of the effect of the minimum wage on employment can be distinguished as either technical or substantive. The primary considerations in the technical category, corrections needed for a reliable result, include adjusting for study or author effects, for estimates' precision, and for publication bias. Study (author) effects include both lack of independence across estimates from the same study (author) and variation in the number of estimates from each study (author). The main type of substantive control concerns whether the estimated effects for youth and for the food and drink sector differ from the overall effect. It will be useful to present these separately so that the consequences of the technical factors can be understood. For clarity of presentation, new equations will be presented below.

Equation (4.5a), describing the meta-estimated effect uncorrected for anything is the same as Equation (4.1):

(4.5a) $Effect_k = \overline{Effect} + u_k = b_1 + u_k$

Correcting only for the estimates' precision gives equation (4.5b):[9]

(4.5b) $t_k = b_1 precision_k + v_k$

Neither of these two equations corrects for publication bias. Equation (4.5a) has only a constant term (no standard error term), and when that constant term is weighted by precision to generate Equation (4.5b), the result is an equation with only one right-hand-side variable, precision, and in particular, no constant term. The effect of correcting for publication bias, which will introduce the standard error into Equation (4.5a) and a corresponding constant term in Equation (4.5b), is being deferred until after considering the effects of weighting the observations and of controlling for the imbalance resulting from the widely varying number of observations drawn from each study.

Equations (4.6a) and (4.6b) build on (4.5a) and (4.5b) by adjusting for lack of independence among estimates from the same study:[10]

(4.6a) $Effect_k = b_1 + \sum_{s=2}^{S} c_s Study_s + u_k$

(4.6b) $t_k = b_1 precision_k + precision_k \sum_{s=2}^{S} c_s Study_s + v_k$

The $Study_s$ variables are indicator variables that are 1 if observation k comes from study s, -1 if from study 1, and 0 otherwise; that is, they are indicator variables for the study, coded in deviation form and where the excluded indicator corresponds to the first study. The difference between Equations (4.5a) and (4.6a) is that (4.6a) includes fixed effects for the study. The difference between Equations (4.5b), which includes no constant term, and (4.6b) is that (4.6b) includes interactions between precision and the study indicator variables. Finally, Equations (4.7a) and (4.7b) use random effects (μ_s) and random coefficients (ρ_s), respectively, to control for study effects:

(4.7a) $Effect_k = b_1 + u_k$, $u_k = \mu_s + e_k$

(4.7b) $t_k = b_1 precision_k + v_k$, $v_k = \rho_s precision_k + w_k$

Table 4.3 presents estimates of b_1 from these equations. The raw mean, the employment elasticity of the minimum wage as meta-

Table 4.3 Preliminary Meta-Estimates of the Minimum Wage Elasticity, b_1

Equation estimated	b_1	t
Equation (4.5a): raw mean	−0.075 (0.013)	−5.77
Equation (4.5b): precision-weighted mean	−0.034 (0.004)	−9.57
Equation (4.6a): (4.5a) + study fixed effects	−0.092 (0.016)	−5.76
Equation (4.6b): precision-weighted (4.6a)	−0.050 (0.007)	−7.04
Equation (4.7a): (4.5a) + study random effects	−0.099 (0.037)	−2.67
Equation (4.7b): precision-weighted (4.7a)	−0.050 (0.015)	−3.30
Mean of the unweighted estimates (4.5a, 4.6a, 4.7a)	−0.089 (0.024)	−3.62
Mean of the precision-weighted estimates (4.5b, 4.6b, 4.7b)	−0.044 (0.010)	−4.52
Precision-weighted mean of the unweighted estimates	−0.085 (0.020)	−4.25
Precision-weighted mean of the precision-weighted estimates	−0.040 (0.007)	−5.60

NOTE: Standard errors are in parentheses.
SOURCE: Authors' calculations.

estimated by Equation (4.5a), is −0.075 with a very small standard error of 0.013. When precisely estimated values are given more weight, Equation (4.5b), the effect drops by more than half to −0.034, and the standard error drops by more than three quarters to 0.004. When we return to the unweighted mean but instead control for lack of independence within each study using fixed effects (4.6a), the meta-estimated effect rises by about one-fourth from the first value of −0.075 to −0.092 (and the standard error rises by about the same proportion, to 0.016). The corresponding precision-weighted value (4.6b) is −0.050, half again as large as the initial weighted mean and one-third less than the initial unweighted value; the standard error is about twice as large as that for the original weighted value, although the meta-estimate remains statistically significant by any standard (including particle physics) and is about half that of the raw mean. Using random effects (or random coefficients) in place of fixed effects leads to point values of the meta-estimates that are about the same size as those from the corresponding fixed-effects equations, and to standard errors that are about twice as large.[11] Despite the increase in the standard errors, the coefficients from the specification with random effects are strongly statistically significant.

Two patterns in Table 4.3 stand out. One is that precision weighting reduces the meta-estimated magnitude of the employment effect. The other is that identifying estimates that are from the same study and accounting for their lack of independence increases the magnitude of the meta-estimated effect. The first result is consistent with an editorial preference for statistically significant results, at least when they are negative. The second tells us that in this sample, studies that presented a large number of usable estimates (usable in that they included both elasticities and their standard errors) had smaller average magnitudes of the estimates than those that presented fewer. It may be well be that authors of studies that presented evidence against a negative minimum wage effect provide a larger set of robustness and sensitivity tests (or their editors or referees requested them) than those with more conventional results.[12] Including study controls will prevent this issue, if it exists, from contaminating the metaregression.

The next step is to incorporate the standard error term into the equations to control for any bias toward statistically significant results in the sample. This gives the following six equations (the first being the same as Equation [4.2]):

OLS models:

$$(4.5a')\quad Effect_k = b_1 + b_0 SE_k + u_k$$

$$(4.5b')\quad t_k = b_0 + b_1 precision_k + v_k$$

Fixed-effects models:

$$(4.6a')\quad Effect_k = b_1 + b_0 SE_k + \sum_{s=2}^{S} c_s Study_s + u_k$$

$$(4.6b')\quad t_k = b_0 + b_1 precision_k + precision_k \sum_{s=2}^{S} c_s Study_s + v_k$$

Random-effects models:

(4.7a′) $Effect_k = b_1 + b_0 SE_k + u_k$, $u_k = \mu_s + e_k$

(4.7b′) $t_k = b_0 + b_1 precision_k + v_k$, $v_k = \rho_s precision_k + w_k$

In addition, the controls for study should be interacted with standard error:

(4.6a″) $Effect_k = b_1 + b_0 SE_k + \sum_{s=2}^{S} c_s Study_z + SE_k \sum_{s=2}^{S} d_s Study_s + u_k$

(4.6b″) $t_k = b_0 + b_1 precision_k + precision_k \left(\sum_{s=2}^{S} c_s Study_s \right)$
$+ \sum_{s=2}^{S} d_s Study_s + v_k$

(4.7a″) $Effect_k = b_1 + b_0 SE_k + u_k$, $u_k = \mu_s + \gamma_s SE_k + e_k$

(4.7b″) $t_k = b_0 + b_1 precision_k + v_k$, $v_k = \rho_s precision_k + \delta_s + w_k$

Table 4.4 displays estimates of b_1 and b_0 from these equations.[13] Start with the estimates of b_1. In Equations (4.5a′)–(4.7b′), the patterns identified in Table 4.3 are present but weaker. With one slight exception in each pattern, precision weighting results in meta-estimates of smaller magnitude than not weighting, and accounting for the study effects raises the meta-estimate.[14] Including the standard error in the equation to control for (some types of) publication bias reduces the meta-estimate of the effect size in each of these six equations relative to their Table 4.3 counterparts. Third, including terms for the interaction of the study effects with the standard error, Equations (4.6a″)–(4.7b″), has little effect on the first of the fixed-effects meta-estimates (compare [4.6a′] and [4.6a″]) but increases the precision-weighted fixed-effects meta-estimate by a factor of three ([4.6b′] and [4.6b″]). In the random-effect specifications, this change has little effect on the point values of the meta-estimates, although the standard errors drop. The final noteworthy point is that the only meta-estimates in this table that are not statistically significant are three of these last four estimates for b_1, those that include the fixed-effect interactions, and the unweighted meta-estimate with the random coefficients for standard error.

Table 4.4 Meta-Estimates of the Minimum Wage Elasticity of Employment, b_1, When a Correction for Publication Bias Is Included

	b_1 (Minimum wage elasticity of employment)		b_0	
	Meta-estimate	t	Meta-estimate	t
Equation (4.5a′)	−0.020 (0.019)	−1.05	−0.426 (0.106)	−4.02
Equation (4.5b′): precision-weighted (4.5a′)	−0.022 (0.004)	−5.12	−0.487 (0.111)	−4.39
Equation (4.6a′): (4.5a′) + study fixed effects	−0.059 (0.020)	−2.96	−0.300 (0.109)	−2.76
Equation (4.6b′): precision-weighted (4.6a′)	−0.018 (0.010)	−1.86	−0.599 (0.128)	−4.67
Equation (4.7a′): (4.5a′) + study random effects	−0.060 (0.037)	−1.62	−0.341 (0.108)	−3.16
Equation (4.7b′): precision-weighted (4.7a′)	−0.022 (0.017)	−1.32	−0.568 (0.128)	−4.45
Equation (4.6a″): (4.6a′) + fixed effects interacted w/standard error	−0.051 (0.043)	−1.18	−0.292 (0.925)	−0.32
Equation (4.6b″): precision-weighted (4.6a″)	−0.048 (0.019)	−2.59	0.193 (0.339)	0.57
Equation (4.7a″): (4.7a′) + random coefs. for standard error	−0.059 (0.020)	−2.91	−0.276 (0.277)	−1.00
Equation (4.7b″): precision-weighted (4.7a″)	−0.025 (0.012)	−2.03	−0.603 (0.252)	−2.39
Mean of the unweighted estimates (4.5a′, 4.6a′, 4.7a′, 4.6a″, 4.7a″)	−0.050 (0.052)	−0.96	−0.327 (0.331)	−0.99
Mean of the precision-weighted estimates (4.5b′, 4.6b′, 4.7b′, 4.6b″, 4.7b″)	−0.027 (0.029)	−0.93	−0.413 (0.515)	−0.80
Precision-weighted mean of the unweighted estimates (4.5a′, 4.6a′, 4.7a′, 4.6a″, 4.7a″)	−0.048 (0.026)	−1.84	−0.345 (0.215)	−1.60
Precision-weighted mean of the precision-weighted estimates (4.5b′, 4.6b′, 4.7b′, 4.6b″, 4.7b″)	−0.024 (0.011)	−2.28	−0.487 (0.173)	2.81

NOTE: Standard errors are in parentheses.

So far, we have seen a range of meta-estimates for the minimum wage employment effect, from −0.018 to −0.099. Only four of the meta-estimates, however, are from equations that control for dependence within study, precision, and (a type of) publication bias: Equations (4.6b′), (4.6b″), (4.7b′), and (4.7b″). In this group, the range is about one-third as large, from −0.022 to −0.048 (Equations [4.7b′] and [4.6b″], respectively). The mean of these four is −0.028 (and the precision-weighted mean is slightly smaller in magnitude, −0.026).

METAREGRESSIONS—PART 2

Finally, we turn to equations in which we control for not just the study effects but for several other factors that are common to various studies and which we suspect may systematically affect the estimated elasticities. To this end, we include (deviation coded) indicator variables for whether the estimates:

1) have reliable standard errors, i.e., are free of the problems that Bertrand, Duflo, and Mullainathan (2004) identified, as well as those that Donald and Lang (2007) identified (called *reliable*);

2) are based on a quasi experiment or a more conventional regression framework (called *regression*);

3) are based on data from the United States or from other countries (called *USA*);

4) are based on employment or on hours of employment (called *employment*).[15]

We present two sets of results, all of which include these variables. One set also includes (deviation coded) indicators for whether the estimates are based on data for teenagers and young adults (*youth*) or for eating and drinking places (*E&D*).

The addition of the first four variables, but not the last two variables, *Youth* and *E&D*, turns Equations (4.6b′), (4.6b″), (4.7b′), and (4.7b″) into (4.8b′), (4.8b″), (4.9b′), and (4.9b″):[16]

Fixed-effects models:

$$(4.8b') \quad t_k = b_0 + b_1 precision_k + precision_k \sum_{s=2}^{S} c_s Study_s +$$

$$b_1^{reliable} reliable_k \times precision_k + b_1^{regression} regression_k \times precision_k +$$

$$b_1^{USA} USA_k \times precision_k \qquad + b_1^{employment} employment_k \times precision_k + v_k$$

$$(4.8b'') \quad t_k = b_0 + b_1 precision_k + precision_k \sum_{s=2}^{S} c_s Study_s + \sum_{s=2}^{S} d_s Study_s +$$

$$b_1^{reliable} reliable_k \times precision_k + b_1^{regression} regression_k \times precision_k +$$

$$b_1^{USA} USA_k \times precision_k \qquad + b_1^{employment} employment_k \times precision_k + v_k$$

Random-effects models:

$$(4.9b') \quad b_0 + b_1 precision_k + b_1^{reliable} reliable_k \times precision_k +$$

$$b_1^{regression} regression_k \times precision_k \qquad + b_1^{USA} USA_k \times precision_k +$$

$$b_1^{employment} employment_k \times precision_k + v_k$$

$$v_k = \rho_s precision_k + w_k$$

$$(4.9b'') \quad t_k = b_0 + b_1 precision_k + b_1^{reliable} reliable_k \times precision_k +$$

$$b_1^{regression} regression_k \times precision_k \qquad + b_1^{USA} USA_k \times precision_k +$$

$$b_1^{employment} employment_k \times precision_k + v_k$$

$$v_k = \rho_s precision_k + \delta_s + w_k$$

k indexes each estimate (observation)
s indexes the study from which each estimate is drawn.

Meta-Estimates of Overall Models

Although the literature on the minimum wage is particularly concerned with the effect of the minimum wage on young workers and
on the eating and drinking places, we start with meta-estimates of the
overall effect, and hold off considering these more specific effects until
later in this chapter. Table 4.5 provides both coefficient meta-estimates
and sums of the coefficients for Equations (4.8b')–(4.9b''). The table
includes not only the meta-estimates for each equation but also two

means of these meta-estimates, the first a simple mean, the second a precision-weighted mean.[17] Because there are so many meta-estimates, and because we are agnostic as to which of the models (4.8b′)–(4.9b′′) is the "correct" model, our discussion focuses on these means and, in particular, the precision-weighted mean. We favor the precision-weighted mean, as this places the greatest weight on the meta-estimates that are estimated with the least variance.[18] As it turns out, however, there is little difference in the point value or statistical significance between the two means.

Our assessments of statistical significance deviate somewhat from the standard we have used elsewhere in this book. To this point we have used a two-tailed 0.05 standard to assess the statistical significance of estimates. Given that conventional economic theory suggests that the minimum wage should have a negative effect on employment and hours, and that this view is held by many who follow this topic, we will also use a 0.05 test for a negative effect against the null of no effect or a positive effect. Using these criteria, we find weak evidence of a small negative effect on employment, but even this effect does not appear in studies of the United States. In terms of overall effects, the United States has a far more favorable situation with respect to the effect of the minimum wage on employment than the balance of the countries covered by this research.

Table 4.5 is laid out in two panels. The upper panel, panel A, reports point estimates, standard errors, and t-statistics for the coefficients; the lower panel, Panel B, reports similar statistics for relevant sums of the coefficients. Panel A provides meta-estimates of the average employment and hours elasticity (hereafter the average elasticity), the additional response associated with regression-based estimates (in contrast with those based on quasi experiments), the additional effect for estimates that likely have reliable standard errors (against those that are likely not reliable), the additional effect for those drawn from models of employment (vs. models of hours), and the additional effect for those drawn from analyses of U.S. data (against the balance of the world). The sums in Panel B address issues such as what is the effect of the minimum wage on employment and what is the effect of the minimum wage on employment in the United States. These sums will be the focus of our discussion, but we first need to consider the coefficient meta-estimates.

Table 4.5 Meta-Estimates of the Minimum Wage Elasticity of Employment and Hours

	4.8b′	4.8b″	4.9b′	4.9b″	Mean	Precision-weighted mean
		Panel A: Coefficient estimates				
b_1	−0.099	−0.237	−0.041	−0.024	−0.100	−0.057
	(0.089)	(0.089)	(0.019)	(0.020)	(0.0645)	(0.0418)
t	−1.12	−2.65	−2.13	−1.23	−1.55	−1.37
$b_1^{regression}$	−0.006	−0.020	−0.018	0.009	−0.009	−0.009
	(0.016)	(0.018)	(0.011)	(0.014)	(0.015)	(0.014)
t	−0.37	−1.13	−1.64	0.68	−0.59	−0.60
$b_1^{reliable}$	−0.029	0.044	0.015	0.031	0.015	0.019
	(0.053)	(0.055)	(0.017)	(0.018)	(0.040)	(0.031)
t	−0.56	0.80	0.87	1.69	0.37	0.60
$b_1^{employment}$	−0.011	−0.006	−0.013	−0.008	−0.010	−0.010
	(0.007)	(0.008)	(0.007)	(0.011)	(0.008)	(0.008)
t	−1.49	−0.81	−1.84	−0.75	−1.14	−1.21
b_1^{USA}	0.147	0.240	0.037	−0.011	0.103	0.045
	(0.106)	(0.099)	(0.020)	(0.022)	(0.074)	(0.047)
t	1.39	2.42	1.83	−0.48	1.39	0.97
		Panel B: Sums of coefficients				
b_1	−0.099	−0.237	−0.041	−0.024	−0.100	−0.057
	(0.089)	(0.089)	(0.019)	(0.020)	(0.0645)	(0.0418)
t	−1.12	−2.65	−2.13	−1.23	−1.55	−1.37
$b_1 + b_1^{employment}$	−0.110	−0.243	−0.054	−0.032	−0.110	−0.067
	(0.089)	(0.089)	(0.019)	(0.019)	(0.064)	(0.041)
t	−1.24	−2.73	−2.88	−1.72	−1.71	−1.63
$b_1 + b_1^{USA}$	0.048	0.003	−0.004	−0.035	0.003	−0.003
	(0.037)	(0.039)	(0.022)	(0.022)	(0.031)	(0.029)
t	1.29	0.08	−0.19	−1.58	0.10	−0.10
$b_1 + b_1^{employment} + b_1^{USA}$	0.037	−0.003	−0.017	−0.043	−0.006	−0.013
	(0.037)	(0.039)	(0.021)	(0.021)	(0.031)	(0.028)
	1.01	−0.08	−0.80	−2.01	−0.21	−0.45

NOTE: Standard errors are in parentheses.

Before discussing this table, it is useful to clarify the interpretation of the coefficients when the indicators for regression, reliability, employments, and USA are meta-estimated in deviation form. The overall meta-estimate, b_1, is the grand mean across all of the categories of controls. Consider the meta-estimate of b_1 for Equation (4.8b′) in the upper left-hand corner of Panel A. Putting aside its lack of statistical significance, the coefficient of −0.099 indicates that a 10 percent increase in the minimum wage would result in a 0.99 percent reduction in employment and hours. If we want to know the effect on employment alone, that is, the elasticity drawn only from estimates based on models of employment and excluding those drawn from models of hours, we need to add the coefficient on $b_1^{employment}$, −0.011, to b_1. With this addition, the mean effect on employment of the 10 percent increase would be a 1.1 percent decline in employment. If we wished to know the effect on hours, we would subtract the coefficient on $b_1^{employment}$ to find that the effect on hours would be a decline of −0.88 percent. Given this coding, we are most interested in the sums of coefficients, and most of our discussion will be about the sums in Panel B.

Turning briefly to Panel A, we are faced with five coefficients for each of four equations. Although the meta-estimates are often similar across equations, this is not always the case. For example, estimates of the average elasticity, $\hat{b}_1$, take on the values of −0.099, −0.237, −0.041, and −0.024, and the t-statistics range between −2.65 and −1.12. We do not have strong priors about which of the equations provide the correct meta-estimates, and it therefore seems appropriate to average them. We calculate two means: the first a simple average, the second weighted by the precision of the meta-estimate. Allowing for statistical significance, there are not meaningful differences between the two.

Considering specific coefficient meta-estimates and their means, meta-estimates of the average elasticity show the largest range in both coefficients and statistical significance. The fixed-effects models produce the largest effects, but only the (4.8b′′) coefficient meets the 0.05 test. The random-effects coefficients are far smaller in magnitude and (4.9b′) reject the null of no effect, but (4.9b′′) does not. Neither the simple mean nor the precision-weighted mean are statistically significant, but the simple mean is not greatly below a 0.05 one-tailed test criteria. Most of the other coefficients—$b_1^{regression}$, $b_1^{reliable}$, and $b_1^{employment}$—

are very small, less than 0.01 in absolute value, and not significant; b_1^{USA} is an exception to this statement.

Consider next the sums reported in Panel B, starting with the elasticity employment, $b_1 + b_1^{employment}$.[19] The simple mean indicates that employment declines by 1.1 percent when the minimum wage is raised by 10 percent and the precision-weighted mean is −0.67 percent; the former passes a one-tailed 0.05 test, and the latter is very close to passing. The meta-analysis then indicates a small negative employment effect across all studies without regard to the country of origin.

The estimates of b_1^{USA} are considerably different from those for the other controls. It is positive in three out of four cases, and in those instances it is virtually the mirror image of the average elasticity. This is particularly striking for Equation (4.8b″), in which the meta-estimate of b_1 is −0.237 and the meta-estimate of b_1^{USA} is 0.240. Both are statistically significant, and, as a result, when the average elasticity for the United States is calculated in Panel B, $b_1 + b_1^{USA}$, it is a tiny, statistically nonsignificant 0.003; in the United States, a 10 percent increase in the minimum wage is meta-estimated to cause a 0.03 percent decline in employment (whether measured by jobs or hours). Both the simple and precision-weighted means of b_1^{USA} are sufficiently similar in absolute value but opposite in sign to the b_1 means that the meta-estimated elasticity in the United States is, in essence, 0.0.

These meta-estimates also find that the minimum wage does not affect employment in the United States. Meta-estimates of $b_1 + b_1^{employment} + b_1^{USA}$, the minimum wage elasticity of employment in the United States (i.e., excluding studies of hours), are in the bottom row of Panel B. The point estimates range between +0.037 and −0.043; the means indicate that a 10 percent rise in the minimum wage would result in a change in employment between +0.06 percent and −0.13 percent, but neither is close to passing a conventional standard of statistical significance.

The meta-estimates in Table 4.5 show that increases in the minimum wage do not affect employment and hours, but there is evidence of a small negative effect on employment alone. This effect is, however, an effect in countries other than the United States. The meta-estimated effect on employment in the United States, $b_1 + b_1^{USA}$, is both vanishingly small and not statistically significant in even the most generous test. These initial results set the stage for investigating the effect of the minimum wage on two groups of particular interest, younger workers, and those working in the eating and drinking places.

Separating Out the Effects for Youth and Eating and Drinking Places

Next, we include the *Youth* and *E&D* variables in the equations to allow for different elasticities for young workers and for eating and drinking places:

Fixed-effects models:

$$(4.10b') \quad t_k = b_0 + b_1 precision_k + precision_k \sum_{s=2}^{S} c_s Study_s +$$

$$b_1^{reliable} reliable_k \times precision_k + b_1^{regression} regression_k \times precision_k +$$

$$b_1^{USA} USA_k \times precision_k \qquad + b_1^{employment} employment_k \times precision_k +$$

$$b_1^{YouthY} Youth_k \times precision_k \quad + b_1^{E\&D} E\&D_k \times precision_k + v_k$$

$$(4.10b'')$$

$$t_k = b_0 + b_1 precision_k + precision_k \left(\sum_{s=2}^{S} c_s Study_s \right) + \sum_{s=2}^{S} d_s Study_s +$$

$$b_1^{reliable} reliable_k \times precision_k + b_1^{regression} regression_k \times precision_k +$$

$$b_1^{USA} USA_k \times precision_k \qquad + b_1^{employment} employment_k \times precision_k +$$

$$b_1^{YouthY} Youth_k \times precision_k \quad + b_1^{E\&D} E\&D_k \times precision_k + v_k$$

Random-effects models:

$$(4.11b') \quad t_k = b_0 + b_1 precision_k + b_1^{reliable} reliable_k \times precision_k +$$

$$b_1^{regression} regression_k \times precision_k \qquad + b_1^{USA} USA_k \times precision_k +$$

$$b_1^{employment} employment_k \times precision_k +$$

$$b_1^{YouthY} Youth_k \times precision_k \qquad + b_1^{E\&D} E\&D_k \times precision_k + v_k$$

$$v_k = \rho_s precision_k + w_k$$

$$(4.11b'') \quad t_k = b_0 + b_1 precision_k + b_1^{reliable} reliable_k \times precision_k +$$

$$b_1^{regression} regression_k \times precision_k \quad + b_1^{USA} USA_k \times precision_k +$$

$$b_1^{employment} employment_k \times precision_k +$$

$$b_1^{YouthY} Youth_k \times precision_k \quad + b_1^{E\&D} E\&D_k \times precision_k + v_k$$

$$v_k = \rho_s precision_k + \delta_s + w_k$$

Estimates Separating Out the Effect of Youth and Eating and Drinking Places

Table 4.6 presents the coefficient estimates for Equations (4.10b′)–(4.11b″). As we are interested in parsing out not only the average elasticity but also the effect on employment of youth and in eating and drinking places, Table 4.7 presents sums that include the terms b_1^{youth}, $b_1^{E\&D}$, and $b_1^{employment}$.

Parallel to Table 4.5, Table 4.6 presents the estimates for the seven coefficients of interest. Estimates of the additional effect on youth, b_1^{youth}, are small, ranging from +0.022 to −0.029, and none are statistically significant even in a one-tailed 0.05 test. In contrast, the estimated additional effect on eating and drinking places, $b_1^{E\&D}$, which range between +0.001 and −0.093, are negative and statistically significant in three of the four specifications. The mean values hover around −0.04, and the precision-weighted mean is significant in a one-tailed 0.05 test. The average elasticity, b_1, is marginally more negative compared to the estimates in Table 4.5, which do not include indicator variables for youth or eating and drinking places, but the means remain small in magnitude and do not achieve statistical significance in a one-tailed 0.05 test. The point estimates for $b_1^{regression}$, $b_1^{reliable}$, $b_1^{employment}$, and b_1^{USA} barely move, with no changes occurring to the left of the second decimal position.

Panel B1 in Table 4.7 presents the same sums as Panel B in Table 4.5. As the youth and eating and drinking places indicators are in deviation form, the sums are very similar to those for the same terms in Table 4.5. The estimates of the employment elasticity, $b_1 + b_1^{employment}$, differ from the Table 4.5 estimates at the second or third decimal point, and both means are statistically significant in better than a one-tailed 0.05 test, as before. A 10 percent increase in the minimum wage is estimated to reduce employment between 1 percent and 0.64 percent. Studies of

Table 4.6 Meta-Estimates of the Minimum Wage Elasticity of Employment and Hours for Models with Controls for Youth and Eating and Drinking Places

	4.10b′	4.10b″	4.11b′	4.11b″	Mean	Elasticity-weighted mean
b_1	−0.112	−0.222	−0.043	−0.035	−0.103	−0.064
	(0.086)	(0.088)	(0.020)	(0.022)	(0.063)	(0.043)
t	−1.30	−2.53	−2.16	−1.60	−1.63	−1.50
$b_1^{regression}$	−0.006	−0.020	−0.018	0.010	−0.008	−0.008
	(0.015)	(0.018)	(0.011)	(0.014)	(0.015)	(0.014)
t	−0.40	−1.14	−1.61	0.75	−0.58	−0.59
$b_1^{reliable}$	−0.015	0.050	0.017	0.036	0.022	0.024
	(0.051)	(0.054)	(0.017)	(0.019)	(0.039)	(0.031)
t	−0.28	0.94	1.00	1.90	0.57	0.78
$b_1^{employment}$	−0.011	−0.006	−0.012	−0.003	−0.008	−0.009
	(0.007)	(0.008)	(0.007)	(0.011)	(0.008)	(0.008)
t	−1.52	−0.77	−1.77	−0.31	−0.96	−1.07
b_1^{USA}	0.148	0.218	0.041	−0.002	0.101	0.049
	(0.103)	(0.098)	(0.021)	(0.023)	(0.073)	(0.047)
t	1.44	2.24	1.95	−0.11	1.39	1.06
b_1^{youth}	0.022	−0.029	−0.011	−0.005	−0.006	−0.004
	(0.014)	(0.022)	(0.011)	(0.012)	(0.015)	(0.014)
t	1.56	−1.33	−1.08	−0.38	−0.38	−0.30
$b_1^{E\&D}$	−0.093	0.001	−0.030	−0.037	−0.040	−0.043
	(0.023)	(0.043)	(0.016)	(0.018)	(0.027)	(0.023)
t	−3.98	0.02	−1.92	−2.05	−1.46	−1.84

NOTE: Standard errors are in parentheses.

the United States produce much smaller estimates of minimum wage effects. The two means of the estimates for $b_1 + b_1^{USA}$ are −0.002 and −0.006, and neither is close to statistical significance. The estimates of the employment-only elasticity, $b_1 + b_1^{employment} + b_1^{USA}$, are −0.01 for the simple mean and 0.014 for the weighted mean; t-statistics for both are very small.

Table 4.7 Meta-Estimates of the Minimum Wage Elasticity of Employment and Hours for Models with Controls for Youth and Eating and Drinking Places

Panel B1: Employment, hours, and U.S. coefficients						
b_1	−0.112	−0.222	−0.043	−0.035	−0.103	−0.064
	(0.086)	(0.088)	(0.020)	(0.022)	(0.063)	(0.043)
t	−1.30	−2.53	−2.16	−1.60	−1.63	−1.50
$b_1 + b_1^{employment}$	−0.122	−0.228	−0.055	−0.038	−0.111	−0.070
	(0.086)	(0.088)	(0.019)	(0.020)	(0.063)	(0.041)
t	−1.42	−2.61	−2.87	−1.94	−1.76	−1.71
$b_1 + b_1^{USA}$	0.036	−0.004	−0.003	−0.037	−0.002	−0.006
	(0.036)	(0.039)	(0.022)	(0.023)	(0.031)	(0.029)
t	1.00	−0.09	−0.13	−1.62	−0.06	−0.21
$b_1 + b_1^{employment} + b_1^{USA}$	0.025	−0.010	−0.015	−0.041	−0.010	−0.014
	(0.036)	(0.038)	(0.021)	(0.022)	(0.030)	(0.028)
t	0.71	−0.25	−0.71	−1.86	−0.33	−0.51
	4.10b′	4.10b″	4.11b′	4.11b″	Mean	Precision-weighted mean
Panel B2: Sums that include the coefficient for youth, b_1^{youth}						
$b_1 + b_1^{youth}$	−0.090	−0.251	−0.055	−0.040	−0.109	−0.070
	(0.086)	(0.091)	(0.020)	(0.021)	(0.064)	(0.043)
t	−1.04	−2.76	−2.68	−1.86	−1.69	−1.64
$b_1 + b_1^{employment} + b_1^{youth}$	−0.101	−0.257	−0.067	−0.043	−0.117	−0.078
	(0.086)	(0.091)	(0.020)	(0.021)	(0.064)	(0.043)
t	−1.16	−2.84	−3.33	−2.03	−1.82	−1.83
$b_1 + b_1^{USA} + b_1^{youth}$	0.058	−0.033	−0.014	−0.042	−0.008	−0.012
	(0.039)	(0.045)	(0.023)	(0.024)	(0.034)	(0.031)
t	1.49	−0.73	−0.61	−1.75	−0.23	−0.38
$b_1 + b_1^{employment} + b_1^{USA} + b_1^{youth}$	0.047	−0.039	−0.026	−0.045	−0.016	−0.020
	(0.038)	(0.044)	(0.023)	(0.025)	(0.034)	(0.031)
t	1.23	−0.88	−1.14	−1.85	−0.47	−0.63

Table 4.7 (continued)

	4.10b′	4.10b″	4.11b′	4.11b″	Mean	Precision-weighted mean
Panel B3: Sums that include the coefficient for eating and drinking places, $b_1^{E\&D}$						
$b_1 + b_1^{E\&D}$	−0.204	−0.221	−0.074	−0.072	−0.143	−0.107
	(0.091)	(0.096)	(0.028)	(0.033)	(0.070)	(0.053)
t	−2.25	−2.29	−2.61	−2.19	−2.05	−2.01
$b_1 + b_1^{employment} + b_1^{E\&D}$	−0.215	−0.227	−0.086	−0.076	−0.151	−0.114
	(0.091)	(0.096)	(0.027)	(0.030)	(0.069)	(0.052)
t	−2.37	−2.36	−3.14	−2.56	−2.18	−2.21
$b_1 + b_1^{USA} + b_1^{E\&D}$	−0.057	−0.003	−0.033	−0.075	−0.042	−0.045
	(0.044)	(0.058)	(0.028)	(0.032)	(0.042)	(0.039)
t	−1.30	−0.05	−1.21	−2.34	−1.00	−1.17
$b_1 + b_1^{employment} + b_1^{USA} + b_1^{E\&D}$	−0.067	−0.009	−0.045	−0.078	−0.050	−0.054
	(0.043)	(0.057)	(0.027)	(0.029)	(0.041)	(0.037)
t	−1.55	−0.15	−1.69	−2.70	−1.22	−1.46

NOTE: Standard errors are in parentheses.

The estimates of b_1^{youth} are small, and the sums that include b_1^{youth} (Table 4.7, Panel B2) are similar to those without it (Table 4.7, Panel B1). The means of the estimated elasticities for young workers, $b_1 + b_1^{youth}$, indicate that a 10 percent increase in the minimum wage reduces youth employment by between −0.7 percent and −1.1 percent, their t-statistics closely straddling the value that marks a one-tailed 0.05 test (the former not passing the test, the latter passing it). Estimates of the youth elasticity that do not incorporate analyses of hours data, $b_1 + b_1^{youth} + b_1^{employment}$, are slightly larger in magnitude and have larger t-statistics. For the USA, values of the elasticity for youth, both with and without observations derived from analyses of hours studies, $b_1 + b_1^{youth} + b_1^{USA}$ and $b_1 + b_1^{youth} + b_1^{employment} + b_1^{USA}$, indicate that higher minimum wages do not reduce youth employment. Six of the eight coefficients and all of the means are very small. Neither the means nor these six meta-estimates are statistically significant. The other two meta-estimates are negative and statistically significant but not large; a 10 percent increase in the minimum wage leads employment to decline by less than 0.5 percent. Although the minimum wage is estimated to have a small negative effect on youth across all studies, this is an issue for countries other than the United States. Higher minimum wages are not associated with reduced youth employment in the United States.

The minimum wage is associated with reduced employment in eating and drinking places in the full sample, but again, there is no effect in the United States (Table 4.7, Panel B3). The average elasticity, $b_1 + b_1^{E\&D}$, indicates that a 10 percent increase in the minimum wage would result in a decline of 1.1 percent to 1.4 percent in employment and hours; the effect strictly on employment, measured by $b_1 + b_1^{E\&D} + b_1^{employment}$, is slightly greater, ranging from 1.1 percent to 1.5 percent. Again, the effect on employment and employment and hours is much smaller in the United States. Three of the four estimates for the effect on hours and employment are not statistically significant in a 0.05 one-tailed test; two of the four estimates for the employment effect are likewise not statistically significant. The means for $b_1 + b_1^{E\&D} + b_1^{employment} + b_1^{USA}$ and $b_1 + b_1^{E\&D} + b_1^{USA}$ indicate that a 10 percent increase in the minimum wage would cause a decline in the corresponding measure of between 0.42 percent and 0.54 percent, but none of the means passes a one-tailed 0.05 test.[20] Although the evidence for higher minimum wages being associated with reduced employment in eating and drinking places in the United States is stronger than the evidence for there being an effect on young workers in the United States, it does not meet conventional statistical tests and is small in magnitude.

CONCLUSION

In what must be the most cited review of research into the employment effect of the minimum wage, Brown, Gilroy, and Kohen (1982) concluded, "Time series studies typically find that a 10 percent increase in the minimum wage reduces teenage employment by one to three percent. . . . We believe that the lower half of that range is to be preferred" (p. 524). Nearly two decades later, Brown (1999) wrote in another review, "My reading of the new and old evidence suggests that the short-term effect of the minimum wage on teenage employment is small. Time-series estimates that centered on an elasticity of −0.10 moved closer to zero in samples that included the 1980s" (p. 2154). Based on this meta-analysis of results from the most recent work from the NMWR, Brown's judgment concerning the minimum wage elasticity of employment remains valid, not just for youth but more broadly.

We have provided a very large number of meta-estimates of the employment elasticity. The range of the simplest estimates, found in Table 4.3, is [−0.099, −0.034], with the precision-weighted estimates falling in the interval [−0.050, −0.034]. Including a correction for publication bias (Table 4.4) shifts the range toward zero [−0.06, −0.018], with the precision-weighted estimates in the interval [−0.048, −0.018].

Tables 4.5–4.7 include 64 estimates of employment and employment/hours effects. Estimates and the statistical significance of the estimates vary systematically according to the method of estimation, the population under study, the controls, and whether employment or employment and hours are considered. Using a weaker but appropriate standard of statistical significance than in the balance of our work, we find some evidence that increases in the minimum wage results in modest reductions in employment. Applying a one-tailed 0.05 standard of significance to our more complete models, we find some evidence that increases in the minimum wage result in very small reductions in employment. Considering estimates that reflect the effect on both employment and hours and on employment alone, a 10 percent increase in the minimum wage is associated with a reduction of between 0.0 percent and −2.6 percent. Somewhat less than half of the estimates are statistically significant, and of those, more than half find an employment decline toward the lower end of a range between −0.1 percent and −0.03 percent. Not allowing for differences between studies of the United States and other countries, the evidence suggests that there may be no effect or a very small negative effect.

The means, which average across estimation methods, are somewhat easier to summarize because they reduce the sometimes substantial variance in estimates between methods of estimation. Considering the 16 means that do not include the U.S. effect, somewhat more than half indicate a small but statistically significant effect on employment or employment and hours. Seven of the estimates do not meet any criteria for statistical significance, 5 meet a one-tailed 5 percent standard, and 4 meet a two-tailed 5 percent standard or better. Statistically significant estimates fall in a range from −0.110 to −0.057, with the precision-weighted mean being consistently smaller than the simple mean.

The United States, however, faces a far more favorable situation. Considering the 16 means of sums that include the term b_1^{USA}, a 10 percent increase in the minimum wage is estimated to reduce employment between 0.03 percent and 0.6 percent, but none of these estimates pass even a one-tailed 0.05 test of statistical significance.[21] Bearing in mind that the estimates for the United States reflect a historic experience of moderate increases in the minimum wage, it appears that if negative effects on employment are present, they are too small to be statistically detectable. Such effects would be too modest to have meaningful consequences in the dynamically changing labor markets of the United States.

We must hedge our conclusion because a number of articles could not be incorporated into the analysis. Doucouliagos and Stanley (2009) excluded about one-third of the 100 studies that they identified, either because they would make the sample too heterogeneous to be meaningful or because they lack an important piece of data to enable comparison with other studies, i.e., an employment elasticity or its standard error. In this analysis, more than two-thirds of the 80 studies could not be used. Heterogeneity is the hallmark of the NMWR, and if a common measure can be calculated, it would be preferable to control for heterogeneity in the metaregression. The problem is that in the minimum wage literature, the elasticity couplet (point estimate, standard error) is too much a rare bird. One reason is that for some measures of the minimum wage—the fraction affected and the wage gap, which may well be better measures in this context than the real minimum wage itself—it is necessary to jump through more hoops in order to derive a minimum wage elasticity of employment. However, without some common measure, and an elasticity is surely the most common measure in economics, it is not possible to compare or aggregate research results. Without presenting some common measure as well as an estimate of its precision, the contribution to empirical knowledge of a particular piece of research is self-limiting.

Notes

1. This presentation draws heavily on Stanley (2001, 2005, 2008) and follows the order in which he presents the equations.
2. Notice that with the heteroskedasticity correction, the constant term in Equation (4.2) becomes the precision variable in Equation (4.3b), and the standard error variable in Equation (4.2) becomes the constant term in Equation (4.3b). If, for whatever reason, the metaregression does not include the term that corrects publication bias for statistical significance, Equation (4.3b) will have no constant term. We return to this on p. 159 in the section titled "Metaregressions—Part 1."
3. A good discussion of deviation coding is to be found in Chen et al. (2003).
4. In addition to metaregression, Doucouliagos and Stanley (2009) present a graphical analysis that is useful in exploring publication bias. Because this issue is not of particular interest here, beyond purging its effect so as not to distort the results of meta-analysis, the focus is on their metaregression.
5. The formula is $r = \dfrac{t}{\sqrt{t^2 + df}}$,

   where t is the t-value of the estimated coefficient for the minimum wage variable, and df is its degrees of freedom. We do not use this approach in our own analysis as, according to the derivation in Greene (2011, pp. 36–37), the partial correlation coefficient is related to the OLS t-statistic but not to t-statistics based on other formulas, e.g., those derived from robust standard errors.
6. More robust but cruder measures of precision are sometimes used, including sample size or its square root, and the degrees of freedom,
7. The terminology begins to be confusing at this point. The primary variable in this meta-analysis is a collection of point estimates of an elasticity. A very important secondary variable is the collection of standard errors, the standard error associated with each point estimate: so far, so good. These two variables have a bivariate distribution, and each variable by itself has a mean and a standard deviation. Because the point estimates of the elasticities are themselves means, and the standard deviation of a set of means is a standard error, the one-standard-deviation lines in the graph indicate a standard error. This is obviously distinct from the collection of standard errors that make up the important secondary variable. For clarity, although the standard deviation associated with the lines is indeed a standard error, that term (*standard error*) will refer only to the variable in this discussion and not to the standard deviation indicated by the lines.
8. "Reliable" does not mean here that the standard errors are entirely or largely without problem, only that issues that Bertrand, Duflo, and Mullainathan (2004) and Donald and Lang (2007) identified give no cause for concern.
9. Recall Note 4 concerning the source (or, in this case, lack thereof) of a constant term in Equation (4.3b).
10. Two studies, each of which contributes only one elasticity estimate to the sample, do not have a corresponding indicator variable in the list {2, 3, ... A}.

Some authors were responsible for more than one study in the sample. Correcting by author-group instead of study has almost no impact on either the point estimates or their standard errors. To avoid overwhelming the reader with redundant results, those corrected for study are presented here.

11. Clark and Linzer (2013) make two observations about the choice between fixed and random effects, both without any claim of originality. The first is that the random effects specification occupies the continuum between two extremes, one identified with the pooled model and the other with the fixed-effects model.

> As Gelman and Hill (2007, 258) note, . . . (the random effects estimator) is equivalent to . . . (the fixed effects estimator) when we assume that $\alpha_j \sim N(\mu_\alpha, \infty)$ rather than $\alpha_j \sim N(\mu_\alpha, \sigma_\alpha^2)$. In other words, the random effects specification models the intercepts as arising from a distribution with a finite|and estimable|variance sigma-alpha-squared, whereas the fixed effects specification assumes the intercepts are distributed with infinite variance. The pooled model, by contrast, implicitly assumes $\sigma_\alpha^2 = 0$. (p. 4)

The second observation is the conventional wisdom that "under certain conditions [i.e., correlation between the effects and regressors], random effects models can introduce bias but reduce the variance of estimates of coefficients of interest. Fixed effects estimates will be unbiased but may be subject to high variance." Two common responses to this conundrum are to abjure bias and stick only to fixed effects or to make the decision based on the results of a Hausman test. The Hausman test is not ideal for several reasons. Based on results from their Monte Carlo simulations, Clark and Linzer (2013) observe that it often lacks power necessary to detect the correlation that it is intended to detect. In our own experience below comparing Equations (4.6b) and (4.7b), the difference of the covariance matrices that is used to construct the test statistic was not positive definite, and consequently, the test statistic could not be calculated. Most persuasively in our view, Clark and Linzer remind us that the trade-off between bias and variance is pervasive in statistical analysis and that some bias may be a reasonable price cost for a sufficiently large reduction in variance; a biased estimate may well be better in a finite sample, closer to the true value of the parameter, than an unbiased estimate with high variance. Their simulation results provide examples in support of this point.

Rather than choose sides in this argument, we present estimates from both fixed- and random-effects specifications, and later fixed- and random-coefficient specifications. As we shall see in the results presented in Tables 4.3 and 4.4, for simple models without any control variables for the estimates that make up our sample, there is little difference between either the point estimates or their standard errors for otherwise corresponding models that differ on this dimension. In the results with control variables, presented in Tables 4.5–4.7, this pattern changes. Overall (but not uniformly), results for the parameters of interest from the fixed-effects and fixed-coefficient specifications are point estimates and standard errors that are larger in magnitude, and t-statistics that are smaller in magnitude than from the random-effects and random-coefficients specifications.

12. In this case, the characterization of the phenomenon in the previous sentence is less accurate than "studies with smaller average magnitudes of the estimates presented more of them, as well as their standard errors."

13. A Hausman test of the random-effects model, Equation (4.7b′), vs. the fixed-effects model, Equation (6b′), was attempted, but as in Table 4.3, the difference of the covariance matrices was not positive definite. However, for the corresponding test with the more parameterized models, Equations (4.7b′′) and (4.6b′′), the test statistic is 2.34 with a p-value of 0.13. This suggests that we have no statistical reason for preferring one or the other of Equations (4.6b′) and (4.7b′). That we do not reject the null hypothesis in the test comparing Equations (4.6b′′) and (4.7b′′) suggests that the latter, the random-coefficients specification, is to be preferred since it is less parameterized and more efficient. Both of the random parameter terms in Equation 4.(7b′′) have statistically significant standard deviations, each with a t-statistic near 4, which suggests that in the event of a substantive difference between Equations (4.7b′) and (4.7b′′), the latter is to be preferred on statistical grounds.

14. The exception for the consequence of precision weighting occurs in the equation pair (4.5a′) and (4.5b′), where the magnitude of the precision-weighted estimate of the effect, Equation (4.5b′), is 10 percent larger than the former. Note that the estimate's standard error falls by 80 percent; the estimate in Equation (4.5a′) is not statistically significant, while that in Equation (4.5b′) is. The exception for the consequences of including study effects occurs in the transition from Equation (4.5b′) to Equation (4.6b′), where the point estimate falls by nearly one-fifth and the standard error more than doubles.

15. Because the costs of varying hours of employment may differ from those of varying the level of employment, the respective elasticities with respect to the minimum wage may differ, and this allows for that possibility.

16. There are no Equations (4.8a) or (4.8b). We retain the primes and use only b to label the equations so that the provenance of each equation is easier to trace.

17. The standard errors shown beneath each mean are calculated as the square roots of the corresponding means of the squared standard errors (i.e., square roots of the mean variances) in the row. This assumes that the meta-estimates have zero covariance; since the most likely covariance is positive, these values are likely a floor.

18. A primary concern is that many of the point meta-estimates from Equation (8b′′) are outliers relative to the corresponding meta-estimates from the other three specifications. Ignoring these values entirely in the calculation of the means is one response, though perhaps an overreaction. Because the standard errors of these meta-estimates are typically quite high, precision weighting is an alternative approach that reduces their contributions to the means without throwing them out entirely.

19. We do not use the coefficients for regression or reliability in our summed effects, as these controls are not of interest in obtaining measures of the impact of the minimum wage on employment or hours. They can be of interest in understanding any biases associated with econometric techniques. We include the coefficient for

the overall effect as the first entry for panel B of Tables 4.5 and 4.6 to facilitate comparison with other summed effects.

20. One can speculate that the effect on youth employment in eating and drinking places is quite strong. Because none of the estimates included in this analysis are based on that conjecture, sums that include $b_1^{Youth} + b_1^{E\&D}$ extrapolate outside the sample, so we do not pursue this.

21. Of the 32 sums of coefficients themselves, 7 pass this test for statistical significance, 6 from random-effects–random-coefficients specifications, and 8 from a random-coefficients specification (that does not include random effects). None of the 16 fixed-effects specifications, the specifications for which we can be reasonably certain are unbiased, are statistically significant.

5
Wages and Earnings

How do increases in the minimum wage affect wages, earnings, and income? On its face, the answer is obvious: Those who are earning less than the new minimum wage will see their hourly rates rise, and if the effect on hours is not too severe, their earnings will also rise, as will their household incomes. Once we know the effect on employment and hours, straightforward calculations provide the answers to our question on wages, earnings, and income. Case closed. Or is it?

The effect of the minimum wage on earnings may reach further into the wage distribution and pose more challenging measurement issues. For example, does the minimum wage affect the earnings of those who, prior to the increase, earned slightly more than the new minimum? Are their wages unchanged, or do they too rise with the increase in the minimum wage? Another issue is whether increases in the minimum wage have a meaningful effect over time on the earnings of those affected by the minimum wage. If the pay of those at the minimum wage rises rapidly after they are first hired, then the minimum wage can only modestly improve their earnings trajectories and incomes over time. If the wages of those earning the minimum wage remain close to the minimum for extended periods, an increase in the minimum wage will result in a meaningful increase in both current and future earnings. There are a number of such issues, and, as a result, the case is not quite as easy to close as it seemed initially.

Our discussion of wage effects is organized around six questions:

1) How is the average wage affected by the minimum wage?

2) How does the minimum wage affect the wages of those who are at or below the new minimum wage?

3) How does the minimum wage affect the wages of those who, prior to an increase, were earning more than the new minimum wage?

4) What are the dynamics of wage increases of those who are at or are close to the minimum wage?

5) How does the minimum wage affect the distribution of earnings?

6) How does the minimum wage affect the income of low-income households, particularly those at or near the poverty line?

Answers to these questions provide a comprehensive portrait of the impact of the minimum wage on wages, earnings, and income. In this chapter we limit ourselves to the first three questions; the questions on wage dynamics, wage growth, inequality, and poverty are addressed in later chapters. Before turning to these three questions, we address issues regarding measurement of wage effects and introduce some data on the minimum wage in the United States.

MEASURING THE EFFECTS OF THE MINIMUM WAGE

The interest of readers is seldom peaked with substantive discussion of definitions. However, the terms *wages* and *earnings* are used inconsistently across studies, and it is often challenging to know what is being measured. In order to better navigate the rough semantic terrain, we have to define how these terms will be used in this review, and then we discuss each of the studies using our terminology. For the purposes of this review, *wage rate* refers to the straight-time hourly wage an individual is paid. *Earnings* is the pretax amount an employee receives in her paychecks over some period. For those paid weekly (or biweekly or monthly), hourly earnings would be the amount they are paid per week (or fortnight or month) divided by the number of hours they worked that week (or fortnight or month). For those paid by the hour, hourly earnings might also be their wage rate, but if they worked overtime at time and one-half or better, hourly earnings might be greater than their wage rate. While earnings can be computed for all employees, wage rates are only available for those who are paid by the hour.[1] In this review, we use *wages* as a general term referring to employee pay. It encompasses both wage rates and earnings, but, unlike wage rates or earnings, it is not a specific measure. Payments for benefits and for the employer share of payroll taxes are not included in any of these measures.[2]

A challenge to measuring the effect of the minimum wage on wages is that observed and average wages, whether measured as wage rates or earnings, will almost certainly increase whether or not an increase in the minimum wage causes any individual's wage to increase. If wages rise in response to an increase in the minimum wage, and if the minimum wage is not so far below the market rate that no workers are bound by the increase, two outcomes are possible, and both result in the minimum wage becoming the floor on the wage structure. First, if the increase in the minimum wage does not cause employers to lay off workers, the case when the labor demand curve is entirely inelastic, then workers who previously earned less than the new minimum wage have their wages boosted to that minimum wage. Their wage rate rises, and, if working hours are not reduced, weekly and monthly earnings also rise. Average hourly wage rates and earnings increase.

The second, opposite case can be derived from an economic model of a single labor market with workers of varying productivity. In the extreme, an increase in the minimum wage would cause the layoff of workers whose productivity was less than the new minimum wage, all of the workers bound by the new minimum wage.[3] As in the first case, the new minimum wage is now the lowest wage rate in the labor market. The average wage rate and hourly earnings will also have increased, and the average wage will be higher than in the case with no layoffs. However, none of the previously bound workers will be better off, as they are all without employment. We cannot then simply assume that a rise in wage rates and hourly earnings following an increase in the minimum wage corresponds to an increase in individuals' wages.[4]

What would be evidence that the minimum wage increases workers' wages and earnings? This depends in part on the structure of the data. Longitudinal data enable the analyst to follow individuals across minimum wage increases and to estimate the effect of the minimum on both wage and employment outcomes for bound workers (Currie and Fallick 1996). Both cross-sectional surveys of individuals and data aggregated by city, county, or state pose greater challenges because there is no inherent connection between the before and after group in studies over time, or the low and high minimum wage group in studies across places. An increase in average wages cannot be taken as evidence that any person is actually better off. One approach to this challenge has been to estimate both employment and wage effects. The estimates of employment effects can be used to determine the degree to which higher average ex post wages are due to disemployment, rather than to higher wages for bound workers. If employment effects are small or entirely missing, then the effect of the minimum wage is due in large part to increases in wages for bound workers.[5] Wolfson and Belman (2004, 2010) explicitly consider the effects of the minimum wage on wages, employment, and hours. This allows them to both focus on those industries in which there is a wage effect and consider the degree to which any wage effects are offset by declines in employment. In their most recent study, they find that increases in the federal minimum wage had a positive and significant effect on the average wage in 16 of 23 low-wage industries (70 percent), with little evidence of an employment effect.

Another approach to determining the effect on bound workers is to compare the distribution of hourly wages before and after a change in the minimum wage.[6] Absent clumping in the distribution of individual productivity, wage distributions should be reasonably smooth with little clumping of observations at any particular wage rate. This is not entirely the case in survey data, because employers tend to pay in round increments, and respondents tend to round their hourly earnings to even dollar amounts. Consequently, mass points or "spikes" occur at even dollar amounts. If an increase in the minimum wage causes bound workers to lose their employment, then we would expect the distribution to be truncated at the new minimum wage with little or no spiking at the point. If, on the other hand, those who are bound are moved up to the new minimum wage, and retain their job, we would expect a spike at the minimum wage. This occurs because employers who move lower-wage employees up in response to the minimum wage are likely to pay them at or close to the minimum no matter how far below the new minimum they previously were.

WAGE DISTRIBUTION

Measurement of wage distributions is central to much of this chapter, and it is useful to define this concept, provide background on current wage distributions, and consider descriptive evidence on spikes in recent and past distributions. A wage distribution charts the relationship between a wage, or range of wages, and the proportion of the employed labor force earning that wage. Tables 5.1, 5.2, and 5.3 present these different ways of considering hourly earnings for those earning between $3.00 and $100 per hour in 2010.[7] Table 5.1, a cumulative distribution, reports the percentage of workers earning less than a given dollar amount. The first two columns report these percentages for all respondents who report working for pay; the third and fourth column exclude those aged 16–24 who report being enrolled in school. Within each pair

Table 5.1 The Distribution of Hourly Wages and Hourly Earnings by Dollar Amount, 2010

Earnings ($)	All compensated employees		Exclude full- and part-time students	
	Percent of those paid hourly earnings below	Percent below including salaried workers	Percent of those paid hourly earnings below	Percent below including salaried workers
< 7	1.5	2.0	1.2	1.8
<= 7.50 (minimum wage)[a]	6.0	5.0	4.7	4.1
< 8	9.4	7.4	7.3	6.0
< 9	20.3	14.8	16.9	12.5
< 10	28.3	20.4	24.7	17.8
< 12	44.1	32.1	40.6	29.3
< 14	56.3	42.0	53.2	39.4
<15	61.0	46.2	58.2	43.7
<16	66.7	51.0	64.1	48.7
< 18	73.6	58.1	71.6	56.1
< 20	78.6	64.1	77.0	62.4
< 25	87.7	76.0	86.7	74.7
< 30	93.1	84.3	92.5	83.5
< 50	98.9	97.0	98.7	96.9
>= 100	100.0	100.0	100.0	100.0

[a] The minimum wage is $7.25. Following conventional practice to allow for measurement error (i.e., inaccurate reporting), any wage reported to be between $7 and $7.50 is considered to be at the minimum wage .

SOURCE: Authors' calculations from the 2010 CPS ORG. Calculations of average hourly earnings (inclusive of salaried workers) do not include those who report variable hours.

of columns, the first reports the distribution of wage rates for only those who are paid by the hour; the second includes individuals who are paid weekly, biweekly, or monthly and for whom average hourly earnings can be computed. Hourly earnings in columns two and four are computed as the ratio of average weekly earnings to average weekly hours.[8]

The difference between these measures can be illustrated by looking at the row for the federal minimum wage (<= $7.50).[9] Following Aaronson, Agarwal, and French (2011), we address reporting error by creating a "thick" band that extends from $7.00 to $7.50. If we consider those who are paid hourly without regard to whether they are enrolled in school, 6.0 percent of workers are paid at or below the minimum wage.[10] This declines to 4.7 percent if we exclude students from the sample (column 3). We can broaden our sample by moving from individuals who are paid hourly to all employees, including those paid a salary. Considering the full workforce, 5.0 percent of the workforce earns the minimum wage or less; if we exclude students, then this declines to 4.1 percent. Inclusion of the salaried workforce consistently reduces the proportion of the workforce at a given pay level as salaried workers tend to earn more on an hourly basis than employees who are paid by the hour; how many doctors are paid hourly? Although the proportion working at or below the minimum varies across the four samples, we can summarize by saying about 1 in 20 employees earns the minimum wage or less.

What happens as we move up the wage distribution? Between one in eight (12.5 percent) and one in five (20 percent) workers earn no more than $9.00, $1.50 above the (thick) minimum wage band. From one in six (18 percent) to one in four (28 percent) employees earn no more than $10.00, $2.50 above the minimum wage. We complete our tour of Table 5.1 at $14.00, almost twice the minimum wage. Between 39 percent and 56 percent of employees are paid no more than $14.00. Even at the low end of these estimates, in excess of two in every five employees earn no more than twice the federal minimum wage.

Table 5.2 provides another cut on this data. Here, we calculate the wage or hourly earnings at a given percentile of the wage distribution. Five percent of all workers who are paid by the hour earn no more than the federal minimum wage. If we exclude students, the 5 percent cutoff rises to $7.50. Eight dollars per hour cuts off 10 percent of hourly employees both when students are, and are not, part of the sample. Ten

Table 5.2 The Distribution of Hourly Wages and Hourly Earnings by Percentile, 2010

Percentile	All compensated employees		Exclude full- and part-time students	
	Highest wage for those paid hourly	Highest wage, including salaried workers	Highest wage for those paid hourly	Highest wage, including sala-ried workers
5th	7.25	7.50	7.50	7.50
10th	8.00	8.00	8.00	8.50
20th	9.00	10.00	9.25	10.00
30th	10.00	11.54	10.25	12.00
40th	11.25	13.60	12.00	14.00
50th (median)	13.00	15.85	13.50	16.34
60th	15.00	18.70	15.00	19.23
70th	17.00	22.00	17.50	22.67
80th	20.00	26.92	21.00	27.60
90th	26.00	35.19	27.00	36.05

SOURCE: Authors' calculations from the 2010 CPS ORG. Calculations of average hourly earnings (inclusive of salaried workers) do not include those who report variable hours.

percent of all employees inclusive of salaried employees also earn no more than $8.00 per hour, but this rises to $8.50 when students are excluded (fourth column). The ceiling for the 20th percentile is between the hourly wages of $9.00 and $10.00, and for the 30th percentile, between $10.00 and $12.00. The median splits the paid workforce into two equally large parts. Half of the hourly workforce earns less than twice the federal minimum wage. If we include salaried workers, the median earner is paid between 210 and 220 percent of the minimum wage. Although a small minority of workers earn close to the minimum wage, the federal minimum is not far from the wages of 30 percent of the labor force.

The measure used for Table 5.3 accounts for state minimum wages in excess of the federal minimum and provides a more comprehensive measure of the fraction of the workforce that is "close to" the applicable minimum wage. For this table, we first calculate the ratio of an individual's wage to the higher of the federal wage or the minimum wage

Table 5.3 The Distribution of Hourly Wages and Earnings Relative to the Minimum Wage, 2010

	All compensated employees		Exclude full- and part-time students	
	Percent of those paid hourly earnings below	Percent below including sala- ried workers	Percent of those paid hourly earnings below	Percent below including sala- ried workers
Less than the mini- mum wage	3.7	3.6	2.9	3.0
At the minimum wage	7.4	5.9	5.9	4.8
Less than 110% of the minimum wage	13.3	9.9	10.7	8.1
Less than 120% of the minimum wage	21.8	15.6	18.3	13.2
No more than 150% of the minimum wage	40.2	28.9	36.4	26.0
No more than 175% of the minimum wage	52.1	38.5	48.7	35.7
No more than 200% of the minimum wage	61.5	46.6	58.7	44.1
No more than 300% of the minimum wage	84.3	70.8	83.0	69.4

SOURCE: Authors' calculations from the 2010 CPS ORG. Calculations of average hourly earnings (inclusive of salaried workers) do not include those who report vari- able hours.

of the state in which they live and then form the distribution from this ratio. The table is organized similarly to Table 5.1 but uses these ratios instead of dollar amounts: those earning no more than the minimum wage (up to 103 percent of the minimum wage to allow for reporting error), those earning no more than 110 percent of the minimum, those earning no more than 120 percent of the minimum, and so on. The col- umns of Table 5.3 are arranged in the same manner as Tables 5.1 and 5.2.

The fraction of the workforce that earns no more than the applicable minimum varies from 1 in 20 (5 percent) to 1 in 14 (7 percent). The higher estimate includes all hourly paid workers without regard to educational status, and the low estimate includes all salaried and hourly workers except students. Moving up the distribution, the fraction of workers earning close to the minimum wage rises substantially relative to Tables 5.1 and 5.2. Between one in eight (13 percent) and one in five (22 percent) employees earn no more than 120 percent of the applicable minimum. At 150 percent of the minimum wage, the ratio varies between two in eight (26 percent) and two in five (40 percent), depending on how the sample is defined. At twice the minimum wage, the smallest estimate, 44 percent, is close to half the workforce, while the largest is greater than 60 percent.

What conclusions can we draw from these tables? First, that a modest but nontrivial fraction of the workforce is paid no more than the minimum wage. Table 5.3 indicates that between 4.8 percent and 7.4 percent of the workforce, at least 1 in 20 workers, earn no more than the higher of the federal or state minimum wage. Second, the hourly earnings of a large fraction of the workforce is not greatly above the minimum wage. Between 13 percent and 20 percent of workers earn no more than $1.50 above the federal minimum wage (Table 5.1). Between 18 percent and 28 percent earn no more than $2.50 above the federal minimum wage (Table 5.1), and between 13 percent and 22 percent earn no more than 150 percent of the applicable federal or state minimum wage (Table 5.3). Third, increases in the minimum wage likely reach a considerable proportion of the labor force. Research discussed below suggests that the minimum wage boosts the earnings not only of those of who were bound by the new minimum but also of those who previously earned more than the new minimum. This increase in the earnings of those already above the new minimum is termed a "spillover effect." Spillovers may reach as high as the third decile of the wage distribution, positively affecting the earnings of workers earning between $10.00 and $12.00 per hour. The minimum is then not simply a very low wage reserved for teenagers and workers with impossibly low productivity and poor work habits, irrelevant to the overwhelming majority of the workforce. Rather, for large proportions of the labor force, the minimum wage is closer than it appears.

Spikes in the Wage Distribution

The next issue is whether there is a spike at the minimum wage. One of our issues is whether "those bound by the new minimum lose their jobs or do they receive wage increases?" If the latter, then there will be a spike at the new minimum as employers move bound workers up to but no further than the new minimum. If the former, if bound workers are dismissed, then the distribution should be relatively smooth and there shouldn't be a pronounced spike. Evidence of a spike can be found in Table 5.3. Between 1.8 and 3.7 percent of the workforce was paid exactly the applicable minimum wage (the difference between the proportion of workers earning no more than the minimum wage, row 2 in the table, and the proportion earning less than the minimum wage, row 1).

The period 2006–2010 is good for examining the effects of the minimum wage visually. The minimum wage remained at $5.15 per hour from September 1, 1997, until July 23, 2007. It rose to $5.85 on July 24, 2007, to $6.55 a year later and finally to $7.25 on July 24, 2009. With a low inflation during this period, we would not expect wages to be rising rapidly.

What Happened to the Distribution of Wages over This Period?

We present nominal and relative dollar wage distributions computed from the outgoing rotation files of the Current Population Survey (CPS). Both are computed for average hourly earnings, the ratio of average weekly earnings to average weekly hours.[11] In both Figures 5.1 and 5.2, the upper panels are the year prior to the 2007 federal increase, and the lower panels are the year following the 2009 federal increase. The distribution is formed using a kernel density smoothing process.[12] Figure 5.1 represents the distribution of hourly earnings in nominal dollars. The minimum wage line only references the federal minimum wage; state minimum wage in excess of the federal minimum is not depicted. Figure 5.2 compares the ratio of individual hourly earnings to the applicable minimum wage, the higher of the state or federal minimum wage, for the same two periods. A ratio of 1 means the individual earned exactly the applicable minimum wage for the individual's state

Figure 5.1 Kernel Density Estimate of Hourly Earnings

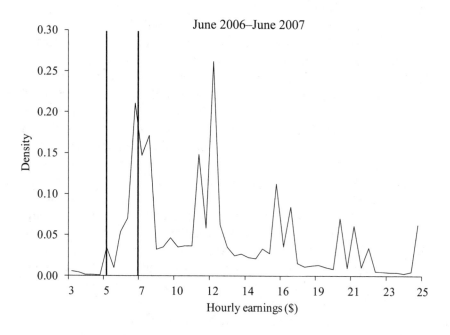

June 2006–June 2007

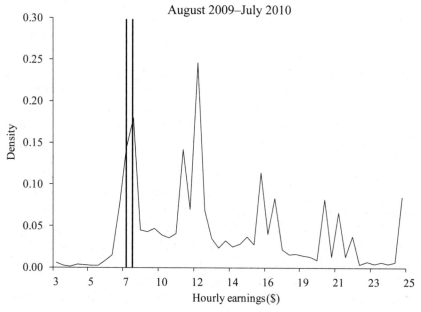

August 2009–July 2010

of residence; a value of greater than 1 indicates the individual earned more than the minimum wage.

Figure 5.1 depicts the distribution of nominal hourly wages between $3 and $25. The wages are on the horizontal axis, and the density (proportional to the fraction of the labor force earning near that wage) is on the vertical axis. The upper panel depicts the distribution for July 1, 2006, through June 30, 2007, prior to the first of the recent increases in the minimum wage. There are numerous spikes in the wage distribution, typically, but not always, at even dollar amounts, and large spikes at $7.00, $11.00, $12.00, and $16.00. A small spike at $5.15, then the federal minimum wage, is consistent with the view that the minimum wage causes employers to pay more for workers who, absent the minimum wage, would receive less. The story that emerges from this distribution is that, although there is a spike at the federal minimum, the minimum wage is not having much effect by 2007. The labor market had passed it by during its seven-year sojourn at $5.15.

The lower panel depicts the wage distribution in the year following the 2009 increase in the federal minimum wage. Here the new minimum wage, $7.25 per hour, is close to an inflection point in the second-largest spike in the wage distribution, but the peak of the spike is at $7.90 per hour. Although the wage distribution is not the cliff followed by a smooth distribution that would occur if all bound workers were disemployed, neither is the minimum wage the spike's peak, as would be the case if most bound workers received an increase to precisely the minimum wage. Again, as this is the nominal minimum wage, we cannot be sure if the spike at $7.90 is due to the presence of higher state minimum wages or some other factor.

Figure 5.2, which measures individuals' hourly earnings relative to the higher of the applicable state or federal minimum, provides additional insights. The upper panel again depicts the year prior to the federal 2007 increase. There is an inflection point at a value of 1, the ratio at which the individual's hourly earnings are exactly equal to the minimum wage, and a more marked inflection point at 1.1, where the distribution flattens out. The lower panel, the 2009–2010 relative minimum wage distribution, has a marked inflection point slightly above 1.0 (at 1.02) and achieves an absolute peak at 1.09 times the applicable minimum wage. This is evidence of some change in the effect of the state and federal minimum wage on the wage distribution. Rather

Figure 5.2   Kernel Density Estimates of the Ratio of Hourly Earnings to the Applicable Minimum Wage

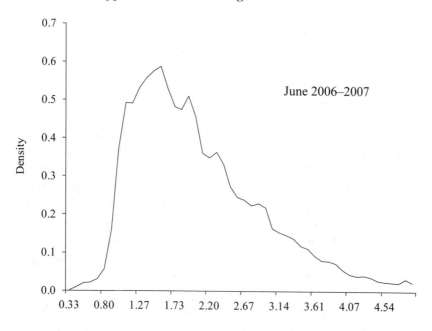

June 2006–2007

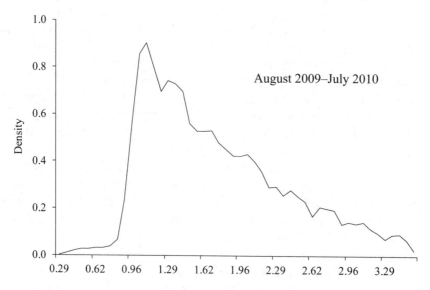

August 2009–July 2010

than just creating a single large spike at the minimum wage, it appears that the minimum wage is affecting wages that are above the applicable minimum.

An initial conclusion emerging from Figures 5.1 and 5.2 is that while both the nominal and relative wage distributions are useful to chart the effect of the minimum wage, with the increasing number of states with minimum wages above the federal minimum, the relative distributions better portray the effect of the applicable minimum wage. Second, Figure 5.2 indicates that state minimum wages matter. Third, the increases in federal and state minimum wages during this period caused a large spike to form close to, but not at, the minimum wage. The effect of the upward movement of the minimum wage is apparent from comparing the two panels in Figure 5.2. While the peak in the distribution in the upper panel, prior to the increase in the federal minimum wage, is at about 1.5 times the applicable minimum wage, the peak in the lower panel, after the federal minimum wage had been increased to $7.25, is only 1.1 times the applicable minimum wage. This is consistent with minimum wage increases altering the distribution in a fashion that market forces, by themselves, would not have done.

Why is the peak often some distance above the minimum wage? At one time, there was a very sharp peak immediately at the federal minimum wage. Figure 5.3 is a kernel density estimate of the hourly wage rate of those paid by the hour in 1981 following the increase in the federal minimum wage to $3.35 on January 1.[13] Here the peak of the distribution is just to the right of the reference line at the federal minimum wage, and the distribution quickly flattens above the minimum wage. Why the difference between this 1981 result, where the minimum wage is the largest spike, and the results for 2009–2010, where the peak is above (although still close to) the applicable minimum wage? Results from experimental economics suggest that the minimum wage has become a benchmark from which a minimally acceptable wage is determined. Falk, Fehr, and Zehnder (2006) argue that the minimum wage is currently viewed as the wage that anyone can earn without serious work effort or application. To motivate workers, employers must pay them above the minimum wage, if by only a small amount. Consistent with this interpretation, experiments indicate that when informed about a minimum wage, participants set their desired wage just a bit above the minimum wage. Why would these perceptions affect labor market

Figure 5.3 Kernel Density Estimate of Average Hourly Earnings, 1981

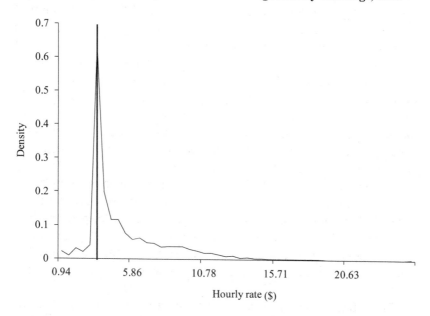

outcomes in 2010 but not 1981? Perhaps because the minimum wage was increased annually or biannually from 1961 to 1981, keeping pace with trends in the labor market, it was considered a reasonable entry-level wage. The two extended periods in which the federal minimum wage remained fixed between 1981 and 2007, each about a decade long, may have altered perceptions, turning the minimum wage from an acceptable entry wage to a benchmark from which the lowest acceptable wage is determined.

Having seen this initial evidence that the minimum wage raises the floor on the wage distribution, we now turn to the literature on the effect of the minimum wage on wage rates and earnings. In the following sections we consider how the minimum wage affects those bound by the minimum wage, and how it affects those earning above the minimum wage.

The average wage

How the minimum wage affects the average wage is often the first question in minimum wage analysis. If the average wage does not respond, and in the same direction as the minimum wage, then it is likely that the latter is set too low to affect the labor market.[14] In addition, if the average wage does not respond, it is hard to argue that the minimum wage improves outcomes for any workers.

The employees in a labor market are readily divided into those who were earning between the previous and the current minimum wage, workers bound by the new minimum, and those who were previously earning more than the current minimum wage. Economic theory has focused much of its attention on the effect on the bound workers, as it is their earnings and employment that are most obviously affected by the new minimum. The second group is less obviously affected, as their employment is not in doubt, and any effects on their earnings could only occur if the rise in wages of the less-skilled increases demand for, and thus the wages of, the more-skilled and already better-paid employees. While a minimum wage increase could affect the wages of those earning above the new minimum, such cross-price effects are viewed as relatively small in magnitude and secondary in interest when addressed at all.

The effects of an increase in the minimum wage on the wages of both bound and higher-paid workers are captured in studies of the effect of the minimum wage on average wages. As discussed in the beginning of this chapter, there is no simple correspondence that assures that an increase in the average wage is associated with individuals receiving higher earnings. Although we would expect at least some employees to receive higher wages even when there is job loss, it is not possible a priori to determine how much of a change in the average wage is due to higher wages for previously bound workers and how much is due to job loss among the previously bound. Additional evidence about the presence and size of the employment loss is needed to interpret an increase in the average wage.

Mindful of Galbraith's (1972) observation that an advantage of writing nonfiction is that one need not maintain suspense, we venture our own observation that almost every study of average wages finds that increases in the minimum wage result in higher earnings. There is very strong evidence that higher minimum wages are associated with higher individual earnings even after sorting out the studies where, because of the limitations of the average wage measure, it is not possible to entirely know the effect of the minimum on individuals' earnings.[15] We present

31 studies of the effect of the minimum wage. To facilitate the discussion and provide an orange-to-tangerine comparison, we first consider several hypothetical examples to explore how change in the average wage depends on the level of job loss for bound workers. This provides some useful background for trying to interpret the results in the work that we survey. Only after having considered these examples do we turn to the literature, studies of vulnerable groups, and especially of teens.[16] We then move on to sectoral and industry studies and end with studies of the United Kingdom.

What happens to the average wage following a boost in the minimum wage?

Consider a simple hypothetical example. Suppose we have an economy in which half the workforce earns $10.00 per hour and half earns $5 per hour. The average wage would be $7.50 per hour. Next, suppose that the minimum wage rises to $7.50 per hour. If all of the lower-paid workers remain employed and their hourly wage rises from $5.00 to $7.50, then the new average would be $8.75 per hour. However, if all bound workers were laid off, the new average wage would be $10.00 per hour. If some but not all bound workers lose their jobs, the average wage will end up somewhere between $8.75 and $10.00. The smaller the job loss, the lower the ex post average wage.

Let us now complicate this a bit and consider only teens. Assume a national labor market in which the minimum wage is $5.00 per hour, to be raised by 10 percent to $5.50 per hour. Twenty percent of teens are bound by the new minimum, earning between $5.00 and $5.49 per hour, and the remaining 80 percent earn at least $5.50 but no more than $10 per hour. Also assume that the teens are uniformly distributed within the low-wage and high-wage groupings. Under these assumptions low-wage teens are overrepresented, comprising 20 rather than the 10 percent of employment they would represent if earnings were completely uniformly distributed between $5.00 and $10.00. The average wage of the low-wage group is $5.25, the average wage of the high-wage group is $7.75; the overall average is $7.25.

What happens to the average wage when the minimum wage rises to $5.50/hour? In minimum wage studies that focus on teenagers, the elasticity of employment with respect to the minimum wage varies between 0 and −0.3, with statistically significant elasticities between −0.2 and −0.3.[17] According to these latter figures, a 10 percent increase in the minimum wage results in employment declines between 2 and 3 percent; limiting these job losses to the lowest-paid bound workers in our example implies that 10–15 percent of the low-wage labor force would lose their positions, and 85–90 percent would receive wage increases of between $0.01 and $0.39 per hour.[18] Allowing for layoffs, the average wage would rise to $7.34 when the employment elasticity is −0.2, or $7.36 when the employment elasticity is −0.3. This suggests an elasticity of the average wage with respect to the minimum wage between 0.12 and 0.15. In contrast, were all bound workers to remain employed and earning the new minimum of $5.50, the average wage would rise only to $7.30 and the elasticity would be only 0.07.

Having explored these hypothetical examples, we now turn to a realistic situation using data on teens from the 2010 CPS, when the minimum wage was $7.25, and the average wage of teens was $8.89. Forty percent of teens earned $7.99 or less, and 60 percent earned $8.00 or more. Some teens earn less than the adult minimum wage as employers may pay those under age 20 as little as $4.25 per hour for the first 90 calendar days following initial employment.[19] A 10 percent increase in the minimum wage would result in a new minimum of $8.00.[20] With a negative employment elasticity of −0.2, teens earning $6.75 or less would become unemployed, and teen employment among the bound would decline by 5.0 percent. With an employment elasticity of −0.3, teens earning $6.99 or less would lose their positions, and bound teen employment would fall by 7.5 percent.[21]

As relatively few individuals would lose their positions, more than 92 percent of those bound would benefit from the new higher minimum wage. The average wage following the 7.5 percent layoffs under the new minimum wage would be between $9.20 and $9.21. The elasticity of the average wage with respect to the minimum wage would be 0.35. Absent layoffs, the average wage would rise to $9.18, and the average wage elasticity would be 0.32; if all bound working teens lost their jobs, then the average wage would rise to $9.96, and the wage elasticity would be 1.2.

Studies of vulnerable groups

Teens. In contrast to research on employment, research on the effect of the minimum wage on wages is not as dominated by a focus on the experience on teens. Nonetheless, there are more studies of teen wages, nine in all, than any of the other groups that we review in this chapter. In all instances, higher minimum wages resulted in higher average wages. In most cases in which elasticities were provided, they were quite large.

Allegretto, Dube, and Reich (2011); Dube, Lester, and Reich (2011); Thompson (2009); Sabia (2009); Orrenius and Zavodny (2008); Portugal and Cardoso (2006); and Neumark and Wascher (2011) each use state-by-time panels or repeated cross sections to estimate wage equations in which the average teen wage is a function of state and federal minimum wages along with a set of controls (see Table 5.4). All of the studies cluster observations by state when calculating standard errors to address the issue of serial correlation and avoid downward-biased estimates of standard errors. The studies consider different time periods and use similar but not identical specifications. Sabia and Thompson both report large and significant average earning elasticities, ranging between 0.16 and 0.5 for Sabia and 0.4 and 0.6 for Thompson. (Thompson argues that the large wage effect found in his work reflects compositional change in the minimum wage labor force.) Both also report negative employment effects for employment (Sabia) or employment share (Thompson) with elasticities in the range of −0.2 to −0.3. Neumark and Wascher report a positive and significant relationship between the minimum wage and the hourly earnings, but no effect on either weekly earnings or employment.[22] Elasticity of average earnings ranges from 0.22 to 0.37 when considering all teens and teens other than Hispanic and black.[23] The positive elasticity for women is partially offset by a negative and significant interaction between the minimum wage and eligibility for the earned income tax credit. Allegretto, Dube, and Reich (2011), whose work parallels that of Sabia and Thompson but better controls for heterogeneity in spatial-employment patterns, report smaller but still highly significant earnings elasticities, with a preferred value of 0.15, and no employment effects. Dube, Lester, and Reich estimate the effect of the minimum wage on teens and on employment in eating and drinking places. Using Quarterly Workforce Indicators for

Table 5.4 The Effect of the Minimum Wage on Average Wages, Vulnerable Groups: Teens

Study	Effect	Target	Country	Sample period	Analytic approach	Unit of observation	Data structure	Type of standard error	Data set[a]
Allegretto, Dube, and Reich (2011)	The average wage elasticity ranges from 0.07 to 0.22, with a favored value of 0.149. Effects larger for women than men. No wage effect for Hispanic, but there is an effect for white, non-Hispanic, and black.	Teenagers	United States	Various	Regression	Individual-quarter	Repeated cross section	Clustered (state)	Census, BLS-EEH, ACS
Dube, Lester, and Reich (2010)									
Orrenius and Zavodny (2008)	The elasticity of the average age wage is 0.18 for teens	Teenagers	United States	1995–2005	Regression	State-year	Panel	Clustered (state)	CPS
Portugal and Cardoso (2006)	Extension of the minimum wage in Portugal (1987) to 17-year-olds and then to those 16 and younger in 1988 resulted in both higher wages and higher wage growth. Wage growth of 18–19-year-olds also raised their wages (1987)	Teenage workers	Portugal	1986–1989	Regression	Firm-worker-year	Panel	Conventional	QP

Neumark and Wascher (2011)	A positive and significant relationship with hourly earnings but no effect on weekly earnings	Women, single mothers, and less-educated women	United States	Regression	Individual-month	Repeated cross section	Clustered (state)	Various, incl. CPS

[a] BLS-EEH = Bureau of Labor Statistics-Employee Earnings and Hours. ACS = American Community Survey. QWI = Quarterly Workforce Indicators. CPS = Current Population Survey. QP = QP (Portugal) *Quadros de Pessoal* (personnel records, Portuguese Ministry of Qualification and Employment.

2001–2009, they find that higher minimum wages are associated with higher monthly earnings for teens, with elasticities varying from 0.11 to 0.14.[24] Orrenius and Zavodny estimate an average earnings equation for teens aged 16–19 as a benchmark for the effect of the minimum wage on less-educated immigrant and native-born workers. Using a state-by-year panel, reporting clustered errors 1994–2005 and including controls for business cycle effects, their estimated elasticity, 0.18, is significant in better than a 1 percent test. When separated by gender, the earnings elasticities are 0.22 for men and 0.14 for women; both are significant at the 0.01 level. Portugal and Cardoso (2006), in a study of the minimum wage in Portugal, find that extending the minimum wage to teens aged 16–17 and increasing the minimum wage of those aged 18–19 raised average wages.[25]

Each of these studies finds a positive wage effect, but three also find a negative and significant employment effect. Can these latter studies be taken as evidence that increases in the minimum wage increase the wages of individuals? As the hypothetical examples show, the estimates of the elasticity of the average wage obtained from these studies are more consistent with significant numbers of bound workers receiving a higher wage than with most of the change in the average wage resulting from the loss of employment.

The less educated. Teens are not the only group that is potentially vulnerable to the employment effects of an increase in the minimum wage. Those with less education and fewer skills have been singled out as potentially vulnerable, as have single women (see Table 5.5 for article summaries for each of these groups). Three articles address the effect of the minimum wage on the less educated, two of which—Easton (2006) and Krashinsky (2008)—find that higher minimum wages are unambiguously associated with higher earnings. Neumark and Wascher (2011), who allow for complex interactions between the minimum wage and other federal income assistance programs, find the minimum wage has a positive direct effect. The effect net of the interactions with other federal income policies is however, difficult to parse given the available information.

Running regressions on cross sections of CPS data for 1990, 1994, and 1999, Easton (2006) considers the effect of the minimum wage on the earnings of those who live in metropolitan areas and have no more than a high school education. Each regression includes controls for individual characteristics as well as the wage and industrial character-istics of the urban areas. The less educated are divided between those with less than a high school education and those whose education ended with a high school degree. The minimum wage is measured both as a level and as change from the prior minimum wage.

Estimates across all metropolitan areas are strictly positive but vary considerably with respect to statistical significance by gender, year, educational attainment, and measure of the minimum wage. However, when the sample is limited to metropolitan areas for which there are at least 36 observations, the combined effect of the two minimum wage measures in all three years is positive, large, and statistically significant in a 5 percent or better test for each gender and level of education at-tainment. The effect of the minimum wage on average wages persists for some years after the increase, although the persistence is weaker for those without a high school degree than for those with one. For men and women with less than a high school education, Easton estimates that the elasticity of the average wage with respect to the minimum wage ranges from 0.1 to 0.5. The elasticities are smaller for those with no more than a high school degree, with statistically significant estimates ranging be-tween 0.06 and 0.14. Easton provides no employment elasticities, so it is not clear who in particular benefits from higher wages.

Krashinsky (2008) finds that the decline in the real minimum wage from the late 1970s to the early 1990s reduced the earnings of less-educated men working as employees—those with a high school degree or less—relative to similarly educated men who were self-employed. In the United States, employees are protected by a range of laws regarding minimum wage, overtime, union organization, unemployment insur-ance, and workers' compensation. The self-employed are, in contrast, not subject to these laws. All else constant, changes in the labor laws should change the position of employees relative to their self-employed counterparts. Using data on white males with no more than a high school diploma for 1979–1991, the author estimates the effect of the minimum wage on the ratio of the annual median earnings of the self-employed to the annual median earnings of wage and salary workers. This is benchmarked to the corresponding ratio for men with college degrees, a group less affected by changes in the minimum wage and other labor

Table 5.5 The Effect of the Minimum Wage on Average Wages, Vulnerable Groups: Other

Study	Effect	Target	Country	Sample period	Analytic approach	Unit of observation	Data structure	Type of standard error	Data set
Easton (2006)	Higher minimum wages and growth of minimum wages were associated with higher wages among less-educated women in urban areas; only the change in the minimum wage affected men's earnings.	Less-educated workers	United States	1986, 1990, 1994, 1999	Two-stage regression allowing for spatial auto-correlation within a metro-politan area	Individuals in first stage/ MSAs with 250+ observations in second stage	Cross section	Weighted least squares	CPS ORG files
Krashinsky (2008)	The decline in the minimum wage from the 1970s to the 1990s reduced the earnings of less-educated men.	Prime-age white males, salary and wage earners vs. the self-employed	United States	1979–1991	Two-stage regression with industry fixed effects and kernel density estimates	First stage is individual, the second stage is state-industry	State-by-industry cross section	White corrected	CPS ORG, March CPS, and Census
Sabia (2008)	The elasticity of annual earnings of single mothers with less than a high school degree is close to 1 but is not	Low-income single mothers	United States	1991–2004	Regression	Individual-year	Repeated cross section	Clustered (state)	CPS

	significant when estimated for all single mothers, or women with at least a HS degree. With controls, there is no effect even for the less educated.							
Neumark and Wascher (2011)	Minimum wage is either not significant or positive, interaction with EITC and kids is positive for single women 21–44	Women, single mothers and less-educated women	United States	1976–2007	Regression	Individual-month	Repeated cross section	Clustered (state)	Various, incl. CPS

market institutions. For those without a high school degree, the ratio of the median wage of the self-employed to the median wage of wage and salary workers rose steadily in the 1980s and reached equality in 1991. This ratio also rose for those with high school degrees but did not reach equality by 1991. In contrast, the ratio fell to equality for those with a college degree. Regression estimates suggest that both the level and the change in the minimum wage between 1979 and 1991 were negatively and significantly related to the ratio both for those with less than a high school and those with a high school degree. Fifteen to 16 percent of the decline in the relative wages of the less educated of wage and salary earners can be attributed to the decline in the real minimum wage (see Table 5.6). In contrast, the minimum wage did not affect the ratio for those with some college education or a college degree.

Neumark and Wascher (2011) report that higher minimum wages increase the wages of less-educated individuals, but find there is a complex interaction with the earned income tax credit. The model, which uses CPS ORG data for individuals aged 21–44 for 1997–2006, is estimated in the state-by-year panel framework they pioneered in the NMWR and clusters errors by state. Estimates for all childless less-educated individuals suggests that the minimum wage has a positive and significant direct effect on hourly earnings. This is at least partially offset by a negative and statistically significant interaction between the minimum wage and EITC eligibility that, in its turn, may be offset by a positive interaction between the minimum wage, EITC, and having no more than a high school degree. Similarly complex patterns are found for black and Hispanic individuals and for black and Hispanic males.[26] Because of the complexity of these factors, it is not possible to be certain of the minimum wage's net effect on hourly or annual earnings.

Single women. Another group of interest to minimum wage researchers are women, particularly single women. The income of single women and especially single women with children is low relative to many other groups in the population; spells of unemployment and low earnings that place them in poverty are relatively frequent for this group. Compared to other groups, the effects of the minimum wage on the earnings of single women are less certain, with an even division of articles between no effect and a positive effect.

Table 5.6 The Effect of the Minimum Wage on Average Wages

Study	Effect	Target	Country	Sample period	Analytic approach	Unit of observation	Data structure	Type of standard error	Data set[a]
Wolfson and Belman (2004)	Increases in the minimum wage are associated with higher average wages in low-wage industries	Low-wage industries	United States	1947–1997	Regression	Industry-month	Multiple panel time series	Conventional	BLS-EEH
Belman and Wolfson (2010)	Increases in the minimum wage are associated with higher average wages in 16 of 23 low-wage industries	Low-wage industries	United States	1972–2003	Regression	Industry-month	Panel time series	Conventional	BLS-EEH
Dickens et al. (1995)	Increases in the agricultural minimum wage boost both the average wage and the wage at the lower deciles of the wage distribution	Agricultural workers	United Kingdom	1954–1991	Contemporary time series	Country (England, Wales, and Northern Ireland; Scotland), by year	Univariate time series		Variety of governmental data sources

[a] BLS-EEH: Bureau of Labor Statistics-Employee Earnings and Hours.

Studies of single women are not entirely comparable with the other studies as they consider annual earnings, rather than hourly or weekly earnings, and include those who have no annual earnings in the estimates. Sabia (2008) finds that, between 1992 and 2005, increases in the minimum wage had no effect on the annual income of either all single women or single women with at least a high school education. Higher minimum wages had a positive effect on the annual earnings of single women with less than a high school education (the estimated elasticity is 0.992), but this effect vanishes in a regression with conventional controls. Neumark and Wascher (2011) permit the minimum wage to affect the earnings of single women directly, and with interactions with the presence of children, the Earned Income Tax Credit, and both of these factors. The estimated pattern of interaction is complex both with respect to sign, magnitude, and significance. The authors summarize their findings: "These results suggest that the combination of an EITC and a higher minimum wage may be especially powerful in raising the employment and earnings of low-skilled single mothers. However, the estimates also hint at the possibility that the positive labor supply response of single mothers eligible for the EITC may reduce employment and earnings among low-educated or minority single women without children" (p. 730).[27] In some instances, the minimum wage only has an effect through an interaction with the EITC. The estimates of the elasticity of annual earnings with respect to the minimum wage of women with children relative to those without are consistently statistically significant and positive, but are quite small, likely because of the inclusion of those who report no earnings.

Summary

What preliminary summary can we make of the studies by demographic group? Of the 12 studies reviewed, all but 1 report that the minimum wage has a positive and significant effect on the measures of earnings of vulnerable groups. Further, even where there was evidence of a negative employment effect, our analysis suggests that the disemployment effect is moderate in size, and that a very substantial majority of bound workers benefit from the minimum wage increase. Our initial conclusion is that higher minimum wages raise the wage of many members of vulnerable groups, although the evidence on annual earnings of single mothers is mixed.

SECTORAL AND INDUSTRY STUDIES

Studies focused on sectors, industries, and occupations bring advantages and disadvantages. They can incorporate detail about the industries or occupations and better control for factors affecting wages and employment than typical demographic studies, which omit industry and occupational detail. Their implications are potentially more limited, as care is needed in generalizing beyond the sectors, industries, and occupations under study.

Multi-Industry Studies

While most of these studies consider particular sectors or industries, Belman and Wolfson (2004, 2010) apply time-series methods to wage, employment, and hours data to a varying set of low-wage industries (see Table 5.6 for a summary of multi-industry studies). The employment chapter presents this work in detail, and so we limit our discussion to our wage estimates. In the earlier of these studies, all but a handful of the 120 estimates of the effect of the minimum wage on average wages are positive, and about half are statistically significant in a 5 percent test or better. The median elasticity of the average wage with respect to the minimum wage is between 0.02 and 0.05, depending on the panel. The later article, which applies a more flexible estimation method to a single panel of data, and which allows for changes in hours as well as employment, produces stronger evidence for a positive relationship between the minimum wage and average wage in low-wage industries. Estimates for 16 of 23 low-wage industries are positive and significant in a 5 percent test, with elasticities that range from 0.05 to 0.4. Taken together, these estimates suggest that, although increases in the minimum wage do not affect the average wage in all low-wage industries, they boost wages in a majority of these industries.

Restaurants

The food and beverage service industry, consisting of eating and drinking establishments, has been closely studied because much of its labor force is paid close to the minimum wage (see Table 5.7).

The work on fast food establishments (Card and Kreuger 1994, 2000; Katz and Kreuger 1992) is well known. Three of the four studies of the restaurant industry that predate the NMWR find that the minimum wage increases the average wage in the industry.

Dube, Naidu, and Reich (2007) perform an analysis similar to that of Card and Krueger (1994), modified to reflect criticisms of the earlier work, of the 2004–2005 increase in San Francisco's minimum wage on the restaurant industry. The city of San Francisco increased its citywide minimum wage for midsize employers to $8.50 in 2004, exempting small employers until 2005. Using data from a sample of restaurants in San Francisco and the East Bay, the authors compare the change in wages of affected restaurants—those that are midsize with at least some employees earning less than the new minimum wage—with three comparison groups: midsize restaurants in the East Bay, small restaurants in San Francisco, and midsize San Francisco restaurants with no employees earning below the new minimum ex ante.

The models were estimated with two distinct dependent variables: 1) the average wage of the establishment, and 2) the percentage of workers at an establishment earning below $8.50, the new minimum wage (the percent below $8.50 will vary systematically by time and type of restaurant in San Fransisco and by location between San Fransisco and the East Bay). Difference-in-differences estimates of the effect of the minimum wage increase indicate that it was associated with a statistically significant increase in the average wage relative to East Bay restaurants, with an effect that was significant in a 5 percent test, and relative to midsize unaffected San Francisco restaurants, with an effect that was significant in a 10 percent test but not relative to small San Francisco restaurants.

Dube, Lester, and Reich (2010) use data from the Quarterly Census of Employment and Wages (QCEW) to estimate the effect of the minimum wage on earnings and employment in restaurants and other low-wage sectors from 1990 to 2006. Panel regressions are estimated for all U.S. counties, as well as for pairs of adjacent counties on opposite sides of state lines. This pairing is designed to control for an economic climate that is, presumably, similar in small adjacent regions. The pairings of interest are those in which the applicable minimum wages in each county of a pair differ. The pairing of counties does not have a large effect on earnings estimates; the elasticity of the minimum wage on earnings varies between 0.15 and 0.22 when models are estimated with all counties and between 0.19 and 0.23 when only paired counties are used. Significance is likewise not affected; standard errors allow for rejection of the null in better than a 1 percent test for all earnings elasticities. Further estimates find no evidence that the minimum wage spills over from one county to the wages of the other in the county pairs.

The authors broaden their paired county work on restaurants by using Quarterly Workforce Indicators for 2001–2009 to consider the effect of the minimum wage on not only average wages and employment but also on hires, separations and turnover rates by age, and type of restaurant (Dube, Lester, and Reich 2011). Panel regressions are estimated for all U.S. counties, as well as for pairs of counties that are adjacent to each other but on opposite sides of state lines. The estimated effect of the minimum wage on average wages is consistently positive and statistically significant for teens and young adults working in restaurants as well as for restaurant workers as a whole. The estimated elasticities range from 0.17 to 0.22, depending on specification and sample; the elasticities tend to be larger for estimates with paired counties than for the full sample, suggesting that omitted variable bias may be reducing the magnitude of the minimum wage effect in the all-county sample. The estimated effect on the average wage is also strictly positive and significant for both limited- and full-service restaurants for the workforce as a whole. When broken down by age, the estimates show a positive and significant effect on the wages of teens, of young adults, and of all women, but none on those of adults 25 or older, nor those of men (without regard to age).

Addison, Blackburn, and Cotti (2012) use quarterly data from the QCEW to measure the effect of the minimum wage on both limited- and full-service restaurants from 1990 to 2005. These data, which are derived from firms' unemployment insurance filings, cover 98 percent of the labor force, have far more complete coverage than any other survey, and have sufficient observations to allow the study of industries at the county level. This study demonstrates the importance of allowing for

Table 5.7 The Effect of the Minimum Wage on Average Wages: Restaurants

Study	Effect	Target	Country	Sample period	Analytic approach	Unit of observation	Data structure	Type of standard error	Data set[a]
Dube, Naidu, and Reich (2007)	The increase in the San Francisco (SF) minimum wage in 2004 increased the average wage in SF restaurants relative to East Bay restaurants and "high wage" SF restaurants	San Francisco restaurants	United States	2003–2004	Quasi experiment	Firm-year	Firm panel	Robust	Private survey
Dube, Lester, and Reich (2010)	There is a positive effect on the quarterly earnings of teens and young adults but not adults 25+ in full- and limited-service restaurants with elasticities of 0.3 to 0.5. There is a positive effect on women but no effect on men. The average elasticity ranges from 0.17 to 0.22.	Restaurants	United States	1990–2006	Quasi experiment	County-quarter	Aggregate panel with county pairing in some estimates	Clustered (state)	QCEW
Addison, Blackburn, and Cotti (2012)	Higher minimum wages are associated with higher county-industry average weekly compensation in the restaurant	Restaurants	United States	1990–2005	Regression	County-quarter	Aggregate panel	Clustered (state)	QCEW

... industry. The effect is smaller in counties with higher average wages. Weekly earnings are higher when limited to counties that had minimum wage above the federal level.

Study	Findings	Industry/workers	Location	Period	Method	Unit	Data type	Standard errors	Data source
Anderson and Bodvarsson (2005)	Servers' and bartenders' wages are increased by state minimum wages set higher than the federal level but are not benefitted by less generous tip credit rules	Servers and bartenders	United States	1999	Regression, some with selection correction	State	Cross section	Conventional	Constructed from BLS, BEA, and National Restaurant Association data
Even and MacPherson (2014)	Higher cash wages and higher minimum wages are associated with increased weekly earnings	Full- and limited-service restaurants	United States	1990:1–2011:4	Regression	State-quarter and individual-month	Aggregate panel	Clustered (state)	QCEW and CPS

[a]QCEW = Quarterly Census of Employment and Wages. CPS = Current Population Survey.

county-level trends in the estimation of the employment effect of the minimum wage. The estimates almost universally indicate that higher minimum wages are associated with higher weekly compensation among restaurant workers.[28] Elasticities in linear models vary between 0.17 and 0.22; more elaborate models suggest a nonlinear relationship between the minimum wage and compensation, as well as possible interactions between the minimum wage and both county unemployment and weekly earnings. The effect of the minimum wage on the earnings of restaurant workers was larger in limited-service than in full-service restaurants: the estimated elasticities were 0.25 and 0.14, respectively.

Food service workers may receive substantial tip income. Under federal law, employers may pay as little as $2.30 per hour to tipped employees, so long as tip income makes up the difference between this amount and the federal minimum wage.[29] Some states also allow for "tip credits," but there is considerable difference in state policies. Anderson and Bodvarsson (2005) consider the effect of state minimum wage and tip credit legislation on the hourly earnings of wait staff and bartenders. Although the authors divide the states into five categories based on the level of the state minimum wage and the state tip credit, the broad coverage of the federal minimum wage reduces this to three operative categories: those that have no requirements beyond federal requirements, those where the tip credit and/or the state minimum wage is more generous than the federal policy, and those with no tip credit but with a minimum wage above the federal level. It would be expected that servers and bartenders would have higher average wages in states that exceeded federal requirements in one dimension or another. The authors report that there is no gain in the hourly earnings of bartenders and servers in states where tip and/or minimum wage policies are more generous than the federal policy. However, with controls for selection into differing legal regimes, waitstaff and bartenders in states with minimum wages above the federal minimum (and no tip credit) are estimated to earn an additional $1.34 an hour relative to states with laws that are no stronger than the federal requirements.[30]

Even and Macpherson (2014) provide a more recent and sophisticated analysis of the effect of the minimum wage and tip credits on restaurant employees' earnings. Using quarter-by-state observations aggregated from the QCEW, they examine the response of earnings of employees of full- and limited-service restaurants to both state treatment of tipped income and state and federal changes in the minimum wage during 1990:1 to 2011:4 and 1994:1 to 2007:3.[31] The models include state demographic and economic controls and state fixed effects, and they are estimated both with and without state-specific time trends. Increases in the tipped wage are estimated to increase average weekly wages for employees in full-service restaurants, where tipping is common, but not in limited-service restaurants, where tipping is uncommon. A 10 percent increase in the tipped wage is estimated to raise weekly earnings between 0.3 and 0.5 percent. Higher minimum wages are associated with increased average weekly earnings in both full-service and limited-service restaurants. A 10 percent increase in the minimum wage is estimated to increase weekly earnings of employees in full-service restaurants by 1.3 percent and 1.5 percent, and from 1.5 to 2.2 percent in limited-service restaurants.[32]

Other retail industries in the United States

While the early NMWR focused on restaurants as a low-wage sector, more recent work has branched out to retail industries, another large employer of low-wage labor. Of the four studies of retail, three find positive wage effects, and the fourth finds large negative wage effects (see Table 5.8).

The work of Addison, Blackburn, and Cotti (2009) is particularly interesting because of its nuance and creativity in investigating the interaction between the minimum wage and other state employment laws. Paralleling their work on the restaurant industry, they consider the effect of the minimum wage on industries within retail trade, again using county-by-quarter data from the QCEW for 1990–2005.[33] Initial panel regressions indicate that the minimum wage has a positive and statistically significant effect on wages for only beer, wine, and liquor stores, with an elasticity of 0.17. With controls for county-level trends similar to those of Allegretto, Dube, and Reich (2009, 2011), there are positive earnings effects for convenience stores; specialty food stores; and beer, wine, and liquor stores but not for supermarkets or for food and beverage stores as a whole. Moving beyond food and beverage stores, they find positive earnings effects for gasoline stations, sporting goods stores, general merchandise stores, department stores, and miscellaneous store retailers.

Table 5.8 The Effect of the Minimum Wage on Average Wages: Service Industries

Study	Effect	Target	Country	Sample period	Analytic approach	Unit of observation	Data structure	Type of standard error	Data set[a]
Addison, Blackburn, and Cotti (2009)	The average wages of many sectors within retail trade increase when the minimum wage increases. There is an effect in right-to-work states but not in non-right-to-work states.	Retail trade	United States	1990–2005	Regression	County-quarter	Aggregate panel	Clustered by state	QCEW
Orazem and Mattila (2002)	Earnings elasticities are negative, ranging from −0.14 to −0.16.	Retail, service, not professional	Iowa	1989–1992	Regression	County-qtr.-industry	Aggregate panel		
Sabia (2008)	Elasticity ranges from 0.13 to 0.18 for all workers in retail; from 0.32 to 0.38 for teens.	All teens, and in retail	United States	1979–2004	Regression	State-month	Aggregate panel	Clustered (state)	CPS
Giuliano (2013)	For the 1996 increase in the minimum wage, the elasticity of the average wage with respect to the wage gap was 0.75. The effect declines over time as wage trends catch up with the minimum wage.	Teens in retail	United States	1996–1998	Regression	Establishment-period	Panel	Conventional	Private + census

[a] QCEW = Quarterly Census of Employment and Wages. CPS = Current Population Survey.

The authors take this research further by distinguishing between right-to-work and non-right-to-work states. In right-to-work states, they find that the minimum wage has a positive effect on the average wage for food and beverage stores as a whole and for supermarkets and convenience stores in particular (they did not report other industries in these estimates) but no wage effect in states without right-to-work laws. Further, for the industries under study, either the presence of unions or a union threat effect mitigates the effect of minimum wages on earnings and employment.[34] These findings suggest that state minimum wage laws interact with other state employment laws and with the institutional characteristics of state labor markets.

Orazem and Mattila (2002), Sabia (2009), and Giuliano (2013) each consider the effect of the minimum wage on retail earnings. Orazem and Mattila report a large and significant negative elasticity of quarterly earnings with respect to the minimum wage in a model using county-by-quarter and county-by-year regressions for Iowa for 1989–1992; estimated elasticities range from −0.14 to −0.16. Sabia uses a state-by-month panel for 1979–2004 to estimate the effect of the minimum wage on retail earnings and employment for the sector as a whole as well as for teens. Depending on the specification, the elasticity of the average wage with respect to the minimum wage varies from 0.13 to 0.18; the elasticity for teens ranges from 0.32 to 0.38. Guiliano's (2013) study of a single retail firm with more than 700 establishments considers the effect of the average wage gap—the proportional increase in the average wage required to bring all workers up to the new minimum wage—to estimate the effect of the increase in the federal minimum wage in 1996 on average wages. As the firm has stores in many states, wage gaps vary systematically with the state minimum wage. Guiliano reports that a 10 percent increase in a store's wage gap resulted in 7–8 percent growth in average wages over two years following the 1996 increase.

British nursing homes

The residential care home industry (nursing homes in the United States) is one of the larger low-wage industries in the United Kingdom, and, as a result, it plays a role in studies of the minimum wage similar to that of teenagers or the restaurant industry in studies of U.S. data. In 1999, the United Kingdom implemented its NMW, which has since been increased several times. Each of the three articles on care homes discussed below find that the implementation of, and increases in, the minimum wage raised wages (see Table 5.9).

Machin, Manning, and Rahmin (2003) surveyed residential care homes before and after the implementation of the NMW.[35] Care assistants are among the most common and lowest-paid workers in residential care homes; in all homes in the pre-NMW sample, 32–38 percent of them were bound by the minimum wage. On average, their earnings were 4–5 percent below the NMW. Following implementation, average earnings of care assistants rose by 6 percent. Regression estimates indicate that average hourly and weekly earnings grew faster in homes with a larger fraction of care assistants bound by the NMW, and in homes where there was a larger difference between the minimum wage and the average earnings of care assistants. Further, the growth of earnings accelerated relative to an earlier period before the NMW was implemented. The authors indicate that there was "some evidence" of reductions in employment and hours subsequent to the implementation of the NMW.[36]

Machin and Wilson (2004) extended this work with a survey of residential care homes along the South Coast of England to examine the 2001 increase in the NMW. Consistent with prior studies, they found larger increases in the average wage in homes that had more workers bound by the minimum wage during the 1999 implementation and 2001 increase in the minimum wage. In addition, there was a statistically significant decline in employment in care homes following the implementation of the NMW, but not in response to the 2001 increase.[37] The pattern of employment decline suggests that the initial increase in the average wage was due to both employment decline and an increase in wages for those bound workers who kept their jobs, but that the subsequent average wage increase reflected solely an increase in wages.

As part of a broader study of the effect of the NMW on care homes, Georgiadis (2008) revisited the same survey data on the 1999 implementation of the NMW. Regression estimates indicate that the increase in the average earnings in a care home was positively and significantly related to both the proportion of staff bound by the new minimum wage or by the wage gap—the proportional increase in earnings needed to bring all workers to the new minimum wage. Wage-gap elasticities—

Table 5.9 The Effect of the Minimum Wage on Average Wages: Studies of the United Kingdom

Study	Effect	Target	Country	Sample period	Analytic approach	Unit of observation	Data structure	Type of standard error	Data set
		Care homes							
Machin, Manning, and Rahman (2003)	Implementation of the NMW increased the average wages of care assistants, with the largest increases in homes with the largest proportion of care assistants bound by the minimum wage.	Home care	United Kingdom	1992–1999	Quasi experiment	Firm-survey response	Two-period panel	Conventional	Private survey
Machin and Wilson (2004)	Average wages of cared assistants in care homes rose most rapidly in homes with larger numbers of bound workers.	Home care	United Kingdom	1998–1999	Regression	Firm-survey response	Two-period panel	Conventional	Private survey
Georgiadis (2006)	A positive relationship between the proportion of workers bound by the minimum wage and the increase in the average wage in care homes.	Home care	United Kingdom	1999–2001		Care home	Care home by year	Conventional	Private survey

the change in average earnings associated with a 1 percent decline in an establishment's wage gap—are close to 0.9.

Summary

Research on the effect of the minimum wage on average wages is surprisingly strong, given the divided results obtained for other outcomes; higher minimum wages are associated with higher average wages. Of the 29 empirical articles on the effect of the minimum wage on average wages, 26 report that higher minimum wages or increases in the minimum wage result in a higher average wage. Nine of 10 articles on teens and vulnerable groups report a positive wage effect; the one contrary article (Sabia 2008) estimates the effect on the unconditional average annual wage as the dependent variable (that is, the average wage is calculated over all single women rather than the employed). Twelve of 14 articles on industries and sectors report that a higher minimum wage is associated with higher average wages.

This is not to assert that the effect of the minimum wage is consistent across all groups and industries. For example, Belman and Wolfson (2010) find positive and significant effects in 16 of 23 low-wage industries, suggesting that there is no effect in some low-wage industries. Addison, Blackburn, and Cotti (2009) find that the minimum wage does not affect weekly earnings of service industry employees in states without right-to-work legislation but does have a large effect in states with such laws. Sabia (2008) finds that increases in the minimum wage do not improve the unconditional annual earnings of single women. Nuance is then the order of the day. The evidence also indicates that the increase in the average wage is benefitting a substantial majority of bound workers and may raise the wages of those who were already earning more than the new minimum wage. Results from studies that consider both employment and the average wage do not suggest that the increase in the latter is simply due to job loss among bound workers. Some studies report no employment effect, but even where negative employment elasticities are found, they are consistent with large majorities of bound workers retaining their positions and receiving higher wages because of the increase in the minimum wage. Estimates of the average wage elasticity are sufficiently large that wages of workers not previously bound are, in all likelihood, also rising.

WORKERS WHO ARE BOUND BY THE NEW MINIMUM WAGE

To this point, we have considered the overall effect of the minimum wage on the wages of the whole labor force. We now consider our second question, does an increase in the minimum wage raise the hourly earnings of those who had been earning less than the new value? Differing from much of the work in this chapter and book, some of this research is descriptive, rather than organizing itself around hypotheses. The richness of the description and care taken in consideration of both employment and earnings issues make it useful for understanding the impact of the minimum wage on bound workers. All but one of these descriptive studies are from the United Kingdom. All provide strong evidence that a higher minimum wage raises the earnings of those previously bound by the minimum wage. We finish this discussion with three articles using longitudinal data to formally test the impact of increases in the minimum wage on the wages of bound workers (see Table 5.10).

Descriptive Studies

Reich and Hall (2001) describe the effects of the increase in the federal and California minimum wages from 1994 to 1999 on wages and employment. In 1994, both the federal and California minimum wage stood at $4.25. They both rose to $4.75 in 1996 and then to $5.15 in 1997. The California minimum wage rose again in 1998 to $5.75. In 1994, prior to the increase in the minimum wage, 11.7 percent of wage and salary earners in California were earning less than $5.75. In contrast, in 1999 only 3.9 percent were earning less than $5.75 (their Table 10, reprinted as Table 5.11).[38] Reich and Hall's employment analysis finds that the increase in the minimum wage did not depress employment or employment growth. Consequently, the increases in the minimum wage should have benefitted bound workers.

Was this improvement in the earnings of lower-wage Californians truly due to the minimum wage, or was it something that would have occurred regardless of changes in the minimum wage, perhaps because the California economy was booming through this period? If a strong

Table 5.10 The Effect of the Minimum Wage on Those Bound by the New Minimum Wage

Study	Effect	Target	Country	Sample period	Analytic approach	Unit of observation	Data structure	Type of standard error	Data set	Comments
Reich and Hall (2001)	Wages of those bound by the minimum wage and those at low wages were increased.	California labor force	United States	1994–1999	Descriptive	Individuals	Description statistics from successive cross sections	n/a	CPS Outgoing Rotation Group	Only provides descriptive statistics, but the magnitude of the changes and size of the samples would likely result in significant tests of appropriate hypothesis.
Burton and Dorset (2001)	But for the agricultural minimum wage, about half of English and Welsh agricultural workers would have earned less than the minimum wage.	Agricultural labor force	England and Wales	1991–1995	Regression corrected for selection	Individuals	Multiple cross sections	Selection corrected	Survey of Earnings and Hours	Study considers the effect of the Agricultural Wages Boards, a regime that has since been supplanted by the NMW.
Dickens and Manning (2004)	The imposition of the NMW raised the wage of the lowest-paid workers, about 6–7% of the labor force.	Adult population 22 and older	United Kingdom	1999–2001	Estimated density functions	Individuals	Cross section	n/a	Labor Force Survey	The NMW had no detectable effect on earnings at the 10th percentile, possibly because the initial level was deliberately set very low.

Lam et al. (2006)	Implementation and increase in the NMW caused distinct spikes in the earnings distribution.	Individuals earning within £3 of the NMW	United Kingdom	1998–2004	Descriptive	Individuals in employer survey	Descriptive statistics from cross section and longitudinal data	n/a	Annual Survey of Hours and Earnings
Butcher (2005)	Wage growth of individuals in the lower part of UK earnings distribution accelerated following implementation of the NMW.	Low-wage workers relative to balance of employed workers	United Kingdom	1998–2003	Descriptive	Individuals	Cross section	n/a	New Earnings Survey

Table 5.11 The Effects of Minimum Wage Increases in California, 1994–1999

	Percentage earning below ($):		
	5.75	6.50	7.25
1994	11.7	15.0	21.2
1995	12.8	17.9	21.7
1996	11.8	18.2	21.8
1997	10.9	16.9	20.4
1998	5.8	14.9	20.8
1999	3.9	13.7	20.6
Change 1994–1999	7.8	1.3	0.6

NOTE: The California minimum wage rose from $4.25 in 1995 to $5.75 in 1998. Reich and Hall measure change from 1995, the year prior to the first increase in the minimum wage, to 1999, the year following the increase in the minimum wage. We have recalculated the result using 1994 as the base year, as there was a bump up in the percent of workers at below $5.75 and $6.50 in 1995. By starting in 1994, we avoid using 1995, with Reich and Hall's (2001) "bump up" as a base. The choice of base year does not materially affect description of the effect of the minimum wage.
SOURCE: Reich and Hall (2001, Table 10), using data from CPS ORG.

economy were the cause of the reduction in the proportion of individuals working at very low wages, one would expect that the entire lower end of the wage distribution would have shifted up. This did not happen. The fraction of workers earning less than $6.50 declined by 1.3 percentage points from 1995 to 1999, about one-sixth the decline in the fraction below the 1999 minimum wage ($5.75), and there was virtually no decline in the percent earning less than $7.25. Reich and Hall (2001) report that while the wage at the 5th percentile of the income distribution rose by 19 percent, from $4.85 in 1995 to $5.75 in 1999, the increase at the 10th percentile was half as large, 10 percent, from $5.49 to $6.04: at the median (50th percentile) the increase was $0.37 (less than 3 percent), from $12.63 to $13.00. There was then no large, general upward movement in the lower half of the wage distribution. For bound workers, those directly affected by the new minimum wage, the shift was substantially larger than for those higher up the wage distribution.

Several Studies from Overseas

While studies of effects of the minimum wage on bound workers are relatively rare in the United States, four European studies have examined this issue. This greater interest may reflect recent changes in European minimum wage policies. In contrast with the United States, where the minimum wage has been in place for more than 70 years and has risen in modest increments in the last several decades, the British implemented an entirely new minimum wage system in 1999. Several other European countries have recently raised their minimum wages proportionally more than the United States has ever done.

Studying the earnings of English and Welch agricultural workers in 1991–1994 under the supplanted Agricultural Wage Board system, Burton and Dorsett (2001) find distinct spikes among the different grades of agricultural workers, with each spike corresponding to the minimum wage for a particular grade of worker. Forty percent of "craft" workers and 20 percent of ungraded workers earned exactly the minimum wage in their "grade" in 1991–1992. Selection adjustment is a technique that corrects for the change in the characteristics of workers caused by minimum-wage-induced job loss.[39] Using data on agricultural workers from the Survey of Earnings and Hours from 1991–1995 and making this adjustment, the authors estimate that without the minimum wage, half or more of the agricultural labor force would have earned less than the applicable minimum.[40] Based on work that was particularly attentive to limitations of United Kingdom data, Dickens and Manning (2004a) find that increases in the minimum wage increased the earnings of those directly affected, between 6 and 7 percent of the employed.

In a dramatic policy change, the United Kingdom implemented an economy-wide minimum wage, an NMW of £3.60/hour in April 1999. The NMW was further increased to £3.70 in 2001, £4.10 in 2002, £4.20 in 2003, and £4.50 in 2004. The initial NMW was intentionally set relatively low so as not to impose too great a burden on industry. Subsequent increases raised the NMW to a level at which it might be expected to affect a larger proportion of individuals. While it is unlikely that the reasons for implementation included creation of an opportunity for research, several seized this unique chance, providing detailed descriptive studies of both the implementation and initial increases in the NMW; Lam et al. (2006) and Butcher (2005), all associated with governmental organizations in the United Kingdom, report faster wage growth at the bottom of the wage distribution due to the NMW.

Using the Annual Survey of Hours and Earnings (ASHE), Lam et al. (2006) construct distributions of straight-time hourly earnings for a range of £0–£3 above the NMW for the period 1998–2004.[41] The data demonstrate increasingly large spikes at the applicable NMW following the 1999 implementation and the 2003 and 2004 increases in the NMW, as increases in the NMW affect increasing numbers of workers (Lam et al. 2006, see Figure 5.4).

There is a distinct spike at the NMW in the 1999 data, the year in which the NMW was implemented, which is higher than any other spike that year. The spike at the NMW in 2003 is also distinct but below the spikes at £5 and £6. This changes in 2004, when the spike at £4.5, the NMW, is well above any of the other spikes in the data. The spikes at the NMW are consistent with employers upgrading bound workers to, but not beyond, the required minimum wage. Lam et al.'s

Figure 5.4 Distribution of Hourly Wages in the United Kingdom, 1998–2004

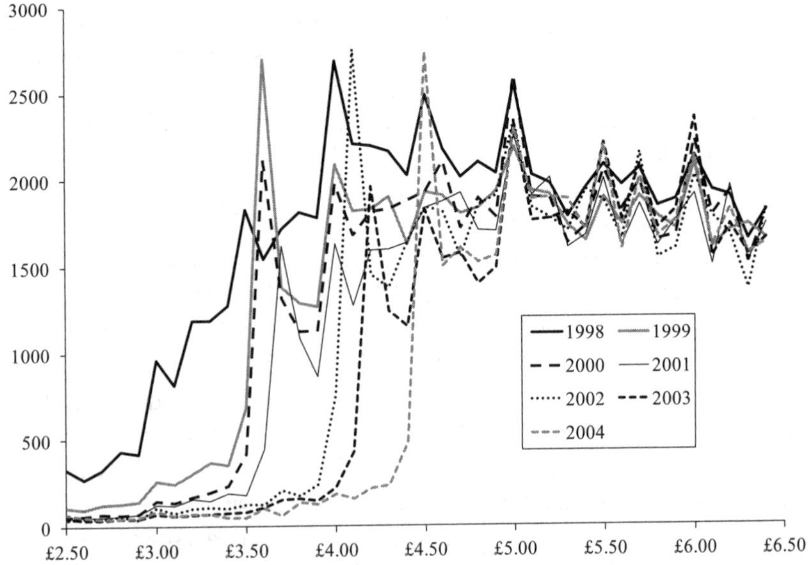

SOURCE: Lam et al. (2006).

(2006) findings are particularly interesting because they are obtained from employer data. A concern with household data is that spikes may be the result of rounding by respondents rather than the actual distribution of wages. Because data from employer surveys come from payroll records, spikes in employer data are more likely to reflect the true distribution of earnings.

Butcher (2005) takes a different approach to measuring the impact of the NMW, comparing wage growth by percentile under the NMW to wage growth in the period before implementation. Using data from the New Earnings Survey, an employer-based longitudinal survey, Butcher calculates the growth of hourly earnings, excluding overtime, throughout the earnings distribution for the period 1992–1997, prior to the implementation of the NMW, and for 1998–2003. Economy-wide economic trends are incorporated by subtracting the growth rate of the median earnings from the growth rate at each percentile in the earnings distribution. Earnings growth relative to the growth of median earnings is graphed by percentile of the earnings distribution and the period in which the NMW was implemented and increased compared to the period prior to the implementation.

Prior to the implementation of the NMW, there was a simple positive relationship between an individual's position in the earnings distribution and earnings growth. The higher one's place in the distribution, the faster one's earnings grew relative to median growth. The distinctly slower growth of those at the bottom of the distribution is apparent in Figures 5.5 and 5.6. The growth in earnings of both men and women in the lowest 10 percent of the wage distribution is notably slower than growth at the median of the wage distribution. The reduced rate of wage growth at the low end is visible up to the 30th percentile of the wage distribution. In contrast, in the period following the implementation of the NMW, wage growth at the bottom of the wage distribution is very high relative to growth at the median. It is perhaps as much as 5 percent faster than median wage growth at the 5th percentile for women, and up to the 20th percentile for both women and men, it is higher or equal to growth at the median. Parallel results are found for both part-time and full-time employees (see Figures 5.5 and 5.6), and when those employees are distinguished by gender (see Figures 5.7 and 5.8).

Although this analysis does not include measures of statistical significance or go beyond using the median to control for other conditions

Figure 5.5 Increase in Percentile Gross Hourly Earnings Excluding Overtime Minus Increase in the Median, Male Employees (Aged 22 and Over), 1992–2003

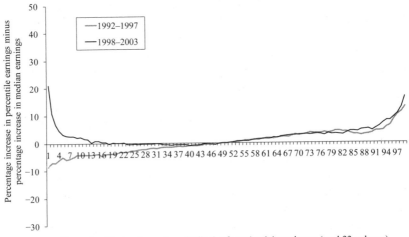

Percentile of the hourly earnings distribution for male adult employees (aged 22 and over)

Figure 5.6 Increase in Percentile Gross Hourly Earnings Excluding Overtime Minus Increase in the Median, Female Employees (Aged 22 and Over), 1992–2003

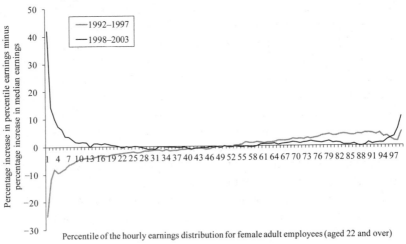

Percentile of the hourly earnings distribution for female adult employees (aged 22 and over)

SOURCE: Lam et al. (2006).

Figure 5.7 Increase in Percentile Gross Hourly Earnings Excluding Overtime Minus Increase in the Median, Full-Time Employees (Aged 22 and Over), 1992–2003

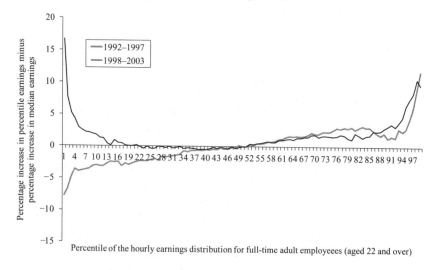

Percentile of the hourly earnings distribution for full-time adult employeees (aged 22 and over)

Figure 5.8 Increase in Percentile Gross Hourly Earnings Excluding Overtime Minus Increase in the Median, Part-Time Employees (Aged 22 and Over), 1992–2003

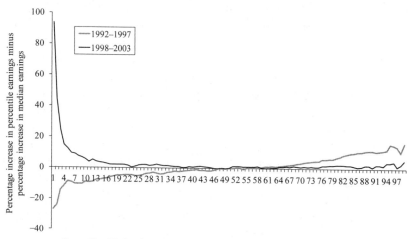

Percentile of the hourly earnings distribution for part-time adult employees (aged 22 and over)

SOURCE: Lam et al. (2006).

affecting the growth of hourly earnings, both the magnitude of the effect and its size in the lowest-earnings deciles suggest that increases in the minimum wage have a large effect on the earnings growth of those at the lowest-earnings levels.[42]

Longitudinal Studies

A challenge in measuring the effect of the minimum wage on bound workers is that most surveys do not follow the same individuals across changes in the minimum wage. As a result, although researchers are able to measure the effect of the minimum wage on similar workers prior to and after a change in the minimum wage, they rarely observe the experience of bound workers across the change. Longitudinal data, which follow individuals over time, sometimes over many years, open the possibility for following the same bound individuals through changes in the minimum wage. It also makes it possible to remove unobserved individual characteristics that may affect individuals' employability and earnings, thereby getting a better measure of the effect of the minimum wage on wage and employment outcomes. (Longitudinal studies are summarized in Table 5.12.) Currie and Fallick (1996), Zavodny (2000), and Stewart (2004b) each estimate models of the effect of the minimum wage on wages and employment with longitudinal data. While the latter two studies find that higher minimum wages are associated with higher earnings, Currie and Fallick's work, which covers a period of peak inflation in the United States, suggests either a negative or nonsignificant relationship. A synthesis of these studies provides a window into the effect of the minimum wage during periods of high and low inflation.

As part of a study of the effect of the minimum wage on the employment of teens and young workers, Currie and Fallick (1996) estimate the effect of the minimum wage on earnings. They follow individuals who were between 14 and 21 years old in 1979 through the 1979 and 1980 increases in the minimum wage. Individuals' wages, the dependent variable, are measured as the level and the change in log wage (which is a good approximation of wage growth). The wage gap, the difference between an individual's ex ante wage and the new minimum wage, is used as the measure of the magnitude of the effect of the minimum wage.[43]

Table 5.12 The Effect of the Minimum Wage on Those Bound by the New Minimum Longitudinal Studies

Study	Effect	Target	Country	Sample period	Analytic approach	Unit of observation	Data structure	Type of standard error	Data set[a]
Currie and Fallick (1996)	Increases in the minimum reduce the real earnings of bound workers.	Bound workers	United States	1979–1987	OLS and fixed effect regression	Individual	Longitudinal	Conventional	NLSY
Zavodny (2000)	Larger wage gaps are associated with larger increases in post-minimum wage increase wages. At the mean wage gap for bound workers, those who are bound have wage increases of $0.50 to $0.55 more per hour than the unbound.	Teenagers	United States	1979–1993	Regression, D-D	State-year and individual-year	Panel and longitudinal	Conventional	CPS
Stewart (2004b)	Wage growth is considerably higher for bound employees than for those earning above the NMW.	Bound workers	United Kingdom	Various	Quasi-experiment	Individual-year	Panel	Conventional	Matched LFS, BHPS, NES

[a]NLSY = National Longitudinal Survey of Youth. CPS = Current Population Survey. LFS = Labour Force Survey. BHPS = British Household Panel Survey. NES = New Earnings Survey.

Consistent with the expectations of economic theory, Currie and Fallick (1996) find that higher minimum wages reduce employment. Their initial estimates for wage increases are, on their face, counterintuitive: higher minimum wages do not affect the rate of wage change and have a negative effect on the level of the wage. This changes considerably when individuals with unusually high wage growth between any two years, 100 percent or more, are excluded from the sample.[44] With this exclusion, there is a large and statistically significant relationship between the wage gap and the change in the wage. Those with larger wage gaps have faster wage growth following an increase in the minimum wage. The coefficient on the wage-gap measure remains negative in the model in which the wage (rather than wage growth) is the dependent variable, but it is far from statistically significant. The results are, in the end, puzzling and difficult to reconcile. The authors raise some doubts about the accuracy of National Longitudinal Survey of Youth (NLSY) wage data and conclude that their estimates must be interpreted with caution, as coefficient estimates are sensitive to outliers and changes in specification.

Building on this approach, Zavodny (2000) estimates a model of employment, hours, and hourly earnings for teens between 1979 and 1993 using CPS data matched across years to create longitudinal data consisting of two observations on each person. Utilizing a specification similar to that of Currie and Fallick (1996), she finds that each $0.01 increase in the wage gap results in a $0.023 additional increase in hourly earnings following an increase in the minimum wage. Zavodny then constructs a comparison group of teens who earn close to but above the minimum wage in periods in which inflation is relatively low. She compares the effect of a minimum wage increase on this group to the effect of the increase in the minimum wage on the bound group and on a group of high-wage teenagers. She finds that while the average wage of bound teens rose by $0.57 relative to the high-wage group following a minimum wage increase, the wage of the comparison group of low-wage but unbound teens rose by $0.36 cents following the increase in the minimum wage.

Stewart (2004) also adopted Currie and Fallick's method for longitudinal models of the effect of the implementation of the NMW in the United Kingdom. Three sets of difference-in-differences, each relying on a different survey (the British Labour Force Survey, the New Economic Survey, and the British Household Panel Survey), indicate that the group of workers bound by the minimum wage increase experienced a 4–10 percent faster wage growth than a control group composed of individuals previously earning just above the new minimum wage. While the magnitude of the effect varied between surveys, results were invariant to use of a wage gap measure or a variable that simply indicated whether an individual was bound by the minimum wage (and invariant to controls for additional factors).

The three longitudinal studies point in somewhat different directions. While Currie and Fallick (1996) suggest that the minimum wage has an uncertain effect on the wages of the bound, both Zavodny (2000) and Stewart (2004) find a strong positive effect. How might these differences be explained, particularly given the similarity in methods? While it may lie in part in differences between countries, or differences in implementing and raising a minimum wage, the economic circumstances of the studies are quite different. Currie and Fallick focus on minimum wage changes during a period of rapid inflation. While this period is part of Zavodny's study, her work also includes increases in a period of stable prices. Stewart's study covers a period of price stability in the United Kingdom. Inflation is then a prime suspect; it was so rapid from the mid-1970s to the early 1980s that, in an attempt at least to keep pace with inflation, the minimum wage was raised annually for eight years. From 1979 to 1982, the period considered by Currie and Fallick, the minimum wage rose by 14 percent, consumer prices rose by 33 percent, and the wages of production and nonsupervisory workers by 25 percent. As earnings of those whose wages were determined by the minimum wage fell behind wages in the broader economy, Currie and Fallick's finding of an uncertain relationship between the wage gap, wages, and wage growth is not surprising.

In contrast, in periods of price and relative wage stability, which characterize the period studied by Stewart (2004b) and much of the period studied by Zavodny (2000), legislated increases in the minimum wage often substantially exceed price and average wage growth. In such periods, we would expect to find a positive relationship between minimum wage increases and wage growth for bound workers.

Current research does not provide a clear answer with respect to the relationship between inflation, the average wage, and the minimum wage. These three studies suggest that, in periods of moderate price inflation, increases in the minimum wage have a substantial positive effect on the wages and wage growth of bound workers, but that this does not hold in periods of rapid inflation. In such periods, those whose wages are determined by the minimum wage are likely to lag both inflation and general wage growth.[45]

Inclusive of the longitudinal studies, eight examine how the earnings of bound workers respond to the level, the increase, or the imposition of a minimum wage. Of these, seven find a positive effect and one finds a mixed effect; this last appears to be a product of a macroeconomic climate characterized by rapid inflation in which, as a consequence, the minimum wage was lagging the inflation-driven increases in the wage structure.

SPILLOVER EFFECTS

Does the minimum wage affect only those who were bound by the new minimum wage, or is there also a pay increase for those who were previously earning more than the new minimum? If it affects this group, how far up the wage distribution does it extend?

The possibility that minimum wage increases raise the wages of those already earning above the new minimum wage, referred to as a spillover effect, has been part of the discussion of minimum wages since before passage of the Fair Labor Standards Act in 1938. Why would there be spillover effects? In a neoclassical model, the wages of those earning above the new minimum may increase if these workers are substitutes for workers bound by the minimum wage. When the minimum wage rises, employers substitute capital and more productive, higher-wage workers for those whose productivity is below the new minimum. The increased demand for higher-wage workers will increase their equilibrium wage. This increase will depend on the size of the increase in demand for their labor, which in turn depends on the degree to which they are close—good—substitutes, and the degree to which their wage rises in response to the additional demand. Grossman (1983) styles this market-driven increase as an *indirect effect*, as employers are responding to market forces rather than directly to the legislated increase in the minimum wage.

Some economists—particularly those associated with the institution-alist, neoinstitutionalist, and behavioral streams of economics, but also some more neoclassically oriented—locate the source of the spillover effect in the way workers and their employers determine their appro-priate wages and in the functioning of competitive markets. Although each study—from Commons and Andrews (1916) and Webb and Webb (1897) to Dunlop (1950) and Ross (1948) and on to Grossman (1983); Falk, Fehr, and Zehnder (2006); Falk and Huffman (2007); Spriggs (1994); and Hirsch, Kaufman, and Zelenska (2011)—has a different explanation of the wage structures and linkages that underlie spillover effects, broad agreement exists that workers form their expectations of wages and wage increases through comparison with other workers.[46] The importance of comparing wages is variously attributed to work-ers' desire to maintain their social status, to psychological processes, or the method workers use to collect information about reasonable wage increases. In a world in which workers form their wage expectations from the wage improvements of a self-defined peer group, an increase in the minimum wage will cause an upward revision in the wage expec-tations of those ex ante earning not far above the new minimum wage. These higher expectations place pressure on employers, since failure to meet such expectations may result in being viewed as unfair, with con-sequences for labor efficiency and turnover (Grossman 1983, p. 360). The importance of comparison in forming a view of a reasonable wage is not limited to individual comparisons; Ross's (1948) description of "orbits of coercive comparison" and their impact on wage formation is another example of the view that comparison permeates wage setting institutions.

This logic is supported by experimental economics. The minimum wage creates a target that workers use to judge the adequacy of their wage. When everyone is assured a minimum wage, the minimum is identified as the wage that even the least capable employee is paid. Those who identify themselves as better than minimum wage workers adopt a reservation wage above the minimum wage (Falk, Fehr, and Zehnder 2006).[47] When the minimum wage is raised, employers who wish to maintain morale and productivity must raise the wages of em-ployees who use the minimum as a benchmark.

Several studies have searched for evidence of spillover effects, some in particular industries or occupations, others at the national level. Evidence on spillovers from industry- and occupation-specific studies is mixed, with the balance tending against there being meaningful spillover effects. Broader studies of the U.S. labor market suggest the presence of spillover effects, particularly for women. Studies of the United Kingdom find large spillovers for both sexes that reach a considerable distance up the wage distribution.

Industry- and Occupation-Specific Studies

If the spillover effect of the minimum wage operates through the expectations of employees who, ex ante, earn the minimum wage, then it will only appear ex post, when substantial groups of employees associate with or compare themselves to minimum wage workers. One might expect the minimum wage to have a large effect in establishments where many workers earn the minimum wage or close to the minimum wage (e.g., restaurants and fast food establishments), but little effect in establishments where the minimum wage is far from binding. Spriggs (1994) investigates this in a survey of restaurants in Greensboro, North Carolina, and Jackson, Mississippi, two states with relatively low wage structures before and after the 1991 increase in the minimum wage. (Studies of spillover effects are summarized in Table 5.13.)

The survey suggests that restaurants can be divided into three broad categories with respect to wage policies: 1) those that pay high wages and whose wage structure is not influenced by increases in the minimum wage; 2) those for which the minimum wage is a key or focal wage, and which respond to increases in the minimum wage by moving up their entire wage distribution; and 3) those that choose to minimize wage costs by increasing the wages only of those for whom it is legally required.[48] The 1991 increase in the minimum wage caused wage increases for bound workers in which the minimum wage is a key wage, and for those who view the minimum wage as a narrow legal requirement. The wages also rose for many workers in restaurants in which the minimum wage is a key wage, creating some degree of spillover in the industry. The wage difference between high-wage restaurants, which ignored the increase altogether, and low-wage restaurants declined. Overall, spillover effects dominated, and the average restaurant wage rose by between the amount that would occur if the typical restaurant increased the wage of each employee by $0.45, the increase in the nominal minimum wage, and that which would occur if the typical restaurant increased all wages by 12 percent, the proportional increase in the minimum wage (Spriggs 1994, p. 227). The increase in wages was affected by the proportion of workers below the new minimum wage but not by the average difference between bound workers' wages and the new minimum wage. Spriggs also finds that the wages of restaurants with a larger proportion of African Americans in their workforces increased less than those with a smaller proportion of African Americans.

Although primarily interested in the effect of the 2007–2009 increases in the minimum wage on employment, Hirsch, Kaufman, and Zelenska's (2011) study of three quick-food restaurant chains in Georgia and Alabama addresses issues similar to those considered by Spriggs (1994). They report that the increase in the minimum wage resulted in increased wage compression. While wages of workers bound by the increase in the minimum wage rose, employees earning more than the new minimum wage received smaller than normal (or no) wage increases. Compression was limited by the effect on the morale of the higher-paid workers, who were generally more experienced and better-performing employees. Consistent with Spriggs's research, the employees of these chains were heavily African American (64 percent).[49] Grossman (1983) studied the effect of minimum wage increases on nine blue- and white-collar occupations earning slightly above the minimum wage in 16 cities between 1960 and 1975.

Wages among white-collar workers were compressed for a time after a minimum wage increase, as lower-wage white-collar occupations realize larger increases in earnings than higher-wage white-collar workers. However, within a year and a half of the increase, the relative distribution of earnings among white-collar occupations was largely restored. Four of the six white-collar occupations realized earnings increases associated with minimum wage increases one year after the increase, and only two of the six still realized increases after an additional six months. There is no evidence that the minimum wage affects the nonproduction blue-collar occupations of laborer, janitor, and order filler.[50]

Dickens and Manning (2004a,b) find little to no evidence of spillover effects associated with the implementation of the NMW in 1999. Using their survey of care homes, they find that home care workers who earned more than the NMW prior to its implementation realized a

Table 5.13 Spillover Effects: The Effect of the Minimum Wage on Those Earning More but Close to the New Minimum Wage

Study	Effect	Target	Country	Sample period	Analytic approach	Unit of observation	Data structure	Type of standard error	Data set[a]	Comments
Falk, Fehr, and Zehnder (2006)	The minimum wage serves as a benchmark for low-wage workers and employers to set wages rather than a floor.	University students	Switzerland	Experimental in the 2000s	Regression	Individuals	Regression	Robust clustered on sessions	Data collected from 240 subjects in 10 experimental simulations	There may be an issue with non-independence of observations, as the number of reported observations, up to 5,400, substantially exceeds the number of subjects (240).
Spriggs (1994)	Increases in the minimum wage affected earnings of those above the minimum in particular types of restaurants.	Restaurant industry in low-wage areas	United States	1991 increase in the minimum wage	Regression	Restaurants	Regression	Conventional	Private survey of restaurants in two southern towns	
Hirsch, Kaufman, and Zelenska (2011)	Increases in the minimum wage resulted in increased wage compression.	Fast food market	United States (Georgia and Alabama)	2007–2009	Regression	Individual employee	Longitudinal by restaurant	Clustered	81 quick-service restaurants	

(continued)

	as employees earning above the minimum received smaller increases than those inbound.								
Grossman (1983)	Increases in the minimum wage initially causes wage compression among white-collar workers, but wage relativities are restored within 18 months.	Labor force	United States	1960–1975	Time series regression with a lag structure on wages	SMSA (metro area)	City-by-year panel	Conventional (considered appropriate at the time)	BLS Area Wage Survey
Dickens and Manning (2004a)	Very modest spillover, in the range of 1% to 2.4%.	Care home workers	United Kingdom	1999	Regression	Care home	Cross section with pre- and post-observations on care homes	Conventional	Private postal survey

Table 5.13 (continued)

Study	Effect	Target	Country	Sample period	Analytic approach	Unit of observation	Data structure	Type of standard error	Data set[a]	Comments
Dickens and Manning (2004b)	The imposition of the NMW raised the wage of the lowest-paid workers, about 6–7% of the labor force, but there was no spillover effect.	Adult population aged 22 and older	United Kingdom	1999–2001	Estimated density functions	Individuals	Cross section	n/a	LFS	The NMW had no detectable effect on earnings at the 10th percentile, possibly because the initial level was deliberately set very low.
Harvey and Bernstein (2003)	Increases in the minimum wage affect the first two deciles of the female wage distribution but not the first decile of the male distribution.	Individuals aged 18–64	United States	1979–2002	Contemporary time series	Individuals	Quarterly wage deciles derived from the CPS	Appropriate to contemporary time-series methods	CPS	
Luttmer (2007)	Increases in the minimum wage affect workers up to $1.75 above the new minimum.	Individuals aged 16–65	United States	1989–1992	Regression used to group observations by skill	Individuals	Short panels (two periods)	Robust	CPS	

Reich and Hall (2001)	An increase in the minimum wage pushes up the lower part of the wage distribution, including some earning above the new minimum.	California labor force	United States	1994–1999	Descriptive	Individuals	Description statistics from successive cross sections	n/a	CPS ORG	Only provides descriptive statistics, but the magnitude of the changes and size of the samples would likely result in significant tests of appropriate hypothesis.
Aaronson, Agarwal, and French (2007, 2011)	Increases wages of workers earning between 120 and 200% of the minimum.	Households	United States	1979–2008	Regression	Individual	Repeat cross section or longitudinal, depending on the data set	Cluster corrected by household	SIPP, CPS, and CES	
Butcher (2005)	NMW affected wages up to the third decile of the wage distribution.	Employed labor force	United Kingdom	1992–2003	Descriptive	Individuals	Series of cross sections	Conventional	NES	
Stewart (2004a)	Wage growth increases among those whose initial wage was above the NMW, but it is slower than that of bound workers.	Low-wage workers	United Kingdom	Various	Quasi experiment	Individual-year	Panel	Conventional	Matched LFS, BHPS, NES	

(continued)

Table 5.13 (continued)

Study	Effect	Target	Country	Sample period	Analytic approach	Unit of observation	Data structure	Type of standard error	Data set[a]	Comments
Lam et al. (2006)	Spillover effects were observed up to £6.50 for minimum wage increases of up to £4.50.	Adult workers aged 22 or older	United Kingdom	1998–2004	Descriptive statistics and regression	Individual	Series of cross sections	Conventional (uncertain)	Annual Survey of Hours and Earnings	

[a] LFS = Labour Force Survey. CPS = Current Population Survey. ORG = Outgoing Rotation Groups. SIPP = Survey of Income and Program Participation. CES = Consumer Expenditure Survey. NES = New Earnings Survey. BHPS = British Household Panel Survey.

substantial wage gain afterwards, between 6 and 8 percent. However, once adjustment is made for normal wage growth, estimated spillover effect ranges between 1 and 2.5 percent; the lower estimate is not statistically significant in even a 10 percent test. In their work with national United Kingdom data (2004b), they report that despite an increase in the earnings of those bound by the NMW due to its implementation, there was not a statistically significant spillover effect. They conclude that the NMW had little effect on the overall wage distribution because relatively few employees were directly affected.

If firms' wage distributions change differently in response to increases in the minimum wage, even within an industry, as Spriggs suggests, what additional issues need to be addressed in investigating spillover effects? One is whether there is evidence of broad spillover effects throughout the labor market. Is it isolated to a few firms or industries, or does it substantially affect the wages of many of those earning above the new minimum wage? If there is a spillover effect, where are we likely to find it? Which workers are likely to gain from spillovers, and which firms are likely to increase the wages of their employees who were previously earning more than the new legally mandated minimum? Finally, how high up the wage distribution do spillover effects reach? No one article addresses all of these questions, but answers can be synthesized from the articles that address some of these issues.

The U.S. Experience

Many studies limit their inquiry to specific industries or occupations, but several consider national wage structures. Harvey and Bernstein (2003) consider the impact of the minimum wage on the trends in hourly wage deciles from 1979 to 2000 using modern time-series methods. They find a wage spillover effect in the first and second deciles of the female wage distribution but no evidence of a spillover even within the first male decile. Luttmer's (2007) examination of the effect of the minimum wage on employment by skill group finds that the 1990–1991 increase in the federal minimum wage to $4.25 resulted in higher rates of wage increase for workers whose ex ante wage was as high as $6 per hour (see Figure 5.2 and discussion). Reich and Hall (2001, Table 10) provide evidence for both spillover and compression (a narrowing of wage differences) following the rise in the minimum wage to $5.75 in the mid-1990s.

This suggests that although the bottom of the California wage structure moved up considerably between 1995 and 1999, there was little or no movement of wages above the top of the 2nd decile (20th percentile). Any spillover effects were occurring within the first two deciles.[51]

Aaronson, Agarwal, and French (2011) find that minimum wage increases are associated with detectable increases in the earnings of workers making between 120 percent and 300 percent of the minimum wage.[52] The authors analyze the Survey of Income and Program Participation (SIPP) for 1986–2007, the CPS for 1979–2007, and the Consumer Expenditure Survey for 1983–2008. The estimate models of family income in which pretax nonasset income is determined by leads and lags on the effective minimum wage (the higher of the state or federal minimum wage), a fixed family effect, and dummies for year and quarter.[53] The regressions are also organized by the proportion of family income originating from minimum wage employment: those with no minimum wage income, those with some family income (but less than 20 percent) originating from minimum wage employment, and those families for which at least 20 percent of family income originates from minimum wage jobs. Although this research considers the effect of the minimum wage on family income rather than individual earnings, the link between individual earnings and family income is sufficiently direct and these results sufficiently useful in understanding of the effect of the minimum wage on earnings to consider in this part of the review.

Aaronson, Agarwal, and French (2011) report, unsurprisingly, that the income of families with no income from the minimum wage is not affected by changes in the minimum wage. When the sample is limited to families with some of their income originating from a minimum wage job, the average effect was $255 per quarter, significant in a 1 percent test.[54] When limited to families that obtain at least 20 percent of their income from minimum wage employment, the weighted average effect was $209, again significant in a 1 percent test.

More relevant to the measure of spillover effects, the models differentiate among families that receive income from an adult earning an hourly wage within 120 percent of the new minimum, and between 120 and 300 percent of the new minimum. They further subdivide this latter broad category into smaller bands of 120–200 percent and 200–300 percent of the new minimum.[55] Considering families that have at least some income from the minimum wage and an adult earning between 120 and 300 percent of the highest applicable minimum, the weighted average effect is small in magnitude, $58 per quarter, and does not satisfy a 5 percent significance test. Similar results are obtained when the estimates are limited to families that obtain at least 20 percent of their income from minimum wage employment. When this group is divided into those earning 120–200 percent and 200–300 percent of the minimum, the effect estimated for the latter group is very small in magnitude and far from being statistically significant. The effect of a higher minimum wage on families with members earning 120–200 percent of the minimum wage are both larger and statistically significant. Higher minimum wages are associated with an additional $110 per quarter for families with some minimum wage income, and $123 higher for families for which a minimum wage job provides at least 20 percent of family income. Both weighted estimates are significant in a 5 percent test. If we convert these findings from "individuals' wages as a percent of the minimum" to "percentiles of the wage distribution (for those who are not enrolled in high school or college)," the group earning no more than 120 percent ($6.18) of the minimum wage in 2000 composed 8 percent of the employed population, while those earning 120–200 percent ($10.30) of the minimum wage composed an additional 30 percent of the employed workforce. In this study, the effect of the minimum wage reaches beyond the first decile, but not as high as the fourth decile, of the wage distribution.

The United Kingdom Experience

Butcher (2005) finds that the NMW affected the growth of wages of men and women up to the third decile of the earnings distribution. While wage growth of the first three deciles of the British wage distribution was less than the growth of the median wage between 1992 and 1997, it exceeded that figure from 1998 to 2003. The gain in wage growth was larger and it extended further up the wage distribution for full-time than for part-time employees.

According to Stewart's (2004a) study of the introduction of the NMW in 1999, wage growth among bound workers accelerated substantially following implementation. Wage growth among those who were ex ante earning more than the NMW, between £4.00 and £5.00, also accelerated following implementation, but by a smaller amount. There is some ambiguity about the effect on those whose ex ante wages were between £3.60 and £4.00.

Lam et al. (2006) find that spillover effects reached as high as £6.50 following the implementation of the NMW in 1999 and its subsequent increases through 2004. In the absence of a spillover effect, ongoing increases in the minimum wage would gather an increasing fraction of the labor force in a spike at the new minimum.[56] However, the spike at the minimum wage that occurred with the imposition of the NMW in 1999 did not become ever larger with successive increases in the minimum. Instead, the spike represented a relatively constant proportion of the population with low earnings throughout the increases in 2001–2004. Following the 2003 and 2004 increases, the distribution of earnings above the NMW remained similar to that observed after the 1999 imposition of the NMW.

The clumping of observations at focal values of earnings, such as between £1.00 and £1.50 more than the NMW, remained roughly similar in 2003 and 2004 to what it had been in 1999. The fraction of workers at round numbers such as £5.00, £5.50, and £6.00 becomes more marked over time with the upward movement of the NMW, suggesting that the earnings structure was stable relative to the NMW, with earnings above the minimum rising with the successive increases in the minimum.

Further evidence that the low-wage market as a whole adjusts to increases in the minimum wage is provided by regressions for individuals earning up to £2.00 more than the contemporaneous value of the NMW. The greater an individual's wage relative to the contemporaneous value of the NMW, the larger his relative wage in the following year. For example, those earning £1.00 more than the NMW in 1999, 2000, 2001, and 2003 were, on average, earning between £1.25 and £1.50 above the new value of the NMW in the following year. Those at £1.50 more than the minimum in those years earned, on average, between £1.70 and £2.10 in the following year. Lam et al. (2006) report that the likelihood of receiving a wage increase of a given size relative to the value of the NMW in the following year stays constant over time, providing additional evidence that the minimum wage serves as a benchmark for the lower part of the wage distribution.[57]

Summary

In the modest number of studies of spillover effects, the reported outcomes are less cohesive than those of studies of the average wage or wages of bound workers. Of the 10 nonexperimental studies, 8 report at least some evidence of spillovers at or above the 10th decile of the earnings distribution. The magnitude of spillovers, how far they extend up the wage distribution, and the groups, occupations, and industries where they exist, are less certain. There is broad evidence of spillovers in the United States. Aaronson, Agarwal, and French (2011) and Luttmer (2007) both find spillovers for employed workers. Harvey and Bernstein (2003) report a spillover effect up to the 3rd decile for women, but no spillover effect for men. Spriggs (1993–94) finds evidence of spillovers for U.S. restaurants, and Grossman's work suggests spillovers for some white-collar occupations for a year following the increase.

The evidence for the United Kingdom is mixed, with disagreement over whether the introduction of the NMW spilled over into the wages of those not directly affected. Dickens and Manning (2004) find no spillovers in their national data and very small effects in their care home data. Stewart (2004a), Lam et al. (2006), and Butcher (2005) each suggest some spillover in response to implementation. Research on later increases by Lam et al. and Butcher provide considerable evidence of spillovers as the NMW continued to rise in 2003 and 2004.

It then appears that spillover effects occur, but we are uncertain about what groups realize spillover effects, which demographic groups, occupations and industries they are likely to affect, or the magnitude of the increase in the minimum wage that would initiate spillovers. It may be that, as both Spriggs and Grossman suggest, more detailed studies of specific wage and employment structures are needed to determine when and where spillovers occur.

CONCLUSION

We began this chapter with three questions about the effect of the minimum wage on wages: 1) does the minimum wage affect the earnings of bound workers, 2) are there spillover effects, and 3) does the minimum wage affect average wages? Summed over the three classifications of articles, and permitting double counting where articles address multiple issues, 37 of 41 studies of average wages, bound workers, and spillovers reviewed in this chapter indicate a positive relationship between the minimum wage and some aspect of wages.

Although the results are not one-sided, the preponderance of evidence is that higher minimum wages raise the wages of both bound workers and workers who had previously been earning above but close to the new minimum. Average wages are almost always estimated to rise in response to increases in the minimum wage. Even where higher minimum wages are found to cause the loss of jobs, large majorities of bound workers benefitted from the increase in the minimum wage. The impact of spillovers varies considerably by study, but they may reach as high as or beyond the 20th percentile of the wage distribution.

Several patterns emerge from this research. First, minimum wages and minimum wage increases have a greater impact on women than on men. Minimum wage increases are estimated to reach further in women's wage distributions than men's. Some studies indicate that up to 20 percent of women are affected by increases in the minimum wage, but likely only 10 percent of men. This result should not be surprising given the lower earnings of women, but the difference in the fractions of women and men affected is very large. The minimum wage is then particularly important to women's earnings.

Second, there is evidence that the effect of the minimum wage has become more complex over time in the United States. While at one time the minimum wage was the entry wage for many workers, it has evolved into a benchmark used to establish an acceptable entry wage for workers who have completed their schooling. The spike in the wage distribution that was formerly at the minimum wage is now somewhat above the applicable minimum wage. As Falk, Fehr, and Zehnder (2006) suggest, this change is consistent with workers' seeing the minimum as the wage paid to anyone who is employable. Inducing more than minimal work effort from employees requires the employer to demonstrate that employees are not viewed as plain vanilla minimum wage workers, by paying more than the minimum. This change in the psychology of the minimum wage might be caused by the decline in its real value over the last 50 years. What was once a substantial wage is now too low to call forth effort in jobs in which employee effort is important, and this, in turn, transforms the minimum wage into a benchmark rather than a true floor.

There is also diversity and richness in the results, particularly when specific industries and occupations are considered. Spriggs (1994) suggests that restaurants' response to increases in the minimum wage depend on their work organization and salary structure. Further, restaurants that have found other ways to achieve productivity goals increase only the wages of bound workers when the minimum wage increases. This parallels the finding that the implementation of the NMW only moved bound workers at care homes up to the NMW and did not affect the wages of those earning above the NMW (Dickens and Manning 2004a).

The implication is that differences in the work organization of low-wage firms lead to differences both in response to increases in the minimum wage, and in the number of workers affected by those minimum wages. Similarly, Belman and Wolfson's (2004, 2010) work suggests that the average wage of many low-wage industries rises in response to increases in the minimum wage, but that this is not universal. Besides finding differences in the wage response of detailed industries within the food and beverage industry, Addison, Blackburn, and Cotti 2009) find differences in the impact of the minimum wage on wages between states with and without right-to-work laws.

Notes

1. An additional problem, mentioned in Chapter 3, is that the CPS does not collect hours data for those who report that their hours vary, that is, that they have no usual hours. A measure of the wage, and thus of hourly earnings, is still available for those who report being paid hourly. It is not possible, however, to calculate hourly earnings for those who are both paid by the week or month and report variable usual hours.

2. When based on data gathered from the employee in a household survey such as the CPS, the earnings distribution exhibits spikes not seen in data gathered from employers and tax records—that is, data gathered from employees are less smooth and more concentrated at certain values. It is believed that this is due to rounding or the use of proxy respondents. Figures gathered from tax or employer records are considered to be more accurate. In the United States, spikes appear in household survey data at even dollar amounts or figures evenly divisible by $0.25.

3. We abstract from diminishing marginal returns for this example. In a more realistic world, in which the reduction in the workforce resulted in rising productivity, some of the previously bound workers would remain employed as the marginal product of the labor force rose in response to layoffs.

4. A third possibility is that no workers are bound by the increase in the minimum wage. In this instance, an increase in the minimum wage would have no effect on employment, and neither wage rates nor earnings would be affected. Economic theory suggests that, if labor demand curves are neither infinitely elastic nor completely inelastic, then there will be a mix of some layoffs and some bound workers moving up to the new minimum wage.

5. In addition, finding a wage effect is necessary for there to be an employment effect. If the minimum wage doesn't have a detectable effect on wages, then we would not expect it to affect employment. We return to the effect of the minimum wage on the average wage in the next section of the chapter.

6. Or between high- and low-minimum-wage locations.

7. The tables are computed from the Outgoing Rotation files of the Current Population Survey. The tables use wage rates for individuals who report being paid by the hour, and average hourly earnings when samples include both those paid by the hour and those paid on some other basis.

8. The organization of the data in Tables 5.1 and 5.2 does not allow us to adjust for those instances in which the state minimum wage exceeds the federal minimum.

9. The federal minimum wage was $7.25/hour in 2010.

10. Because the minimum wage is supposed to be the lowest wage that can be paid to employees, the reader deserves some explanation of the less than minimum wage grouping. We use the applicable federal minimum wage for Tables 5.1 and 5.2, and certain groups of employees, domestics, those in agriculture, and those working for small firms that are deemed not to be engaged in interstate commerce, can be paid less than the minimum wage. The federal minimum wage for tipped workers permits part of the value of the tips received to be counted against the employers' minimum wage requirement. As a result, employers only need to pay tipped employees $2.30 per hour, so long as their tips make up the difference between $2.30 and the applicable minimum wage. Mistakes in reporting by tipped employees, in which these employees only report the employer portion of their pay, and employees' reluctance to inform employers when tips do not fully top up the earnings of tipped employees, is another source of individuals' reporting earnings less than the minimum wage. Finally, not all employers obey the law and pay the full minimum to their employees.

11. The estimates with wage rates are visually similar to those obtained using average hourly earnings. For all figures, the data used in their construction run from August through July. Because the data in the CPS refer to a week in the middle of the month, the data for the year preceding the 2007 increases do not straddle that increase.

12. The parameters for the kernel density smoothing are taken from Neumark, Schweitzer, and Wascher (2004).

13. At this time, only Alaska and Connecticut had state minimum wages in excess of the $3.35 federal minimum. Alaska's minimum was $3.85, and Connecticut's was $3.37, $0.02 above federal minimum.

14. As a mathematical possibility, increases in the wages of low-paid workers and decreases in those of higher-paid workers can offset each other to leave the average wage unchanged. The literature offers neither evidence nor explanation for such an outcome, so we do not take it up.

15. In this review of the literature, we generally do not discuss articles in which the empirical results were found to be suspect. These include Böckerman and Uusitalo (2009); Neumark and Nizalova (2007); Neumark, Schweitzer, and Wascher (2004); and Pereira (2003). In addition, we mention, but do not place great weight on, state-by-time panels that do not cluster their errors by state and find a significant relationship between the minimum and average wage.

    This is not the case for state-by-time panels that do not cluster and do not find an effect. As discussed in the employment chapter, the downward bias in the estimate of standard errors results in rejecting the hypothesis of no effect too frequently. Given the bias against finding "no effect," such studies can dependably be used when the hypothesis of no effect is not rejected.

16. The differences between studies are sufficient that, even with topical grouping, it is difficult to argue we are making an apples-to-apples comparison. However, the flavor and color are sufficiently similar within topics that an orange-to-tangerine comparison is possible.

17. The −0.2 to −0.3 range is the top of the range obtained from the older minimum wage research. Using this high a figure, which is considerably larger in magnitude than obtained from the new minimum wage research, suffices for the current computation work.

18. If we suppose that those bound workers who are laid off were all previously paid less than those who kept their jobs, then those who had been earning $5.10 or less lose their positions, when the elasticity is −0.2. With an elasticity of −0.3, those who had earned no more than $5.15 lose their jobs. The maximum wage increase for those retaining their positions is then $0.39 per hour.

19. See http://www.dol.gov/whd/regs/compliance/whdfs32.htm (accessed August 9, 2012).

20. Actually, $7.98, but we use $8.00 for simplicity.

21. We assume that all currently employed teens will complete their 90 days of employment at the youth subminimum wage and, if they remain employed, have their wage increased to the full adult minimum wage. We also assume that teens will be laid off in order from lowest to highest paid.

22. The lack of any effect on weekly earnings is likely related to including the unemployed and those not in the labor force in the calculation of weekly earnings, and defining those individuals' weekly earnings to be zero.

23. Although there is still no employment effect for male or female black or Hispanic teens, the minimum wage is *negatively* and significantly associated with average hourly earnings and very negatively associated with average weekly earnings for males. For black or Hispanic women, a higher minimum wage is associated

with higher average hourly earnings, but it does not affect weekly earnings except through a negative interaction with the EITC.

24. When the model is estimated for teens who have been employed for more than one quarter, there is not a statistically significant effect on monthly earnings for the all-county sample but a positive and significant effect when controls for omitted economic variables in spatially separated countries are implemented.

25. Other studies also find that a higher minimum wage is associated with higher average wages for teens (Burkhauser, Couch, and Wittenburg 2000; Campolieti, Gunderson, and Riddell 2006). However, as the errors are not clustered, we cannot tell whether their findings pass a 5 percent test for statistical significance.

26. The minimum wage generally is positively related to employment, but its interaction with the EITC is negatively related to employment for less-educated individuals who are not eligible for the EITC. The minimum wage is found to have a positive effect on weekly earnings, where weekly earnings includes nonworking individuals who are assigned a zero for earnings, but the interaction between the minimum wage and EITC is strongly negative. In net, the authors calculate that a 10 percent increase in the minimum wage has no effect on weekly labor earnings.

27. Because Neumark and Wascher (2011) use the logarithm of the wage as their dependant variable, they assign values of $1 to hourly earnings for those who have no earnings because of unemployment or not being in the labor force. Sabia (2008) follows this approach in including those who are not employed in his estimates of annual income.

28. The QCEW provides data on quarterly payroll inclusive of direct hourly pay, overtime, tips, bonuses, stock options, and employer contributions to retirement funds. Payroll is divided by total employment during the quarter to provide a measure of average (weekly) earnings per employee. As such, the compensation measure used in this study is considerably broader than the typical measure of earnings.

29. When first applied to restaurant employees, employers of tipped employees were required to pay half of the minimum wage to employees, if the balance were made up by tip income. However, since the 1990s, the minimum required pay for tipped employees has remained at $2.30. This may reflect the influence of the restaurant and bar industry in obtaining a quid pro quo for not strongly opposing increases in these requirements.

30. There is a positive but nonsignificant effect in models that do not allow for selection. Anderson and Bodvarsson's (2005) approach to classification, which mixes the tip credit and level of the minimum wage laws, makes it difficult to distinguish the effect of these two aspects of minimum wage policy. In addition, the data are a cross section of states for 1999 with two observations per state, one each for servers and bartenders, so there are only 100 observations that are pairwise nonindependent. Standard errors are then likely to be large relative to other studies reported in this review and may be mismeasured, as the nonindependence is not accounted for.

31. The shorter sample excludes the recessions at the beginning and end of the longer sample.

32. A limitation of this study is the failure to allow for the time-series structure of the QCEW data. It assumes that effects are contemporaneous and that there is no inertia in economic processes. Although the clustering of the standard error by state addresses the issue of serial correlation, equally important issues with unit roots and cointegration are not addressed.

33. As the standard errors are clustered by state, there are not issues of an underestimate of standard errors.

34. An advantage of the QCEW is illustrated in these latter estimates. The county-level detail provides many more observations than the more frequently analyzed state-by-time panel, and this detail may be critical to obtaining precise estimates of the interaction between the minimum wage and right-to-work laws.

35. Earlier work on the effect of minimum wages in the United Kingdom includes Machin, Manning, and Rahman (2003), who report that between 1950 and 1980, the elasticity of average earnings with respect to the minimum wage was 0.4–0.5 in England and Wales and 0.6–1.0 in Scotland and Ireland, with no effect on employment.

36. Wage data from the 1999 survey were reanalyzed as part of a study on the effect of the implementation of the NMW on care home profitability and survival (Draca, Machin, and Van Reenen 2011). The authors report that the implementation of the NMW had a large positive effect on average wages, and that a 10 percent wage gap was associated with an 8.86 percent increase in the average wage in a regression with controls. The magnitude of wage change was substantially larger than in an equivalent period in which there was no increase in the minimum wage (pp. 13–14).

37. Although the authors do not suggest this, the pattern is consistent with there being a "shock" effect associated with the implementation of the new wage—firms reconfigure their workforces in response to the initial implementation of new labor regulations. However, the reconfiguration is a one-time event, and further increases in the minimum wage do not result in as large a displacement of workers.

38. Reich and Hall (2001, p. 9) indicate that the spike associated with the minimum wage moved up with increases in the minimum wage.

39. Economic models suggest that the least-productive individuals would not be employed when a sufficiently high minimum wage is in place because their marginal product would be less than the minimum wage. If the wage equation were straightforwardly estimated with only the currently employed, it would be biased by the exclusion of the lower-productivity workers and would provide an inaccurate estimate of the wage equation that would apply if the lower-productivity workers remained employed. Selection correction allows estimation of a wage equation appropriate to the workforce that would be employed in the absence of a minimum wage.

40. Burton and Dorsett (2001, Figure 3) provide data for the income distribution without a minimum wage but do not calculate the proportion of the labor force that would be earning less than the minimum. Examination of the figures suggests that half or more of the labor force would have earnings below the minimum. The

absence of formal testing of the effect of the minimum wage on the estimated proportion earning below the minimum is a limitation of this study.

41. Wage rates are straight-time hourly pay.

42. The evidence that the effect on wage growth extends as far up as the 20th percentile of earners will be addressed in the section on wage spillovers.

43. The wage-gap variable takes a value of zero if the individual's wage is equal to or greater than the new minimum wage. Currie and Fallick (1996) do not indicate whether they use the wage rate or hourly earnings measures for their wage and wage-gap calculations.

44. Currie and Fallick (1996) find that excluding the small number of high-growth outliers greatly affects the regression coefficients but not the standard errors (pp. 415–416).

45. This is similar to the finding that union/nonunion wage gaps close during periods of inflation and tight labor markets, when market-determined nonunion wages move upward rapidly while contractually determined union wages adjust slowly.

46. A detailed and useful explication of, broadly defined, institutional economists' views of the minimum wage and the role it plays in labor markets and the economy is found in Kaufman (2007). It explicitly develops Commons's, Perlman's and many less well-known institutionalists' views. This article is recommended for those who are interested in a deeper understanding of theories of economics as these apply to labor markets and a thoughtful contrast between neoclassical and other economic theories with regard to the minimum wage. It is particularly enlightening in developing the institutional economists' self-understanding that they were explicating the framework within which neoclassical markets operated, rather than developing an alternative to a neoclassical theory.

47. Experimental research also indicates that the effect of minimum wage boosts are not reversible—once the minimum wage has created a standard for the wage, removal of the minimum wage does not automatically reduce workers' expectations about an appropriate wage.

48. Spriggs (1994) speculates that there may be a group of low-wage-restaurant firms that can maintain productivity without maintaining their intra-firm wage structure.

49. Hirsch, Kaufman, and Zelenska (2011) find considerable evidence that these restaurants adjust employment in ways consistent with institutionalist views. While part of the adjustment took place through modest increases in prices, a considerable part of the adjustment resulted from taking advantage of reduced turnover and improved human resource practices. The latter, in particular, is consistent with a shock effect.

50. Grossman (1983) notes that this must be taken with some caution, as the data set is small and the standard errors are large. The techniques used in this study, appropriate for when it was conducted but currently dated, also suggest the need for caution in interpreting these findings.

51. Reich and Hall (2001) investigate and reject the hypotheses that increases in the minimum wage adversely affected employment. Their observed change in the wage distribution was therefore not due to truncation.

52. We also cite estimates provided by the authors but not incorporated into the paper.

53. Families are referred to as *units* in this study; we use the term *family* for clarity about the "unit of observation."

54. Aaronson, Agarwal, and French (2011) estimate their models with three different surveys and report the estimates from each survey and calculate a cross-survey weighted estimate and standard error. We report the cross-survey effect, as this uses the largest sample and greatest range of data. The estimated effect based on data from the CPS declines from $311 to $218 per quarter when the sample is restricted to families receiving at least 20 percent of their income from minimum wage jobs. There is also a modest decline in the CEX coefficient but an increase in the coefficient for the SIPP, which becomes significant in a 10 percent test.

55. For the purposes of measuring spillover effects, treating those earning up to 120 percent of the minimum wage as minimum wage workers potentially results in some spillover effects being attributed to those earning the minimum wage. We thank Aaronson, Agarwal, and French (2011) for providing their estimates of the effect from 120–200 percent, and 200–300 percent of the new minimum, as these do not appear in the 2011 version of the paper.

    The estimates of these effects are sensitive to the period under study. In the prior paper, in which data series ended in 2005 rather than 2008, CPS estimates ranged from $336 to $419, and SIPP estimates ranged from $195 to $210, both with statistically significant estimates in a 5 percent test. In this study, the CPS estimates ranged from $45 to $83, with the lower estimate far from significant; SIPP estimates ranged from $110 to $123 and were significant in a 1 percent test.

56. Inflation was very low during this period, averaging 1.2 percent annually. Any effect it had on upward movement of the lower part of the wage distribution was likely to be very small and would not substantially complicate this descriptive analysis.

57. As these changes are not compared to wage growth prior to the implementation of the NMW, it was unfortunately not possible to distinguish the portion that might be attributed to "regular" wage growth from that attributable to spillover effects.

6
Human Capital

While research on the minimum wage most often examines its consequences for employment and wages, the minimum wage also potentially affects decisions about schooling, training, and the provision of nonwage benefits. The largest body of research on these decisions considers the effect of the minimum wage on education and training—the accumulation of human capital. Behind this is the concern that teenagers may discontinue their education to pursue the improved earnings afforded by increased minimum wages, and that employers will reduce the training they provide to employees. Furthermore, a reduction in the development of skills might have negative consequences for individuals and society, as it would reduce future productivity and earnings, particularly for low-wage workers.

This concern originates in the predictions of human capital theory. Individuals' productivity—their capacity to produce goods and services—is closely related to their knowledge, skills, and abilities. Although some part of an individual's productivity is associated with innate abilities, their productivity can be increased through education, training, and work experience. This investment requires both time and money, and individuals' choices about investing in themselves through education and training can be framed in a fashion parallel to investing in physical capital. Developing human capital has a direct cost: money invested in education and training, and an indirect cost, the earnings and output forgone while the individual trains. The gain from these costs is the increase in future output and earnings associated with improved human capital. With this conceptualization of education and training, the logic used to evaluate investments in physical capital can be applied to investments in human capital. It is possible to compare the costs of a particular investment in human capital to the discounted increase in income associated with the investment. Alternative investments in human capital can be compared to one another, and to the returns from an investment of the same resources in other markets. One might, for instance, compare the return on a college degree with the income that would otherwise be earned from starting work after high school.

Human capital theory can be used to evaluate the effects of social policies on human capital formation and economic welfare. For example, laws that limit the types of work in which children can engage alter the returns to leaving school at a young age. As children's employment opportunities are restricted, and their wages decline with the demand for their labor, the cost of remaining in school declines, and returns to continued investment in human capital rise. This would, in turn, result in increased school attendance, the development of additional human capital in society as a whole, and perhaps in an increase in national income in the long term. A wide range of government policies, including those on college loans and grants, training, and subsidies to educational institutions, affect individuals' and firms' returns to investments in human capital and their choices about such investments. By altering the wages individuals and firms face, labor market policies change the costs and returns to investments in human capital, possibly in a complex fashion.

The effect of an increase in the minimum wage on the accumulation of human capital cannot be derived from theory alone. An increased minimum wage may tempt low-performing high school students to leave school because of the greater income available from working. If employers are, however, less willing to employ teenagers at the new higher minimum wage, the reduced likelihood of employment may instead cause the teen to reassess the decision to leave high school. A minimum wage increase may cause a high school graduate to forgo further education and training or may provide the income needed to support improvements in their human capital. As theory does not posit a certain outcome, the effects of changes in the minimum wage on human capital are, in the end, an empirical issue.

THE LOGIC OF INDIVIDUAL AND FIRM INVESTMENT IN HUMAN CAPITAL

Both individuals and firms invest in human capital. The issues facing individuals and firms are different, and we develop the individual's decision before turning to the firm's decision. For the individual, the decision about investing in human capital, either in the form of education or more specific training, is one of comparing direct and indirect current costs in the present with the discounted increase in future income. The costs associated with investment in human capital are both the direct costs of the training and the income that is forgone as training time displaces paid employment. The gains are the improved earnings realized by the individual in the future. Because the gains are in the future, they need to be discounted to reflect their current value. In making decisions about investing in themselves, individuals compare the costs of obtaining a particular form of human capital to the discounted gain in earnings associated with that investment. If the net benefit is positive, it is economically rational to undertake the investment. However, before deciding on a course of action, individuals will compare various human capital investments and choose among them based on their net return, their rate of return, and other relevant criteria, choosing the one providing the largest net benefit.

Firms also invest in human capital to improve the productivity of their employees and processes. Such investments make the firm more efficient and profitable, and firms will invest as long as the discounted net benefit is positive and better than other available investments.

Firms face a somewhat different problem than individuals in making decisions about investing in human capital.[1] When people invest in themselves, there is no question about who will benefit from that investment. Because there is no certainty that individuals will remain with the firm, there is no assurance that the firm will reap the benefits of investments in their employees. From the firm's perspective, investments in employees range along a continuum from investments that improve employee productivity in any setting, such as developing reading and math skills, to investments that improve only employee productivity with their current employer. The former is termed *general human capital*, the latter is *firm-specific human capital*.

The problem facing the firm is that the benefits of its investments in general human capital may not accrue to employers. If a firm is to invest in an employee's general human capital, it must be able to recoup the investment through the employee's increased productivity. Even if the firm shares some of the return with the employee, the firm cannot share too much if it is to benefit from the investment. The wage paid to the employee needs to be below, possibly substantially below, the value produced by the employee so that the firm can realize a reasonable return on its investment. Firms that do not invest in training are in a position to entice a trained employee away by offering a wage more in line with the employee's improved productivity. They can do this because they do not need to recover training costs. Because of the problem of recapturing their investments, firms rarely invest in general human capital. An exception occurs when an employee is willing to accept a reduced wage in return for general training, in which case the employee and not the employer is funding the training.[2]

The same problem is not present with firm-specific training. This training, such as training on firm-specific machinery or procedures, is not useful to other firms, and no incentive exists for other firms to offer the employee a wage greater than the employee's current one. The firm that provides the training captures the gains as long as the worker remains an employee of the firm. It may choose to share some of the productivity gain with the employee, setting his wage above what he could earn from other employers, to reduce the likelihood that he will leave the firm.

HUMAN CAPITAL AND THE MINIMUM WAGE

Changes in the minimum wage may affect decisions of individuals and firms to invest in human capital. The effects of an increase in the minimum wage are potentially complex and may occur among different types of employees. While a higher minimum wage may induce a teen to abandon school to pursue a job at the now higher wage, it might also induce retired workers to invest in training that would enable them to qualify for jobs. Although the effects of the minimum wage on training might occur throughout the labor force, the literature has focused its effect on the decisions of teenagers to remain in school, and its effect on the training decisions of firms.

THE EFFECT OF THE MINIMUM WAGE ON SCHOOL
ENROLLMENT: THEORY AND FINDINGS

Economic theory provides no certain prediction about the effect of increases in the minimum wage on teen school enrollment. Individuals are assumed to maximize their lifetime earnings by balancing the present discounted value of the gains from additional education against the costs of that additional education, mostly forgone earnings while in school. Increases in the minimum wage compress the lower end of the earnings distribution in a fashion favorable to low-wage workers. For teens who can find employment following a minimum wage increase, it raises the cost of forgone earnings, reduces the net benefit of continuing in school, and, where the net benefit becomes a net cost, induces leaving school. However, if a higher minimum wage results in employers requiring higher productivity from their now more expensive low-wage employees and reducing the number of low-wage jobs available to teens, then teens are less likely to find employment, the cost of forgone work declines, and the returns to schooling increase. The return to schooling rises further if additional schooling increases the likelihood of being hired into a job at the new higher minimum wage in the future. If these factors sufficiently increase the net benefit of continued schooling sufficiently, increases in the minimum wage could be associated with increased school attendance.[3]

Empirical Work on the Effect of Minimum Wage Increases on School Enrollment

In *The New Industrial State* (1972), John Kenneth Galbraith indicated that an advantage of writing nonfiction is an absence of a need to maintain suspense. We follow that dictum. Although the effect of the minimum wage on schooling is an important topic and has been addressed in 14 articles published between 1981 and 2007, conceptual and methodological problems are sufficiently pervasive that little can be concluded (see Table 6.1 for a summary of these studies).[4]

A pervasive methodological issue is that almost all of the recent articles predate the work by Bertrand, Duflo, and Mullainathan (2004) and use panel structures likely subject to serial correlation. Standard

Table 6.1 Schooling and Human Capital

Study	Effect	Country	Target	Data	Data structure	Period	Comments
Ehrenberg and Marcus (1982)	Higher relative minimum wages cause white males and white females in low-income families to shift from enrolled/employed to full-time schooling. Results for nonwhites are not statistically significant.	United States	Males and females, 14–19	National Labour Force Survey	Cross sectional	1966 (male) and 1968 (female)	A 10% increase in the minimum wage would be associated with a 0.7 to 0.8% increase in the enrollment of 14–17-year olds and a 1.3 to 1.4 % increase in the enrollment of 18–19-year-olds. The estimates are adjusted for auto correlation. There is generally a positive effect on employment for those in school and a negative effect for those not in school.
Mattila (1981)	Increases in the minimum wage positively affect enrollment for both genders and both age categories.	United States	Teenagers, 14–17 and 18–19, by gender	October, CPS Education Supplement, 1947–1977	Annual observations from October CPS with correction for autocorrelation	1947–1977	
Cunningham (1981)	Effect varies systematically by race and age group	United States	Teens and young adults	1960 and 1970 census	Cross section with 1970 state enrollment and employment outcomes a function of the change in the minimum wage, adjusted 1960 state outcomes, and other state characteristics	1970	Higher minimum wages reduce school enrollment for white teens 16–19 but do not affect white 20–24-year-olds. Enrollments for black teens is increased by higher minimum wages. When the model for the white population is estimated distinguishing between covered and uncovered sectors, there is no effect on teens or young adults who are in school but not employed, but a negative effect on enrollment of teens who are in school and in covered employment.

Neumark and Wascher (1995a)	Higher minimum wage results in a greater fraction of teens in the not enrolled/ not employed status.	United States	Teenagers and young adults	CPS	State-by-year panel	1978– 1989	As with other state-by-year research prior to 2004, there are issues of significance tests being biased toward rejecting the null. Although there is clear evidence that the fraction of teens in the not enrolled/ not employed category rises, the minimum wage does not have statistically significant negative effects in other categories, complicating the understanding of whether the increase affects enrollment, employment, or both.
Neumark and Wascher (1995b)	Increases the likelihood that teens move into the not enrolled/not employed category	United States	Teens 16–19	Matched CPS	Matched individual observations in a state-by-year panel	1977– 1989	This article is greatly expanded in Neumark and Wascher (1996).
Neumark and Wascher (1996)	Increases the likelihood that teens move into the not enrolled/not employed category but effects vary greatly by period, age, and initial wage level.	United States	Teens 16–19	Match CPS	Matched Individual observations in a state-by-year panel estimated by multinomial logit	1979– 1992	The estimates are rich and varied according to time period, sample, and estimation method. In general, only the transition into not enrolled/not employed is statistically significant, leaving questions about whether the measured effect is an enrollment or employment effect or both. The estimated effect is large and significant for the 1980–1984 period, but is not for 1985–1992. The RCS structure raises issues with downward bias in estimated standard errors.

(continued)

Table 6.1 (continued)

Study	Effect	Country	Target	Data	Data structure	Period	Comments
Neumark and Wascher (2003)	Higher minimum wage results in greater fraction of teens in not enrolled/not employed status	United States	Teenagers	CPS	State-by-year panel	1978–1989, 1980–1989, 1980–1998	Results generally show that an increase in the minimum wage increases the fraction of teens who are not enrolled/not employed but doesn't have a statistically significant effect on other categories. Results are sensitive to the period under consideration and the error structure. Concerns about the downward bias of estimated standard errors in state-by-year panels apply to this research.
Campolieti, Fang, and Gunderson (2005b)	Increases in the minimum wage do not affect school enrollment.	Canada	Teens 16–19	Survey of Labour and Income Dynamics	Matched individual observations in a province and year panel estimated with multinomial logit.	1993–1999	Builds on Neumark and Wascher (1995b, 1996).
Baker (2005)	No effect on enrollment for those aged 15–19 or 20–24	Canada	15–24-year-olds	Canadian Labour Force Survey	Province-by-year panel	1983–2000	
Hyslop and Stillman (2007)	The minimum wage does not systematically affect enrollments, but some significant effects are found for particular age groups and years.	New Zealand	Teenagers	New Zealand Household Labour Force Survey	Individual-annual panel	1997–2003	Once business cycle controls are included, of the nine estimates of minimum wage effects, there are significant effects for 16–17-year-olds in 2002 and for 20–21-year-olds in 2001.
Pacheco and Cruickshank (2007)	Increased coverage increases school enrollment, while increases in the real minimum wage reduce school enrollment for 16–19-year-olds. There is no effect on 20–24-year-olds.	New Zealand	Teens 16–19 and young adults 20–24	New Zealand Labour Force Survey combined with school enrollment data	Year-by-age group panels	1986–2004	Unpacks the effect of coverage, which is positive, from the effect of increases in the real minimum wage, which is negative. As with other work with unit-by-time panels, there may be issues with under estimation of the standard errors.

Study	Findings	Country	Sample	Data source	Research design	Years	Notes
Landon (1997)	Increases in the provincial minimum wage reduce school enrollments for 16-year-old males and 17-year-old males and females. A $0.50 increase in the relative minimum wage would reduce enrollment by about 0.7 percent.	Canada	16- and 17-year-old males and females in six Canadian provinces	Assembled from a variety of Canadian Education and Labour Market data sources	Year-by-province panel	1975–1989	Differs from most other studies in using education, rather than labor force data and focusing on high school enrollment.
Chaplin, Turner, and Pape (2003)	Increased minimum wages are associated with lower continuation ratios in states that allow school leaving at age 16 and younger. There is no effect on states that do not allow school leaving after age 17.	United States	High school students	Common core data from the U.S. Department of Education	State-by-year panels	1989–1990 to 1996–1997 school year	Differs from most other studies in using a school-based education rather than a labor market data set and focusing on high school education.
Warren and Hamrock (2010)	Although the minimum wage is never significant of itself, the elasticity of the interaction with the state unemployment rate is negative and significant.	United States	High school students	Common core data	State-by-year panels	1982–2005	
Crofton, Anderson, and Rawe (2009)	The level of the minimum wage does not affect dropout rates for all high school students or any subgroup except Hispanics. The errors are not clustered, so significance may be over stated.	United States (Maryland)	High school students	Maryland Report Card (http://www.mdreportcard.org)	County-by-year panels	1993–2004	

errors are never clustered by cross-sectional unit: state, province, or age. This would not be an issue if the data were not serially correlated. However, there is reason to believe, and perhaps hope, that there is considerable inertia, and therefore serial correlation, in enrollment ratios or other measures of schooling.[5] The Pearson correlation of the enrollment to population ratio between its current value and its first lag is 0.99 in U.S. national data for 14–17-year-olds between 1900 and 2000; both Dickey-Fuller Generalized Least Squares and Kwiatkowski-Phillips-Schmidt-Shin tests indicate unit roots in enrollment to population ratios. Although not necessarily determinative for state data, the factors that cause such a high level of serial correlation in the national data also characterize state data. As the errors are not clustered, the standard errors of all but short panels will be systematically underestimated, and the null hypothesis, that the minimum wage has no effect on enrollment, will be rejected too frequently. Given this problem, the estimates are reliable only when they do not reject the null, but they are unreliable when they do. Of the 15 articles on this topic listed in Table 6.1, only Ehrenberg and Marcus (1982) and Hyslop and Stillman (2007) provide reliable hypothesis tests.

A second issue, one that is important to future research, concerns the differences in approach arising from analysts' home disciplines, labor economics, and education. Labor economists have tended to approach enrollment models as extensions of their employment models. The most serious consequence of this has been conflation of the decision about remaining in high school with that of going to college. Dividing populations into teens aged 16–19 and young adults aged 20–24 is standard in labor market studies, but it is not consistent with decisions about schooling. Most students complete high school at age 18 and, if they choose, enter college at age 18 or 19. By constructing samples of teens 16–19, the research mixes decisions about remaining in high school with the decision to continue education beyond high school. Mixing these decisions complicates measurement issues, estimation, and application of findings to policy decisions.

Evidence for differences between these decisions can be found in Neumark and Wascher (1996). Although the authors do not get beyond descriptive statistics that distinguish outcomes for 16- and 17-year-olds from 18- and 19-year-olds, their data suggest considerable differences in the responses of enrollment for the two age groups to a higher minimum wage. Research that distinguishes the effects of the minimum wage on decisions about staying in high school and entering college will be more interesting and more useful than much of the current research.

The failure to embed studies of the effect of the minimum wage on enrollment in generally accepted models of school staying or college entrance also raises issues about research originating in the labor economic tradition. Although fixed effects by year and state control for many factors, it is not reasonable to assert that such models can capture the effect of state minimum wage variables on enrollment without also allowing that state education requirements, finance, and related factors should not also be incorporated into these models. There has been progress on this over time. Some of the work of Neumark and Wascher, and the research by Baker (2005), Chaplin, Turner, and Pape (2003), Landon (1997), and Pacheco and Cruickshank (2007) make important contributions to a specification that integrates the factors favored by labor economists with those that education scholars believe to be important in the determination of enrollment and graduation.

A final issue is that, despite the small number of articles, it is difficult to synthesize the results because of differences in definitions, groups under consideration, methods, and the period studied. Where findings differ, it is challenging to determine the source of differences among articles. As current researchers seldom embed their work in specifications used by prior researchers, one is unsure whether differences emerge because of the use of data for different time periods, different model specifications, different measures of the minimum wage, or other sources. Most researchers wish to make their particular mark, to bring their insight to an issue; this creativity is central to the evolution of research. This drive toward originality should not preclude explicit exploration of the sources of differences between earlier work and their own; indeed, it highlights their contribution.

Early Research

Research on school attendance and the minimum wage first appeared in 1979 in papers presented at a conference on the minimum wage at the American Enterprise Institute. Establishing a pattern for future research, the studies by Mattila (1981) and Cunningham (1981) reached opposite conclusions. Mattila's time-series models of the enrollment rate of men and women aged 14–17 and 18–19 from 1947 to 1977 find a consistent positive relationship between the minimum wage index and school enrollment. Cunningham uses 1960 and 1970 census data aggregated by state to consider the effect of the increase in the level and coverage of the minimum wage between 1960 and 1970 on youth school enrollment and employment. Estimates from models with extensive controls for changes in demographic, economic, and industrial characteristics of states find that the minimum wage is associated with a modest decline in the fraction of white male and female teens not in school but does not affect the schooling decisions of 20–24-year-olds. The elasticity for white male teens is −0.15, −0.21 for white female teens. The effect on black youth is quite different: the minimum wage has a statistically significant positive effect on the enrollment of black male teens and no effect on other black populations.[6]

Ehrenberg and Marcus (1982) provide many of the concepts and methods used in more recent research on whether the minimum wage has different effects on teens from high- and low-income families, and on the relationship between the minimum wage, employment, and schooling and initiated work. They divide 1966 and 1968 NLS respondents aged 16–19 into four statuses: 1) those who are enrolled in school but are not employed (ENE); 2) those who are enrolled and employed (EE); 3) those who are not enrolled but employed (NEE); and 4) those who are neither enrolled nor employed (NENE). The probability that an individual is in one of the EE, NEE, or NENE categories relative to being in ENE is determined by the relative coverage-adjusted minimum wage and control variables. The effect of the minimum wage on individuals from households with an annual income no greater than $4,000 is compared to those from households with incomes of at least $8,000.[7] Higher relative minimum wages induce white females to move from working to not working while enrolled in school (from EE to ENE); this same effect is found for white males from high-income families. The relative minimum wage has no effect on the behavior of nonwhite females, but it induces ENE nonwhite males to move out of school into employment (from ENE to NEE). Broadly, higher minimum wages either do not affect enrollment outcomes or encourage greater schooling among white teenagers. Results for nonwhites are distinct, with higher minimum wages inducing black male teens, but not black female teens, to leave school for employment.

The work by Mattila (1981) and Cunningham (1981) has not aged as well as might be hoped, and their methods are, for the most part, no longer used. They are then more suggestive than conclusive. In contrast, Ehrenberg and Marcus's (1982) work provides a foundation for much of the research of the 1990s and 2000s.

Contemporary Research

Neumark and Wascher are the most prolific authors on this topic, having published four articles on the relationship between the minimum wage and school enrollments. Their work builds on Ehrenberg and Marcus (1982) but adds a time dimension by using state-by-year aggregate panels or repeat cross sections. As these articles all predate the work of Bertrand, Duflo, and Mullainathan (2004), errors are not clustered by state, and hypothesis tests may be biased toward rejecting the null hypothesis. We first consider the two articles using aggregate panels.

Neumark and Wascher's initial work (1995a) adapts the approach of Ehrenberg and Marcus to aggregate panel data. The CPS is used to calculate annual values of the fraction of teens aged 16–19 in each state who are in each of the four enrollment/employment categories (EE, ENE, NEE, and NENE) between 1977 and 1989. The fraction of each state's teens in each of these four categories is determined by the coverage-adjusted effective relative minimum wage and its lagged value; the fraction of the population aged 16–19; the prime-age male unemployment rate; a set of dummies indicating whether students are allowed to leave school without graduating if they are less than 16, if they are 17, and if they are 18; and average teacher salaries by state along with year and state fixed effect.[8] Other than the minimum wage, only the adult male unemployment rate has a statistically significant effect on enrollment/employment status: it is positively related to the teens' being enrolled and not employed (ENE) and negatively associated with employment outcomes (both EE and NEE). Neither enrollment laws nor teacher salaries affect the outcomes.

The effect of the minimum wage on enrollment is not certain. Putting aside the issue of bias in hypothesis testing, only the elasticity of the NENE outcome with respect to the minimum wage is substantially larger than its estimated standard error in Neumark and Wascher's

(1995a) preferred model. A 10 percent increase in the relative minimum wage would increase the fraction of teens who were neither in school nor employed by 6.4 percent. While elasticities of enrollment for both the EE and ENE, the two outcomes related to school enrollment, are negative, they are small in magnitude and far from statistical significance.[9] In 10 additional estimates, the elasticity of ENE with respect to the minimum wage is smaller than its standard error in eight estimates and never achieves 5 percent significance standard in any estimate. Only 2 of the 10 estimates of the elasticity of the EE outcome meet a 5 percent test of significance. When the minimum wage is measured relative to inflation, rather than the state average wage, all decline elasticities fall in magnitude and none approach 5 percent significance.

Responding to issues raised by Evans and Turner (1995), Neumark and Wascher (2003) further update and expand their 1995 work. A number of estimates use the more reliable measures of enrollment provided by the CPS October school enrollment supplement. Models are estimated for 1979–1989 and for 1980–1998. Results for the four-way division of outcomes are qualitatively similar to those obtained in the 1995 work. Although the elasticity of NENE is positive and significant, albeit biased, neither EE nor the ENE outcome is affected by the minimum wage. Coefficients are small in magnitude and do not achieve a 5 percent level of significance across eight variants in specification and sample.

More relevant to the issues of this chapter, the authors also estimate models of enrollment without respect to employment. Twelve variants of the model are estimated with models differing by period, error structure, and measure of enrollment. All 12 estimates find that the minimum wage has negative effects on enrollment, but only 5 are significant in a 5 percent test. There is some evidence in additional models that state laws that establish the age at which teens can leave high school moderate the effect of the minimum wage, with the minimum wage effect attenuating as the age of leaving is increased. However, given the problems with hypothesis testing in this work, the interaction between the minimum wage and state enrollment laws is only suggestive of issues to be pursued in future research.

Neumark and Wascher's (1995b, 1996) second approach takes advantage of the rotation of CPS respondents to examine the work and schooling transitions among teenagers between 1979 and 1992.[10] Individuals' observations can be matched between their fourth and eighth month in the survey, a one-year interval, in the outgoing rotation files of the CPS. Although there is some loss in respondents between the fourth and eighth month, most individuals' transitions between employment and unemployment and between school enrollment and nonenrollment can be observed. Using the four employment enrollment categories, individuals' second-year outcomes are modeled as an outcome of their category in the first year, the contemporaneous and lagged level of the effective relative minimum wage, and controls for adult unemployment, age, race, and sex as well as state and year fixed effects. More than 36,000 records on teens can be matched between 1979 and 1992.

Neumark and Wascher estimate a number of models, and the effect of the minimum wage varies considerably by specification. The variants that are most similar to their prior work find that higher minimum wages are associated with a transition from EE to NENE, but they do not affect other outcomes. When controls for unobserved individual characteristics, individual fixed effects, are incorporated, the minimum wage no longer has a statistically significant effect on schooling or labor market transitions. Although the authors express doubts about the value of this estimate, the results suggest that unobserved individual characteristics impact the estimates. Additional estimates by level of schooling, age, period, race and ethnicity, and the level of the initial wage suggest considerable variation in the effect of the minimum wage on enrollment. The negative effect of higher minimum wages on enrollment and employment are larger for black and Hispanic teens than other teens; black and Hispanic teens are at greater risk for transitioning into NENE.

Estimates are sensitive to the study period and initial wage. The authors estimate a number of models, dividing the data into 1980–1984 and 1985–1992, roughly the period affected by the double-dip recession of the early 1980s, and the period of strong growth following that recession. During the recessionary period, the estimated likelihood of transitioning into NENE is large in magnitude and generally considerably larger than its standard error. In contrast, the size of the effect of the minimum wage on the transition between enrollment status and labor market status is consistently small and small relative to its standard error, in the latter period. This suggests that estimates in the earlier period are affected by the depth of the recession. We may be observing the transition of teens who entered a particularly difficult job market upon graduating high school.

Where does Neumark and Wascher's extensive and vigorous investigation leave us? The lack of reliable hypothesis tests limits what may be concluded. If the minimum wage has an effect, it is likely on the movement of those who are in school and employed to being out of school and out of employment, from EE to NENE. Nonwhite teens appear more vulnerable to the effects of the minimum wage than white teens. The effect of the minimum wage on enrollment and employment may be limited to, or greatly exacerbated by, deep recession and unemployment. Although the models included a control for adult unemployment, the marked difference in the 1980–1984 and 1985–1992 results suggests that the effect of macroeconomic performance was not fully controlled and that the performance of the U.S. economy is an important moderator of the impact of the minimum wage. Finally, and perhaps most important, the estimates with matched data suggest that the minimum wage measure is picking up unobserved characteristics that affect individual transitions from enrollment and employment into nonenrollment and nonemployment, from EE to NENE. Further investigation with a data set, such as the NLSY, which is better adapted to controlling for unobserved individual characteristics, may produce interesting findings. Although this prolific and interesting work has not accomplished as much as the authors had hoped in answering questions about how the minimum wage affected school enrollments, it has provided a foundation for further inquiry.

Studies of Other Countries

Economic research on other countries builds on the work of Neumark and Wascher. In addition to providing estimates for other countries, it innovates with a more sophisticated approach to modeling school policies and financing and household factors. Campolieti, Fang, and Gunderson (2005b) use longitudinal data, with which they can follow individuals over time, to study the experience of Canadian teens, aged 16–19 from 1993 to 1999. Baker (2005) uses a province-by-year panel for 1983–2000 to consider similar issues. Hyslop and Stillman (2007) consider the effect of the 2001 increase in the New Zealand minimum wage on the enrollment of individuals aged 16–17, 18–19, and 20–21 in 2001, 2002, and 2003. Building on Hyslop and Stillman, Pacheco and Cruickshank (2007) combine data from the Ministry of Education and the LFS to construct an age-by-year panel of 16–24-year-olds for 1986–2004 to distinguish the effect of broadening minimum wage coverage from the effect of changes in the real minimum wage.

In Canada the minimum wage is determined solely by provincial legislation. Lacking a national floor on the minimum wage, statutory minimum wages in Canada have greater variation than their U.S. counterparts. The greater variation can improve the precision of estimates. The specification adopted by Campolieti, Fang, and Gunderson (2005b) is also a step forward in incorporating a wider set of individual factors that likely affect enrollment decisions such as household income. The estimated elasticity of school enrollment with respect to the minimum wage index is positive but not significant, and the authors conclude that, at least in the Canadian case, the provincial minimum wage does not affect school enrollments.[11] Baker (2005) also finds that provincial minimum wages do not affect school enrollment in Canada.

New Zealand introduced a minimum wage for those aged 20 and older in 1983 and extended coverage, at rates below the adult rate, to 16–19-year-olds in 1994. In 2001, the rate for 18–19-year-olds was increased from 60 percent of the adult wage to the full adult minimum. The wage for those younger than 18 was raised to 80 percent of the adult wage. These reforms raised the minimum wage by 69 percent for 18–19-year-olds, and by 41 percent for younger workers. These substantial increases provided an opportunity to consider the effect of both the extension of coverage and large increases to employment and schooling outcomes of young workers in New Zealand. Hyslop and Stillman (2007) construct a panel of age-by-quarter cells from 1997 to 2003 from the New Zealand Household Labour Force Survey (HLFS) of those aged 16–25. Four of the six enrollment elasticities were not statistically significant in a model with controls for business cycle effects. Enrollment among 16–17-year-olds was estimated to decline by 3 percent in 2002, while it fell by 4 percent among 20–21-year-olds in 2000.[12]

Pacheco and Cruickshank (2007) find that the 1994 extension of coverage increased the enrollment of those 16–19 by 1.1 to 1.5 percent, while changes in the real minimum wage had no effect on enrollments in the full sample. When the sample was limited to 16–19-year-olds, broadening coverage raised enrollments, but the real minimum wage itself was negatively related to enrollments, with an elasticity of −0.15. Projections from these estimates found that the introduction of the minimum wage for teenagers resulted in a permanent increase in enrollments of between 1 and 1.5 percent, while the 2001 increase in the minimum wage reduced enrollments of 18–19-year-olds by 10 percent, and of 16–17-year-olds by 6 percent.[13]

Studies Informed by Research on Education

The work reviewed to this point is anchored in labor economics and has been little influenced by the education literature on school enrollment. The definition of samples, specification models, and the data sets used to construct variables reflect this approach. In particular, samples that conflate the decision to remain in high school with the decision to go to college, and equations that include no more than the minimal controls for the state education policies, raise the possibility of omitted variable bias and render it challenging to sort out the policy implications of the research.

Baker (2005); Chaplin, Turner, and Pape (2003); Crofton, Anderson and Rawe (2009); Landon (1997); and Warren and Hamrock (2010) take important steps toward a more interdisciplinary approach to the minimum wage enrollment issue. Landon estimates a province-by-year model of enrollment of 16–17-year-olds for six Canadian provinces for 1975–1998. The sample of 16–17-year-olds focuses the research on the decision to remain in high school. The use of enrollment data from educational databases rather than from surveys with a primary focus on labor market issues improves our confidence in the accuracy of the enrollment measures. In addition to conventional economic controls, Landon incorporates five measures of school finance; three measures of educational characteristics, including the average number of pupils per school; and demographic controls, including divorce rates, the percentage of immigrants, the fraction of provincial GDP from agriculture, and real per capita income. The minimum wage is measured as the ratio of the provincial minimum wage to the average hourly wage. We focus on the estimates that include province and year fixed effects.[14] Landon estimates separate equations by age and gender, resulting in four estimates of the effect of the minimum wage.

Higher minimum wages were associated with lower enrollment levels for three of the four groups studied, but the magnitude of the effect is small, and, because the standard errors are not corrected for serial correlation, the statistical significance is uncertain.[15] The elasticities of enrollment with respect to the minimum wage range from −0.08 (for 16-year-old males) to −0.17 (17-year-old males). Landon (1997) calculates that a $0.50 wage increase in 1989 would have resulted in a decline in enrollment of 3,074 students across six provinces (out of about 475,000 students total), between 0.6 percent and 0.8 percent of 16–17-year-olds.

Chaplin, Turner, and Pape (2003) examine the effect of the minimum wage and its interaction with laws regulating when students can leave high school with a state-by-year panel. The dependent variable, the proportion of high school students completing their degrees by state, is constructed from the common core of data, an annual survey of all public schools conducted by the U.S. Department of Education, for the 1989–1990 to 1996–1997 school years. As the data pertain only to high school students, the study avoids conflating decisions about leaving high school and entering college. Measures of state policies on school leaving—the age at which teens are allowed to leave school, whether the state requires an exit examination for graduation, and total school credits required in high school—are included in the model, and the real effective minimum wage is interacted with the age-of-leaving indicator variables. As with other work predating Bertrand, Duflo, and Mullainathan (2004), the errors are not clustered.

Higher minimum wages are associated with reduced continuation rates among states that allow students to leave school at age 16. In these states, the elasticity of continuation with respect to the minimum wage ranged from −0.042 to −0.057.[16] However, the minimum wage does not affect continuation rates among states that only allow school leaving at age 17 or age 18. These results are consistent with the findings from Neumark and Wascher (2003)—that the minimum wage did not affect enrollment in states in which students could not leave high school until age 18—but not with Neumark and Wascher (1995a), which finds that legal restrictions on when students could leave school did not affect enrollments.

Baker (2005) reports that higher provincial minimum wages are not associated with reduced enrollments. Although this study conflates the decision to leave high school with that of entering college, it is otherwise especially thoughtful in synthesizing the economic and education variables incorporated in panel data studies.

Warren and Hamrock (2010) add to this literature with a broad discussion of factors affecting graduation as understood in economics and education, better measures of state high school completion rates, and more extensive controls for graduation requirements. Educational theories of high school completion are structured around push and pull factors as well as psychological processes. Push factors include a range of state education policies, while pull factors include labor market conditions and family and peer influences. These factors are embedded in a developmental process that is affected by success and failure in school; student psychological orientations toward school, work, and family; and other individual-level factors. In this context, the effect of the push-pull factors are contingent.

The data for the model are structured as a state-by-year panel with year and state fixed effects. Explanatory variables include not only the usual suspects (measures of the minimum wage and state unemployment rates) but also measures of compulsory school attendance ages, the presence and stringency of graduation exams, and the courses required for graduation measured in Carnegie units.[17] The dependent variable is a cohort-specific measure of the percent of 9th graders in public high school who complete high school from 1982 to 2005.[18] Errors are clustered by state.

To allow for contingency, Warren and Hamrock (2010) estimate five models, four of which allow the minimum wage to interact with education policy variables or the unemployment rate. The coefficient on the uninteracted minimum wage term is small in magnitude and never statistically significant, with a standard error that is 2–10 times the magnitude of the point estimate. The interaction of the minimum wage with the state unemployment rate is negative and significant in a 0.05 test. In this variant of the model, a 10 percent increase of the mean minimum wage would result in a 1 percent decline in high school completion. Other specifications in which the minimum wage is interacted with compulsory schooling laws and graduation requirements are not statistically significant.[19]

The one state-specific study, an estimate of the effect of the minimum wage on dropout rates by county in Maryland between 1993 and

2004, finds no relationship between the real minimum wage and drop-out rates for their full sample or for the white, African American, or Asian samples, but it finds a large negative effect for Hispanics (Crofton, Anderson, and Rawe 2009).[20] An interesting addition to this panel data model is a control for teen pregnancy rates, which has a strongly significant positive effect on dropout rates.

The Minimum Wage and School Enrollment

Where do we then stand with respect to understanding the effect of the minimum wage on school enrollment? One possible conclusion is that we know little or nothing. Because of the likely problem with rejecting the null hypothesis (of no effect) too frequently, most recent studies cannot be used with any assurance to determine whether the minimum wage affects schooling. Three of the remaining four studies, Mattile (1981), Ehrenberg and Marcus (1982), and Hyslop and Stillman (2007), generally find that the minimum wage does not affect enrollment, but Cunningham (1981) finds the opposite. A number of the studies for which there are issues with bias find no statistically significant effect, and in those instances we can accept the result. In contrast, we cannot know with certainty whether the studies that find a negative effect would, once estimated correctly, continue to find that effect. We are left with a suspicion that there is likely no effect, but, as so much of the evidence cannot be used, what appears to be reliable is not sufficiently conclusive to argue against an effect with confidence.

Research on the effect of the minimum wage on enrollment and attainment has advanced over the last decade, but it has not provided a definitive answer about the effects of the minimum wage. Past research has shown how to synthesize economic and education approaches. We know that we need to distinguish between the decisions to remain in high school and to enter college. We know that we need to address serial correlation by clustering observations when calculating standard errors where appropriate, and by other approaches where clustering is not appropriate, in order to get accurate hypothesis tests. Prior research has also provided a considerable range of controls that should be considered for inclusion in empirical models. Building on this knowledge, it should be possible to obtain useful estimates of the effect of the minimum wage on schooling.

THE MINIMUM WAGE AND EMPLOYER-SUPPLIED
TRAINING: THEORY AND FINDINGS

As discussed, firms will not provide general training to employees unless the employees pay for that training, possibly by accepting lower wages. This insight is readily incorporated into a model of compensation by stylizing general training as a fringe benefit, a component of total compensation. Employers offer some package of direct wages, fringe benefits, and training to workers of a given marginal productivity. Packages with more general training will have lower levels of other compensation. Workers choose the package that maximizes their lifetime discounted income (utility) by choosing among employers, but the value of the package, total compensation, is fixed by their productivity. Employees who place greater value on future income chose compensation packages that provide training and higher future income. Movement away from their voluntary choice can only, in an economic model, make the employee worse off.

Increases in the minimum wage potentially move employees away from their "preferred" mix of wages, training, and other fringes. Higher minimum wages increase direct wages as a share of total compensation. Unless a higher minimum wage results in greater productivity, employers will reduce the value of voluntary fringes, such as training.[21] The reduction in employee training reduces employees' future productivity and earnings. A higher minimum wage would then be associated with less general training, reduced earnings growth, and lower levels of future income.

Although not specifically considered in the literature, increases in the minimum wage may also cause firms to reduce firm-specific training. Specific training is more analogous to other forms of capital investment than general training, as there is no incentive for other firms to poach these employees. Even if the firm shares some of the gains with workers, it captures the lion's share of productivity gains. As with increases in the price of other capital goods, by lowering the rate of return on specific training, increases in the minimum wage would cause firms to reduce investment in specific training.

When labor markets are not fully competitive, firms may respond to higher minimum wages by increasing training (Acemoglu and Pischke

1999, 2003). An increase in the minimum wage compresses wages and sets the wage above the marginal revenue product of less-skilled workers. In a competitive market, firms will lay off workers whose productivity is less than the minimum wage. Where labor markets are not fully competitive, and firms earn rents, it may be profitable to hire less-productive workers and provide training.[22] As long as training costs are less than the rents earned from a worker, firms will employ and train workers; the training becomes a form of rent sharing.

Institutionalist theories also suggest a positive relationship between the minimum wage and firm-supplied training. Constrained from using low-cost labor, firms can only maintain their output and profitability through better management of labor and improving its productivity. Although firms can take many steps to improve labor performance, increased training plays an important role in these steps.

The "Old" New Minimum Wage Research

Just as the minimum wage increases of 1990 and 1991 spurred the "new" minimum wage research, the increases in the minimum wage and expansion of coverage in 1967 and 1968 was followed by a burst of research. This work was creative and wide ranging, addressing many issues revisited in the "new" minimum wage research, including school enrollment and on-the-job training. The expansion of coverage to smaller retail establishments raised concerns about the effect on positions that provide entry to employment and the development of on-the-job human capital.[23] A particular concern was whether the combination of reduced employment opportunities and firms' reduction in the provision of training to early-career employees would reduce employees' earnings throughout their careers. Hashimoto's (1982) work provides the most developed theory linking higher minimum wages to reductions in employer-provided general training and, in turn, to reduced earnings growth. The effect of the minimum wage on training and wage growth depends on the magnitude of the difference between the wage the individual would receive absent the minimum wage and the minimum wage itself. Those with the largest differences suffer the largest reductions in training and wage growth.

The early research on training followed two broad paths. Researchers with data on training measured the relationship between the minimum wage and training directly. Those without training data measured the response of wage growth to the minimum wage and, like Hashimoto (1982), relied on economic theory to link results to training. We focus our discussion on the former work, as the relationship is direct and less dependent on theory to link the minimum wage and training. (A summary of articles on the minimum wage and training is found in Table 6.2.[24])

Both the NLSY and PSID ask respondents about training, the former about whether the employer provided formal training, the latter about whether skills learned in the current job would be useful in future jobs. Leighton and Mincer (1981) use both to directly estimate the effect of the minimum wage on training. Few of the estimates are statistically significant: only 1 of 5 PSID and 2 of 14 with NLSY estimates approach 5 percent significance.[25] As part of his work with the NLSY, Schiller (1994) finds limited evidence that higher minimum wages reduce training. Although only 1 out of 8 of the minimum wage workers perceived a total lack of training, regression with controls for age, gender, marital and minority status, academic enrollment and achievement, intelligence, location, firm size and broad industry group find a weak, negative relationship, only significant in a 10 percent test, between being employed at exactly the minimum wage and training.

Grossberg and Sicilian (1999) provide the most explicit examination of the minimum wage's effect on training, and the relationship between the minimum wage, training, and wage growth. They adopt a difference-in-difference regression methodology, dividing employees into three groups: 1) those hired at the minimum wage, 2) those hired above but no more than $0.25 above the new minimum, and 3) those hired at higher wages. Comparisons between those hired at the minimum wage and those hired at low but above the minimum wage determine whether the minimum wage's hires are less likely to obtain training than other low-wage workers. Comparison between the high-wage group and these two low-wage groups further delineates the impact of wages on training. While being hired at the minimum wage was associated with lower wage growth, it was not associated with reduced hours of training.[26] Those hired at the minimum wage and those hired at low wages received less training than those hired at high wages, but training hours were not significantly different between the minimum-wage and low-wage workers. Lower levels of training for men seems to be an outcome of being hired at low wages rather than the minimum wage. For women, starting at the minimum wage does not affect training hours relative to the low-wage or high-wage group.[27] Although Grossberg and Sicilian's (1999) work supports the view that the minimum wage is associated with slower growth of wages, their work casts doubt on there being a link from the minimum wage through training to slower wage growth.

More recent studies of training effects include the work of Acemoglu and Pischke (2003); Arulampalam, Booth, and Bryan (2004); Baker (2005); Fairris and Pedace (2004); and Neumark and Wascher (2001). Neumark and Wascher use the 1983 and 1991 CPS, which include questions about formal and informal training, to estimate the effect of the minimum wage on employer-provided training and on pre-job training undertaken by individuals. The analysis of the 1991 data compares individuals aged 16–24 with those aged 35–54. The joint analysis of data from 1991 and 1983 compares 16–24-year-olds in 1991 with those in the 1983 survey. Individuals' training outcomes are modeled as a function of the individual characteristics, state indicator variables, an age indicator variable, and the average ratio of the state to the federal minimum wage by year interacted with age.[28]

The comparison of younger and older workers in 1991 finds no connection between the minimum wage ratio and training, whether training is measured as a whole or disaggregated into formal and informal training. Disaggregating teens and young adults finds no effect on teens, but a 10 percent higher minimum wage is associated with a 1.8 percent reduction in the formal training for young adults aged 20–24. Higher minimum wages are associated with lower levels of training when younger workers are compared between 1991 and 1983. A 10 percent higher state relative minimum wage causes a 1.2 percent reduction in the likelihood of training among those 16–24 and a 1.8 percent reduction in the likelihood of formal training among those 20–24. There is no effect on informal training for the any-age group. Estimates are robust with respect to the period over which the minimum wage is averaged but are sensitive to the CPS survey used for the estimates.[29] There is no evidence that higher minimum wages cause individuals to seek more pre-job training to qualify for a position.[30]

Baker (2005) considers the minimum wage/training relationship in Canada with the 1992, 1994, and 1998 Adult Education and Training Survey.[31] The model incorporates controls for individual, province, and

Table 6.2 Firm-Provided Training

Study	Effect	Country	Target	Data	Data structure	Period	Comments
Hashimoto (1982)	The effect on training is measured indirectly through the effect on wage growth. The minimum wage, measured as the ratio of the effective minimum wage to the wage the individual would have earned absent the minimum wage, is not significant in the OLS model. With selection correction, the minimum wage has a large negative and significant effect on training, while its interaction with experience is large, positive, and significant. The implied elasticity of training with respect to the minimum wage is between -0.3 and -1.6.	United States	White males age 14 to 24 in 1966 who were not enrolled in school in 1966 or 1969	NLSY	Cross section of change in wages between 1966 and 1969	1966–1969	
Leighton and Mincer (1981)	When measured indirectly through the effect on wage growth, PSID estimates find a significant negative effect. NLSY estimates find a significant negative effect for white males in 1969–1971, but not in the earlier period. There is no effect on black males. When the effect on training is measured directly, PSID estimates are mixed with most being nonsignificant. There is no evidence of	United States	White and black men. NLSY comprises younger workers; PSID is a cross section of the population.	PSID and NLSY	Cross section of individuals; NLSY is younger workers	1973 and 1975 PSID; 1967–1971 NLSY	

	an effect on white males in the NLSY, but some evidence of an effect on black males in the 1967–1969 panel but not in the later panel.					
Baker (2005)	No effect in a difference-in-differences specification, some evidence in a negative effect for younger workers but it is not statistically different than that for older workers.	Canada	Workers aged 17–24	Adult Education and Training Survey	Repeat cross sections for 1992, 1994, and 1998	1992–1998
Arulampalam, Booth, and Bryan (2004)	Possible positive effect on training, no evidence of a negative effect	United Kingdom	Workers aged 18–60	British Household Panel Survey	Waves 8–10 of BHPS. Model estimated with control for unobserved individual effects.	1998–2000
Acemoglu and Pischke (1999, 2003)	No effect on training	United States	Bound workers and workers earning up to 150 percent of minimum wage, aged 24–34	NLSY		1988–1992 Both difference-in-differences and simple regressions
Fairris and Pedace (2004)	No effect on training hours, mixed and problematic estimates for likelihood of training	United States	Establishments	National Employer Survey	Cross-sectional regression	1997

year effects; the minimum wage is measured as the ratio of the provincial minimum wage to the average industrial wage for the province. While there is evidence of a negative relationship between the minimum wage and training in the 1994 and 1998 data for those aged 17–24, the measured effect is not different from that of those aged 35–44, a group unlikely to be greatly affected by the minimum wage. Baker concludes that "a prudent conclusion would be at this stage the analysis is uniformative about the relationship between minimum wages and training" (p. 40).

Arulampalam, Booth, and Bryan (2004) find no evidence that the United Kingdom's introduction of the NMW in 1999 led to a decline in training, and some evidence that training of those aged 18–60 increased. This main result, the absence of a negative effect, was robust to distinctions between changes in both the provision and the intensity of training and to the definition of the treatment group.

Fairris and Pedace (2004) use a difference-in-difference approach with establishment data from the 1997 National Employer Survey to measure the effect of state relative minimum wages on the likelihood of employees' receiving training and the average hours of training. Higher minimum wages reduce the likelihood of training within establishments. However, when the sample is disaggregated by broad occupation, there is no difference in the effect of the minimum wage on the likelihood of training between frontline workers, support staff, technical, and supervisory and managerial workers. The authors suggest that, as the training of managerial and supervisory workers is unlikely to be affected by the minimum wage, it is likely that the negative training effect of the minimum wage is proxying other factors affecting training within establishments. When the minimum wage is measured as the ratio of the effective minimum wage to the establishment-specific occupational wage, there is a large negative and significant effect for support staff and for supervisory workers but no effect on frontline or technical workers.[32] The effect of the minimum wage on average hours of training is never significant in any specification. The authors conclude that the evidence on the provision of training is mixed and problematic for the provision of training, but that there is no effect on hours of training.

Acemoglu and Pischke (1999, 2003) theorize that higher minimum wages are associated with increased training in less-competitive labor markets. They use the 1988–1992 NLSY to examine this with longitudinal data on those aged 24–34 with no more than a high school degree. Difference-in-difference estimates with several definitions of the treatment group are positive but far from significant. The estimates from simple regressions are more varied but are qualitatively similar. Of estimates from 40 specifications that are differentiated by the definition of the affected group of workers, the way in which the minimum wage is deflated and the control variables, only 9 are significant in a 5 percent test. Of these, 3 are negative and 6 positive. Given little reason to prefer one regression estimate over another, and the lack of statistical significance of the difference-in-difference estimates, the authors conclude that there is not sufficient evidence for establishing a systematic relationship between the minimum wage and training.

Little empirical work explicitly addresses institutionalist hypotheses about the minimum wage and training. Hirsch, Kaufman, and Zelenska (2011) report that 68 percent of managers at the quick-food restaurants in their survey indicated that cross-training workers for multitasking was a very important part of their response to the increase in the minimum wage. McLaughlin's (2009) qualitative comparison between Denmark's and New Zealand's training responses to increased minimum wages suggests that whether small- and medium-sized employers respond to such increases with increased training depends very much on the legal and institutional framework in which the increase occurs. Minimum wage increases are more likely to occur and be more robust in coordinated market economies such as Denmark than in liberal market economies such as New Zealand, which depend on firms' individually making training decisions.

Summary

What does the current research say about the effect of the minimum wage on firm-provided training?[33] Leighton and Mincer's (1981) research is sensitive to data set, with those based on the PSID indicating a negative relationship and those derived from the NLSY generally not. Grossberg and Sicilian (1999) find that for men the apparent negative relationship between the minimum wage and training is, in fact, a negative relationship between low-wage employment and training. They find no evidence of higher minimum wages' reducing training for women. More recent work generally but not universally finds no relationship between the minimum wage and training. Neumark and Wascher (2001) report that based on comparisons of young adults to older workers, higher minimum wages reduce formal training for those aged 20–24 but do not affect formal training for teen or informal training for any age group; they also report stronger evidence that higher minimum wages between 1983 and 1991 reduced training of those aged 16–24.[34] In contrast, Acemoglu and Pischke (1999, 2003); Arulampalam, Booth, and Bryan (2004); Baker (2005); and Fairris and Pedace (2004) report little or no evidence that higher minimum wages are associated with reduced training. The mixed evidence on the proposition that higher minimum wages induce firms to provide less training supports a verdict of "not proven" and perhaps "not guilty." There is less support for the view that higher minimum wages result in increased training.

THE MINIMUM WAGE AND EMPLOYER-PROVIDED BENEFITS: HEALTH CARE AND PENSIONS

Although wages constitute the lion's share of low-wage employees' compensation, some receive benefits such as health insurance, pensions, holidays and vacations, and, of course, training. Economic theory suggests that the composition of the compensation packages will be determined by the reconciliation of employer and employee preferences through markets. The result is an optimal combination of wages and fringe benefits.

When the only form of compensation is the wage, employers' response to the imposition or increase in the minimum wage is, in an economic model, to reduce employment to a level where the marginal revenue product of the marginal worker is equal to the minimum wage. Other margins of adjustment become available once the compensation package includes voluntary benefits. Suppose an employer provides $5.00 in total compensation for each hour worked, of which $4.00 are direct wages and $1.00 are voluntary fringe benefits. In this situation, the imposition of a $4.50 per hour minimum wage leaves the employer with a range of responses. At one extreme, the employer can continue to pay the same fringe benefits and reduce employment to the point where marginal revenue product equals $5.50/hour; compensation rises by the difference between the new minimum wage and ex ante direct wages. At the other extreme, the employer can maintain ex ante employment and reduce voluntary fringe benefits by $0.50 per hour, leaving the value of the compensation package at $5.00 per hour. The first situation is the familiar one where the minimum wage improves the situation for those who remain employed, but those who are unemployed yet willing and qualified to work at the original level of compensation are worse off. In comparison, the second situation appears harmless since none lose jobs, but employees are moved away from their optimal compensation package to another that is overweighted toward direct wages and underweighted toward benefits. Where compensation packages include voluntary fringe benefits, the adverse effects of the minimum wage may not show up in reduction in employment but rather in the modification of compensation packages.

Firms' ability to alter fringe benefits is limited. Employers cannot reduce contributions to legally mandated fringe benefits, including Social Security, Medicare, unemployment insurance, and workers' compensation. Employers may also be reluctant to reduce voluntary benefits such as health insurance and pensions. Under IRS regulations, these benefits have to be provided in a nondiscriminatory fashion to qualify for pretax treatment.[35] Firms with large numbers of non–minimum wage workers may find that withdrawing benefits from minimum wage workers, and losing the privileged tax treatment for their other workers, is very expensive. Other benefits, such as training, holidays, vacation, and sick pay are not regulated and could be reduced without tax consequences.[36]

Early Research

In his book on the minimum wage in the restaurant industry, Alpert (1986) investigates the effect of the minimum wage on fringe benefits. He uses data from the *Employer Expenditures from Selected Compensation Practices* survey, a rich source of measures of fringe benefits developed by the Bureau of Labor Statistics (see Table 6.3 for a summary of the articles on the minimum wage and benefits).[37] The 20 benefits in the series are merged with demographic variables from the CPS to form short time series in which each benefit is measured on both a per-hour and an annual per-firm basis. Four of the 40 estimates were significant in a 5 percent test or better. The real minimum wage had a negative and significant effect on vacation expenditures and on total leave hours when these were measured on a per-hour basis and on severance pay and shift premiums when measured on an annual-firm basis. In a less wide-ranging study, Card and Krueger (1994) find that fast food restaurants did not respond to minimum wage increases by limiting the provision of meals at reduced prices.

Recent Research

Two more recent studies, Simon and Kaestner (2004) and Marks (2011), use the Annual Demographic Files in the March CPS to study different aspects of the relationship between the minimum wage and health and pension benefits.[38] These surveys collect retrospective information on pension and health insurance eligibility and coverage at the firm where the employee spent the most time in the prior year. The surveys include questions on whether workers participate in their employers' plan, whether they participate in a family health insurance plan, whether the employer pays the full cost of the health insurance, and whether the respondent participated in a pension plan sponsored by their employer.[39] The survey also includes a question on firm size, a measure central to Marks's (2011) work concerns.

Simon and Kaestner (2004) hypothesize that if the minimum wage affects benefits, the effect should be smaller for better-educated and higher-income workers. They use a quasi-experimental design, with treatment and comparison groups defined by education or income, and estimate models for 1979–1986, a period in which there was little state variation in minimum wages, and 1987–2000, when there was considerable variation in state minimum wages. They find no evidence that higher minimum wages resulted in worse outcomes for the treatment group with respect to whether the individual participates in an employer-provided health insurance plan, whether they participate in a family health insurance plan, whether the employer pays the full cost of the health insurance, and whether the respondent participated in a pension plan sponsored by their employer.[40]

For more than 100 years, economists have noted that larger firms pay higher wages and benefits to their employees and debated why this is the case.[41] One reason may be differences in the legal treatment of large and small firms with respect to labor market regulation.[42] Recognizing this, Marks (2011) extends Simon and Kaestner's (2004) work by investigating the interaction between minimum wages, benefits, educational attainment, and firm size. Although building on Simon and Kaestner's issues and the March CPS, she uses a regression methodology that includes a sample of the employed 18–64-year-olds in place of Simon and Kaestner's quasi experiment. The periods under examination, 1988–1993 and 1998–2005, overlap but differ from Simon and Kaestner.[43]

Marks (2011) finds that the minimum wage influences the provision of health benefits at small, but not large, firms; this does not occur with pension benefits for which the small and large firms face similar regulation. In models that do not divide the sample by educational attainment, the minimum wage does not have a statistically significant effect on health insurance provision in either large or small firms. When the minimum wage is interacted with educational attainment, less than high school, high school degree, and more than high school, there is still no relationship between the minimum wage and health insurance coverage for any group at large firms. There is, however, a negative and significant relationship between a higher real minimum wage and the provision of health insurance for those without high school degrees at small firms.[44] The elasticity of the health insurance coverage with respect to the real minimum wage at small firms is 0.13 in 1988–1993 and 0.10 in 1998–2005.[45] A higher real minimum wage is also associated with a reduced probability that employers would fully cover the cost of health plans of less-educated employees at small firms; the minimum wage had no effect on the likelihood of full coverage of any employees at larger firms.[46]

The effect of the minimum wage on pension coverage is markedly different. Small firms are not exempt from nondiscrimination standards with respect to pension participation. Consistent with the hypothesis that firms are constrained by the effects of regulations that restrict discrimination against lower-earning workers, higher minimum wages are not associated with a reduction in pension participation among less-educated workers in smaller firms.[47]

Although Marks (2011) builds on Simon and Kaestner (2004), differences in methodologies reduce certainty about why the estimates are different. Simon and Kaestner find no difference in the effect of the minimum wage on whether an employer provides health insurance be-

Table 6.3 The Minimum Wage and Benefits

Study	Effect	Country	Target	Data	Data structure	Period	Comments
Alpert (1986)	Four of 20 estimates find that higher real minimum wages are associated with reduced provision of particular benefits	United States	Restaurant industry	Combined CPS and employer expenditures on selected compensation practices	Time series	1970–1977	The strength of this study is the use of a data set with considerable detail on the types of fringe benefits available. A limitation is that there are few observations, 32, for each type of fringe benefit. The author assumes first-order auto correlation but does not test for the appropriateness of this structure.
Simon and Kaestner (2004)	Using a difference-in-differences approach, there is no difference in health and pension coverage between the group affected by the minimum wage and the comparison group.	United States	U.S. workforce	Annual demographic files of the CPS	A difference-in-differences approach using annual repeat cross section of individuals with state and year fixed effects	1979–2000	Estimates are corrected for clustering by state, addressing the bias in hypothesis tests of unclustered estimates.
Marks (2011)	Higher state real minimum wages are associated with lower health care coverage for employees with less than a high school degree at firms	United States	U.S. employed workforce	Annual Demographic Files of the CPS	A regression model using annual repeat cross section with	1988–1993 1998–2005	Estimates are corrected for clustering by state, addressing the bias in hypothesis testing of unclustered samples. The average minimum-wage induced decline in health insurance cov-

293

erage over the period covered by the sample is in the range of 2%.

state and year fixed effects and a time trend

with fewer than 500 employees. Other groups are unaffected. The reverse effect is found with pension coverage, firms with 500 or more employees are likely to reduce pension coverage of their lowest-educated employees in response to an increase in the minimum wage, but there is no effect on small firms.

Dube, Naidu, and Reich (2007)

Increases in the minimum wage in San Francisco did not affect health insurance coverage in restaurants.

tween those with less than a high school degree and those with a high school degree. In a model that also does not distinguish outcomes by firm size, Marks finds a negative relationship between the minimum wage and health insurance coverage for the least-educated workers. Given this difference in outcome, it may be that the differences between Simon and Kaestner's and Marks's results originate in differences in the periods under study, or between a quasi-experimental and regression methodology rather than in allowing for the effects of firm size. Resolution of this matter is necessary before conclusions can be drawn about the impact of the minimum wage on benefit coverage or the effects of firm size.

The San Francisco Minimum Wage

In their quasi-experimental study of the effects of the San Francisco minimum wage, described in detail in Chapter 2, Dube, Naidu, and Reich (2007) examine the impact of the minimum wage on health insurance coverage. Although the coefficients on the minimum wage term are positive (with one exception), the standard errors are usually as large or larger than the coefficients. The increase in the minimum wage in San Francisco does not appear to have reduced or improved health insurance coverage in restaurants.

SUMMARY

As with many of the topics other than employment and wages, research on the effect of the minimum wage on fringe benefits is thin. Alpert's (1986) work suggests that, in restaurants, there may be some effect on some voluntary fringes, leave, shift pay, and severance pay. More recent work finds that although there is not an effect on health insurance across all firms, there may be a negative relationship between the minimum wage and health insurance for firms with fewer than 500 employees. There appears to be no effect on pension coverage, even among small firms. However, findings for San Fransisco restaurants, a small part of the national small-firm universe, also suggest no effect on health insurance.

Our ability to reach a conclusion is limited by authors' not building explicitly on the work of prior authors. The work of Simon and Kaestner (2004) and Marks (2011) is a case in point. Marks's work builds on Simon and Kaestner and uses the same survey. However, Marks uses different time periods and a simple regression rather than a difference-in-differences regression. As a result, it cannot be said with certainty whether the difference in Marks's results are to be attributed to her innovation, distinguishing the effect of the minimum wage by firm size and education, or differences in samples and methods. Authors should not be bound by prior work—they need to follow the logic of their work and creativity. Taking a page or two to systematically investigate whether, using the same approach as prior researchers, the innovations developed in the current research would have the anticipated effect would do much to fill the gaps in our knowledge.

Notes

1. See, for example, the discussion of firm human capital decision in Ehrenberg and Smith (2012, pp. 152–156). Rosen (1972) laid the foundations for the current approach.
2. An alternative is for the employee to agree to work off the training debt by remaining with the firm for a fixed period after completing the training. This has been used by trucking firms that train employees to drive large trucks. The employee incurs a "debt" for the training, which is then paid down as the employee drives for the firm. If they leave the firm before the debt is paid, they are required to pay the remaining debt.
3. This assumes that there is a close connection between worker productivity and wages and an understanding by workers that additional education will improve their likelihood of gaining employment at the higher minimum wage (Ravn and Sorensen 1997).
4. Because the literature studying the effect of the minimum wage on schooling is small relative to the employment and wage literature, we review articles as early as 1981.
5. The enrollment ratio is the ratio of the population enrolled in school relative to the population. As with the employment ratio, the enrollment ratio can be calculated for specific demographic groups such as teens.
6. Although at the time, work by Mattila (1981) and Cunningham (1981) represented estimates and hypothesis tests that are subject to question. The time-series methods used by Mattila have largely been superseded. There are reasons to be concerned that Cunningham's adjustments to the 1960 census data and other variables

have induced forms of heteroskedasticity that are not accounted for in the error, throwing off the hypothesis testing.

7. Those from families with incomes of $4,001–$7,999 are excluded from the sample. The model includes controls for a variety of demographic and labor market factors. The inclusion of a control for whether the individual has graduated from high school helps resolve the problem of mixing the decision to remain in high school from entering college.

8. Neumark and Wascher (1995a) use two specifications of the outcomes, one that aggregates the EE and NEE category into a single employed group, and one that uses all four categories. We use the latter, as it better addresses the issue of enrollment.

9. Neither is sufficiently large relative to the standard error to reject the null of no effect in a 5 percent test. Neumark and Wascher (1995a) do not provide a joint enrollment elasticity or include the weights needed to construct such an elasticity.

10. Neumark and Wascher (1996) is more fully developed than the 1995 paper, and we draw on it for this discussion.

11. As with other state-by-year panels, there may be an issue with downward-biased standard errors. However, given that the null is not rejected, it is reasonable to believe this result would have been obtained in a model with errors that were computed correctly. The problem of computation of the elasticities without weights applies to the enrollment as well as employment results.

12. Both New Zealand studies use a time-by-cross-sectional-unit data structure and, as a result, may be biased toward rejecting the null of no effect. Lacking information on whether the New Zealand real minimum wage or enrollments by age are characterized by serial correlation, and the lack of clustering, we cannot be certain about the presence of bias. As Hyslop and Stillman (2007) use relatively short panels, 1996–2004, there is less likelihood of bias than Pacheco and Cruickshank (2007), whose work covers 18 years.

13. Because 20–24-year-olds were already covered by the minimum wage during the estimation period, the effect of the introduction of the minimum wage cannot be estimated for that group.

14. Landon's (1997) time indicators cover two years, an unusual and unexplained choice.

15. Because of the small number of provinces, clustering does not resolve the issue of serial correlation.

16. Further estimates with grade-specific continuation ratios suggest that the effect of the minimum wage occurs between the 9th and 10th grades.

17. Models were also estimated with variants on the minimum wage, including the average of the minimum wage in the students' junior and senior year, a four-year average, or an indicator for any change in the minimum wage during the junior and senior year or during the four years of high school. Estimates were not qualitatively sensitive to the minimum wage. A Carnegie Unit is 120 hours of class time over the course of a year at the secondary (U.S. high school) level.

18. The Warren and Hamrock (2010) measure of completion is constructed from the Common Core data (CCD), but the authors adjust that data for net migration and student's repetition of grades. Warren has previously written about the accuracy

of CPS and CCD measures of high school completion. He reports that the CPS overestimates completion because of adult respondent's tendency to report enrollment or completion when children have left school without a degree (Warren and Halpern-Manners 2007). He also finds that the CCD is biased by net migration and retention of students (Warren 2003).

19. Warren and Hamrock (2010) argue that the positive effect of unemployment on completion is convex and that the interaction with the minimum wage is picking up this convexity. This might be resolved by including the squares of both the unemployment and minimum wage terms as well as their interaction, thereby distinguishing nonlinearities from interactions.

20. As errors are not clustered by county, the significance for Hispanics may be overstated.

21. The phenomenon of worker productivity rising with the minimum wage is known as the shock effect and is not part of the conventional analysis.

22. See Burdett and Mortensen (1998) for a search model in which labor market outcomes are not fully competitive.

23. See Rottenberg (1981) for a broad-ranging set of papers on the effects of the minimum wage.

24. Grossberg and Sicilian (1999), Hashimoto (1982), and Leighton and Mincer (1981) measure the effect of the minimum wage on training through the indirect approach suggested by Hashimoto. Using the NLSY to study young white males who had completed their education, Hashimoto finds no effect when his model was estimated with OLS, but once corrected for sample selection, higher minimum wages are associated with reduced wage growth and training. Using NLSY and PSID for young white and black males under age 25, Leighton and Mincer find higher minimum wages are associated with lower wage growth for white, but not black males. Using the Employment Opportunities Pilot Project data on the last employee hired by a firm between 1980 and 1982, Grossberg and Sicilian also find that the wages of men hired at the minimum wage grew more slowly than the wages of those hired at low but above minimum wages and 47 percent more slowly than the wages of those hired at high wages. Women's wage growth was not influenced by the wage at which they were hired. Schiller (1994) finds that higher minimum wages are associated with higher wage growth among individuals aged 15–23.

25. The authors also estimate a series of models that incorporate the effect of state minimum wage levels and distinguish the effects of coverage and the level of the minimum wage. The results are again mixed and somewhat confusing. The standardized minimum wage generally has a positive or nonsignificant effect on wage growth, while coverage is negative or nonsignificant. With respect to job tenure, the effects of coverage and the standardized minimum wage are opposite signed in the PSID; the standardized wage effect is generally not significant in the NLSY estimates, the effect of coverage is generally significant, but opposite signed between the white and black equations. Results from the training equations are equally mixed.

26. As Leighton and Mincer (1981) provide only the coefficients for the logistic regressions, it is not possible to determine the reduced likelihood of training that those at the minimum wage experience.

27. Grossberg and Sicilian's (1999) wage growth results are discussed in Chapter 7.

28. The estimates include controls for firm-side measures, including firm size, weekly hours, whether the individual was in a permanent job, and industry of employment, and individual measures, including related experience, union membership, hours of work, occupation, job complexity, the firm's capital stock, and whether the individual had been employed for more than three months. The models are estimated in a Tobit model, which allows for the part of the sample that received no training.

29. See Table 8 of Neumark and Wascher (2001). Both coefficients and standard errors shift, and the estimated effects are no longer statistically significant if the model uses the outgoing rotation file rather than the full training file. Given that even the smallest sample has more than 2,000 observations, the shifts in magnitude and standard errors is unexpected.

30. The rigor of the assumptions and magnitude of the effects is critically discussed by Acemoglu and Pischke (1999, p. 131 and Note 8).

31. The Adult Education and Training Survey is a Canadian survey intended to capture all types of training received by 17–24-year-olds in the previous year. The survey asks whether the individual received any training, whether they received employer-supported education or training, and the type of employer-provided training received. It is similar but not identical to the CPS training supplement survey.

32. Estimates with establishment-specific wages are instrumented because of the endogeneity of the establishment wage.

33. We do not place great weight on older indirect approaches to measuring training effects, as Grossberg and Sicilian's (1999) research calls into question whether there is an empirical linkage between the wage growth and training and because there are now sufficient direct estimates of the minimum wage/training relationship to reduce the need for indirect approaches.

34. As with all state-by-year panels prior to 2004, the bias of the hypothesis tests toward rejecting the null makes the results difficult to interpret.

35. Employee pretax benefits are not counted as part of employee income and are not subject to income tax. This tax treatment makes them valued by employees, and it reduces employer tax liability, as they do not pay social security, unemployment, workers' compensation, or other taxes on these benefits.

36. Simon and Kaestner (2004) suggest that firms may be reluctant to adjust fringe benefits packages if, because of inflation, the increase in the real minimum wage is temporary and there are costs associated with ending and starting fringe benefit programs. Minimum enrollment requirements of insurance firms may also limit smaller firms' ability to reduce fringe benefit coverage, particularly health insurance (see Simon and Kaestner [2004]). However, firms that are not self-insured for health insurance are not covered by the IRS regulations on nondiscrimination

and therefore may be in a better position to withdraw or reduce health insurance coverage of minimum wage employees (Marks 2011).

37. The list is long and includes the value of private fringes; overtime pay; pension expense; holiday expenditures; health, accident and life insurance expenditures; severance pay; shift premiums; sick pay; other private fringes; and a measure of total hours of leave

38. An unpublished article by Royalty (2001) is cited in some research on this topic. She finds a negative relationship between higher minimum wages, and pension and health coverage. There are issues with the methodology, specification, and interpretation. It has not been published to date, and we do not include it in our discussion.

39. Other measures might include whether a respondent works for an employer that offers a plan or has coverage through a spouse or some other plan, such as veterans' benefits. Measures of participation in one's employer plan best measures the effect of the minimum wage.

40. The models are estimated with between 24,500 and 255,000 observations, depending on the outcome, group, and period; standard errors are clustered by state.

41. For a discussion of this literature through 1998, see Belman and Groshen (1998).

42. Marks (2011) suggests that one cause may be differences in the legal treatment of large and small firms with respect to regulation of working conditions. Under Internal Revenue Service codes, the health plans of self-insured firms, a type of plan found mainly among larger firms, must not discriminate in favor of highly compensated employees. These rules do not apply to firms that purchase insurance, mainly smaller firms, and they are permitted to discriminate in their provision of insurance.

   The nondiscrimination requirement increases the cost of excluding low-wage employees, including those hired at the minimum wage. Particularly for those firms with large numbers of higher-wage employees who expect health insurance coverage, the cost of excluding lower-wage employees from health insurance is very high. For firms not covered by such requirements, the cost of discrimination is lower, and we might expect to see them reducing health insurance coverage of its lower-wage workforce in the face of higher minimum wages.

43. There are about 183,000 individuals in Marks's (2011) large-firm sample and 244,000 individuals in the small-firm sample. The sample does not include the self-employed and students.

44. Although the coefficient is significant in a 5 percent test, this standard may not be sufficiently stringent for a sample with almost one-quarter million observations.

45. The elasticities are calculated at the average real minimum wage of $2.97 reported by Marks (2011) for her sample.

46. Similar results are found with measures of the state relative minimum wage, the ratio of the state minimum wage to the median wage for workers with a high school degree or less. The effect on health insurance coverage is more marked when the sample is limited to industries in which at least 20 percent of the labor force has less than a high school degree. The elasticity of health insurance coverage for the less educated ranged from 0.18 to 0.23, depending on time period.

47. There is, however, evidence that both the least- and highest-educated workers in large firms and the highest-educated workers in small firms have lower probabilities of pension coverage when the minimum wage is higher. The cause of the negative relationship between the minimum wage and pension plan participation among the best-educated workers is uncertain; it may be proxying effects of other variables related to the minimum wage.

7
Poverty and Inequality

An intent of the Fair Labor Standards Act and preceding state minimum wage laws was to assure that those who worked were able to afford a modest lifestyle. In this chapter we review the literature on how the minimum wage affects both the absolute and relative standard of living of those at the lower end of the income distribution in the United States. We begin with the research on the effect of the minimum wage on income inequality, the relative standard of living. Researchers are unanimous in finding that increases in the minimum wage act to reduce income inequality. The results with respect to absolute standards of living are less sanguine, as current research does not indicate that the minimum wage affects the number of individuals living in poverty. This may be due to the loose attachment of many of the low-income families to the labor force.

INEQUALITY AND THE DISTRIBUTION OF WAGES

Reversing a trend that started during the Great Depression, wage and income inequality in the United States has increased over the last four decades. The greatest changes have been the divergence in the upper and lower ends of the income distribution. In the later 1960s and throughout the 1970s, the mean household income of the 5 percent of families with the most income was 16 times the mean of the 20 percent of families with the least income. This ratio began to rise in the 1980s, when it averaged 18, continued to rise into the 1990s, when it averaged 22, and rose again in the 2000s, averaging 26. The ratio peaked in 2011 at 28 (U.S. Census Bureau 2011). The growth of inequality has been due mainly to the rapid growth in the income of the highest earning families. Between 1979 and 2007, the top 1 percent of families captured 60 percent of income gains, while the bottom 90 percent received about 9 percent of income gains (see, for example, Bivens [2011]).

The rise in inequality has become a topic of public controversy and academic discussion.[1] Recent research has both documented the change and examined plausible causes. Many have been considered, but most attention has been on differential change in levels of education and skill across demographic groups, on shifts in the supply and demand for different types of labor, on the effects of technology and of international trade, and on the change in the industrial and occupational structure of the economy. Changes in labor market institutions have also received attention as important causal factors in the increase in inequality. At issue is whether the weakening of labor market institutions, specifically declines in both the real minimum wage and the bargaining power of unions, has been an important factor in the relative decrease in wages and incomes of those in the lower tail of the income distribution. In the context of this study, we are interested in what the research says about the effect of changes in the minimum wage on lower-wage workers, as well as the channels through which these increases raise the wages of bound workers and near minimum wage workers.

The issues raised by this research revolve around how increases in the minimum wage affect wages, particularly in the lower ranges of the wage distribution. Does an increase in the minimum wage result in a compression of the wage structure, thereby reducing inequality, or does the wage structure as a whole move up, leaving inequality unaffected? We discussed the effect of the minimum wage on the earnings of low-wage workers in Chapter 5, and we limit the current discussion to research that addresses inequality directly.

Economists use many different measures to gauge inequality. Inequality, or change in inequality, can be measured by comparing the income of individuals at different points in the earnings distribution. For example, the 50/10 ratio is the ratio of the earnings of an individual at the 50th percentile of the earnings distribution to the earnings of an individual at the 10th percentile. This ratio is used to measure how the bottom of the earnings distribution is doing relative to an individual in the middle of the distribution. The 90/10 ratio is the ratio of the earnings of individuals at the 90th percentile to those at the 10th percentile. It measures how well those close to the top of the earnings distribution are doing relative to those toward the bottom. By considering these two measures, along with the 90/50 ratio, we can form a clear idea of not only how the overall distribution of earnings is shifting but also how individuals at various points in the distribution are doing relative to one another. The more commonly used ratios are 90/10, 90/50, 50/10, and 75/25. The last ratio measures how the middle of the lower half of the earnings distribution is doing relative to the middle of the upper half. Measures of variance are also used; higher variance in earnings corresponds to greater income inequality. Variance measures can be decomposed to allow changes in variance over time to be associated with particular sources of change, such as the minimum wage. Decomposition of variance allows us to understand both the magnitude of the effect of individual factors and the relative magnitude of the factors affecting earnings inequality. Other measures, such as the difference in earnings between those with only a high school degree and those with a college degree, provide another approach to measuring changes in earnings inequality.

Current research supports the view that the minimum wage reduces inequality in the lower half of the wage distribution through raising the minimum wage relative to the mean or median wage. (Table 7.1 provides information on the 8 studies of inequality.) There is considerably less agreement about the size of the effect, and whether there is an effect for men. The initial research, DiNardo, Fortin, and Lemieux (1996), focuses on the effect of labor market institutions on wage distributions between 1973 and 1992. Using CPS data and controlling for the effects on the distribution of wages of individual attributes such as education and age, macroeconomic factors such as shocks to supply and demand, and institutional factors including unionization and the minimum wage, the authors report that the decline in the real minimum wage between 1979 and 1988 accounted for about one-quarter of the increase in the standard deviation of men's wages, and nearly one-third of the increase in the standard deviation of women's wages. Other factors individually contributed considerably less to the rise in inequality. Changes with respect to unions and individual attributes each accounted for about one-seventh of the increase in standard deviation, and supply and demand for two-ninths for men. For women, the corresponding figures were one-thirtieth, one-quarter, and nearly one-fifth.

The minimum wage mainly affected the lower tail of both the male and female wage distributions. The decline in the real minimum wage accounts for between 45 and 60 percent of the increase in the difference in earnings between the 10th and 50th percentiles of the male distribu-

Table 7.1 The Effect of the Minimum Wage on the Distribution of Wages

Study	Effect	Target	Country	Sample period	Analytic approach	Unit of observation	Data structure	Type of standard error	Data set[a]
DiNardo, Fortin, and Lemieux (1996)	The decline in the real minimum wage was the source of one quarter of the increase in inequality.	Labor force	United States	1973–1992	Kernel density	Individual	Cross sectional	n/a	May CPS and CPS ORG
Lee (1999)	Lower minimum wages are associated with greater wage inequality in the lower tail of the wage distribution, particularly among women.	Labor force	United States	1979–1989	Regression	Individual aggregated to state	State-by-year panel	Hetero-skedasticity adjusted and clustered by state	CPS ORG
Card and DiNardo (2002)	A simple model finds that 90% of the change in the 90/10 wage gap is due to a declining real minimum wage.	Employed labor force	United States	1973–2000	Regression	Individual	Series of cross sections	n/a	March CPS and CPS ORG
Lemieux (2002)	Minimum wages affect the wage distribution; higher minimum wages are associated with reduced inequality in the lower tail of the wage distribution.	Employed labor force	Canada and United States	2000 for Canada; 1973, 1979, 1989, 1999	Regression supplemented by a logistic or probit	Individual	Cross sections	n/a	Canadian LFS for Alberta and BC; May CPS and CPS ORG

Study	Finding	Sample	Country	Period	Method	Unit	Structure	Clustering	Data
Lemieux (2006)	The decline in the real minimum wage was an important source of increased inequality.	Employed labor force	United States	1973–1993	Reweighting of residual wage variance	Individual	Cross sections	n/a	May CPS and CPS ORG
Autor, Katz, and Kearney (2008)	23% of the increase in the 50/10 wage gap is attributable to the declining real minimum wage.	College high school wage gap	United States	1963–2005	Regression	Experience group by year	Time series	Conventional	March CPS
Autor, Manning, Smith (2010)	If the real minimum wage had stayed at its 1979 level, 50/10 inequality would have been 28 to 39% smaller.	Labor force 18–64	United States	1979–2009	Regression; quantile and two stage	State-by-year	State-by-year panel	Clustered by state	CPS ORG
Dolton, Rosazza, and Wadsworth (2012)	The deeper the "bite" of the minimum wage, the greater the reduction in lower tail inequality.	Bound workers	United Kingdom	1999–2007	Incremental difference-in-differences regression	Region-year	Aggregate panel	Clustered by region	NES and ASHE

aCPS ORG = Current Population Survey Outgoing Rotation Groups. LFS = Labour Force Survey. NES = New Earnings Survey. ASHE = Annual Survey of Hours and Earnings.

tion, and 57–66 percent of the increase in the difference in women's 50/10 ratio. It has had a very small effect on the 75/25 ratio for the wages of men, and it accounts for less than one-tenth of the increase in the 75/25 ratio for women.[2] Consistent with the discussion of wage spillovers, the influence of the minimum wage does not reach as high as the 25th percentile for men but has some effect at the 25th percentile for women. Examination of data for 1973–1979, a period when the real minimum wage rose, suggests that the minimum wage accounted for between 25 and 33 percent of the decline in the standard deviation of women's wages and 33 percent of the decline in the standard deviation of men's wages. The minimum wage had a larger effect on the ratios of those with no more than a high school degree than those with a college degree for both genders in both 1973–1979 and 1979–1988.

Using a technique that better accounted for differences in labor market performance among the states in the 1980s and early 1990s, Lee (1999) finds that the decline in the minimum wage relative to state mean and median wages accounted for at least 70 percent of the growth in earnings inequality in the 50/10 ratio for women, and 70 percent of the growth in the 50/10 and 25 percent of the growth in the 50/25 ratio for men. Consistent with spillover effects occurring above the level of the binding minimum wage, the minimum wage reduced female wage inequality relative to the median as high as the third decile; the effect on men does not extend as high and is more sensitive to specification. Nevertheless, the effect on the 50/25 ratio for men suggests some spillover effect for men. A 10 percent increase in the minimum wage relative to a state's mean earnings is estimated to reduce women's 50/10 ratio by between 3 and 6 percent; for men the reduction is between 1 and 4 percent, but it is estimated with little precision.[3]

Additional research by Card and DiNardo (2002) and Lemieux (2002, 2006) provides further evidence that a higher minimum wage raises the bottom of the wage distribution and reduces wage inequality in the lower tail of that distribution. In an analysis that they describe as "somewhat informal," Card and DiNardo suggest that factors such as the decline in the real minimum wage played an important role in the 17 percent rise in the 90/10 wage gap between 1979 and 1999. Using a variety of measures and techniques, Lemieux (2002) finds that relative to Alberta, British Columbia's higher minimum wage was associated with smaller wage inequality in 2000. The increase in the U.S. minimum wage in the early 1990s similarly reduced inequality in the lower half of the wage distribution. Lemieux (2006) finds that, after adjusting for changes in workforce characteristics between 1972 and 2003, changes in the minimum wage accounted for 80 percent of the change in male inequality and 90 percent of the change in female inequality.

More recent work by Autor, Katz, and Kearney (2008) and Autor, Manning, and Smith (2010) suggests that the minimum wage has a smaller but still substantial effect on wage inequality. The first analysis measures the effects of the minimum wage, of supply and demand factors, and of unemployment on the ratio the wages of college graduates to those of high school graduates wages 1963 to 2005. A 10 percent higher real minimum wage is estimated to reduce the college/high school wage ratio by less than 1 percent; one-tenth the magnitude of that of aggregate labor supply conditions. There is also evidence that the minimum wage only affects the college/high school wage ratio for the initial 20 years after an individual's education is completed. Models that estimate the effect of the minimum wage on the 50/10 wage ratio without regard to educational attainment suggest that the decline in the real minimum wage from 1973 to 2005 accounted for 23 percent of the increase in inequality over the period.

The second study addresses concerns with measures used by Lee (1999). These estimates indicate that from 1979 to 2009, the decline in the minimum wage was associated with a third of the 11 percent increase in 50/10 inequality. This contrasts with Lee's method, which attributes all of the increase in inequality to the declining minimum wage. Effects differ considerably by gender. Had the minimum wage remained at its 1979 level, women's 50/10 ratio would have been 38 percent lower, while male inequality would have remained unchanged between 1979 and 2009.

Although considerably smaller than those reported by Lee (1999), the magnitude of the effect remains substantial—too large to be explained only by the effect of the minimum wage on bound workers. Separate regressions for different percentiles of the wage distribution indicate that the effect of the minimum wage extends up to the 30th percentile of the female wage distribution but only up through the 10th percentile of the male wage distribution. Again, the male result in particular contrasts with Lee, who finds effects in the male 50/25 ratio. The authors indicate that spillovers account for half of the effect of the minimum wage on wage inequality and provide some evidence that the spillover effect is larger in periods in which the real minimum wage falls. However, because of issues with self-reported wages, the degree to which the estimated spillover is due to reporting errors is uncertain.

As part of an analysis of the regional effect of the NMW in England, Scotland, and Wales, Dolton, Rosazza, and Wadsworth (2012) consider the effect of the NMW on lower-tail inequality.[4] They apply an incremental difference-in-differences estimator to earnings measures from the New Earnings Survey and the Annual Survey of Hours and Earnings from 1999 to 2007 to estimate whether the 5/50 and 10/50 income ratio has responded to changes in the NMW. Their regressions, structured as a geographic area-by-year panel, include a variety of controls as well as year and area effects, and the reported standard errors are corrected for heteroskedasticity and unspecified serial correlation. They report that an increase in the proportion paid at or below the minimum wage was associated with reduced lower-tail inequality and that the effect became more pronounced with the increases in the NMW between 1999 and 2007.

THE EFFECT OF THE MINIMUM WAGE ON POVERTY AND ECONOMIC INEQUALITY

As articulated in the preamble to the Fair Labor Standards Act, a central goal of the minimum wage is to assure that low-wage workers have sufficient earnings to support a modest standard of living. While the minimum wage targets low-wage workers (and firms), what we ultimately want to know about the minimum wage is whether it improves the lot of low-income workers—are they better off than they would otherwise be because of the minimum wage or an increase in the minimum wage? Are they absolutely better off? Are they better off in comparison with other, higher-income workers? Does the minimum wage raise living standards for those whose living standards are below average? If so, does it do this as a stand-alone policy or in combination with other policies? Does it enable them to afford better housing, diet, health care, or any of the other things that together make up a standard of living?

It is surprising how little work on this issue exists. Most of the literature considers one of two issues. The first is the relationship between the minimum wage and poverty, in particular, how the minimum wage affects either transitions of households into and out of poverty or, at a more aggregate level, how it affects the poverty rate. The second issue concerns interactions between the minimum wage and other anti-poverty policies.

To understand the first strand, it is necessary to know what is meant by poverty. The colloquial meaning is a bit vague, but dictionaries give the following definitions:

- The state of one who lacks a usual or socially acceptable amount of money or material possessions. Poverty may cover a range from extreme want of necessities to absence of material comforts.[5]

- The condition of having little or no wealth or few material possessions; indigence, destitution.[6]

Neither definition provides the quantitative precision that statistical analysis typically requires, but both suggest that what is considered to be poverty can change over time.

In the United States, there is a widely accepted definition of what it means to be in poverty that varies over time and with the size and structure of the household.[7] In the 1950s, the U.S. Department of Agriculture (USDA) developed four different food plans, with the least expensive one known as the "thrifty food plan." In the mid-1960s, Orshansky (1963, 1965) determined the cost of this plan and extrapolated that to total household income based on results from the 1955 Household Food Consumption Survey (also of the USDA), which indicated that families of three or more spent about one-third of their annual income on food (Fisher 1992). Families with incomes less than three times the amount needed to buy the thrifty food plan were judged to be in poverty.

The definition of poverty-level income has been a contentious, heavily politicized issue, as it can lead to sound bites about increases or decreases in the poverty rate during politicians' tenure in office. Since originally defined, poverty-level income has been updated only for inflation, and it has not been adjusted for changes in spending patterns on food, other consumer goods, or changes in housing and commuting patterns, in particular, the growth of suburbs. Correcting for these would substantially raise the level of income needed to be above the poverty line. The income share of food expenditures had already fallen from one-third to one-quarter by 1965, and, had the poverty-level income been adjusted, the poverty line would have been one-third more than it was. By 2007 food expenditures had declined to one-tenth of family income; adjusting the definition for this change would have raised the poverty line to three times its then current level (Clauson 2008). Income used to calculate the poverty line also does not include many government transfers, which would either reduce the income needed to escape poverty or increase the amount of income attributed to many households, in either case reducing the number of households in poverty. While the poverty line may have reflected reality when first defined, it does not any longer.[8]

Table 7.2 shows the minimum levels of income needed for families of different sizes to be classified as being above poverty. A family of one adult and two children would be considered not to be in poverty if annual income exceeds $17,568, while one of two adults and two children requires a minimum of $22,113. The poverty line defines a very low standard of living, possibly destitution. For example, working single parents almost always require child care. According to the National Association of Child Care Resource and Referral Agencies (2011, p. 23), in 2010, the average cost of child care for two children (an infant and a four-year-old) in Mississippi, the least expensive state, would be at least $7,280, more than 40 percent of the poverty-level income of $15,030.[9] There would be little income for anything else.

The poverty line(s) and the minimum wage make almost no contact with each other. First consider a single-parent family with one or two children. In each case, the 2010 poverty line is $17,552 and $17,568, respectively. If this parent worked full time at minimum wage, she would earn $14,500, not enough for the family income to exceed the poverty line. The minimum wage, which was $7.25 per hour at the time of writing, would have to rise by more than $1.50/hour, in excess of 20 percent, to bring this household to the poverty line. None of the increases in the federal minimum wage since the Korean War, except for those of 1956 and 1974, have been as large as 20 percent, and most have been about half that.

Next, consider two-parent families. If both parents work full time at the minimum wage, annual income is $29,000/year. Unless the family

Table 7.2 Poverty Thresholds for 2010 by Size of Family and Number of Related Children under 18 Years ($, 2010)

Size of family unit	Related children under 18 years								
	None	One	Two	Three	Four	Five	Six	Seven	Eight or more
One person (unrelated individual)									
Under 65 years	11,344								
65 years and over	10,458								
Two people									
Householder under 65 years	14,602	15,030							
Householder 65 years and over	13,180	14,973							
Three people	17,057	17,552	17,568						
Four people	22,491	22,859	22,113	22,190					
Five people	27,123	27,518	26,675	26,023	25,625				
Six people	31,197	31,320	30,675	30,056	29,137	28,591			
Seven people	35,896	36,120	35,347	34,809	33,805	32,635	31,351		
Eight people	40,146	40,501	39,772	39,133	38,227	37,076	35,879	35,575	
Nine people or more	48,293	48,527	47,882	47,340	46,451	45,227	44,120	43,845	42,156

SOURCE: U.S. Census Bureau, http://www.census.gov/hhes/www/poverty/data/threshld/thresh10.xls, (accessed August 24, 2011).

has more than three children, this is above the poverty line and would require that the minimum wage drop to $6.50 an hour (a decline of more than 10 percent) for the family to be at the poverty line if it has three children, and to about $5.50/hour for a family with two children (the federal minimum wage has not declined in dollar terms since it was first established). If the family has more than three children, it would be $137 below the poverty income with two full-time minimum wage workers. An increase in the minimum wage of less than a nickel would bring this family to the poverty line. Larger families would require increases in the minimum wage between $0.90 and $2.75 (between 12 and 38 percent) to earn more than a poverty-level income.

Transitions across the officially defined poverty line are too crude a measure to discern the effect of the minimum wage. Although the minimum wage may affect the standard of living of low-income families that include a bound worker, the definition of the poverty line and the size of a typical minimum wage increase make it unlikely that changes in the minimum wage will succeed in moving families out of poverty as officially defined.

A second reason not to expect those in poverty to benefit from the minimum wage is their low employment and labor force participation rates. Burkhauser, Couch, and Glenn (1995, Table 4) report that in 1989, a quarter of households below the poverty line had no employed workers. Using data from the 2006 CPS, the last full year of the CPS prior to the start of the Great Recession, Table 7.3 displays the percentage of households in each of 16 income categories and tabulates the percentage in which at least one adult was employed, and if not employed, whether at least one was nevertheless in the labor force (i.e., unemployed, defined as not employed but actively looking for work). The first two columns define the income categories for family income over the prior 12 months: the first one shows the percentage of households in each income category, and the next displays the cumulative percentage in that income category or a lower one. The next three columns give information about labor force status—whether anyone in the household is employed, and if not, whether anyone is actively looking for work and thus counted as unemployed; if no one is employed or unemployed, the household is classified as having no one in the labor force.

Only half (51 percent) of the households in the lowest income categories had any members employed at the time they were surveyed by the CPS. As we go up the (2006) income distribution, this fraction increases until, near the top, virtually all households have at least one employed member. The percentage of households that had nobody employed but somebody unemployed falls from 12 percent at the lowest income levels to nearly zero. The combination of these two categories is households that had at least one member who was in the labor force. If we consider the percentage of households with no labor force participants, we see that it falls from a high value of 45 percent in households with a family income over the last 12 months between $5,000 and $7,499 to a low of 3 percent in households with a 12-month income between $100,000 and $149,999. Sixty-two percent of households with incomes less than $25,000 had any earner; in families that make at least $25,000, 92 percent include someone who is employed. Given the low level of employment among households that earned income under $20,000 annually, opportunities for the minimum wage to affect household income are limited.

The last four columns in Table 7.3 highlight other differences between low- and higher-income households. Not only is it the case that higher-income households are more likely to have at least one employed person, but as household income rises, so too do both the average number of employed individuals in households and the average number of paid hours per household. In 2006, the federal minimum wage was $5.15 per hour, and the poverty line for a single parent of two children was an annual income of $16,242 (U.S. Census Bureau 2006). The parents would have had to work more than 60 hours per week at a minimum wage job for the whole year to exceed that level. More than half of households with 2005 incomes below $20,000 worked no more than 40 hours per week in the week before the survey. Too many low-income households have no one in the labor force, much less employed, for the minimum wage to have much effect on poverty. Even for those that do, the minimum wage is too low and households work too few hours for an increase to change poverty status.

Empirical Studies of the Minimum Wage and Poverty

Table 7.4 lists more than a dozen statistical analyses of the response of poverty to the minimum wage. In this group, there are four data structures, the most common of which is a state-year panel (or province-year

Table 7.3 **Labor Force Status in 2006 by Family Income in 2005**

| Total family income in 2006 ($) | Share of labor force (%) | Cumulative share (%) | Earner (%) | No earners (%) | | Labor force status | | | |
| | | | | Unemployed (at least 1) | None in the labor force | Number of earners | | Hours last week | |
						Mean	Median	Mean[a]	Median[b]
Less than 5,000	2.8	2.8	51	12.0	37.0	0.72	1	52	40
5,000–7,499	2.1	4.8	47	7.7	45.0	0.67	0	52	40
7,500–9,999	2.2	6.8	49	6.2	45.0	0.68	0	51	40
10,000–12,499	3.0	10.0	56	6.2	38.0	0.78	1	53	40
12,500–14,999	2.8	12.8	61	5.9	33.0	0.89	1	57	40
15,000–19,999	4.7	17.5	69	3.7	27.0	0.98	1	56	40
20,000–24,999	5.6	23.2	74	2.9	23.0	1.10	1	59	46
25,000–29,999	6.0	29.0	80	2.3	18.0	1.20	1	62	52
30,000–34,999	6.5	35.6	84	1.6	14.0	1.40	1	65	60
35,000–39,999	5.8	41.4	87	1.0	12.0	1.50	1	67	63
40,000–49,999	9.1	50.5	90	1.1	9.3	1.60	2	71	70
50,000–59,999	9.2	59.6	91	0.8	7.8	1.70	2	75	78
60,000–74,999	10.9	70.5	94	0.6	5.7	1.80	2	81	80
75,000–99,999	12.2	82.7	96	0.4	3.9	1.90	2	83	80
100,000–149,999	10.2	92.9	97	0.2	3.0	2.00	2	87	80
At least 150,000	7.1	100.0	97	0.2	3.1	1.90	2	88	83
Overall mean/median			85	1.9	13.0	1.50	2	74	75
Less than 15,000	12.8	12.8	54	7.6	39.0	0.76	1	53	40
Less than 25,000	23.2	23.2	62	5.6	33.0	0.89	1	55	43

| Greater than 10,000 | 17.0 | 83.0 | 97 | 0.2 | 3.0 | 2.00 | 2 | 88 |

[a] Approximately one-sixth of respondents did not provide an answer to the income category question. The figures for total and cumulative total are calculated with reference to the remaining 83% of the sample.

[b] Calculated only over households with at least one earner last week.

SOURCE: 2006 CPS ORG files.

panels in the case of Sen, Rybczynski, and Van de Waal [2011] and Campolieti, Gunderson, and Lee [2012]).

The other three structures are a state-year repeat cross section (Sabia 2008), an aggregate time series (Vedder and Gallaway 2002), and longitudinal panels (Neumark, Schweitzer, and Wascher 2005; Sabia and Nielsen 2013). Of these last two studies, the former has two observations per family, while the latter is a more conventional longitudinal structure with considerably more observations on each individual and a variety of outcome measures. Except for three studies, those that use a state-year panel or aggregate time series relate poverty rates to the minimum wage, and the one based on a repeated cross section is conceptually similar, relating a family's poverty status to the minimum wage and other factors. The panel with two observations on each family, Neumark, Schweitzer, and Wascher (2005), relates transitions into and out of poverty to the minimum wage and other factors in a difference-in-differences framework. The analyses of Gundersen (2006) and Gundersen and Ziliak (2004), both of which use state-by-year panels, are unusual in that they consider not only the poverty status of families (i.e., changes in the poverty rate) but also the severity of poverty, that is, whether families below the poverty line move closer to it while nevertheless remaining in poverty. Sabia and Neilsen (2013) are likewise unusual in going beyond poverty status to consider effects on the income-to-poverty ratio and material hardship. The three exceptions mentioned above are Grogger (2003, 2004), who relates the minimum wage to whether families receive welfare benefits, and Page, Spetz, and Millar (2005), who relate it to welfare caseloads.

Those studies in the first panel in Table 7.4 are, with the exception of Sabia and Nielsen (2013), all vulnerable to the critique of Bertrand, Duflo, and Mullainathan (2004). This has no consequences for findings of no relationship between the minimum wage and poverty, but it raises doubts about the reliability of any results reported to be statistically significant: Addison and Blackburn (1999); DeFina (2008); Grogger (2003, 2004); Gundersen and Ziliak (2004); Gundersen (2006); Neumark and Wascher (2002); Page, Spetz, and Millar (2005); Morgan and Kickham (2001); and Stevans and Sessions (2001). Four of the remaining regression analyses find no response of poverty to the minimum wage. Two find that the poverty rate rises when the minimum wage is higher, but both are problematic. Vedder and Gallaway (2002) are markedly nonchalant about the serial correlation that is almost certainly a part of the aggregate time series that they analyze. (This analysis is treated in slightly more detail in Chapter 3.) The difficulties of Sen, Rybczynski, and Van de Waal's (2011) analysis are more interesting. They analyze a 25-year-long panel of nine Canadian provinces and present standard errors that are clustered by both province and year in the calculation. Bertrand, Duflo, and Mullainathan (2004) document that clustering does not resolve the problem of serial correlation when the number of clusters is too small; in their Monte Carlo example, nearly 11 percent of their simulations using only 10 clusters (corresponding to states or provinces) incorrectly reject the null of no effect at test size of 0.05, and more than 15 percent using only 6 clusters do so. (Hansen [2007b] and Cameron, Gelbach, and Miller [2008] confirm this result.)

Sabia and Nielsen (2013) are among the more interesting analyses of the effect of the minimum wage on poverty. Using the Survey of Income Program Participation (SIPP), a longitudinal survey with extensive information on sources of income and participation in welfare and income maintenance programs, the authors estimate the relationship between federal and state minimum wages and poverty, material hardship, and income for the years 1996–2007. Models are estimated for all workers aged 16–64, for the employed, for those aged 16–29 without a high school diploma, for blacks aged 16–24, and, as a falsification test, for individuals aged 30–54 with a high school degree or better. The estimates of standard errors in the regression models are clustered by state. Estimates for poverty and income take advantage of the longitudinal structure to control for individual heterogeneity.

The authors find little or no evidence that the minimum wage is related to any of the outcomes. In their sample with all individuals aged 16–64, the coefficient on the minimum wage is very small and never significant for indicator measures of being below poverty, or of being within 125 percent or 150 percent of the poverty line. It is also not significant for either the ratio of income to poverty or being below poverty inclusive of transfer payments. Similar results are obtained with the subsamples of workers, of those aged 16–29 without a high school diploma, and for blacks aged 16–24. However, several estimates with state time trends find that a higher minimum wage increases the likelihood that 16–29-year-olds with a high school diploma will be below 125 percent and 150 percent of poverty.

Table 7.4 Statistical Studies of the Minimum Wage and Poverty

Study	Minimum wage and poverty relationship	Target group	Country	Sample period	Unit of observation	Data structure	Analytic approach	Type of standard error	Data set[a]
Addison and Blackburn (1999)	Negative	Teens, young adults, jr. high dropouts	United States	1983–1996	State	State-year panel	Regression	Conventional	March CPS
Burkhauser and Sabia (2007)	None	Individuals in poverty	United States	1989–2003	State	State-year panel	Regression + simulation[b]	PCSE[c]	March CPS
DeFina (2008)	Negative	Kids in female-headed households	United States	1992–2003	State	State-year panel	(Robust) Regression	Conventional	CPS
Grogger (2003)[d]	Varies with age of children	Female-headed families	United States	1979–2000	Family	Repeated cross section	Regression	Clustered (state-year)	March CPS
Grogger (2004)[d]	Contradictory, varies by specification	Female-headed families	United States	1979–2000	Family	Repeated cross section	Regression	Clustered (state-year)	March CPS
Gundersen and Ziliak (2004)	Negative to none	Families (2+ related individuals)	United States	1981–2000	State	State-year panel	Regression	Robust	March CPS
Gundersen (2006)	None except for metro area female-headed households	Families (2+ related individuals)	United States	1988–2003	State	State-year panel	Regression	Conventional	March CPS
Neumark and Wascher (2002)	Net small positive	Families with income < 2 × poverty level	United States	1986–1995	Family	State-year panel	Diff-in-diff. and regression	Conventional	March CPS

Study	Effect	Population	Country	Years	Level	Model	Method	Standard errors	Data
Page, Spetz, and Millar (2005)[d]	Positive	Individuals on Welfare	United States	1983–1996	State	State-year panel	Regression	Newey-West HAC SEs[e]	Various
Morgan and Kickham (2001)	Negative	Children (in poverty)	United States	1987–1996	State	State-year panel	Regression	PCSE[c]	CPS
Stevans and Sessions (2001)	None to negative	Families	United States	1984–1998	State	State-year panel	Regression	Conventional	CPS
Sabia (2008)	None	Single mothers	United States	1992–2005	Individual	State-year RCS[f]	Regression	Clustered	March CPS
Sabia and Burkhauser (2010)	None	Families in poverty	United States	2003–2007	State	State-year panel	Regression + simulation[b]	Clustered	March CPS
Sen, Rybczynski, and Van de Waal (2011)	Positive	All families	Canada	1981–2004	Province	Province-year panel	Regression	Two-way clustered[g]	Statistics Canada
Vedder and Gallaway (2002)	None to positive	Full-time workers	United States	1966–1998	U.S.	Aggregate time series	Regression	Conventional	Census data
Neumark, Schweitzer, and Wascher (2005)	None	Families with income < 6 × poverty level	United States	1986–1995	Family	Two-period panel	Diff-in-diff. / kernel regression	Boot-strapped	March CPS
Campolieti, Gunderson, and Lee (2012)[g]	None	Families at the LICO, 1.25 and 1.5 times the LICO[h]	Canada	1979–2007	Province	Province-by-year panel	Regression	Conventional	SLID

(continued)

Table 7.4 (continued)

Authors	Minimum wage and poverty relationship	Target group	Country	Sample period	Unit of observation	Data structure	Analytic approach	Type of SE	Data set
Sabia and Nielsen (2013)	Increases in the minimum wage do not influence the likelihood of being in poverty or the income-to-poverty ratio.		United States	1996–2007	Individual	Longitudinal	Regression	Clustered	SIPP
Maloney and Pacheco (2012)	Increases in the likelihood that a MW worker will be in lower-income deciles.	Minimum wage employees	New Zealand	1997–2008	Individual	Repeat cross section	Probit and multinomial logit	Conventional	Annual income supplement to the Household Labour Force Survey

[a] Note that the March Current Population Survey (CPS) refers to data for the previous year. Thus, 2003–2007 data are for the period 2002–2006, and similarly for other periods. SLID = Survey of Labour and Income Dynamics. SIPP = Survey of Income and Program Participation.

[b] The simulation uses the regression results to estimate the effects of a proposed increase in the minimum wage.

[c] Panel-corrected standard errors.

[d] This article looks not at poverty but at whether the minimum wage moves families onto or off welfare rolls (Grogger 2003, 2004) or affects the size of welfare caseloads (Page, Spetz, and Millar 2005).

[e] Heteroskedasticity- and autocorrelation-consistent standard errors.

[f] Repeated cross section.

[g] Clustering is unlikely to address the Bertrand, Duflo, and Mallainathan issue for Canadian province-year panels because there are too few provinces. See Bertrand, Duflo, and Mallainathan (2004).

[h] Low-income cut-off.

As we have indicated, we are unconvinced that estimates of whether the minimum wage moves individuals across arbitrary thresholds provide useful insights. The estimates with the income-to-poverty ratios move closer to addressing how the minimum wage affects low-income employees and families. Sabia and Nielsen's (2013) specification may, however, be submerging the effect of the minimum wage in an overly broad sample.[10] If, for example, the impact of the minimum wage on family income occurred in the second and third decile of the income distribution, the effect of minimum wage increases on income may be difficult to detect with a linear specification across all income deciles. The narrowing of the sample by age and high school graduation improves this but does not focus sufficiently tightly on the relevant sample. Despite this, there is evidence that a 10 percent increase in the minimum wage would be associated with a 5.7 percent increase in the income-to-poverty ratio of individuals aged 16–29 who do not have a high school degree. It would be better to divide the sample by income quintile or decile and estimate the effects within those samples.[11]

Simulation Studies of the Minimum Wage and Poverty

Table 7.5 lists six studies that simulate the response of poverty or poverty status to the minimum wage. Using estimates of disemployment effects and wage increases from a number of nonsimulation studies, each of these six studies derives estimates for the number of households that a specific minimum wage increase would raise above the poverty threshold and the number that it would move below it. Neumark and Wascher (2008, Section 5.2.3) detail a number of problems that make it difficult to express confidence in the conclusions drawn from these simulations. Briefly, they generally must rely on estimates of minimum wage effects on groups other than poor households, and they ignore the possibility of a variety of behavioral responses to the minimum wage. In both cases, the reason for doing this is that the estimates necessary for avoiding these practices do not exist. Because of the shakiness of the conclusions, we do not discuss the simulation studies.

Both the statistical and simulation studies of the relationship between the minimum wage and poverty leave us where we started, without any strong evidence that the minimum wage affects the poverty rate one way or the other.

Table 7.5 Simulation Studies of the Minimum Wage and Poverty

Study	Minimum wage and poverty relationship	Target group	Country	Sample period	Unit of observation	Data structure	Data set[a]
Formby, Bishop, and Kim (2010)	Slight negative	Poor households	United States	2007	Household	Cross section	CPS (March & ORG)
Horrigan and Mincy (1993)	Negative	Families (with MW workers)	United States	1980–1987	Family	Annual RCS	March CPS
Knabe and Schöb (2008)	Positive	Low-wage workers	Germany	2006	Individual	Cross section	SOEP
Mascella, Teja, and Thompson (2009)	Very slightly negative	All households	Canada	2004	Household	Cross section	SLID
Müller and Steiner (2008)	None	All households	Germany	2008	Household	Cross section	SOEP
Sutherland (2001)	Negative	Poor households	UK	2001	Household	Cross section	HBAI

[a]CPS = Current Population Survey. SOEP = Socio-Economic Panel (Germany). SLID = Survey of Labour and Income Dynamics (Statistics Canada). HBAI = Households Below Average Income (UK).

Interactions between the Minimum Wage and Other Antipoverty Policies

There have been few studies on the interaction of antipoverty policies and the minimum wage; more often the studies focus on the combined effect on employment (see Table 7.6).[12] Kramarz and Philippon (2001) consider not only changes in the French minimum wage but also in the payroll taxes that employers must pay. In the 1990s, those taxes pertaining to low-wage employees were reduced several times to offset increases in the minimum wage. Consequently, despite increases in the minimum wage, employers' costs of hiring of low-wage workers fell, and affected workers had a higher probability of employment than would otherwise have been the case.

The Earned Income Tax Credit (EITC) subsidizes employment by reducing income taxes on labor income, primarily for low-income families with children. Neumark and Wascher (2011) examine the separate and combined effects on employment and earnings of the EITC and minimum wage on both single mothers and members of other demographic groups that are likely to compete with them in the labor market. They report that the minimum wage has a positive effect on both employment and earnings of single mothers, an important part of the target group of the EITC, both by itself and especially in combination with the EITC. This effect carries through to raise the incomes of very poor families with children, enough to reduce the incidence of poverty in this group. The flip side is that both policies—in some cases separately, in others together, and in yet others both separately and together—reduce employment and earnings of individuals who are not eligible for the EITC and who compete in the labor market with individuals who are eligible for the EITC; they identify these individuals as childless individuals who have not gone beyond high school, white teenage boys, and all teenage girls.

The French studies consider policies that differ from the antipoverty policy considered in the United States, making it difficult to compare results across the two countries. The French policies are designed to offset effects of the minimum wage, either to encourage labor demand or to reduce labor supply. The U.S. policy, the EITC, is designed instead to encourage labor supply and income of poor families, and the minimum wage apparently makes it more effective.

Table 7.6 Studies of the Minimum Wage and Antipoverty Policies

Study	Interaction between minimum wage and other policies	Target	Country	Sample period	Unit of observation	Data structure	Analytic approach	Type of standard error	Data set
Neumark and Wascher (2001)	Not examined—EITC vs. minimum wage	EITC recipients	United States	1986–1995	Family	Two-year panel	Regression	Clustered (state-year)	March CPS[a]
Kramarz and Philippon (2001)	Negative effect on employment	Low-wage workers	France	1990–1998	Individual	Repeated cross section	Quasi experiment	Conventional	Labour Force Survey
Laroque and Salanie (2002)	Negative effect on employment	Married women	France	1997	Individual	Cross section	Regression	Conventional	Labour Force Survey
Neumark and Wascher (2011)	Generally complements	EITC recipients, competitors in labor market	United States	1997–2006	Family and individual	Repeated cross section	Regression	Clustered	March CPS

[a] Note that the March CPS refers to data for the previous year. Thus, 2003–2007 data are for the period 2002–2006, and similarly for other periods.

Is the Minimum Wage Well Targeted to Help Low-Income Households?

Another issue is whether the minimum wage is sufficiently well targeted to aid low-income individuals and households. The rationale for the minimum wage has been regularly criticized because too large a proportion of those earning the minimum wage are not in the lowest income deciles. We explore this issue in our discussion in Chapter 5, Tables 5.1–5.3, and find that a substantial proportion of the U.S. labor force and the career labor force were employed at or not far above the minimum wage. As part of a study of antipoverty effects of the minimum wage in New Zealand, Maloney and Pacheco (2012) find that the relevance of the minimum wage to low-income households is strongly related to whether the minimum wage has kept pace with wage growth and inflation. The National Party of New Zealand allowed the minimum wage to languish from 1990 to 1999. As a result, the value of the minimum wage fell by 1.1 percent relative to inflation and by 8.7 percent relative to average hourly earnings. The Labour Party reversed this policy beginning in 2000 and continuing through to 2008.[13] Over this period, the adult minimum wage rose by 32.9 percent relative to inflation and by 22.6 percent relative to average hourly earnings, and the minimum wage of teenagers rose even more rapidly.

Using the annual income supplements to the Household Labor Force survey for 1997 to 2008 to estimate the relationship between the real minimum wage and the likelihood that an employee in an income decile will be a minimum wage worker, Maloney and Pacheco (2012) find that a 10 percent rise in the real minimum wage increases the likelihood that an adult in the 1st decile of the household income distribution is a minimum wage worker by 9 percent, by 6.8 percent for one in the 2nd decile, 3.3 percent in the 3rd decile, 1.5 percent in the 5th decile, 1.5 percent in the 7th decile, and by 0.25 percent in the 10th decile. A parallel analysis on the distribution of minimum wage workers across income deciles finds that a 10 percent rise in the real minimum wage increases the likelihood that an adult minimum wage worker is in the 2nd decile of household income by 3.8 percent, and decreases the likelihood of their being in the 5th or 10th deciles.

Maloney and Pacheco (2012, Figure 5) find that the proportion of minimum wage workers in each income decile was both low and relatively constant across the household income deciles in 1997–1999, the period in which the minimum wage languished. In contrast, the proportion of minimum wage employees in the lower income deciles were markedly higher in 2006–2008, the end of the period in which the minimum wage was substantially raised. For example, the proportion of employees who were employed at the minimum wage in the lowest income decile rose from 5 percent in 1997–1999 to 33 percent in 2006–2008. In the 3rd decile, it rose from 4 percent to 16 percent. In contrast, in the 9th decile, it rose from 1 percent to 5 percent.

These results suggest that, at least in New Zealand, increases in the minimum wage have their largest effect in the lower reaches of the income distribution. Further, the answer to whether the minimum wage appropriately targets low-income populations is not independent of the level of the minimum wage. When the real minimum wage is very low, the proportion of workers employed at the minimum wage is not closely related to household income. As it rises, it affects the lower deciles of the income distribution far more than the upper deciles.[14]

HOW LONG DO MINIMUM WAGE EARNERS CONTINUE TO EARN THE MINIMUM WAGE?

The importance of the minimum wage to the economic well-being of minimum wage earners is related to how long they remain in positions that pay at or near the minimum wage. If those earning the minimum wage are at the minimum for a brief time and ascend the wage distribution rapidly, there is less reason to be concerned about the minimum wage and its effect on workers' earnings. The effect cannot be large because workers spend little time working at or near the minimum wage. If, on the other hand, they spend considerable time at or near the minimum wage, the minimum wage may have substantial effects on their annual and lifetime income. How long individual workers are in minimum wage positions is then an important consideration in assessing the effect and effectiveness of the minimum wage.

Answers to this question are influenced by researchers' decisions about the point in an individual's economic life cycle to begin measuring their wage growth. The wage path of those still in school is quite different from that of individuals who have permanently left school and are beginning career employment. Answers also depend on how far above the minimum wage researchers look for wage effects. Several studies define the minimum wage as exactly the minimum wage and treat any earnings in excess of that minimum wage as above minimum wage earnings. Others treat those earning within $0.25 of the minimum as minimum wage earners and then consider bands of $0.50, $1.00, and $1.50 above the minimum as potentially affected by the minimum wage. While the former approach assures that we will find few workers spending long periods earning the minimum wage, the latter provides better insights into how rapidly workers move beyond the minimum wage.[15]

The most thoughtful study of minimum wage dynamics is the work of Carrington and Fallick (2001) (see Table 7.7). Their use of the NLSY allows them to track individuals over a decade, providing an extended portrait of the wage movement of workers through their early careers. Restricting their sample to individuals who have completed their schooling removes a large number of minimum wage earners whose labor market decisions are secondary to their education decisions. Defining a minimum wage job as one that pays no more than $0.25 above the minimum wage addresses the imprecision in the reports of the hourly earnings from household surveys. Finally, by presenting their results in bands above the minimum wage, the authors allow for spillover effects, for the effects of within-firm pay increases of longer-term workers who entered at the minimum wage, and for increases in the legislated minimum wage. It allows the readers to determine for themselves the wage band at which the minimum wage is no longer relevant, rather than being constrained by the authors' choices.

Carrington and Fallick (2001) report that 8 percent of the career workforce spent at least half of the first 10 years after completing school in positions paying no more than $1 more than the minimum wage. Employees with a typical career spent at least 2 of their first 10 years working within $1.00 of the minimum wage. African Americans and women spent longer periods close to the minimum wage. In the first year of employment after permanently leaving school, 30 percent of employees work at jobs paying within $0.25 per hour of the minimum wage, and 54 percent (including the 30 percent already mentioned) work in jobs within $1.00 of the minimum wage. These percentages decline steadily

Table 7.7 The Dynamics of Minimum Wage Earners: How Long Do Those Earning the Minimum Wage Remain Close to the Minimum?

Study	Effect	Target	Country	Sample period	Analytic approach	Unit of observation	Data structure	Type of SE	Data set[a]
Carrington and Fallick (2001)	"Most workers who begin their careers in minimum wage jobs eventually gain more experience and move on to higher paying jobs; however, some workers spend substantial portions of their early careers consistently working in minimum wage jobs"	Career workforce who began in minimum wage jobs	United States	First 10 years of career employment between 1979 and 1994	Descriptive	Individual across years	Longitudinal	n/a	1979 NLSY
Smith and Vavrichek (1992)	Half of minimum wage workers continue in minimum wage or close to minimum wage jobs one year later.	Individuals paid exactly the minimum wage in the first year of data	United States	1984–1995	Logit and tobit regressions	Individual	Longitudinal	Conventional	SIPP
Long (1999)	Half of minimum wage workers continue in minimum wage or close to minimum wage jobs one year later.	Individuals paid exactly the minimum wage		1992–1993	Logit and tobit regressions	Individual	Longitudinal	Conventional	SIPP

Even and Macpherson (2003)	29% of those earning the minimum are still at exactly the minimum wage one year later.	Individuals earning exactly the minimum in the first year	United States	1979–1999	Regression	Individual	Semilongitudinal (two-year panels)	Conventional	CPS
Phimister and Theodossiou (2009)	The effect of individual characteristics on the likelihood of exiting low-pay employment differs for men and women and in the period prior to and after implementation of the NMW	Labor force	United Kingdom	1991–2005	Discrete time competing risks hazard model	Individual	Longitudinal	Approximate boot strapped	Waves 1–15 of the BHPS

[a] NLSY = National Longitudinal Survey of Youth. SIPP = Survey of Income and Program Participation. CPS = Current Population Survey. BHPS = British Household Panel Survey.

as employees gain experience. Those working at the minimum wage have about a 50 percent chance of remaining at the minimum wage in the next year, and those who are earning above the minimum wage have a better than 90 percent chance of continuing to earn above the minimum wage in the following year. At 10 years, only 7 percent earn the minimum wage, and a total of 12 percent earn no more than $1 above the minimum wage (see Table 7.8).

Rather than looking at snapshots in time (the end of the first year, the end of the first decade), the data can also be arranged according to the time spent in various wage bands. Only 4 percent of the respondents spent 5 years of the 10 years within $0.50 of the minimum wage, but larger proportions of the workforce spent considerably more time within $1 of the minimum wage. Almost 20 percent of the postschool workforce spend a quarter of their first 10 years within $1 of the minimum wage, and 8 percent spent 5 years within $1 of the minimum wage. Again, fractions of women and African Americans who spent extended periods at or close to the minimum wage were higher than the general population. Carrington and Fallick (2001) conclude that "most workers who begin their careers in minimum wage jobs eventually gain more experience and move on to higher paying jobs; however, some workers

Table 7.8 Share of Population in Minimum Wage or Near-Minimum-Wage Jobs by Years into Career

Years into career	Above prevailing minimum wage by no more than				
	$0.25	$0.50	$1.00	$1.50	$2.00
1	30.5	38.7	54.5	64.3	72.6
2	23.4	30.2	42.4	52.4	62.0
3	16.7	21.8	31.9	42.0	50.8
4	13.5	17.2	25.6	33.9	42.9
5	10.5	14.0	21.0	28.0	37.0
6	9.2	12.0	27.9	24.2	32.4
7	8.6	10.4	15.8	20.6	27.5
8	7.7	9.5	14.4	18.2	25.2
9	7.3	8.8	12.7	17.1	22.5
10	7.3	8.6	12.2	15.1	20.3

NOTE: "Years into career" begin immediately after schooling was completed.
SOURCE: Authors' calculations from the NLSY79. Reproduced from Carrington and Fallick (2001, Table 2).

spend substantial portions of their early careers consistently working in minimum wage jobs" (p. 17).

Most studies examine wage dynamics over shorter periods, use more restrictive definitions of minimum wage workers, or consider different populations. Smith and Vavrichek (1992) use data from the SIPP from September 1983 to March 1986 to track employees who are hired at exactly the minimum wage ($3.35 in 1983). As summarized in Table 7.9, 37 percent still earned no more than the minimum wage a year later: 16 percent earned an hourly wage up to 7.5 percent more than the minimum wage (between $3.36 and to $3.50); 24 percent earned between 7.5 percent and 19.5 percent more than the minimum wage (between $3.51 and $3.99); and 23 percent earned at least 120 percent of the minimum wage (at least $4.00). Similar patterns, again reported in Table 7.9, are found in a replication of this study with data from 1991 to 1994 (Long 1999). Nineteen percent remained exactly at the minimum wage after two years. Another 45 percent of respondents were earning at least 124 percent of the minimum wage two years after being paid the minimum.[16] These results are comparable to those of Carrington and Fallick (2001), who report that of those earning the minimum wage, between 34 and 54 percent earned an hourly wage more than $0.25 above the minimum wage a year later.

The CPS follows individuals for no more than two years, and until 1994, linking individuals across even these two years was technically challenging and incomplete. Thus, the CPS is less suited for tracking the wage dynamics of individuals than true longitudinal data.[17] These limits are counterbalanced by the size of the CPS sample, its representativeness, and the long time period for which CPS data are available. Using the CPS monthly surveys for 1979–1999 and matching individuals across the two years in which they are respondents to the survey, Even and Macpherson (2003) consider wage change in the year following employment at exactly the minimum wage. Twenty-nine percent of respondents continue at exactly the minimum wage, 47 percent have earnings at least $0.01 above the minimum wage, and 24 percent leave employment. Of those who earned exactly the minimum wage in their second year in the survey, Even and Macpherson report that 39 percent were not previously employed, 32 percent had been earning less than or exactly the minimum wage, and 28 percent had wages above the minimum in the previous year. That some workers "fall back" to the

Table 7.9 The Dynamics of the Minimum Wage

Study	Smith and Vavrichek (1992)		Long (1999)		Even and Macpherson (2003)	
Period studied	September 1983–March 1986		October 1991–December 1995		January 1979–December 1999	
Minimum wage	$3.35		$4.25		Varies	
Definition of MW worker	Individual earns exactly the federal minimim wage of $3.35		Individual earns exactly the binding minimum wage		Individual earns exactly the binding minimum wage	
	Distribution of the earnings of minimum wage (MW) workers					
	Wage bands used	% of sample	Wage bands used	% of sample	Wage bands used	% of sample
One year later	No more than MW	37	No more than MW	30	No more than MW	29
	Above the MW to 105% of minimum	16	Above the MW to 111.5% of minimum	21	More than MW	47
	Above 105%	11	Above 115% to 123%	20		
	More than 119%	21	More than 123%	29		
Two years later			No more than MW	19		
			Above MW to 111.5%	15		
			Above 111.5% to 123%	21		
			More than 123%	25		
One year before					No more than MW	33
					More than MW	28

minimum wage suggests that the dynamics of the minimum wage are more complex than its simply being an entry-level wage that individuals rise above over some time. Although this study does not estimate how far back individuals fell, it indicates the possibility of retrograde movement.

Factors Affecting Wage Growth

What factors affect whether individuals remain at or near the minimum wage? There is broad agreement among studies. All of the research indicates that minimum wage earners are more likely to remain at the minimum wage, however defined, if they are female, younger, have less education, or are Hispanic. Most studies indicate that African Americans are more likely to remain at or close to the minimum wage. Studies that include older workers indicate that those approaching the end of their working lives have lower wage growth and, if near the minimum wage, are more likely to remain there than younger workers. The unmarried are more likely than those who are married to have lower wage growth and to remain at the minimum wage, although some studies suggest this is only true of unmarried men.

Is the pattern of wage growth among workers exactly at the minimum wage different from that of other low-wage workers? At issue is whether earning the minimum wage either identifies workers with particularly low productivity or permanently affects them—"scars them," in the colorful terminology of economists—so that their wage growth is adversely affected. Comparing those earning the minimum wage with those earning slightly more, Grossberg and Sicilian (1999, p. 547) find the wage growth of women in these two categories does not differ, but that the difference for men is large, with the minimum wage group experiencing slower growth.

What explains wage growth of men at the minimum wage being slower than that of men earning a bit above the minimum? One possibility is that those who are hired at the minimum wage are less productive. Another is that there is scarring, that time spent at the minimum wage reduces wage growth either by reducing a worker's productivity (bad habits) or labeling the worker so that employers are unwilling to grant the types of increases granted other low-wage workers. Neumark and Nizalova (2007) investigate this issue, but, as we have suggested in

Chapter 2, their methods are not adequate to their purpose. Jones et al. (2007) use the British Household Panel Study, a longitudinal data set that follows the members of families over time, to investigate whether the lower-wage growth of minimum wage workers is due to unobserved lower productivity or scarring (see Table 7.10). Their panel, which runs from 1999 to 2004, includes the initial implementation and early increases in the NMW. Those earning at or below the minimum wage have a 29–36 percent probability of remaining at a wage no higher than the minimum wage the following year; 50 percent of those no higher than the NMW earn more than the NMW in the following year. The rest move out of employment. After allowing for individuals' observable characteristics, Jones et al. estimate that those at the NMW are 14 percent more likely to be employed at that wage in the next year than an employee who is currently earning more than the NMW. However, once the estimates allow for unobserved individual differences, those at the NMW are only 4 percent more likely to earn that amount in the next year than are those currently earning a bit above the NMW. Much of the persistence in individuals' remaining at the minimum wage is then associated with their characteristics; working at the minimum wage does not per se reduce prospects for future wage growth.

Phimister and Theodossiu (2009) use the British Household Panel Survey to investigate how the implementation of the NMW affected wage growth among low-wage men and women. They estimate competing risk-hazard rate models that allow for individual heterogeneity for a pre-NMW panel running from 1992 to 1998 and a post-NMW panel running from 1999 to 2005. Individuals potentially exit low-wage employment into a high-paid job, unemployment, or inactivity. The authors report a complex relationship between personal characteristics and gender, the duration of low-pay spells, and the likelihood of exiting a low-pay spell that makes it difficult to "draw out a single pattern in gender differences" (p. 33). Broadly, personal characteristics have a smaller influence on women than men, but these differences decline after implementation of the NMW. The gender difference in the likelihood of exiting to a high-pay job declines after implementation, as does the difference in the duration of low-pay spells. Simulations for the "typical" characteristics of those observed in low pay suggest that the duration of low-pay spells rises after the NMW, and there is a substantial increase in the probability of exiting to a high-pay job. The NMW

Table 7.10 The Dynamics of Minimum Wage Earners: How Is Wage Growth Affected by Receiving the Minimum Wage?

Study	Effect	Target	Country	Sample period	Analytic approach	Unit of observation	Data structure	Type of standard error	Data set[a]
Grossberg and Sicilian (1999)	Minimum wage earners' wages grow more slowly than those earning close to the minimum wage.	Small and low-wage firms concentrated in the South and Midwest	United States	1982	Regression	Firm	Cross-section	Conventional	EOPP
Jones et al. (2007)	Continued work at the minimum wage is associated with employees' characteristics rather than scarring effects of the minimum wage.	Males 18–65; women 18–60	United Kingdom	1999–2004	Pooled and random effects probit	Individuals over time	Longitudinal	Corrected for unobserved heterogeneity and initial conditions	BHPS waves 9–14

[a] BHPS = British Household Panel Survey; EOPP = Employment Opportunities Pilot Projects.

is then associated with complicated alterations in the low-wage labor market, narrowing gender differences, increasing time spent at low—if higher than before—wages, and increased probabilities of moving into better-paid work.

CONCLUSION

What can we conclude about the effect of the minimum wage on inequality and poverty and on the duration of employment at the minimum wage? Although the magnitude of the effect remains in play, all eight articles that consider the effect of the minimum wage on the wage inequality find that higher minimum wages reduced wage inequality by raising the wages of those in the lower tail of the earnings distribution.[18] The effect is stronger for women than for men. This research supplements the research on bound workers and spillovers, as it indicates that minimum wage affects the wages of bound workers and spillover into higher deciles of the wage distribution, particularly among women.

Research also suggests that the minimum wage may have not have much effect on poverty. This result is not entirely surprising, given that those in poverty are substantially less likely to be working than higher-income groups. Broadening the focus of research on this topic to low-wage workers would likely produce more interesting results. The near poor, families with incomes between 100 and 150 percent of the experimental poverty line, compose one-sixth of the U.S. population. Half live in households headed by a married couple, and more than a quarter have a family member working in a full-time, year-round position. Research that focuses on the effect of the minimum wage on the near poor is a natural step in establishing whether the minimum wage aids low-income workers.

Finally, a broad conclusion about the dynamics of employment at the minimum wage is that most career workers who start in minimum wage jobs move on to higher-wage jobs fairly rapidly, but a substantial proportion spend the first decade of their careers employed at or near minimum wage. This conclusion is universal among the studies that examined how fast those employed at the minimum wage move out of minimum wage employment (Carrington and Fallick 2001; Even and

Macpherson 2003; Long 1999; and Smith and Vavricheck 1992). Of the three studies of the effect of the minimum wage on future wage growth, one suggests that the lower rate of wage growth among minimum wage employees is due to personal characteristics (Jones et al. 2007), and the other suggests that minimum wages scar workers and result in lower wage growth (Grossberg and Sicilian 1999).

For a large minority of the working population, including the part that has completed its schooling, earnings remain close to the minimum wage. Given the effect of the minimum wage in setting a floor under the wage structure, and the evidence for spillover effects, the minimum wage positively affects the income of part of the working population for more than a brief period. Although few workers remain at the minimum wage for long, substantial numbers do not pass through the neighborhood quickly.

Notes

1. Edsall (2013) summarizes discussions of the importance of increases, or lack thereof, on income inequality. Although he finds the arguments of those concerned with inequality more compelling than the arguments of those who find it to be unimportant, he provides links to the key arguments and evidence on both sides of the controversy.
2. The effect of the minimum wage is sensitive to the order in which the effects are entered into the model. There is no "right" order of introducing the effects into the model, so we include the highest and lowest estimates reported by DiNardo, Fortin, and Lemieux (1996).

   Although the effect of the real minimum wage on wages appears to be limited to the lower portion of the wage distribution, the upward movement of wages caused by the minimum wage has had a large effect on inequality by reducing the 90/10 and 95/5 wage differential. For example, the decline in the real minimum wage between 1979 and 1988 accounted for between 25 and 30 percent of the increase in the 10/90 differential and 44–48 percent of the 5/95 differential (for men and women, respectively).
3. Lee (1999) and Autor, Katz, and Kearney (2008) note the somewhat puzzling positive relationship between the minimum wage and inequality between the 90th and 50th percentiles of the wage distribution. Although the latter suggests that the minimum wage variables are picking up spurious economic relationships, an alternative possibility is that legislated changes in the minimum wage are reflective of broad changes in legislation affecting wage inequality. For example, the most recent period of stagnation in the minimum wage was also a period in which taxes and market regulations were reduced, likely increasing the growth of wages and salaries at the upper end of the wage distribution.

4. The analysis of inequality is used to determine whether the NMW is so binding as to produce the employment effects that are the main concern of their work.

5. *Merriam-Webster's Collegiate Dictionary*. 9th ed. Springfield, MA: Merriam-Webster, 1985.

6. *The Compact Edition of the Oxford English Dictionary*. Vol. 2. Oxford: Oxford University Press, 1971.

7. Fisher (1992) presents a detailed history of the development and evolution of the poverty line, and the bulk of our discussion of this topic is based on this article. Fisher mentions that at the same time as Orshansky was doing her analysis, at least one other government economist derived a similar figure for the poverty line with a different approach, suggesting that this figure was reasonable at the time.

8. Current work by the U.S. Census Bureau with experimental poverty measures represents an effort to better align poverty measures with the needs of families relative to their income (see Short [2010]). The experimental measures account for the effects of income transfer programs and better allow for the costs that different types of families face. In terms of the interests of this study, the experimental measures result in a larger proportion of those who are working part- or full time being classified as poor.

9. Note that this is for care in someone's home, which is less than it would be in an accredited child care center.

10. Further reason to be concerned with the effectiveness of this method for measuring state-level effects are the results with other state variables. It would be expected that the prime-age male unemployment rate, the prime-age wage rate, and EITC coverage would have substantial effects on poverty levels, but, with a single exception among 15 estimates, they are not significant.

11. There would potentially be issues of sample selection in the division of the sample by income decile, but these matters are well understood, and the appropriate corrections are incorporated into modern software.

12. As a result, these analyses are described more fully in Chapter 2.

13. Inflation was measured by the New Zealand Consumer Price Index.

14. Maloney and Pacheco's (2012) work applies multinomial logit and probit to repeat cross-section data and are likely subject to issues with the correct estimation of standard errors that characterize regression models. Such issues, which are not discussed in their paper, limit the usefulness of the hypothesis tests. This research nevertheless begins to address how the minimum wage affects low-income workers.

15. We omit Schiller (1994) from this review. Although interesting, 80 percent of the sample was in school at the beginning of the study. Their labor market decisions were likely secondary to their decisions about school, making their wage dynamics less relevant to our concerns.

16. Both sets of estimates include both individuals who are in school and individuals who have completed their schooling. Both studies provided distributions restricted to those employed as hourly workers in their second and third years, as well as for the full sample, including those who were unemployed, who were not

in the workforce, who were no longer hourly employees, and those who were self-employed. We present the distribution for those who remained hourly employees.

17. Until 1994, linking individuals across time was uncertain because, while households carried the same identifiers across years, individuals were not identified. Matching within households was done by age, gender, and race, and, due to the "hot carding" of incomplete records, there were a significant number of individuals who appeared to change sex, race, or both between years. Since 1994, individual identifiers allow for exact matching. Because the CPS is a geographic survey rather than a survey of individuals, there is significant attrition of respondents between their first and second rotations. In contrast, longitudinal data sets follow individuals when they move and make heroic efforts to retain individuals in the survey.

18. A ninth article, Neumark, Schweitzer, and Wascher (2004), also considers the effect of the minimum wage on the distribution of wage by creating wage bands relative to the minimum wage. There are issues with the construction of the data and the lack of clustering of errors. Because the authors believe that there are considerable lags in the effect of the minimum wage, and their model is based on annual changes in wages in matched data, they need to measure wage change over a two-year period. Unfortunately, the rotation structure of the CPS only allows the observation of individuals' wages over one year. The authors build a specification that may capture the lagged effects over this longer period, but the assumptions about the wage formation process are rigorous. The estimates find a positive effect of the contemporary minimum wage on wages but a strictly negative effect of the constructed lagged minimum wage. This raises the question of whether the lagged effect is a result of the construction of the lagged data. Adding to this concern is that they find a positive effect of the contemporary minimum wage, and a negative effect of the lagged minimum wage, among individuals earning six to eight times the minimum wage. This is well above the level at which effects are found in any other study. These suggest sufficient issues that lead us, here as in Chapter 2, not to include this analysis in this review.

Part 2

Macro

8
Gross Flows in the Labor Market

As both the survey and meta-analysis of employment studies indicate, the effect of the minimum wage on employment is at most small. One way to understand why this is so is to examine the effect of the minimum wage on gross flows—the flows into and out of employment over time.

If Emp_t is employment at a single moment, say, the beginning of year t, Equation (8.1) defines the change in employment during year t:

$$(8.1) \quad dEmp_t = Emp_{t+1} - Emp_t$$

The first thing to notice about this is that the two variables on the right are stock variables, measured at different moments of time, while $dEmp_t$ on the left is a flow variable, measured over the period separating the two stock variables. The second is that even as definitions go, it is not especially interesting. However, rearranging to read

$$(8.2) \quad Emp_{t+1} = Emp_t + dEmp_t$$

redirects our attention. Employment at the beginning of year $t + 1$ is determined by employment one year earlier and the change in employment over the intervening year. The flow variable, $dEmp_t$, is the net change in employment during year t. A useful next step is to decompose it into its positive and negative components, the gross changes or gross flows, and separately examine their responses to the minimum wage.

The positive gross flow is accessions, the number of people who are working in positions at the beginning of one year that they were not working in at the beginning of the previous year. The jobs in question may have existed, but someone else may have been working in them; or they may be newly created, perhaps as a result of a firm that opened for business during the year; or they may result from an expansion or reorganization at a firm that was already in business at the year's start. The negative gross flow is separations, the number of people who at the end of the year are no longer working in the same position as at the

343

beginning. Some separations consist of positions that no longer exist, either at firms that downsized their workforces or that are no longer in business. Others are positions that not only existed previously but continue to be occupied, just not by the same person as before.[1] As defined here, both accessions and separations are quantities, but each can also be defined as a rate, where the quantity is divided by employment at the beginning of the year. The accession rate, $Accessions_t/Emp_t$, is the number of people who move into new jobs during the year (the number of accessions) divided by employment at the start of the year. The separations rate is $Separations_t/Emp_t$. The result is either of the following equations:

(8.3a) $dEmp_t = Accessions_t - Separations_t$

(8.3b) $\dfrac{dEmp_t}{Emp_t} = \dfrac{Accessions_t}{Emp_t} - \dfrac{Separations_t}{Emp_t}$

When employment is growing over time, $dEmp_t$, the change in employment, is positive and accessions exceed separation; when employment is shrinking, $dEmp_t$ is negative and separations exceed accessions.

Table 8.1 lists one dozen studies of gross labor market flows. For descriptive purposes, studies of gross flows can be organized into three groups. Analyses in the first group rely on models of the labor market other than a perfectly competitive one. Pinoli (2010); Portugal and Cardoso (2006); and Dube, Lester, and Reich (2012) appeal to search models that incorporate frictions so that minimum wage increases have the potential for increasing employment. Georgiadis (2013) examines efficiency wage models in which it is cost minimizing for firms to pay a higher than competitive wage. Studies in the second group make no appeal to any theoretical model of the labor market: Dube, Naidu, and Reich (2007); Thompson (2009); and Skedinger (2006). Giuliano (2013) straddles the two groups, taking an agnostic view of these models. Studies in the third group focus on quits, a part of separations; because most of these studies predate the NMWR and grow out of a different literature, human capital and compensation, they are treated separately in the last section of this chapter.

DATA ISSUES

Although it is the Swiss Army knife for the examination of many economic issues concerning the U.S. population, the CPS is far from ideal for the study of gross flows (Bjelland et al. 2007; Davis and Haltiwanger 1998).[2] It is a retrospective household survey in which one adult often responds for all household members. Data collection errors that tend to cancel out in the measurement of stocks reinforce each other in the measurement of flows. Systematic biases and attrition that can be adjusted for in the measurement of stocks are more difficult to correct in the measurement of flows. The rotation structure of the CPS interferes with the construction of any but short-term employment histories. Finally, before the 1994 revision that included the question, "Do you still work for [company name]?" in order to improve data consistency, use of the CPS to measure gross flows between jobs was not possible.[3] Although the federal structure of the government that is reflected in the CPS complicates some of these problems, household labor force surveys in other countries also exhibit them.

Long-term longitudinal surveys such as the NLSY and the PSID overcome some (not all) of the shortcomings of the CPS but introduce other problems, such as samples that are not representative of the entire labor force (Fallick and Fleischman 2004).

Data that link employers and employees, especially tax data, are better than either one of those surveys for the examination of flows to or from jobs. In the United States, recent work on gross flows has moved to reliance on data sets that link employer and employee survey data through data collected by state unemployment insurance programs (Abowd and Vilhuber 2011a,b; Bjelland et al. 2007; Hyatt and Spletzer 2013).[4] Because not all employers must pay taxes for unemployment insurance (the self-employed, most employers of domestic and agricultural workers, government), these data do not capture all flows. Nevertheless, this type of data, such as the Longitudinal Employer-Household Dynamics Program of the Census Bureau, is not only extensive but also unique in tracking both individuals and firms over time and including characteristics of each. Its increasing use in the study of gross flows suggests a belief that it is the most appropriate public data available.[5]

Table 8.1 Gross Labor Flows

Study	Target	Country	Sample period	Data set[a]	Variable	Response	Comments
Dube, Naidu, and Reich (2007)	SF restaurants	United States	2003–2004	Private survey	Separation rate	None	
Dube, Lester, and Reich (2012)	Teenagers, restaurants	United States	2001–2008	QWI	Accessions, separations	Negative	Accessions, ≈ separations
Georgiadis (2013)	Home care sector	United Kingdom	1999–2001	Private survey	Accession rate, separation rate	None	
Giuliano (2013)	Teens in retail	United States	1996–1998	Personnel data	Teen share of accessions and of separations	Varied, none	Teen share in accessions doubles only when using both preferred sample and specification.
Grossberg and Sicilian (2004)	Minimum wage workers (men, women)	United States	1988–1994	NLSY	Quits (women) Quits (men)	None. Negative if MW is relatively low, positive if MW is relatively high	
Leighton and Mincer (1981)	White and black men	United States	1967–71 (NLSY) 1973, 1975 (PSID)	NLSY and PSID	Job tenure	None (NLSY), negative (PSID)	
Pinoli (2010)	Youth	Spain	2000–2006	EPAS	Accessions, separations	Varied, positive	No hiring response to unexpected increases, negative after a large, expected increase
Portugal and Cardoso (2006)	Teenage workers	Portugal	1986–1989	QP	Teen share of accessions and of separations	Negative, negative	Accessions-separations > 0

Study	Description	Country	Years	Data	Variables	Result	Notes
Skedinger (2006)	Unskilled workers	Sweden	1979–1999	CSE	Accessions, separations	Negative, varied	Separations positive 1979–1991, mixed later in the 1990s
Sicilian and Grossberg (1993)	3,000 small firms in the South and Midwest	United States	1982 (back to 1978)	EOPP	Quit rates	Net negative	Interaction with tenure dominates direct effect on quits
Thompson (2009)	Teenagers	United States	1996–2000	QWI	Accessions (teen share)	Negative	
Wessels (1980)	Manufacturing industries	United States	1909–1972	EE	Quits	Mixed	

[a] QWI: Quarterly Workforce Indicators (based on Unemployment Insurance records). NLSY = National Longitudinal Survey of Youths; PSID = Panel Study of Income Dynamics; EPAS = Economically Active Population Survey (quarterly household survey, 6 quarters in sample); QP = (Portugal) *Quadros de Pessoal* (personnel records, Portuguese Ministry of Qualification and Employment); CSE = Firm and worker data from the Confederation of Swedish Enterprise; EOPP = Employment Opportunities Pilot Projects. EE = Employment and Earnings (U.S. Bureau of Labor Statistics 1973).

The studies discussed below use many types of data. Dube, Lester, and Reich (2012); Portugal and Cardoso (2006); and Thompson (2009) use tax data. Skedinger (2006) uses payroll data for many firms collected by an employer confederation, and Giuliano (2013) uses personnel and wage data from a single firm. Grossberg and Sicilian (2004) and Leighton and Mincer (1981) rely on long-term longitudinal surveys. Dube, Naidu, and Reich (2007) and Georgiadis (2013) use data from privately conducted surveys of employers, Pinoli (2010) uses the Spanish counterpart to the CPS, and Sicilian and Grossberg (1993) analyze a survey from the late 1970s and early 1980s that was conducted in order to study a program for retraining the unemployed and aiding them in finding work.

STUDIES OF GROSS FLOWS THAT LEAN HEAVILY ON SPECIFIC LABOR MARKET MODELS

Several of the studies that include examinations of the gross flows make appeals to (or firmly embed themselves in) models of the labor market other than the competitive model. Georgiadis (2013) examines implications of one type of efficiency wage model for gross flows. Pinoli (2010) appeals to the search model of Mortensen and Pissarides (1994) to motivate her study. Portugal and Cardoso (2006) and Dube, Lester, and Reich (2012) turn to Burdett and Mortensen (1998) to explain their results concerning the response of gross flows to the minimum wage.

Georgiadis (2013) uses the UK care home industry data of Machin, Manning, and Rahman (2003) to examine the relevance of an efficiency wage model. Efficiency wage models resemble the competitive model of the labor market insofar as prospective employers and employees have no difficulty in finding each other; members of both groups have complete and costless information about who is on the other side of the market. Where these models differ is that in efficiency wage models, a higher wage is associated either with greater productivity or lower nonwage costs. Consequently, it is optimal in these models for firms to pay a wage that is higher than the equilibrium wage of the corresponding competitive model; that is, the two models are identical except for this effect on productivity or costs. At the higher wage, aggregate employment is less than in the competitive equilibrium. Knowing this and the consequence that finding a new job as good as their current one is not so easy (unlike in a competitive equilibrium), employees are less likely to either quit or behave in ways that would lead to being fired. By itself, the lower level of employment results in fewer separations; the employee response adds to this, reducing the separation rate. Similarly, the lower level of employment results in fewer accessions, and the lower separation rate implies a lower vacancy rate (fewer job openings relative to the level of employment), which in turn implies a lower accession rate. Georgiadis (2013) focuses on the turnover efficiency wage model, which emphasizes reduction in turnover as the motivation for the efficiency wage. Firms pay the high wage because turnover is costly; total costs are less despite the higher wage because it reduces the quit rate and, with fewer positions to be filled, the accessions rate. With regard to both rates, Georgiadis reports that "the results are uniformly insignificant across all specifications and minimum wage measures used" (p. 36).

Pinoli (2010) appeals to Mortensen and Pissarides (1994), extending their search model to motivate her focus on the distinction between anticipated and unanticipated increases in the minimum wage. Important features of the original Mortensen and Pissarides model are that only the unemployed search for work, it is costly to firms to create a vacancy, and all jobs pay the same wage. Pinoli (2010) adds an additional friction, a firing tax that firms pay. Since her focus is the lower end of the labor market, the single wage is the (binding) minimum wage. For an unexpected minimum wage increase, all changes to separations and accessions occur only after the fact. Separations rise immediately and then stay constant.[6] Accessions fall immediately, but the increase in unemployment from both their fall and the rise in separations means that unemployment rises; this in turn makes it easier for firms to fill vacancies, leading to a gradual increase in accessions to a higher level than before the minimum wage increase, though not so high as to reduce unemployment to its previous level. Turnover, the sum of accessions and separations, has increased above its initial value by the time accessions have recovered from their initial fall.

For an anticipated minimum wage increase, there are not two periods for the purposes of analysis, before and after the increase, but three: 1) before the increase in the perceived likelihood of the minimum wage increase; 2) after the minimum wage increases; and 3) an intermediate interval, before the minimum wage increases but after its perceived likelihood has risen. In this scenario, separations rise in steps. The first increase in separations occurs immediately upon entering the intermediate period, i.e., when expectations change. Separations rise to their final level, as high as in the case of an unexpected increase, when the minimum wage increase actually occurs. Accessions fall immediately on entering the intermediate period, and then, as in the case of an unexpected increase, rise to a level higher than their initial level because of the increase in unemployment. When the minimum wage actually increases, accessions initially fall to the same level as before the change in expectations, and then, as before, gradually rise to the new long-run level, higher than either the initial or intermediate levels. Because much of the adjustment takes place during the intermediate period before the minimum wage increase, once the increase occurs, accessions approach their new level more rapidly in the anticipated scenario than in the unanticipated one. Not only is turnover higher after the increase than before the change in expectations (at the same level in the long run as in the unanticipated scenario), it first rises in the intermediate period.

Turning to the empirical analysis, Pinoli (2010) reports that the separation rate of teenagers rises by 3 percentage points following the unexpected minimum wage increase, all in the quarter immediately following the increase.[7] For the three largest expected increases in her sample, the separation rate increases by 5.6 percentage points, 4.1 percentage points in the quarter before the increase, and 1.5 in the following two quarters. The accession rate displays no (statistically detectable) response to unexpected minimum wage increases, and a decrease of 4.8 percentage points in the two quarters after a large expected increase.[8] When she distinguishes between permanent and temporary workers (a category that includes 70 percent of employed teenagers), there is no detectable impact on the separation rate for permanent workers, but the effect on the separations rate of temporary workers (those hired for a fixed rather than indefinite term) is the strongest so far: 4 percentage points on impact for unexpected increases and 7.7 percentage points in response to a large, expected increase. More than 6 percentage points of that response immediately precede the increase in the minimum wage, half of the remainder immediately follows the increase, and the other half comes in the next two quarters. She explains that the difference in responses reflects the smaller penalty firms suffer from laying off temporary rather than permanent workers.[9]

How do these estimates compare with Pinoli's (2010) theoretical model? The estimated response of separations in the unexpected scenario are about half the size as that in the expected scenario, not the same size as the theoretical model predicts, and the point estimate during the intermediate interval of the expected scenario is not smaller than that after an unexpected increase but a third again as large. Rather than an increase in accessions, she finds no response to an unexpected minimum wage increase and a decline in response to an expected minimum wage increase.

Portugal and Cardoso (2006) and Dube, Lester, and Reich (2012) both turn to Burdett and Mortensen's (1998) search model as a way of rationalizing their findings.[10] In this model, firms with vacancies post a wage, and with a positive probability some individual learns of it (employment status is not germane to this probability). If the wage is sufficiently high—above the individual's current wage if employed or above the individual's reservation wage if unemployed—then the individual takes the job. Unlike the model of Mortensen and Pissarides (1994), this one generates a distribution of wages. In the absence of a minimum wage, many who are currently employed will take a vacant job because the offered wage is higher than their current one, which sets off a cascade of separations and accessions until someone who is not currently employed fills a position.

A minimum wage raises the entire wage distribution, but more at the bottom than the top, compressing it at the lower end, that is, compressing wages in low-wage labor markets. Because of the compression, workers in low-wage labor markets are less likely (than in the absence of the minimum wage) to find positions with a higher wage than they are already earning, so rather than move to a new job, they stay put.[11] An open position is therefore more likely to go to someone who is currently not employed.[12] With a (higher) minimum wage, the cascade either never begins or it ends more quickly, reducing both accessions and separations.[13]

Portugal and Cardoso (2006) rely on a detailed data set of employees in Portuguese firms to understand the response to a substantial increase in the minimum wages for teenagers in 1987. Theirs is the first study we consider in which gross labor flows are the focus of the analysis.

Their data consist of annual observations on individual firms. They use the recent history of the firm to classify labor flows in finer detail than accessions or separations, distinguishing among accessions and separations at continuing firms, accessions due to births, and separations due to deaths. At continuing firms, the share of teenagers in accessions fell by about four percentage points in both 1988 and 1989, the second and third years after the increase in the teenage minimum wage (see Table 8.2), but their share in separations fell several times as much, 14–15 percentage points in each of these years. At new firms, their share of accessions changed by about the same amount as at continuing firms, about four percentage points in both 1988 and 1989, while their share in separations due to deaths rose by 5 percentage points in 1988 and half as much in 1989. Overall, teenagers' share in accessions fell, and their share in separations fell even more. Portugal and Cardoso conclude that "workers affected by a sharp rise in the minimum wage are not over-represented among those who afterward separate from their employers" (p. 999).[14]

To see how sharply the behavior of accessions and separations for teenagers differed from that of adults, it is necessary to correct for employment change during this period. The accession and separation rates allow us to do this.[15] In 1986, the year before the increases, the teenage accession and separation rates were both about two and a half

Table 8.2 Changes in Teen Shares in Gross Flows in Portugal Following the 1987 Minimum Wage Increase

	Deaths	Continuing firms	Births
Separations			
1988	0.050**	−0.150**	
1989	0.025	−0.140**	
Total	0.075	−0.290	
Accessions			
1988		−0.036**	−0.042**
1989		−0.043**	−0.041**
Total		−0.079	−0.083

NOTE: **statistically significant at the 0.05 level for the annual dummies. Statistical significance for the totals is not known (covariance between annual dummies is needed).
SOURCE: Portugal and Cardoso (2006).

times as large as the corresponding rates for adults: 50 percent versus 19 percent for accessions, and 45 percent versus 16 percent for separations (see Table 8.3). Two years later, in the second year after the increases, the rates for adults increased by about one-third, to 26 percent for accessions and 21 percent for separations. For teenagers, the increases were proportionately smaller, resulting in an accession rate of 57 percent and a separation rate of 48 percent. Teenagers' attachment to jobs did not increase in absolute terms during this period; however, because the adult separation rate grew nearly six times as fast as that of teenagers, the increase in teenagers' share of total private employment was dramatic relative to previous trends, more than a percentage point in two years.

Dube, Lester, and Reich (2012) apply their border-discontinuity approach (Dube, Lester, and Reich 2010) to the 2001–2009 Quarterly Workforce Indicators to examine the minimum wage response of hiring and separation rates of both teenagers and the restaurant industry.[16] Table 8.4 displays their results. They begin with a regression equation, similar to Neumark and Wascher's canonical model, with fixed county and time effects. Their use of a familiar specification enables the reader to determine how dependent the results are on a novel data source. For teenagers, the employment elasticity is −0.2 (standard error = 0.07), and those for accessions and separations are −0.45 (0.09) and −0.46 (0.10), respectively. The employment elasticity equals the midpoint of the consensus range of estimates in the older minimum wage literature. For the restaurant industry, the employment elasticity is −0.12 (0.04), and those for accessions and separations are −0.47 (0.08) and −0.47 (0.08). In each case, the minimum wage responses of the two gross flows effectively cancel each other out, an outcome that is difficult to square with the estimated response of employment.[17]

Table 8.3 Gross Flows for Teens and Adults in Portugal Following the 1987 Minimum Wage Increase (%)

	Separations		Accessions	
	Teens	Adults	Teens	Adults
1986	45	16	50	19
1987	48	22	56	23
1988	48	21	57	26

SOURCE: Portugal and Cardoso (2006, Table 6).

Table 8.4 Estimated Elasticities

	Canonical model		Border-discontinuity model	
	Teens	Restaurant workers	Teens	Restaurant workers
Employment	−0.20**	−0.12**	−0.04	−0.06
Hires	−0.45**	−0.47**	−0.22**	−0.34*
Separations	−0.46**	−0.47**	−0.25**	−0.32
Turnover rate	−0.27**	−0.33**	−0.19**	−0.26**

NOTE: *statistically significant at the 0.01 level; **statistically significant at the 0.05 level.

SOURCE: Dube, Lester, and Reich (2012, Table 3.)

In Dube, Lester, and Reich's (2012) border-discontinuity model, they compare adjacent counties across the borders of states that have different minimum wages. Instead of two-way fixed effects, they include a common time effect for adjacent counties. Although the wage response, which is positive and statistically significant in the canonical model, becomes larger (and remains statistically significant) in the border-discontinuity model, the estimated employment response disappears. For teenagers, the employment elasticity is −0.04 (0.07), the accessions elasticity is −0.22 (0.11), and the separations elasticity is −0.25 (0.10). For restaurants, the three elasticities are −0.06 (0.10), −0.34 (0.17), and −0.32 (0.13). In both cases, the gross flows cancel out, as before, but in contrast with the canonical model, the point estimates for employment elasticity in the border discontinuity model are both small and not statistically significant. An especially telling detail is a comparison of estimates for the border-discontinuity model using the whole sample and using a sample purged of people with less than one-quarter of tenure in the current job, that is, those most likely to be earning the minimum wage. The minimum wage elasticity of the separation rate falls dramatically, for teenagers by more than half, and for restaurant workers by more than 90 percent. In both cases the results are no longer statistically significant despite modest reductions in the estimated standard error. It appears that the minimum wage affects separations of those with little job tenure, not those with greater job tenure; a minimum wage increase leads to greater stability in firms' personnel and reduces high-frequency job changes, something that is costly to firms. It is not possible with the data that Dube, Lester, and Reich use to determine whether this is due to changed behavior on the part of firms and employees or to a compositional effect in the labor force as a result of the minimum wage increase.

The findings of those who rely on formal models in their study of gross flows are mildly contradictory. The model that Georgiadis (2013) uses predicts lower accession and separation rates, which he does not detect. Pinoli's (2010) model predicts higher levels of accessions and separations. She reports higher separation rates, though not quite as her model predicts, and unchanged or lower accession rates. The model that Portugal and Cardoso (2006) and Dube, Lester, and Reich (2012) turn to predicts a decline in both accession and separation rates, and that is what both analyses find, the former reporting greater declines in separations than accessions of teenagers, and the latter reporting declines in the two flows of roughly the same size.

STUDIES OF GROSS FLOWS THAT ARE AGNOSTIC ABOUT LABOR MARKET MODELS

In their analysis of San Francisco's restaurant industry and its response to the introduction of a citywide minimum wage, Dube, Naidu, and Reich (2007) detect no change in the separation rate. In his study of the effect of the minimum wage on teenage employment, Thompson (2009) briefly considers the teenage share of hires, reporting a variety of samples and specifications that make it difficult to summarize his results quantitatively. However, 8 of his 12 results are statistically significant and have the negative sign that Thompson expects. The 1997 increase appears to have reduced the teenage share of new hires by between 8 and 12 percentage points overall, and between 10 and 13 percentage points in small counties where the minimum wage is high relative to the wage distribution.[18]

Skedinger (2006) uses accessions and separations as his primary measures of the response of unskilled employment to changes in the minimum wage in the Swedish hospitality industry. Rather than examine the response of each to changes in the minimum wage, he considers the response of separations only to increases in the minimum wage and the response of accessions only to decreases in the minimum wage. In both cases, the competitive model of the labor market implies an increase in the gross flow under consideration. For the period 1979–1991, the elasticity of the separation rate with respect to minimum wage increases is 0.58 (and highly statistically significant). For the same period, the elasticity of the accession rate to minimum wage decreases is 0.84 (also highly statistically significant). However, when Skedinger turns to the minimum wage increases of the 1990s, the results are more varied, with the elasticity of the separation rate varying by sample and age group. Estimates for older teenagers (18–19-year-olds) are not statistically significant. Depending on the sample of firms used, estimates for adults are larger or smaller than the estimates from the earlier period. The larger adult estimate is statistically significant, and the smaller one is not. As mentioned in the chapter on employment, Skedinger believes that the results with regard to separations are consistent with the standard competitive model, but that the results for accessions are much weaker and may be consistent with a monopsony model.[19]

In a study using personnel data from a large U.S. chain store, Giuliano (2013) reports that the minimum wage has no effect on the share of teenagers in separations and a fragile positive effect on their share in accessions. When she combines her preferred sample with her preferred specification, the share of teenagers in new hires doubles; otherwise the increase in the share is about 50 percent but is not statistically significant.[20]

DISCUSSION OF FINDINGS ON SEPARATIONS AND ACCESSIONS

Several of the analyses consider either only one type of gross flow or both types but only in different situations: Dube, Naidu, and Reich (2007) report only on separations, and Thompson (2009) looks only at accessions. Skedinger (2006) considers both types of employment flows but looks at accessions only following minimum wage decreases and at separations only following minimum wage increases. It is difficult to use these results for further insight on the question of the minimum wage and employment.

Although Giuliano (2013) does not find a robust response of either accessions or separations to the minimum wage, Portugal and Cardoso (2006), studying a highly regulated labor market, and Dube, Lester, and Reich (2012), studying one that is considered very unregulated for a developed economy, report sharp declines in both accessions and separations following an increase in the minimum wage. In both, the decline in separations is at least large enough to cancel out the employment consequences of the decline in accessions. Because Pinoli's (2010) results are less clear, they are difficult to interpret. Contrary to Dube, Lester, and Reich (2012) and Portugal and Cardoso (2006), Pinoli reports that separations rise as a result of both anticipated and unanticipated minimum wage increases. Her findings about accessions are largely inconsistent with her model; they fall after a large expected increase, but apparently do not subsequently rise again, nor do they respond beforehand. Further, she detects no response following the unexpected minimum wage increase, especially surprising since this is also the largest increase in her sample.

It appears that the strongest evidence, the combined findings of Portugal and Cardoso (2006) and Dube, Lester, and Reich (2012), supports declines in both accession and separation rates that roughly cancel each other. This would explain the absence of a clear employment response to the minimum wage in the literature. The evidence is certainly not overwhelming, and there are results that are not consistent with this conclusion. As with the literature on employment, more analysis that carefully controls for confounding factors is necessary to arrive with confidence at a conclusion.

Quits

An accession requires an agreement between two parties who, if they agree, become employer and employee. Separations occur when one or both no longer find the agreement to be beneficial, and can therefore be further divided into quits, sometimes called voluntary separations, and dismissals and layoffs.

Because research on quitting, one component of separations, is embedded in the theories of human capital and employee compensation (see Chapter 6), the relationship between the minimum wage and quit rates is not central in most of the studies below. However, for the purposes of a rough-and-ready history of results in this vein, we shall pretend that it is; it begins with Mixon's (1978) analysis of low-wage industries.[21] Next comes Wessels's (1980) analysis, which incorporated the expanded notion of a compensation package that includes fringe benefits; firms can reduce benefits to offset minimum wage increases, and employees have incomplete information about compensation packages at other firms. In their study of human capital and the minimum wage (see Chapter 6), Leighton and Mincer (1981) report results for a phenomenon closely related to quits, the length of job tenure. Although they do not examine quitting behavior, Holzer, Katz, and Krueger (1991) mention implications of their analysis for aspects of Wessels's; Sicilian and Grossberg (1993) examine quit behavior in the same data set as Holzer, Katz, and Krueger (1991) to refute these points. Finally, Grossberg and Sicilian (2004) make a more expansive use of incomplete information and combine it with De Fraja's (1999) model of jobs.

Wessels (1980) expands the notion of the compensation package to include fringe benefits. The tax treatment of benefits allows firms to provide them at lower after-tax cost than employees can do for themselves, creating a wedge between firm and employee costs. If firms respond to an increase in the minimum wage by reducing benefits, a higher minimum wage can reduce workers' total compensation. Wessels reasons that if those already employed experience this and believe that only their own employer has responded in this way to the minimum wage increase, quit rates may rise until employees understand the marketwide effect of the minimum wage increase.

Wessels (1980) finds some support for the hypothesis that higher minimum wages are associated with higher quit rates among broadly defined manufacturing industries. Estimating models on 13 3- and 4-digit low-wage industries, Wessels reports 8 positive point estimates for the elasticity of the quit rate with respect to the minimum wage. Of these eight, only two are statistically significant, but, consistent with his hypothesis, they are in the highest-wage industries. Leighton and Mincer (1981) consider the effect of the minimum wage on job tenure in the same framework and with the same data used in their study of wage growth and training. They are noncommittal about the expected effect of the minimum wage, emphasizing that human capital theory does not provide an unambiguous prediction about the relationship between the minimum wage and quits. As with their work on the minimum wage and human capital, their estimates vary systematically with data source and specification. Estimates using the Panel Study of Income Dynamics (PSID) indicate that both higher minimum wages and increased coverage have a significantly negative effect on tenure. Estimates using the NLSY indicate that job tenure among white or black men is unaffected by either the level or coverage of the minimum wage.

Sicilian and Grossberg (1993) revisit issues that Wessels (1980) examined, and they compare his analysis to that of Holzer, Katz, and Krueger (1991). Using data collected by the Economic Opportunity Pilot Projects, Holzer, Katz, and Krueger had determined that longer queues formed for minimum wage jobs than others, ceteris paribus, and inferred that these positions had rents that accrued to the employees because firms were unable to fully offset the higher costs from the minimum wage. Sicilian and Grossberg (1993) use the same data set to consider whether workers altered their views of jobs once they were working and had more complete information. If so, quits would rise following minimum wage increases, consistent with Wessels (1980), as the rents would only be expected, not actual.

Sicilian and Grossberg (1993) compare quit rates of those hired at exactly the minimum wage with workers who were hired above the minimum. The "hired at minimum wage" dummy enters the regression equation by itself and interacts with measures of labor market tightness and employee tenure. Although the coefficients for the dummy and its interaction with tightness are both positive, neither satisfies a 0.05 significance test. The only minimum wage coefficient that does is the one for the interaction with tenure, and it is negative; for someone hired at the minimum wage, a one-month increase in tenure reduced the likelihood of quitting by 0.14 percent. The authors conclude that their results are consistent with Wessels's (1980) hypothesis but do not relate them to Holzer, Katz, and Krueger's (1991) hypothesis concerning rents. In fact, their use of a "hired at minimum wage" dummy rather than the percentage change in the minimum wage turns attention from the response of employees earning the minimum wage when it increases to those who begin a position at the minimum wage irrespective of subsequent increases. In doing this, they are focusing on a different issue, one that they analyze more explicitly in their next work.

Grossberg and Sicilian (2004) expand the problem of incomplete information beyond one that applies only to current employees, combining it with De Fraja's (1999) model of the nonpecuniary features of jobs that affect workers' utility. The wedge from the tax treatment of fringe benefits plays no role, and that is also true of mistaken belief in the short term by current employees that only their employer has reduced them. The issue instead explicitly concerns the inferences about a position's intangible characteristics that prospective employees must draw when deciding whether to accept an offer. According to Grossberg and Sicilian's hypothesis, the posted wage is the most important piece of information for these inferences, and only after a perhaps quite lengthy period can the (now) employee determine whether they were reasonably accurate.

The authors agree with Portugal and Cardoso (2006) and Dube, Lester, and Reich (2012) that the amount of wage compression at the low end of the wage distribution will vary monotonically with the relative minimum wage, more salient when it is high than when it is low. Grossberg and Sicilian do not, however, rely on Burdett and Mortensen (1998) and expect this to lead to a decline in quit rates due to the inability of those already in low-wage jobs to find higher paid ones. Rather, they expect that wage compression in low-wage environments results in mistaken inferences about the nature of jobs. In the presence of wage compression, positions that pay minimum wage will not be homogeneous with respect to these intangible qualities that can be judged accurately only with experience. Those newly hired at the minimum wage will then include many who, after some experience of the job, conclude that it is not what they expected. Their hypothesis is similar to that of Wessels (1980) and Sicilian and Grossberg (1993) in the central role played by information loss resulting from compression of the lower tail of the wage distribution due to the minimum wage. It differs from Wessels's (1980) in that this is now a problem not just for those who are employed when the minimum wage increases but for all individuals who start a position at the minimum wage, at least when it binds and leads to much wage compression.

To examine this hypothesis, Grossberg and Sicilian (2004) turn primarily to the NLSY, with a bit of help from the CPS. In addition to much important descriptive data about individuals and their jobs and employers, the NLSY has information about when an individual began a job and the starting wage, when employment in that position ended and why. From the CPS they construct a relative minimum wage variable as the ratio of a state's effective minimum wage in each year to its median that year; the period of their study, 1988–1994, was one of considerably greater variation in the minimum wage, both across states and years, than was available in their earlier work. From these two data sources they can identify quits and model them (i.e., the probability that an employee quits a job) as a function of job tenure, the relative minimum wage, the starting wage relative to the minimum wage, an extensive list of individual and job-specific factors, and local macroeconomic conditions. In presenting their results, they distinguish between state-year cells in which their relative minimum wage was very high and very low.[22]

Grossberg and Sicilian (2004) estimate separate hazard models for men and women, reporting their results in a fashion that calls to mind a difference-in-differences framework. They compare the likelihood of quitting a job when the minimum wage is high, and wage compression is greater, with that when the minimum wage is low. What corresponds to a treatment group consists of those hired at the minimum wage, and the analog to a comparison group is those hired at more than 10 percent above the minimum wage. Their central result is that when the minimum wage is binding and there is (likely) much wage compression, the likelihood of a man's quitting is many times greater for one hired at the minimum wage than for one hired at more than 110 percent of the minimum wage (and the level of statistical significance is phenomenally high). In contrast, when the relative minimum wage is low, the same difference in likelihoods appears to run the other way, although it is both much smaller and not statistically significant. They detect no relationship between starting wage and women's relative quit rates. They conclude that when the minimum wage is relatively high, and wage compression ensues, the minimum wage results in a loss of information that reduces the value of matches in the labor market because job seekers cannot tell without experiencing a position that the previous correlation between wages and intangible characteristics of jobs no longer exists.[23]

Notes

1. Firms that are newly in business are referred to as births, and those that are newly out of business are referred to as deaths. Those that were in business previously and are still operating are called continuing firms.

2. This led the Bureau of Labor Statistics to cease publication after 1952 of estimates for a related set of gross flows, those between labor force states: employed, unemployed, not in the labor force (Frazis et al. [2005]).

3. Fallick and Fleischman (2004) were the first to take advantage of this question to measure flows between jobs.

4. Data from the Unemployment Insurance program and income tax programs can be used to link employer and household data, as they include both social security numbers and employer identification numbers.

5. One drawback is that the Census Bureau limits access to the data and closely controls how the data are used and what is released to prevent the identification of individuals and firms. See http://lehd.ces.census.gov/.

6. This discussion of the behavior of gross flows in Pinoli's theoretical model draws from Figure 3 in Pinoli (2010).

7. In presenting the estimated effects for flows, Pinoli (2010) assumes a 10 percent increase in the minimum wage. While this is an efficient way to convey information, this is at least 50 percent larger than any of the in-sample increases (and more than twice as large as most of them), so involves extrapolating well outside her sample.

8. Pinoli (2010) presents results for other treatment and control groups, but the ones cited here are among the strongest and are based on the best match between treatment and control group: those aged 16–24 and those aged 25–34, respectively. The "large expected increases" were the anticipated ones that occurred under the center-left government and were between two-thirds and five-sixths as large as the unexpected increase that occurred shortly after it came to power.

9. Pinoli (2010) does not present results for accessions of temporary workers.

10. Both report a sharp decline in separations. Portugal and Cardoso (2006) report a decline in accessions that is smaller than the decline in separations, leading to an increase in the teenage share of employment. Dube, Lester, and Reich (2012) report a decline in accessions of both teens and restaurant workers that is roughly equivalent to the decline separations.

11. It is worth noting that this result is not due to the posting of fewer higher-wage jobs when there is a minimum wage but to low-wage workers already occupying a higher-wage job than they would in the absence of the minimum wage.

12. This could happen eventually without a minimum wage, when the cascade of hirings and quits ends with the hiring of an unemployed person, except that the cascade itself raises costs for firms and they end up trying to fill fewer positions than otherwise.

13. A further consequence, relevant later when we come to labor force participation, is that because the wage compression increases the probability of finding a job for

someone who is unemployed, it draws more of those who are not employed into active search.

14. Portugal and Cardoso (2006) report results as changes in relative shares, which complicates straightforward interpretation of the effect of the minimum wage on gross flows. However, because the only changes in the minimum wage were for those of teenagers, we can treat minimum wage–induced changes in gross flows of other groups as zero.

15. All calculations are based on Portugal and Cardoso (2006, Table 6, p. 995). The accession rate is defined as the number of accessions divided by employment at the beginning of the year. An accession is identified as an individual employed at a firm, either continuing or new, at the beginning of one year but not at the same firm at the beginning of the previous year. The separation rate is defined similarly, as the number of separations during a year divided by employment at the beginning of the year, where a separation is identified as an individual employed at a firm, either continuing or one that went out of business, at the beginning of one year but not at the same firm one year later.

16. Teenagers are defined as those aged 14–19 inclusive.

17. Owing to differences in presentation, a quantitative comparison of the results of Dube, Lester, and Reich (2010) with those of Portugal and Cardoso (2006) is not possible.

18. Chapter 2 contains more detailed discussions of Dube, Naidu, and Reich (2007) and Thompson (2009).

19. Böckerman and Uusitalo (2009) apply Skedinger's approach to Finnish teenagers, but their results appear to be internally inconsistent to a degree, and they suspect that their sample period is too short to control adequately for trends in youth employment. Thus, as in the chapter on jobs, this chapter does not discuss their results.

20. Guiliano develops several alternatives to competitive theories in understanding the impact of the minimum wage within firms. Her work is guided by these theories.

21. Because of the use of now-dated time-series methods and strong evidence of uncorrected first-order serial correlation in Mixon's analysis, the account that follows begins with later work.

22. In their mildly confusing terminology, a state-year cell in which the relative minimum wage is high is a low-wage environment (because the median wage is relatively low), and one in which the relative minimum wage is low is a high-wage environment (because the median wage is relatively high). We will instead focus on whether the relative minimum wage is high or low (and thus whether it results in much compression of the distribution of low wages).

23. A serious concern is the reliability of Grossberg and Sicilian's (2004) statistical inference. They report using robust standard errors, a correction for conventional heteroskedasticity (i.e., different variances). The use of state-year cells to define the relative minimum wage immediately calls to mind not only the Moulton (1986, 1990) problem but the critique of Bertrand, Duflo, and Mullainathan (2004), both of which indicate that clustered standard errors are in order. The extremely small

p-value of Grossberg and Sicilian's (2004) most interesting result, the relative probability of quitting for a man hired at minimum wage in a low-wage environment, 0.00001, reinforces this concern.

9
Labor Force Participation Rate, Unemployment, and Vacancies

We have so far considered the effect of the minimum wage on several labor market quantities: the number of jobs filled, the number of people employed, and the number of hours worked, all of which are measures of employment; and gross flows in and out of employment (accessions and separations). These are measures most frequently of interest to labor economists and those interested in the functioning of the labor market. In this chapter, we examine four other labor market measures that are more often considered in discussions of macroeconomic phenomena: the labor force participation rate (LFPR), the unemployment rate, unemployment duration, and the vacancy rate.

Table 9.1 indicates how the population is segmented for the purpose of defining the labor force and its two primary components, the employed and the unemployed—those who are not employed but are actively searching for jobs. Individuals who are neither employed nor actively seeking employment are classified as "not in the labor force." Mincer (1976) suggests that changes in the size of the labor force are a better indication of the effect of minimum wages on the welfare of actual and prospective workers than is the response of employment. He reasons that even if both employment and the probability of finding work decline following a minimum wage increase, an increase in the size of the labor force indicates that, for many, the higher prospective wage offsets these other factors.

As Table 9.2 shows, the LFPR is the number of people in the labor force divided by population size. Like the employment ratio (the number employed divided by the number in the population), the LFPR can be defined for specific demographic groups.

The unemployment rate is the number of the unemployed divided by the number in the labor force, or one minus "the employment ratio divided by the LFPR." At first glance, this is inversely related to the employment ratio, rising when the latter is falling and falling when the latter is rising, so it is not obvious what is to be gained by its study. The

Table 9.1 Labor Force Definitions

Term	Definition
Civilian noninstitutional population (CNIP)	All individuals aged 16 and over who are not in the armed forces or in prison, or other institutions.
Employed	Members of the civilian noninstitutional population who did any work for pay or profit during the survey reference week; persons who did at least 15 hours of unpaid work in a family-operated enterprise; and persons who were temporarily absent from their regular jobs because of illness, vacation, bad weather, industrial dispute, or various personal reasons.
Unemployed	Persons are classified as unemployed if they do not have a job, have actively looked for work in the prior four weeks, and are currently available for work. Persons who were not working and were waiting to be recalled to a job from which they had been temporarily laid off are also included as unemployed.
Labor force	The sum of employed and unemployed persons. The labor force participation rate is the labor force as a percent of the civilian noninstitutional population.

Table 9.2 Labor Force Measures

Measure	Definition	Formula
Labor force participation ratio	The ratio of the number of individuals in the labor force to the number of individuals in the civilian non-institutional population (CNIP).	$LFPR = \dfrac{\#\ in\ LF}{\#\ in\ CNIP}$
Employment ratio	The ratio of the number of individuals employed to the number of individuals in the CNIP.	$ER = \dfrac{\#\ Employed}{\#\ in\ CNIP}$
Unemployment rate	The ratio of the number of individuals unemployed to the number of individuals in the labor force. Measured as a percentage.	$UR = 100 \times \left(\dfrac{\#\ Unemployed}{\#\ in\ LaborForce} \right)$

answer is that the unemployment rate varies not only when the employment ratio does, but also when the LFPR does. Partridge and Partridge (1998) observe that at the state level, the standard deviation of the annual growth rate of teenagers' employment is several times as large as that of the annual teenage unemployment rate (pp. 368–369).[1] They suggest that this higher variability is noise that obscures the signal of the minimum wage and is unrelated to anything that is either of interest or controlled for. At the least, examination of the unemployment rate will complement studies of the employment rate in the minimum wage literature and may well be more fruitful.

Unemployment duration is the average length of time that an unemployed worker has continually sought work.[2] This is of interest because even if none of the other variables already mentioned vary in response to minimum wage changes, a change in unemployment duration contains information about the effect of the minimum wage on (some) workers. It is widely believed that it is undesirable to be unemployed (the song "Hallelujah! I'm a Bum" not withstanding), and longer periods in this condition are worse, perhaps more than in proportion because as skills and networks deteriorate while unemployed, finding a job becomes ever more difficult.

The unemployment rate is a supply-side quantity in the labor market. The vacancy rate is its counterpart on the demand side. Also defined as a fraction, its numerator is the number of positions that firms are trying to fill—the number of vacancies—and its denominator is typically the size of the labor force.[3]

LABOR FORCE PARTICIPATION

Table 9.3 lists Flinn (2006), already discussed in Chapter 2, and three other studies that have problematic standard errors. Flinn (2006) develops two closely related search models, which he calls the endogenous and exogenous models. The difference between them is that the minimum wage influences the contact rate in the endogenous model but not in the exogenous model, which is the one that he believes to be more reliable.[4] To estimate the models' parameters, Flinn relies on CPS data for teenagers and young adults from just before, between, and

Table 9.3 Labor Force Participation Response

Study	Country	Target	Data	Data structure	Period	Comments
Flinn (2006)	United States	White, male teenagers and youth	CPS	Individual repeated cross section	9/96, 2/97, 8/97, 1/98	Very rich search model that models the participation decision. Indicates that the late 1990s increases in the U.S. federal minimum wage most likely increased youth participation, employment, and unemployment, the last because of a larger increase in the LFPR than employment.
Addison and Ozturk (2012)	OECD	Women	OECD	Country-annual panel	1980s– 2000s	Bertrand, Duflo, and Mullainathan (2004) critique applies.
Wessels (2005)	United States	Teenagers	CPS	State-quarter panel	1979– 2001	Bertrand, Duflo, and Mullainathan (2004) critique applies.
Ahn, Arcidiacono, and Wessels (2011)	United States	White, male teenagers	CPS	Repeated cross section	1989– 2000	Search model that builds on Flinn (2006). Identifies compositional effects, where the minimum wage attracts teenagers from more-educated households into the labor force. Bertrand, Duflo, and Mullainathan (2004) critique applies; no standard errors for the elasticities (which are the interesting result).

shortly after the 1996 and 1997 changes in the minimum wage.[5] The exogenous model implies that labor force participation rises until the minimum wage exceeds more than $8.00/hour, above which it declines. The endogenous model pegs this decline as beginning, imperceptibly, at a minimum wage somewhere around $3.00/hour and first becoming perceptible around $3.75/hour.[6]

Considering calculations based only on the range of minimum wage values in the data, the exogenous model indicates a small rise in the LFPR from less than 64 percent at a minimum wage of $4.25/hour to 65 percent at a value of $5.15/hour, while the endogenous model indicates instead a fall from less than the original value of 64 percent to about 59 percent in this interval. As mentioned in the earlier discussion, Flinn (2006) provides no error bias for these results that would allow us to judge whether these movements are the equivalent of statistical noise.[7]

THE UNEMPLOYMENT RATE

Table 9.4 lists 10 studies that examine the effect of the minimum wage on either the unemployment rate or the duration of unemployment.[8] Partridge and Partridge (1998) consider the effect of the minimum wage on teenagers' unemployment rates, and in their 1999 study they look at the long-term unemployment rate.[9] Most of the estimates in each study come from models that include both a contemporaneous and a lagged minimum wage; in these cases, the two-point estimates are always statistically significant but have opposite signs. When they do not include the lagged term, the point estimate of the coefficient on the contemporaneous term is not even remotely near statistical significance. According to the equation with both terms, the response of the unemployment rate is quite large, both initially when it declines in response to a minimum wage increase, and in the next year when an increase in the unemployment rate more than cancels out the previous decline. It would be useful to know the statistical significance of the two coefficients' sum, something that would take into account the correlation between the two terms. It is likely that the sum, the net response of the unemployment rate over two years, is not distinguishable from zero.[10]

In their study of the effect of minimum wage increases on teenagers in New Zealand in 2001, 2002, and 2003, Hyslop and Stillman (2007) report a statistically significant increase in unemployment for those aged 16–17 in response to the largest of the increases, which happened in 2001, but only when they do not include business cycle controls. Once included, none of the increases has a statistically significant effect on unemployment. For older teenagers, aged 18–19, a lack of business controls is associated with a statistically insignificant effect on unemployment. With the inclusion of business cycle controls, the effects on unemployment are statistically significant decreases in the later years, and no statistically significant effect in 2001.

Flinn's (2006) analysis has interesting implications for the unemployment rate. His model has three states for individuals: 1) out of the labor force; 2) unemployed (that is, in the labor force and not employed); and 3) employed. According to the exogenous model, where the contact rate is independent of the minimum wage, the 1996 and 1997 minimum wage increases led to increases in both the employment ratio and the unemployment rate, the latter by 0.2 percentage points. The increase in the unemployment rate was due to a small increase in employment and a slightly larger increase in labor force participation. In the endogenous model, the policy raised the unemployment rate by 0.4 percentage points, resulting from a large drop in employment and a slightly larger drop in labor force participation.

Tulip (2004) examines whether the minimum wage affects the rate of unemployment consistent with a stable inflation rate. The question arises from an interpretation of macroeconomic data, which concludes that prolonged attempts to hold the unemployment rate at a level that is too low can be identified by a rate of inflation that is getting ever larger, while allowing the rate to be too high can be identified by its opposite, an inflation rate that declines over time. NAIRU, the abbreviation for nonaccelerating inflation rate of unemployment, is one acronym for the "Goldilocks value" of the unemployment rate—the value that is just right because it is associated with a stable inflation rate. To address the issue, Tulip derives a regression equation in which the rate of wage inflation depends on the current unemployment rate, on the Kaitz index, on the change in the relative minimum wage, and on several lagged

Table 9.4 Unemployment Rate/Duration

Study	Country	Target	Data	Data structure	Period	Comments
Carmeci and Mauro (2002)	Italy	Regional growth rates	Many Italian sources	Regional-annual panel	1965–1995	Apply cross-country growth framework to Italy's regions; argue that inappropriately high minimum wage leads to high unemployment, slower growth in poorer regions. Minimum wage disappears from view in the course of the model's derivation.
Flinn (2006)	United States	White, male teenagers and youth	CPS	Individual repeated cross section	9/96, 2/97, 8/97, 1/98	Very rich search model that models the participation decision. Indicates that the late 1990s increases in the U.S. federal minimum wage most likely increased youth participation, employment, and unemployment, the last because of a larger increase in the LFPR than employment.
Hyslop and Stillman (2007)	New Zealand	Teenagers	HLFS	Individual-annual panel	1997–2003	Once business cycle controls are included, the only effects are declines in the unemployment rate for 18–19-year-olds.
Partridge and Partridge (1998)	United States	Teenagers	CPS, BEA, others	State-year panel	1984–89	Similar to Neumark and Wascher approach, for unemployment of teens; panel short enough that Bertrand critique not too serious.
Partridge and Partridge (1999)	United States	Long-term unemployment	CPS, BEA, others	State-year panel	1984–89	Similar to Neumark and Wascher approach, for long-term unemployment; panel sufficiently short that Bertrand critique not too serious.
Pedace and Rohm (2011)	United States	Unemployment duration	CPS, Displaced Worker Survey	Individual-year panel; repeated cross section	1984–2000	Hazard model of unemployment duration. Separate estimates for men, women, and various subgroups. Decline in duration for male high school graduates; increase for male high school dropouts, and for women, especially older women and less-skilled women.

Reference	Country	Subject	Data source	Data type	Time period	Description
Tulip (2004)	United States		BLS	Quarterly time series	1948:1–2003:1	Estimate a Phillips curve with minimum wage as a control variable. Then holding inflation constant, solve for the NAIRU, see how the NAIRU responds to minimum wage. NAIRU rises 0.7 percentage points in response to a 10 percent increase in the minimum wage.
van den Berg and Ridder (1998)	Nether-lands	Dutch labor market	OSA Labor Supply Panel Survey	Unbalanced individual-year panel	1985–1990	Apply Burdett and Mortenson's (1998) search model to the Netherlands; partition the labor market into 170 segments; estimate MRPL for each, and analyze effect of the minimum wage. No standard errors provided for the policy analysis, and they express some skepticism about the result.
Fortin, Keil, and Symons (2001)	Canada		Statistics Canada	Regional-annual panel	1967–1991	Why has the unemployment rate risen over this long period? Four sets of estimates, by gender and age. Effect reported for both types of women; Bertrand, Duflo, and Mullainathan (2004) critique applies.
Addison and Ozturk (2012)	OECD	Women	OECD	Country-year panel	1980s–2000	Cross-country analysis of women's labor market outcomes; Bertrand, Duflo, and Mullainathan (2004) critique applies.

measures of wage and price inflation. The intuition for including the minimum wage derives from the following line of reasoning:

- An increase in the minimum wage raises wages.
- Because firms set prices as a percentage over unit costs, they raise prices.
- Higher prices lead to lower demand for output.
- Firms respond by reducing their demand for labor.
- Unemployment rises.

According to the underlying logic of the NAIRU, if policymakers respond by stimulating demand to keep unemployment constant at the original level but make no further changes to the minimum wage, several rounds of ever-smaller price increases will follow that will inflate away the minimum wage increase. In the end, both the unemployment and inflation rates will have returned to their original levels, and the price level will be higher, offsetting the initial rise in the real minimum wage. If policy is instead focused on keeping both the real minimum wage constant at its new, higher level through repeated increases in the nominal minimum wage, and the inflation rate at its original level through tighter monetary policy, the unemployment rate necessarily rises.

Tulip (2004) estimates this equation on aggregate quarterly data for the United States for the period 1947–2003.[11] Based on his estimate, a 10 percent increase in the minimum wage increases the NAIRU by 0.7 percentage points, slowly declining over time until inflation has reduced the real minimum wage to its original value.[12]

Van den Berg and Ridder (1998) use data from the Netherlands to examine how well a search model that generates wage dispersion fits observed data. Previous work in this vein relied on a model in which only unemployed workers searched for work. Van den Berg and Ridder instead use Burdett and Mortensen's (1998) search model, which, by allowing for on-the-job search, is able to generate certain types of heterogeneous results with fewer assumptions made specifically to attain this goal. Observed wages are always between an employee's reservation wage and the corresponding employer's marginal revenue product of labor. Individuals are heterogenous in the value of their reservation wage for a variety of reasons, including their current employment status and their current wage if employed.[13] Firms differ in the value of their marginal product of labor. Wages of employees at the bottom of the wage distribution rise as the minimum wage is increased until it exceeds the value of some firms' marginal revenue product. That firm goes out of business and its employees become unemployed.

To estimate the model, Van den Berg and Ridder (1998) make use of a long-term survey of Dutch households that has information on individuals' employment spells between 1985 and 1990. It allows them to partition the Dutch labor market into nearly 200 segments based on traits of both individuals and jobs. From their estimates of the marginal revenue product of labor in each segment, they calculate that a 10 percent increase in the minimum wage would have no effect on the unemployment rate, but a 25 percent increase would raise the unemployment rate by 16 percentage points. They present no standard errors for this estimate and are wary of placing much weight on its precise value because institutional factors in the Dutch labor market prevent them from being able to distinguish adequately between the effects of search frictions and the minimum wage.[14]

UNEMPLOYMENT DURATION

Pedace and Rohn (2011) study whether (and how) the minimum wage affects the length of unemployment spells by estimating hazard functions on 1984–2000 data from the Displaced Workers Survey (a biennial supplement to the CPS). Hazard functions model durations, how long something lasts, in this case the duration of unemployment spells. In Pedace and Rohn's specification, unemployment duration depends on an individual's demographic traits, including details of the last job held before becoming unemployed, on state and year dummies, and on the level of the minimum wage. In some specifications, they also include the percentage of each states' labor force that receives the minimum wage. As an ad hoc examination of robustness, Pedace and Rohn report results from several different functional forms commonly used to relate duration to regressors, and they perform their estimations separately for each gender as well as for subgroups within each gender:

by age (younger than 25 or not), skill level, and whether or not the individual completed high school.

For males, higher minimum wages reduce the length of unemployment spells of high school graduates, with a $1.00 increase leading to a 21 percent reduction in the average unemployment spell. At the average values in the data for this group, this is a reduction of 5 weeks in unemployment duration, a 27 percent increase in the minimum wage, and an unemployment duration elasticity (with respect to the minimum wage) of −0.8. For males without a high school degree, the corresponding figures are a 63 percent increase in length of unemployment spells, a 28 percent increase in the minimum wage, an elasticity of 2.25, and a more than 21-week increase in the mean length of unemployment spells.[15]

The pattern of results for women is quite different in signs, size, and statistical significance. For the same $1.00 (27 percent) increase, females with a high school degree experience a 55 percent increase in unemployment duration, nearly 18 weeks at the average, for an elasticity of about 2. Lower-skilled women experience a 66 percent increase in unemployment duration, 15 weeks at the average, for an elasticity near 2.4.[16] For those aged 25 and older who experience the same $1 increase in the minimum wage, the increase in women's unemployment duration is 47 percent, for an elasticity of 1.74, and the decline in men's unemployment duration is −17 percent, for an elasticity of −0.62.

As an alternative way to consider their results, Pedace and Rohn (2011) report the response of median unemployment durations to all the federal minimum wage increases during the 1990s. For males with a high school diploma, the minimum wage increases resulted in a decrease in the median duration of unemployment from 17 weeks to 11 weeks. For males without a high school diploma, however, the median unemployment spell more than doubled from 21 weeks to 49 weeks. For women with a high school diploma, the median duration more than doubled, from 16 weeks to 35 weeks, as it also did for women who are lower skilled, from 19 to 47 weeks.

These estimated effects, both the elasticities and the increases in median durations, are substantial. In addition to the compositional effect indicated by the simultaneous reduction in unemployment duration for male high school graduates and increase in duration for women, these results are consistent with incumbents in minimum wage jobs becoming more attached to them, as both Portugal and Cardoso (2006) and Dube, Lester, and Reich (2012) report for teenagers. They are also consistent with Grossberg and Sicilian's (2004) results for men in high-wage states, for whom the minimum wage increases job tenure.[17]

VACANCIES

The Beveridge curve, which plots the vacancy rate against the unemployment rate, is a tool that macroeconomists use to diagnose the state of the economy. In the short run, if the Beveridge curve is not shifting around, a plot of observations is downward sloping, with high values of the vacancy rate observed simultaneously with low values of the unemployment rate, and low values of the vacancy rate observed at the same time as high values of the unemployment rate. The former set of points indicates that the economy is in a boom and the latter that it is in a recession. Over the longer run, it is not uncommon for the Beveridge curve to move toward or away from the origin (also described as shifting in or out). When it shifts out, higher vacancy rates than before are observed with each unemployment rate, and higher unemployment rates with each vacancy rate; the labor market is operating less efficiently as more unfilled jobs coexist with more workers in search of jobs.

Table 9.5 lists two studies that examine the impact of the minimum wage on vacancies. Both—Samson's (1994) study of the Canadian Beveridge curve for the period 1966:1–1988:4 and Singell and Terborg's (2007) study of vacancies in the restaurant and hotel industries of Washington and Oregon in 1994–2001—rely on time-series data. Neither adequately addresses serious problems that time-series data commonly present to the econometrician: unit roots, cointegration, and serially correlated residuals.[18] If serial correlation is not properly addressed, whether in the estimation or in the calculation of standard errors, then the resulting statistical inference is unreliable. If variables in the regression have unit roots that are not addressed, then the point estimates are meaningless.

Table 9.5 Vacancies

Authors	Country	Target	Data	Data structure	Period	Comments
Samson (1994)	Canada	Macro-economy	Various	Quarterly time series and region-quarter panel	1966:4– 1988:4	Estimate unemployment and vacancy equations, including the real minimum wage in both. Lack of attention to time-series issues (unit roots, cointegration, serially correlated residuals) despite the use of time-series data defeats any confidence in the results.
Singell and Terborg (2007)	United States	Restaurant and hotel industries in WA and OR	Classified ads	Monthly time series	1994:1– 2001:12	Analyze monthly want-ad data for restaurant and hotel jobs collected from Portland and Seattle newspapers (one each). (Even) less sensitivity to time-series issues than in the analysis of employment, similar to Samson (above).

CONCLUSION

On balance there is reason to believe that minimum wage increases of the size seen in the U.S. data slightly increase the LFPR of youth, but it is not clear that the size of this response is at all precisely measured. It also appears that the unemployment rate increases in response to minimum wage increases, but here too the lack of appropriately calculated standard errors defeats attempts at reliable inference. Flinn's (2006) model suggests that the increase in the unemployment rate is not big and is in large part due to growth in labor force participation that outstrips employment growth. Pedace and Rohn's (2011) study of employment duration is quite interesting, suggesting that employers substitute toward better-educated male workers and away from both less-educated men and women in all relevant categories, not just less-educated ones. Although they do not mention this, the adverse impact on older women but not younger ones raises the possibility of sexist-age discrimination. Finally, the small bit of work relating the minimum wage to vacancies has statistical problems that keep it from being informative. A fair summary of the research into the consequences of the minimum wage for these macroeconomic variables is that too little of it exists to draw any certain conclusions, and much of what does exist relies heavily on specific models. The models may well be of high quality, and they are certainly interesting, but they are not sufficiently tested yet to inspire great confidence.

Notes

1. Admittedly, focusing on employment growth rates rather than the employment ratio involves a comparison of apples and oranges; the point would be clearer, and substantively the same, if Partridge and Partridge (1998) referred to teen employment ratios instead of employment growth rates.
2. "Duration of unemployment represents the length of time (through the current reference week) that persons classified as unemployed had been continuously looking for work. For persons on layoff, duration of unemployment represents the number of full weeks since the end of their most recent period of employment. Thus, it is a measure of an in-progress spell of joblessness, not a completed spell. Two useful measures of the duration of unemployment are the mean and the median. Mean duration is the arithmetic average computed from single weeks of unemployment.

Median duration is the midpoint of a distribution of weeks of unemployment." See *BLS Handbook of Methods*, Chapter 1, for a discussion of duration and its measurement. http://www.bls.gov/opub/hom/homch1_c.htm (accessed August 15, 2013).

3. Defining the denominator to be the labor force (the sum of the number employed and the number unemployed) rather than the sum of vacancies and the number of jobs filled (which itself is roughly equal to employment) makes the vacancy rate as measured a mix of demand and supply side measures, but it makes it easier to compare the vacancy and unemployment rates.

4. Briefly, the contact rate is the number of job offers that a job seeker can expect to receive in each period of search, or that a firm can expect to make for each vacancy in each period. More precisely, in labor-search models, a contact is defined as a worker's approaching a firm that has a vacancy and asking "How much would you pay me to fill that vacancy?" The firm is able to evaluate how much the worker is worth in that position and makes an offer that reflects that value. The contact rate is defined differently depending, on whether the perspective is that of the job seeker or of the employer. In each period, the numerator is the number of contacts in that period, and the denominator is either the number of job seekers or the number of vacancies that firms are looking to fill.

5. The federal minimum wage rose from $4.25/hour to $4.75/hour on October 1, 1996, and, as part of the same legislation, to $5.15/hour on September 1, 1997. http://www.dol.gov/whd/minwage/chart.htm (accessed August 15, 2013).

6. This is inferred from the behavior of "out of the labor force" in the top part of Flinn's (2006) Figures 1 and 2.

7. Wessels (2005) and Addison and Ozturk (2012) also examine the LFPR, using the empirical approach associated with Neumark and Wascher (1992, 1994). Both report a labor supply response that is negative and statistically significant, Wessels for teenagers in the United States, and Addison and Ozturk for women in OECD countries. In both cases, the statistical significance relies on conventional standard errors, which are likely to be biased downward.

Hyslop and Stillman (2007) consider several variables measuring labor market outcomes, but these are not mutually exclusive and cannot be combined to give labor force participation.

Ahn, Arcidiacono, and Wessels (2011) use a search model similar to Flinn (2006) to study compositional effects of the minimum wage, specifically, the difference in labor market outcomes for teenagers from more- and less-educated households. According to their estimates, as the education level of the head of household increases, teenagers' reservation wages rise, and their search costs fall. The reverse is true if the household head is either unemployed or a single parent. They conclude that a higher minimum wage attracts teenagers from all types of households into the labor force. While most of their point estimates are statistically significant, that is based on conventional standard errors and, given the structure of their data, the Bertrand, Duflo, and Mullainathan (2004) critique is pertinent. In addition, they present no standard errors for the elasticities calculated from these point estimates.

8. One study not listed is Bouvet (2009), which studies unemployment, vacancies, and the minimum wage using both an annual panel of five countries and an annual panel of 60 regions in those five countries. Bouvet's minimum wage variable is a dummy for the existence of a legislated minimum wage; it is difficult to figure out exactly how she carried out her analysis; and unless minimum wage policy in these countries is very different from that in the United States, the Bertrand, Duflo, and Mullainathan (2004) critique is pertinent. Except for the criticism of the minimum wage variable, the same comments apply to Morgan and Mourougane's (2005) analysis of structural unemployment in several EU countries.

9. Both this study and Partridge and Partridge (1999) are short enough (six years of annual data) that the problems may not be especially severe.

10. With a pair of positively correlated variables, this situation (each coefficient statistically significant and with opposite signs when both variables are in the regression, but when only one is in the equation its coefficient is much smaller in magnitude and not statistically significant) suggests that the variables probably do not belong in the equation.

11. Tulip's (2004) residual diagnostics indicate a few of the typical problems from this type of estimation. The exception is a test that indicates that the residuals are not normally distributed. On the one hand, this raises doubts about any statistical inference using the equation. On the other hand, it is rarely evident what sort of adjustments to the equation or estimation will solve this problem.

12. Tulip (2004) recognizes that the relationship between the minimum wage and unemployment or the NAIRU is not likely to be a simple causal one and may in fact be due to a third variable that is both causally related to unemployment and correlated with the minimum wage, but that until this is better understood, the relationship remains useful for forecasting if not policy analysis. Tulip also reports other countries' experiences and explores other variables that may play the role of the third variable. He writes, "If some strong but plausible assumptions are made . . . when wages at the bottom of the distribution are compressed, the NAIRU usually increases. Furthermore, the wide variety of policies across countries suggests that this correlation is not the result of one particular set of institutions or rules. . . . [T]he latter may reflect a causal effect of inequality on unemployment . . . [and] the strong influence of governments in setting wages at the bottom of the distribution" (pp. 17–18).

13. The relevant reservation wage here is not the standard one, the wage necessary to draw someone into the labor force and accept a job, but the lowest wage offer necessary to induce someone to switch jobs.

14. Another study of minimum wage effects in countries other than the United States is Carmeci and Mauro (2002), which uses data for 19 Italian regions during the period 1965–1995. The causal chain linking the minimum wage to unemployment is quite long, in the course of which the minimum wage disappears from view. The minimum wage plays no explicit role in any versions of the equation that they estimate, and in the end, it is both difficult to ascertain the effect of the minimum wage and not at all clear that any effect attributed to the minimum wage is not actually due to other factors.

15. The $1.00 increase is a different percentage increase in the average minimum wage experienced by high school graduates and those without a high school degree because they are distributed differently across states and their different minimum wages.

16. Low-skilled is defined by the occupational category of the last job held before becoming unemployed. Pedace and Rohn (2011) report the details needed to calculate the elasticity only when the results are statistically significant across several specifications of the model: thus, the figures for men without a high school degree versus those for low-skilled women.

17. Recall their interpretation that in low-wage states, the minimum wage results in so much wage compression that the wage alone does not convey useful information about job quality to prospective workers, so there is no discernible effect on tenure.

18. Samson (1994) reports the Durbin-Watson statistic, but the values she reports are typically agnostic about serial correlation. Of greater concern is that it is not an appropriate statistic to report; because of the lagged dependent variables in her equation, the Durbin-Watson statistic is biased away from detecting serial correlation. If there is serial correlation in her residuals, the reported standard errors are inconsistent.

10
The Product Market

How does the product market reflect increases in the minimum wage? In the short run, any adjustment must come through output and prices. If there are important differences in productivity across firms in markets that are affected by the minimum wage, then the degree of competition may change in the long run as less-productive firms shrink or leave the market and more productive ones expand. A number of analyses have examined the price response, a few have examined the effect on profitability, very few have studied the output response, and none have seriously explored any long-term effect on market structure. This chapter discusses studies of the effect on prices and then briefly discusses those that have examined the effects on output or profitability.

PRICES

Most analyses of the price response have examined only the restaurant industry, especially the fast food sector, and by and large they agree that minimum wage increases lead to higher prices at fast food establishments.[1] They do this with a variety of analytic techniques, applied to a variety of data sets drawn from several different time periods in three countries, bolstering the robustness of this finding. There is some disagreement about the strength of the response, but none about its existence or direction. Table 10.1 lists seven studies of the price response to the minimum wage. Those of Fougère, Gautier, and Le Bihan (2010); Lee, Schluter, and O'Roark (2000); and MaCurdy and McIntyre (2001) are based on explicit economic models that relate increases in the minimum wage to price increases in either the restaurant industry or in the broader food sector. Rather than estimating these models directly, parameter values are set according to relevant estimates or measurements that others have calculated elsewhere. The remaining analyses are purely statistical in nature, with no underlying economic model

Table 10.1 Prices

Study	Effect	Target	Country	Sample period	Analytic approach	Unit of observation	Data structure	Type of standard error	Data set[a]
Aaronson (2001)	Positive	Food away from home sector	United States, Canada	1978–1995	Regression	City-month	Panel	Robust	BLS, Stat-Can, Chamber of Commerce
Dube, Naidu, and Reich (2007)	Positive	San Francisco restaurants	United States	2003–2004	Quasi experiment	Firm-year	Panel	Robust	Private survey
Fougère, Gautier, and Le Bihan (2010)	Positive	Restaurants	France	1994–2003	Regression	Meal-establishment-month	Panel	MLE	FSI
Lee, Schluter, and O'Roark (2000)	Positive	Food sector	United States	1992, 1997	I/O analysis	Industry	Cross section	—	Various
MacDonald and Aaronson (2006)	Positive	Food away from home sector	United States	1995–1997	Regression	Item-establishment-month	Panel	Clustered (by est.)	BLS
MaCurdy and McIntyre (2001)	Positive	Minimum wage workers	United States	1996	I/O analysis	Industry	Cross section	—	SIPP, CES
Wadsworth (2010)	Long-term Positive	Minimum wage industries	United Kingdom	1996–2006	Regression	Industry-month	Time series	Newey-West(1)	Various

[a] BLS = Bureau of Labor Statistics. FSI = French Statistical Institute. CES = Consumer Expenditure Survey. SIPP = Survey of Income and Program Participation. Various = CPS-ORG, Census of Manufactures, BEA I/O Tables for the United States.

guiding the attempt to relate the timing and size of price increases in the restaurant industry to the timing and size of minimum wage increases.

Having suggested that monopsonistic competition (also called dynamic monopsony) in the labor market may explain the absence of a decline in employment following minimum wage increases, Card and Krueger (1994, 1995) look for evidence of a decline in prices, one of the implications of this hypothesis. In a labor market that is a dynamic monopsony, a sufficiently small increase in a sufficiently small minimum wage will lead to more employment of low-wage labor, and this will in turn lead to more output. Then, whether or not the output market is competitive, output prices must fall for the market to clear. Both Card and Krueger (1994), in their study of New Jersey and Pennsylvania, and Dube, Naidu, and Reich (2007), in their study of the San Francisco Bay area, report a substantial rise in average prices in the area that experienced the minimum wage increase. Because this result is in both cases based on a simple two-by-two difference-in-differences analysis, its reliability is suspect for the reasons that Donald and Lang (2007) identify. However, each study also presents estimates based on a wage-gap measure of the minimum wage increase, a framework not suspect in this way. In both, the size of the price increase in the treated area does not vary with the wage gap. If not evidence against the presence of dynamic monopsony in the labor market, it is at a minimum not evidence in its favor. While Card and Kreuger draw no inferences from these results about the structure of the labor market, they do conclude that the higher wage bill came out of consumers' pockets (and not from reductions in firm profits).

In a series of studies, both alone and with others, Daniel Aaronson has examined the effect of minimum wage increases on restaurant prices in Canada and the United States, and the implications of these responses for labor market structure.[2] In the earliest study, Aaronson (2001) constructs monthly inflation rates from 1978–1995 using BLS data from 88 U.S. cities to compare changes in the "food away from home" component to changes in the minimum wage, considering both the timing and the size of the changes. He performs a similar analysis for "food at restaurants" in 10 Canadian provinces. In both countries, in the seven-month period centered on the month that a minimum wage increase occurs, the minimum wage elasticity of restaurant prices is about 0.07. One interesting difference is that in the United States, the bulk of the price rise takes place in the three-month period centered on the increase, especially the month before and the month of the increase. In Canada, the price rise appears to begin only a month after the increase, and the largest part of it occurs three months afterward.

Another data set allows Aaronson (2001) to look specifically at three fast food chains in the United States—McDonald's, Kentucky Fried Chicken, and Pizza Hut—and the results are less clear cut. Analyzing the data in several different ways, he consistently finds a response in the price of McDonald's hamburgers that is at least as large, and perhaps twice as large, as that of the restaurant prices already mentioned. The response of Kentucky Fried Chicken prices varies from none to as large as the largest McDonald's hamburger price response, while the response of Pizza Hut prices varies from none to barely a third of that reported above for the restaurant sector.

MacDonald and Aaronson (2006) use the same BLS data for 1995–1997 before it has been aggregated to the level of the city to explore the behavior of price changes in individual establishments, both full-service and limited-service restaurants, and how changes in the minimum wage affect this. Fougère, Gautier, and Le Bihan (2010) perform a similar analysis using French data for 1994–2003. In both surveys, the prices refer to combinations of items called meals (breakfast, lunch, or dinner) rather than to individual items. In both countries, minimum wage labor is an important component of employment (40 percent of restaurant workers in France), and inflation was low during the periods covered. The U.S. data set covers a period in which there were two increases in the national minimum wage, three states each raised their own minimum wages to levels above the new national minimums at the same time as these increases, and six states raised their minimum wages a total of 12 times in other months. During the eight and a half years that the French data cover, the national minimum wage changed in May 1998 and each July, 9 times in all. Complicating the analysis is the changeover of French currency from the franc to the euro in January 2002, a moment at which it was easier than usual to slip price changes through unnoticed.

Both studies document that prices of individual items in restaurants are fairly constant. In the United States, limited-service restaurants (predominantly fast food restaurants) raised prices on about 5.5 percent of items on average in months when they experienced no increase in the minimum wage, and 11 percent in months when they did. For full-service restaurants in France, prices on about 5 percent of items increase each January and September, when they reopen after the holidays, compared to about 3 percent in each of the other months. In fast food restaurants, about 10 percent of prices rise, on average, in each of the months of January, February, and July, versus less than 7 percent in each of the other months. As July is also the month of the annual minimum wage increase, the large July increase may be related to the rise in the minimum wage. The month of minimum wage increases, July, exhibits an unusually high proportion of price increases, but so do two months as far from July as possible, January and February. Fougère, Gautier, and Le Bihan (2010) attribute a larger role to seasonality than to the minimum wage in explaining price increases in French restaurants. In the United States, the corresponding numbers for full-service restaurants are 5.6 percent in months of minimum wage increases (versus 10 percent in France) and 5.4 percent in other months (versus 7–10 percent in France). Presenting data for France, and reporting others' findings for the United States, they show that in other sectors of the economy, larger fractions of prices change each month.

The geographic variation in the U.S. data and the variation in both wage distributions and the level and timing of changes in the minimum wage enable MacDonald and Aaronson (2006) to gain purchase on the data from a number of purely statistical angles. First, controlling for whether the item is typically associated with breakfast, lunch, or dinner; for price changes in other inputs; and for recent price increases and decreases, they report an elasticity of restaurant prices with respect to the minimum wage of about 0.07 in the three two-month periods centered on minimum wage increases.[3] That is, a 10 percent increase in the minimum wage quickly leads to a (roughly) 0.7 percent increase in restaurant prices. When they break out limited-service restaurants separately, the elasticity is more than twice as large (0.16); for full-service restaurants, the elasticity drops by about half. Explicitly exploiting the variation that comes with the geographic reach of the United States, MacDonald and Aaronson interact the minimum wage with terms that locate it relative to the 20th percentile of the local wage distribution. In areas where low-wage workers earn relatively high wages, changes in the minimum wage should have little effect on wages or costs, and therefore, one expects, on prices. That is indeed what they find.

Do restaurants respond to minimum wage increases with larger individual price increases or increases in the prices of more items? To examine this, MacDonald and Aaronson (2006) rely on the reasoning underlying conventional models of price adjustment: that it is costly to the firm not only to change prices but also for prices not to be at the value that equates supply and demand. The cost of having the wrong price depends on its distance from the optimum price. The cost of changing prices, known as an adjustment cost, is attributed to the costs of gathering and evaluating information needed to determine the appropriate price and of changing signs, labels, database values, and advertising. The amount of adjustment costs that the firm incurs depends on the frequency of price changes.[4] To reflect recent incidence of adjustment costs, they constructed a dummy variable, *review*, which was set to one if an establishment had changed any price in the previous period. According to the underlying reasoning, having recently incurred the costs of price adjustment, a restaurant would be less likely to do so again even if the minimum wage had subsequently risen. MacDonald and Aaronson (2006) report exactly this outcome. Of particular interest is the estimate that a 10 percent increase in the minimum wage roughly doubles the probability that an individual item in a fast food restaurant will experience a price increase in the same month.

The French data set had less variation in the timing of minimum wage increases and in the variables that would be expected to vary across large geographic expanses. Consequently, Fougère, Gautier, and Le Bihan (2010) find a more formal approach necessary, modifying and estimating a conventional model of price adjustment that combines the two different parts of the decision that MacDonald and Aaronson (2006) examine separately: the decision to change a price, and the calculation of the appropriate value of the new price. According to their estimate, those prices that change in response to the minimum wage exhibit a minimum wage elasticity of between 0.08 and 0.11, with those in fast food restaurants nearer the upper end, and those in full-service restaurants nearer the lower end. Robustness tests of their model are generally reassuring, although they note that it appears to produce mild overestimates of both the frequency of price changes and the size of both increases and decreases. Both studies find that restaurants do not raise all prices in response to minimum wage increases, but rather groups of prices, leaving others unchanged.

Using their estimates to examine how long it takes for the mouse of minimum wage increases to work its way through the python of French restaurant prices, Fougère, Gautier, and Le Bihan (2010) report a much longer period than Aaronson (2001). Recall his result that nearly all the response of fast food restaurants in both the United States and Canada occurs in a three-month period, which is centered on the increase in the United States, and which follows the increase in Canada. For French fast food establishments, only half of the adjustment occurs within the six months following the increase, and after another year, roughly 10 percent of the adjustment remains. The process is nearly twice as long for full-service restaurants in France.

Lee, Schluter, and O'Roark (2000) also rely on a formal model, though not one of price formation and change, to study the impact of two of the increases of the federal minimum wage in the 1990s.[5] They use a specific model of production that has clear implications for price formation, an input-output model of the food sector. The model begins with data on the distribution of each sector's production costs that are payments to producers in other sectors of the economy and to employees. It combines these data with two important assumptions. The first is that the technology implicit in this distribution is optimal in the short run so that even if relative input costs change, firms will not quickly reorganize production. The second is that residual income (profit, interest payments, and depreciation allowances) does not change; prices adjust fully to reflect any change in costs. As they admit, these are very strong assumptions and imply that their estimates of the price response are an upper bound.[6] Finally, they consider several different assumptions about the effect of minimum wage increases on wages that were higher ex ante than the new value of the minimum wage (known as spillover effects).

Lee, Schluter, and O'Roark (2000) report that had the 1992 minimum wage increased in that year by 12 percent, from $4.25 to $4.75 (something that did not happen until 1996), restaurant prices would have increased by between 1.0 percent and 1.4 percent.[7] The implied price elasticities with respect to the minimum wage are between 0.08 and 0.12. A $0.50 increase in 1997, from $5.15 to $5.65 (10 percent), would have led to restaurant price increases of between 1.0 and 1.2 percent, or price elasticities between 0.09 and 0.13. While greater than both the 0.07 of MacDonald and Aaronson for restaurants (both full-service and limited-service) and the 0.08–0.11 of Fougère, Gautier, and Le Bihan (2010), this is not surprising in light of their recognition that their numbers are an upper bound. In addition, Lee, Schluter, and O'Roark report elasticities for different food manufacturing industries that range between 0.01 and 0.03 in 1992, and 0.01 and 0.03 in 1997.

MaCurdy and McIntyre (2001), as part of a more ambitious analysis to determine which households gain and which lose from minimum wage increases, also perform an input-output analysis to measure price responses to a minimum wage increase. After allowing for their having considered a substantially larger minimum wage increase, their analysis differs from that of Lee, Schluter, and O'Roark (2000) in two important ways: MaCurdy and McIntyre incorporate employer payroll taxes while neglecting spillover effects. These modeling choices lead to offsetting results, with the former choice resulting in larger price increases than otherwise, and the latter in smaller price increases. For the restaurant sector as a whole, they report a price elasticity with respect to the minimum wage of slightly less than 0.12, at the high end of those that Lee, Schluter, and O'Roark estimate when they allow for the greatest spillover effects.

The United Kingdom's National Minimum Wage (NMW) was introduced with the expectation that it would lead to higher prices, according to Grimshaw and Carroll (2006). It was thought that affected firms would either become more efficient (by some combination of reorganizing operations or improving employees' skills) or move into a niche in which they could compete on quality or characteristics other than price. The price response was instead quite tepid, and Grimshaw and Carroll explore this experience in interviews with owners and managers of 36 small British firms in six low-wage industries.[8] The one manufacturing industry faced international competition that prevented pass-through of the increase. In three of the service industries (cleaning, care home, and security), firms dealt with a dominant customer that refused to pay the higher prices. In the security industry, there was both widespread violation of the new law and reductions in service (fewer guards in place) without any reduction in what was charged—possible, it seems, because the customers were unaware of the practice. In the care home industry, there may also have been some attempt to cut service quality, but this was constrained by government regulations (recall Note 1).

Wadsworth (2010) is an extensive exploratory analysis of the relation between the NMW and prices in the United Kingdom. Using a variety of data from several sources, he examines the effect of the minimum wage on prices in both the short run and the long run. He begins with wage data from two sources to determine which industries have a large number of minimum wage employees. His next step is to examine (publicly available) accounts of firms in these industries to identify those in which wages of minimum wage workers are a large share of value added. Having identified 10 "minimum wage" industries, most of which are consumer services including such familiar ones as hotels, restaurants, pubs, and take-out food, Wadsworth turns to monthly retail price data for the corresponding products. His empirical analysis of prices uses these either as is or aggregated up to each industry.

The analysis itself is fairly simple. Recognizing that the connection between changes in costs and changes in prices is not straightforward—Milton Friedman's comment about the long and variable lags relating monetary policy to its effect on the economy comes to mind—Wadsworth (2010) avoids elaborately specified regression equations. To examine the short-run association between price changes and changes in the NMW, he asks, "Is there an association between price increases and the NMW, its implementation, and subsequent increases in the months immediately before or after these changes in the NMW?" To address this, he regresses the monthly inflation rate for each industry on a constant and a dummy variable that indicates whether the NMW increased that month, as well as two leads and two lags of the dummy. The results are underwhelming: 6 out of 41 coefficients on minimum wage dummies are statistically significant. A variety of additional analyses, including combining the individual time series into a panel, also generate no statistically significant estimates. One exception is when he considers inflation rates for individual goods and services rather than the more aggregated ones for each industry: there is then evidence of a weak association starting in the month of the increase and continuing for (at least) the next two months. However, the same exercise performed on non–minimum wage industries and their goods also generates a statistically significant result either one month before the increase (using industry-level data) or two months before and two months after (using item-level data). To this point, there is no strong evidence that the NMW leads to higher prices, at least in the short term.

To examine longer-term effects, Wadsworth (2010) asks, "Has the inflation rate in affected industries been greater since the beginning of the NMW than it would otherwise have been?" His answer involves estimating a difference-in-differences equation where the dummies indicate whether the observation is for an item from a minimum wage industry, and whether the observation was before or during the period in which the NMW was in effect. The coefficient of interest has an estimated *t*-statistic of three, suggesting that over the long run, the NMW is associated with a statistically significant increase of 0.7 percent in the annual inflation rate of minimum wage industries.[9] He concludes, "The extent of any observed relative price increases in minimum-wage sectors does not appear to rise in line with the share of minimum-wage workers in total costs, suggesting that a simple pass-through model of price changes may not hold. . . . [In addition], any effects on prices appear to accumulate gradually over time" (pp. 111–112).

OUTPUT

Little research on the minimum wage considers the response of output from affected firms. Machin, Manning, and Rahman (2003) turn to it briefly near the end of their study of the effects of the introduction of the national minimum wage in 1999 on Britain's home care industry. They report a positive response that is not statistically significant once control variables are included in the analysis. In combination with their finding of "some evidence of employment and hours reductions occurring in homes after minimum wage introduction," this suggests that the minimum wage led to less output than would have otherwise been the case (p. 178).

PROFITABILITY

If firms act as profit maximizers, and if the only immediate effect of the minimum wage increase is higher costs, then profits must fall.

By assumption, firms have no new possibilities available to them.[10] Several responses are possible, all of which were available before the increase in the minimum wage. If the labor market is competitive, then one response is for firms to reduce employment and output. If the labor market is monopsonistic, they may raise employment and output. If they have market power in the product market and are unregulated, then the qualitative effect is likely to resemble that of competitive labor and product markets, with both higher prices and lower employment and output. Firms may substitute capital for labor. Finally, firms may not respond in any way other than to raise wages where necessary. The higher minimum wage does not create any of these possibilities but only changes conditions so that certain choices become relatively more attractive in comparison with what they had been doing. It follows that since firms could have done any of these before but are only choosing to do them following the minimum wage increase, and since costs are higher, lower profits must result. If profits do not fall, something else must be going on (see Note 10).

Do profits in fact fall? Table 10.2 lists seven studies that examine the effect of the minimum wage on profitability or outcomes related that reflect profitability. Card and Krueger (1995) devote a chapter to this question, reporting the results of several event studies. The premise of a typical event study is that a firm's share price reflects the best estimate of its future profits in light of all relevant information that is currently available. An event study is a comparison of changes in the share price relative to the value of the whole market as new information that is especially pertinent to the firm or firms in question becomes available. Card and Krueger identify two sets of publicly traded companies for examination, those in industries with a large number of minimum wage employees, and those whose annual reports include mention of the federal minimum wage hikes of the early 1990s as a source of increased labor costs. The information events they study are headlines in the *Wall Street Journal* over a two-and-a-half-year period preceding final congressional approval of the increases, and the timing of events about a memo leaked during the early Clinton administration concerning plans to push for minimum wage increase (resulting eventually in the increases in the later 1990s).

For both sets of firms, the first set of events provides no consistent support for the hypothesis that the minimum wage is bad for profits.

Table 10.2 Profitability and Failure Rates

Study	Central variable	Effect	Target	Country	Sample period	Analytic approach	Unit of observation	Data structure	Type of standard error	Data set[a]
Card and Krueger (1995)	Profits	Mixed	Firms sensitive to the minimum wage	United States	1987–89, 1992–93	Event study	Daily-firm (stock return)	Panel	OLS	CRSP
Draca, Machin, and Van Reenen (2011)	Profits	Negative	Low-wage firms	United Kingdom	1998–2002	Quasi experiment	Firm-year	Panel	OLS	FAME, LFS, WERS
Machin and Wilson (2004)	Exits	None	Home care	United Kingdom	1998–1999	Regression	Firm-survey response	Two-period panel	OLS	Private survey
Mason, Carter, and Tagg (2006)	Profits	Small decline	Small and midsized enterprises	United Kingdom	2003	Descriptive	Enterprise	Cross section	—	Private survey
Orazem and Mattila (2002)	Failures	Positive	Firms in retail or service, not professional	United States (Iowa)	1989–1992	Regression	County-industry-qtr.	Aggregate panel	OLS	UI records, private survey
Pacheco and Naiker (2006)	Profits	Mixed/ none	Firms in industries with many minimum wage employees	New Zealand	2000–2001	Event study	Daily-firm (stock return)	Panel	OLS	HLFS, IS, IRG
Waltman, McBride, and Camhout (1998)	Failures	Negative	Aggregate failure rate of firms	United States	1948–1983	Regression	Annual aggregates	Time series	OLS	Dun and Bradstreet

a CRSP = Center for Research in Security Prices (US). FAME = Financial Analysis Made Easy (UK). HLFS = Household Labour Force Survey (New Zealand). IRG = Investment Research Group (New Zealand). IS = Income Survey (New Zealand). WERS = Workplace Employment Relations Survey (UK).

Results for the second set of events are different, especially for those firms that had previously referred explicitly to the importance of the minimum wage for their operations. Card and Krueger (1995) conclude that their results are ambiguous and that further work is necessary; on the basis of their analysis, one could make a case that the minimum wage has a noticeable effect on profits of firms that one would expect to be sensitive to it, but one could make the opposite case with equal ease.

Pacheco and Naiker (2006) perform an event study similar to Card and Krueger's (1995), using data from New Zealand, where a substantial reform and increase of the minimum wage for teenagers occurred, starting in early 2001.[11] Using detailed income data to determine which industries are sensitive to the minimum wage, they find four that together employ more than half of minimum wage workers and in which the share of minimum wage workers substantially exceeds the industry's share of the total workforce. Pacheco and Naiker next identify 32 firms that are largely specialized in 1 of these 4 industries, and 10 events that were both related to the revision of the minimum wage between late 1999 and late 2000, and are discussed in published news sources. They judge the results of their event analysis to be ambiguous, with profitability responding to some events as expected but not responding to many others. While expressing concern that the result may be due to extensive noncompliance (between 2 and 3 percent of the employees in the data earned less than the relevant minimum wage), they conclude that "the number of tests and robustness checks performed in this study all point to the same conclusion, implying that some weight should be given to the argument that investors simply find changes in minimum wage value irrelevant" (p. 488).

Mason, Carter, and Tagg (2006) conduct a nationwide survey of small business firms in the United Kingdom to examine the response to the 2003 increase in the NMW and how it varies geographically. The difference between high- and low-wage regions is evident in the effect of the NMW increase. Fifteen percent of firms in high-wage areas (southeastern England and the London metropolitan region) had to raise wages while 25 percent did in low-wage, peripheral areas (Scotland, Wales, Northern Ireland, and both the northeast and northwest of England). The proportion of employees who received wage increases ranged from 6 percent in the high-wage regions, to 13–14 percent in most of the low-wage regions, and to nearly 18 percent of those in Wales.

Mason, Carter, and Tagg's (2006) use of a five-point Likert scale makes interpretation and comparison with other analyses difficult. On the one hand, they report that "London and the South East contained the smallest proportion of businesses that anticipated a decline in profitability, at just 15 percent. In contrast, around one-quarter of businesses in the North East, Northern Ireland, Wales, Yorkshire and the Humber, and the North West anticipated a decrease in their profitability as a result of the national minimum wage uprate" (p. 109). These percentages match those for the proportions of firms that had to raise wages in response to the increase. On the other hand, only 20 percent of firms that had to increase wages for any employee expected this to decrease profitability, and, on the 5-point scale, the mean response for overall profitability was 2.84 (where 3 means no change and 2 means a slight decrease), so the effect on profits appears to be very slight even for firms that had to increase wages. It thus appears that profits declined or were expected to do so, but not by much. Because of their presentation (which is not altogether clear) and the low survey response rate (which raises questions of selection bias), the accuracy of this finding is not certain.

If firms' profits decline following a minimum wage increase, one likely consequence is an increase in firm failure rates. Waltman, McBride, and Camhout (1998) run a simple regression to examine failure rates for the whole economy, comparing years without minimum wage increases to those with them, and do not find a larger rate in the former years. They repeat this for years following those with minimum wage increases relative to other years and produce a similar result.[12]

Orazem and Mattila (2002) study low-wage retail and nonprofessional service firms in Iowa from the middle of 1989 through 1994. Combining quarterly data collected by the unemployment insurance program with tax and other economic data allows them to examine the effect of the minimum wage on firms and workers at the county level. They report statistically significant, negative responses in the number of firms. The minimum wage elasticity of the number of firms is −0.17 within one quarter and −0.25 over four quarters. Peculiarly, there is little difference between the covered and uncovered sectors; that is, the movements are almost identical for firms that must pay the minimum wage and those for which it does not apply. Either all firms feel obliged to pay employees the minimum wage, whether or not legally required to do so, or their minimum wage variable is picking up other phenomena for which Orazem and Mattila have not adequately accounted.

In their study of the British care home industry and its response to the introduction and first increase of the NMW, Machin and Wilson (2004) examine exit of firms from the industry. While the overall rate of exit is high, they are not able to find any indication that it varies with either firms' sensitivity or exposure to the minimum wage.[13] This suggests that the NMW did not have a material effect on profits; otherwise, homes with greater exposure or sensitivity would presumably have experienced a greater decline in profits and would be closing down at greater rates.

Draca, Machin, and Van Reenen (2011) examine two samples of firms. With one, they perform a much more ambitious analysis of the minimum wage and firm profitability than those previously presented, a quasi experiment in which the firms in the treatment and comparison groups differ according to their average wages. In the United Kingdom, even privately held corporations must report considerably more accounting information than U.S. firms, including employment and the total wage bill. This gives Draca, Machin, and Van Reenen a broad sample of firms, including many smaller ones likely to be more sensitive to the NMW than larger, publicly traded firms. The average wage bill in their treatment groups suggests an average wage about 9 percent higher than the NMW at the time it was first introduced. After determining that wages in the treatment group rose relative to those in the comparison group, they report that profits fell in the treatment group, and by an amount that suggests that affected firms made no adjustments other than to raise wages as needed to satisfy the law. Because a given value of the average wage is consistent with many different wage distributions, Draca, Machin, and Van Reenen are not entirely comfortable with their definitions of the treatment and comparison groups, and they poke and prod their specification in a variety of ways to test the robustness of their findings. Their results hold up.

Draca, Machin, and Van Reenen (2011) also conduct a regression analysis on the sample of residential care homes that Machin and Wilson (2004) and others have used to study the NMW; the sample of firms is much narrower than their prior work, but this is balanced by the greater detail, and so more careful measurement of each firm's response to the

NMW. They are able to infer total costs, and from that—defining profits as the difference between revenue and total costs—the rate of profit (as a percentage of revenue). Relating this to the value of a firm's wage gap—the percentage that the wage bill must rise if low-wage employees are to make no less than the minimum wage—Draca, Machin, and Van Reenen report an elasticity of the profit margin of −1.5. A firm with a 10 percent wage gap faces a 15 percent decline in its profit margin (about 5 percentage points on average). However, they confirm the conclusions of Machin and Wilson that the data on firm closings do not reflect this.

For both samples, Draca, Machin, and Van Reenen (2011) consider exits and find no effect of the NMW on this measure. What they cannot examine with these sources is any effect on births of new firms. A different data set based on registration for the value-added tax allows them to study the rates of entry into and exit from low-wage industries, and whether this changed in response to the NMW relative to other industries. They find a small and statistically insignificant relative decline of the rate of firms' entry into low-wage sectors. Rather than study exit alone, they combine entry and exit and report a statistically insignificant (or imprecisely measured) decline in growth rates of low-wage sectors of five percentage points. One response to this estimate is to extrapolate to the long run and infer that after a period of 25–30 years, the NMW will lead to roughly half as many firms in low-wage sectors as would otherwise have been the result.[14] The long horizon, especially in combination with the large standard errors, suggests that other factors would likely swamp this effect. In summary, there is good evidence that the minimum wage reduces profits, certainly in the United Kingdom, but it does not show up where one would expect, in changes in exit rates or firms' share prices. Results of Orazem and Mattila (2002) suggest that the situation may be different in the United States, but the similarity of their results for firms in the covered and uncovered sectors suggests that they have not adequately controlled for other factors affecting the rates of firms' exit and profits.

Notes

1. A handful of articles look at the care home industry in the United Kingdom and find no price response. This is not surprising in light of the heavy price regulation of that sector, which makes any further reference here to this work superfluous.
2. Although Aaronson, French, and MacDonald (2008) have an additional analysis of the same BLS data, it is, empirically, largely a reprise of Aaronson (2001) and MacDonald and Aaronson (2006), its focus being more on the implications for labor market structure of the minimum wage response of prices. For these reasons, we do not discuss it here.
3. Restaurants were each surveyed monthly or bimonthly, thus the use of two-month periods.
4. For big-ticket items especially, frequent price changes may be costly as well to customers, who may respond by more frequent information gathering, which may in turn lead them to switch to a new supplier.
5. These are the second increase, in 1992, and the fourth and last increase, in 1997.
6. If the assumption that inputs cannot be quickly readjusted is correct, but the assumption that cost increases fully pass through to prices in the short run is not, it is likely that profits will suffer.
7. The range results from different assumptions about the extent of spillover effects on the wages of those higher up the wage distribution.
8. The industries are clothing and footwear manufacturing, industrial cleaning services, hospitality, residential care, retail, and security.
9. While Wadsworth (2010) presents results overall and separately for each minimum wage industry, this discussion is limited to the overall results.
10. This rules out, for example, shock effects and effects on labor supply. Shock effects, the sudden rise in costs due to the minimum wage increase, lead firms to search more carefully for efficiencies in production, which in turn reduces the cost of hiring qualified employees.
11. For details, see the discussion of Hyslop and Stillman (2007) in Chapter 2.
12. Taylor and Arnold (1999) identify a serious data mistake but agree that it does not change the results that Waltman, McBride, and Camhout (1998) report.
13. Exposure is measured by the percentage of employees initially paid less than the NMW. Sensitivity is measured by the wage gap, the fraction of the ex ante wage bill needed to bring those who had been paid less than the NMW up to that level.
14. From the discussion, it is not exactly clear what period the entry and exit rates refer to, but it appears to be not a single year but rather the entire period following the treatment, about two and a half years.

11
Conclusion

What have we learned from this exhaustive (and to us, exhausting) review of the minimum wage literature? It is only fair to the possibly equally exhausted reader that we briefly summarize our findings and provide some, but not too many, comments about the implications for the minimum wage as a tool of policy and about how economists go about studying controversial topics.

Evidence leads us to conclude that moderate increases in the minimum wage are a useful means of raising wages in the lower part of the wage distribution that has little or no effect on employment and hours. This is what one seeks in a policy tool, solid benefits with small costs. That said, current research does not speak to whether the same results would hold for large increases in the minimum wage. Our suspicion is that large increases could touch off the disemployment effects that are largely absent for moderate increases, but evidence for the United States is lacking because there have not been large increases in the last generation. Similarly, increases in the minimum wage are not the only policy needed to address issues of low income in the United States. As many others have argued, programs such as the EITC and Food Stamps play a critical role in placing a floor under incomes and consumption, and higher minimum wages are not a substitute for such programs. In other words, the minimum wage is a useful tool for policy and, as with most policy tools, must be used wisely and in coordination with other policies to achieve the desired end.

A SUMMARY OF OUR FINDINGS

Employment

Employment, long square one for disputes about the minimum wage and its effects, has been more intensively studied than any other variable in the minimum wage, both in the NMWR and before. Unfortunately, much work exhibits one or the other of two statistical problems (Bertrand, Duflo, and Mullainathan 2004; Donald and Lang 2007) that make judging the reliability of the analyses impossible. Of the work that has avoided or satisfactorily resolved these issues, little has been able to detect a substantively significant response of employment, measured as the number of jobs, the number of people working, or the number of hours. Although this does not close the issue, the preponderance of the evidence currently leans that way. This is borne out by our own meta-analysis.[1] Once a correction for publication bias is incorporated, overall elasticities for the United States are both statistically insignificant and very close to zero, even when restricting the focus to teenagers and young adults. The corresponding elasticities for eating and drinking establishments in the United States appear to be somewhat larger, with precision weighted means near −0.05, but still not statistically significant.

How long does it take for employment responses to increases in the minimum wage to play out? Baker, Benjamin, and Stanger (1999) is one of the most ingenious and frequently cited analyses by someone other than a participant in the original conference. Providing an interpretation of earlier work, it suggested that the period in question is at least five to six years. Coming, however, before Bertrand, Duflo, and Mullainathan (2004) and the increased recognition of the relevance of the Moulton (1990) problem to panel data research on the minimum wage, the robustness of their interpretation is not clear. Following the logic of the rational expectations hypothesis, Pinoli (2010) argues that much of the response to an anticipated increase occurs before the increase itself. From the little work that is relevant, this does not appear to be the case, at least in the United States. Furthermore, analyses that directly examine the timing indicate that the employment response takes no more than three years to complete (Belman and Wolfson 2010). However, considerably more work, using data from a variety of situations and countries, is necessary before drawing any conclusions with confidence.

Gross Flows

If employment is not affected, what is? For one, there is some evidence of declines in both accessions (hiring) and separations (quits and layoffs). This suggests that jobs do become harder to find following increases in the minimum wage, and that previously employed workers are sufficiently productive, at least afterward, that employers are not inclined to fire them. Explanations for this include a different allocation after the increase of the surplus that the employee creates in this job, a reorganization of the work process following the increase (known as the *shock effect*), and efficiency wage theory, where the higher minimum wage induces greater productive effort from the worker.

The study of the effect of the minimum wage on quits (voluntary separations) is a theoretically and methodologically distinct area of research on gross flows. Although Wessels (1980) reports evidence consistent with his hypothesis that quit rates are temporarily higher following minimum wage increases, the research is old, the result is at odds with more recent work on separations, and new research is needed to establish that Wessels's findings remain relevant.

Unemployment

A few analyses examine the response of the unemployment rate to increases in the minimum wage. The only one that makes no recourse to economic models detects no effect on the unemployment rate of teenagers. Those that begin with well-articulated models report a moderate increase in the unemployment rate. This disagreement raises questions about the extent to which the results are baked in, that is, whether the theoretical models determine the result. One of those that indicates an increase in the unemployment rate attributes it to increases in the labor force participation rate—in other words, increases in the minimum wage induce those without jobs to begin looking for them.

Even if the unemployment rate does not move up and down with the minimum wage, the decline in hiring suggests that it may be harder for those previously unemployed to find work following increases, something that should be reflected in the length of unemployment spells. The one study that examines this reports a decline in unemployment duration for male high school graduates and increases in duration for several groups: men without a high school diploma, women with a high school diploma, low-skilled women, and women older than 24. The one decrease in unemployment duration is slightly more than a month, while the increases range between three and a half months and five months.

Wages and Benefits

What effect does the minimum wage have on wages and their distribution? It is evident that average wages rise along with increases in the minimum wage. Most studies that look specifically at workers who were previously earning less than the new higher minimum wage report higher wages after the fact. It is quite clear that wages of the lowest paid 10 percent of workers are higher following a minimum wage increase, and for women it appears that this is true for the lowest 30 percent. The extent of spillovers varies by country; research on spillovers in the United Kingdom suggests it reaches considerably higher up the wage distribution, and particularly the male wage distribution, than is the case for the United States. Current research also finds that while many incumbents quickly move out of minimum wage jobs after entering the labor market, a substantial fraction of U.S. workers spend much of their first decade at the minimum wage or at wage levels that are affected by the minimum wage. Finally, studies that look at the entire wage distribution report that the minimum wage does indeed raise wages at the bottom and reduce wage inequality.

It has long been suggested that employers may respond to minimum wage increases by reducing spending on training, fringe benefits, and working conditions valued by employees. Results for health insurance are mixed, as are those for training, though some of the evidence for a decline in training after increases in the minimum wage seems to be due to those in low-wage jobs receiving little training irrespective of minimum wage policy.

Enrollment

As with many types of policy, the minimum wage may have unintended consequences. One of the most serious that has received attention is that it may induce teenagers to leave school, interrupting or prematurely ending their formal education. An issue with this literature is how little discussion there is between those approaching the topic from economics and those coming from education policy. Another is statistical problems that likely overstate the precision of the estimates. These problems and the disagreement among results suggest that a definitive answer awaits further work, although a reasonable foundation exists on which to build it.

The Product Market

Broadly speaking, economists use two competing classes of models to understand the minimum wage and its effects in the labor market, competitive models and a variety of models referred to as monopsonistic models, the most important of which involves firms' searching for workers and workers' searching for jobs. Competitive and monopsonistic models have different implications for the response of both employment and product prices. Competitive models imply lower employment and higher output prices in response to a minimum wage increase. Monopsonistic models allow for the possibility of higher employment, which in turn implies lower prices in affected industries. It is quite clear that restaurant prices rise by a small amount following minimum wage increases. In industries that are both sensitive to the minimum wage and face foreign competition, the price response appears to be weaker. In the United Kingdom, there is some evidence that increases in the minimum wage reduce profits at affected firms, but it is difficult to detect this in exit rates, that is, in firms going out of business, suggesting that the response is small. Analyses of the value that financial markets in the United States and New Zealand place on firms that are affected by the minimum wage indicate no pass-through to profits. Perhaps the price response, while weak, protects profits enough to make it worthwhile to remain in business.

WHAT WE KNOW WITH CONFIDENCE

What then can we be reasonably certain of with respect to the minimum wage? As the minimum wage increases considered in this research have been moderate, the conclusions that we draw are premised on moderate increases.

Under such conditions, there is little evidence of negative labor market effects. Hours and employment do not seem to be meaningfully affected. Accessions and separations may slow after minimum wage increases. Decisive evidence that training or benefits responds at all to increases in the minimum wage does not exist.

The evidence on schooling is suggestive but not sufficient to draw conclusions for policy making. This reflects both limitations of the currently available studies and the variety of outcomes across studies. If any conclusion can be drawn from extant studies, it is that any negative effects of the minimum wage on school enrollment is associated with allowing students to leave school in the first two years of high school. Mandatory attendance laws that only allow students to leave in their junior or senior year of high school appear to eliminate any negative effect on school attendance.

There is strong evidence that the minimum wage boosts the earnings of the lowest-wage workers, and it may boost the earnings of those earning moderately higher hourly wages. In almost every wage study, the effect is more marked for women, who are more likely than men to be in low-wage positions.

Considered together, increases in the minimum wage raise the hourly wage and earnings of workers in the lower part of the wage distribution and have very modest or no effects on employment, hours, and other labor market outcomes. The minimum wage can then, as originally intended, be used to improve the conditions of those working in the least remunerative sectors of the labor market. While not a full solution to the issues of low-wage work, it is a useful instrument of policy that has low social costs and clear benefits.

BIG IDEAS

Given the certain predictions of core economic theory, how is it possible that the minimum wage raises wages without the anticipated negative effect on employment and employment-related measures? We are reluctant to spend much time and ink on this, as the ground has been covered repeatedly over the last two decades. Earlier we alluded to the two most widely discussed models of the low-wage labor market, the competitive model and monopsonistic/search models.

Another possibility, which Kaufman (2007) has ably synthesized, is that in the presence of transaction costs and uncertainty about the future, firms do not respond to wage changes mechanistically. In this view, an employment relationship is not the exchange transaction depicted in the core economic model but rather a relationship that persists over time because of transaction costs in the labor market. Moreover, uncertainty about these costs means that firms do not face a precisely defined relationship between wage levels and employment.

In Kaufman's (2007) view, although the use of labor in the production process is universal and labor's place in production can be organized many ways, the labor demand curve used in the core economic analysis presumes an employment relationship: "That is, firms are the 'employer' who go to the labour market and hire people as 'employees' to provide a certain amount of labour services and follow the directions of the employer in return for a certain amount of remuneration per time period" (p. 776).

Such a relationship cannot exist absent transaction costs because without such costs, labor markets become competitive markets for inputs from atomistic independent contractors. Rather than each supplier being an employee of a specific firm, each has a separate relationship with one or more firms to provide a product or service. There is no employment relationship and no labor market that differs in important ways from, say, Summers's (1985) market for ketchup.

Transaction costs arise from the combination of limited human rationality, imperfect information, and ambiguities in property rights. They require that employers and employees establish employment contracts that define the terms under which work will be performed, and so define labor supply curves.[2] Employment contracts are inherently incomplete; they cannot fully specify outcomes because changes in circumstances such as economic environment, technology, and consumer taste necessitate altering the terms of employment. For example, most employment contracts establish compensation but not hours or employment levels. Changes in the circumstances facing an employer can result in large fluctuations in employment and hours. Because of imperfect information and bounded rationality, marginal product schedules and the demand curves derived from those schedules are probabilistic. If future circumstance A occurs, then the demand curve is in position A, but if future circumstance B occurs, then the demand curve will be in the nearby but not identical position B. The firm faces a "set" of demand curves with different likelihoods attached to each curve. The firm does not know which curve will be realized tomorrow and may well be uncertain about which demand curve it is on today. This moves firms away from a deterministic relationship between wages and employment levels and provides some latitude for firms to set wages. Latitude in wage setting is increased because the costs of job search for individuals provide firms limited monopolistic power over employees. Because of the transactions costs, deviation from a market wage will result neither in instantaneous loss of labor if a firm pays a below-market wage nor a long line of individuals seeking employment if it offers an above-market one.

Our own thoughts on why there is such a weak employment effect follow a different and possibly more practical path. Economic theory and models are developed to explore specific topics. This focus makes possible rigorous exploration and full development of the implications associated with an issue of interest. This approach does not replicate the situation of decision makers in the market. Decision makers are daily confronted not with a situation in which all is constant *except* the change in the minimum wage. Rather, they face a world in which little is constant from day to day, week to week, month to month, or year to year. Not only does the minimum wage change, so do prices of supplies, fuel, rental, and myriad other factors. Demand is constantly changing as economic conditions, changes in views and tastes, and chance influence consumers' choices.

In a situation where so much is in flux, the stylization of decision making used in economics does not reasonably approximate decision makers' situations. In determining how much to produce, employers cannot simply take the consumer demand curve as fixed and, having determined their price, know what quantity to produce. Instead, in the face of a shifting demand curve, one must determine both price and quantity and then accept either the excess that could not be sold or the lost profits due to less product than could have been sold at that price. Because the firm's labor demand curve is derived from its product demand curve, the decision maker has no more certainty about the appropriate number of employees to hire than about the price and quantity needed to exactly satisfy demand.

In such a world, one dominated by change rather than comparative static exercises, economic actors are unlikely to make decisions on the knife edge depicted in economic diagrams. Rather, small changes in prices are unlikely to move the decision maker to action. Slight movements in rent, fuel prices, or wages are unlikely to cause decision makers to rethink their use of inputs. While a large price increase might have sufficient effect for one to reconsider how to use that and other inputs, small increases likely get lost in the change of day-to-day operations.

This view is consistent with our results. It does not require that demand curves neither exist nor slope downward; rather, it suggests that the downward slope is not a one-dimensional line but rather a line with some width, implying that for any quantity of employment, the firm is willing to pay a wage within a defined range. Were the minimum wage to increase 50 percent, it would be beyond the range consistent with the current employment level, and firms would reduce their employment. However, when increases are moderate, are within the range consistent with current employment levels, decision makers are too engaged with the world to change their existing arrangements. It is also consistent with the finding that increases in the minimum wage reduce accessions. Both the formation of a firm and the decision to expand require positive action to bring new employees into a business. At such times, decision makers may well consider the cost of inputs, including labor inputs, and alternative arrangements.

If we supplement economic theory with this view of the situation facing economic decision makers, we are then likely to conclude that thresholds, which must be crossed before decision makers act, exist. These thresholds differ by market and individual and are unlikely to be stable over time. Without a doubt, the changes in the value of financial instruments that impel arbitragers and their computers to action are many times smaller than those required to attract the attention of a retailer or fast food franchiser to change their employment policies. The rise in the minimum wage needed to catch the attention of the fast food franchiser in Westchester County, New York, may be far larger than that for exurbia in Alabama. With such an understanding of the world, the lack of a relationship between moderate increases in the minimum wage and employment no longer stands in contradiction to core economic theory. Rather, it points to a research program to investigate the factors affecting thresholds of action in labor markets.

ISSUES OF INNOVATION AND CRAFTSMANSHIP

Although the purpose of this review is not to reflect on the work of the economics profession, our reading and rereading of hundreds of articles reveals a tension between innovation and craftsmanship. The drive toward innovation is strong in economics—witness the popularity of *Freakonomics* (Levitt and Dubner 2005)—and has been productive over the last 50 years in driving a rethinking and expansion of economics thought. Innovators such as Gary Becker, Ronald Coase, William Baulmol, and George Akerlof have done much to advance our understanding of markets and of *homo economicus.*

Answering the important economic questions of the day requires more than novelty. While it can provide new understandings and approaches, unless founded on strong methodological approaches and placed in the context of prior work, it forgoes much of its opportunity to expand knowledge. Too often in our review we have been unable to reconcile results across journal articles because the authors have not systematically explored the sources of differences between what they present and prior work on the topic. Even when articles draw on the same data sources, differences in time period, technique, and measures preclude knowing the source of (the sometimes dramatic) differences in the results. All too often, systematic investigation would have required no more than one table and a page or two of text. Furthermore, in too many cases, authors have failed to investigate important variations of their model to examine the robustness of their results. For example, although it is well established that the choice of comparison group can affect the estimates from difference-in-differences models, most authors choose to present estimates for one or possibly two comparison groups rather than for each of the obvious comparison groups.

Absent greater emphasis on craftsmanship, on the workmanlike investigation of an issue, economists limit their contributions to our understanding of a topic. Without knowing how differences in controls, data, time period, and method influence results, we are left with too many unreconciled findings. Sensitivity to these issues is particularly important when topics are controversial, because there is a greater need to understand the sources of differences between studies and so limit the scope of passion.

How might economics place greater weight on craftsmanship? Partly by training graduate students to be more thoughtful about their research, but more so by reviewers and editors requiring authors to explicitly reconcile their work with prior work and to address reasonable variants on their models. This requires that editors and particularly reviewers be familiar with the topic under study. It also requires that they ask authors to compare and contrast their work with prior work explicitly, and to investigate differences. We believe that reconciliation would not require too much empirical effort or too many journal pages. It will be challenging intellectually, as it is likely to bring to the fore issues of control groups, time periods, and measures.

Redressing the current imbalance between innovation and craftsmanship is then important to advancing our understanding of markets and the investigation of markets. Innovation provides the drive forward, while craftsmanship provides integrity. Both are required for the robust and credible investigation of markets.

INTENDED CONSEQUENCES

Social scientists emphasize, and possibly delight, in pointing to the unintended consequences of social policies. This reflects the dual concern of social science: to document the world and to reveal what cannot be readily seen or understood. Unintended consequences have played a large role in the discussion of the minimum wage, with many arguing that despite the goal of raising the earnings of low-income workers, the minimum wage has resulted not only in higher unemployment but also the receipt of the gains by large numbers of individuals who do not need them, for example, teens in relatively high-income families.

Our review finds that the effect of the minimum wage has largely been one of intended consequences: it achieves the ends initially sought by the originators of the U.S. legislation. The moderate increases seen in the United States have resulted in increased earnings with little to no effect on employment. The increase in earnings has gone largely to households in the lower half of the earnings distribution. While not a stand-alone policy for resolving the issues of low income in the United States, the effectiveness of moderate increases in the minimum wage in raising earnings with few negative consequences makes it an important tool for labor market policy.

Notes

1. *Caveat lector*: As we discuss in Chapter 4, it does not include all articles because too large a number do not report results in a way that makes them comparable to others.

2. Following Rosen (1974), the labor supply curve is defined not only by the wage but also by all the terms and conditions of employment available to employees. The presence of labor supply curves is then premised on there being an employment relationship that specifies those terms and conditions, and following back a step in Kaufman's (2007) logic, on transaction costs.

Appendix A
Data Sources and Variables

Several data sets are used in many analyses of the minimum wage and its effects. The same variables appear in much of this work. For the reader's convenience, we discuss these below rather than discuss them in detail either repeatedly or only the first time each is encountered.

DATA SOURCES

Governments are the source of the most frequently used data in minimum wage research.[1] There are two types of government data sets that are most commonly used in studies of the minimum wage: household surveys and establishment-based data. Other types of data follow individuals or families over long periods of time.

Household Surveys

In many countries, the government conducts a large-scale survey of households at regular intervals, and it provides the data used to calculate unemployment rates, as well as other information about the labor market. Studies of the minimum wage that focus on demographic groups—for instance, teenagers, minorities, young adults, single mothers, or married women—most commonly rely on household surveys. In the United States, the household survey that typically fills these roles is the CPS. Every 10 years, the U.S. census generates a complete listing of all extant residences in the United States. Every month, the U.S. Census Bureau generates a sample from this list of households to interview.[2] Within each household, one person answers questions about all the people in the household. Once selected, a household is interviewed for four consecutive months, is not interviewed for eight months, and is then interviewed over four additional consecutive months. This is known as a 4-8-4 rotation. In the last month of each of the four-month interview cycles, the usual monthly interview is supplemented with questions about hours, earnings, and other economic matters. The households in the last four months of interviews are collectively referred to as the Outgoing Rotation Group (ORG), and it is information from the ORGs—not those from households in any of the other months of their cycle—that is used in most minimum wage studies.

About 50,000 households are interviewed for the CPS each month. Roughly 25 percent of these are in the ORG for either the first or second time and will leave the CPS after this month, either for eight months or permanently. Each month, roughly 12.5 percent of the households are added to the CPS for the first time, and another 12.5 percent start their second cycle of four months. The answers of each household refer not to the whole month but to a reference week, which is defined as the week (Sunday through Saturday) that includes the 12th of the month.

Other countries have similar surveys. In Canada, Statistics Canada conducts the monthly Labor Force Survey. It comprises about 56,000 households each month, each household remains in the survey for six consecutive months, and each month one-sixth of the households are in the survey for the first time and another one-sixth are in for the last time. The reference week is the one that contains the 15th of the month. In the European Union, countries also conduct Labour Force Surveys, often quarterly. In the United Kingdom, it consists of about 60,000 households that remain in the survey for five consecutive quarters, also with a rotation structure similar to the Canadian one. The survey is conducted throughout the quarter, and the reference week is distributed uniformly throughout. New Zealand has the quarterly Household Labor Force Survey, consisting of about 15,000 households, each of which remains in the sample for eight quarters. The survey is conducted throughout the quarter and the questions asked refer to the week before the interview.

In the United States and Canada, these surveys can be aggregated to the level either of states or provinces, respectively, or the entire nation. In the United States, most studies that aggregate to the state level combine the ORGs for an entire calendar year to minimize problems of high variability associated with small samples in the less-populated states. Canadian studies follow the U.S. convention of aggregating the data into calendar years.[3] The studies that use European data, whether individual or more aggregated, are more evenly split between quarterly and annual frequencies.

Establishment-Based Data

An establishment survey is a survey of workplaces: stores, offices, factories, and so forth. In the United States, the most important establishment survey is the Current Employment Survey (CES). The CES collects data from payroll records of about 400,000 establishments. These data include the number of employees, number of paid hours, and total wages paid for both all workers and only production workers, for the payroll period that includes the 12th of the month.[4] Data series are available by industry, state, or both.

Another data set that has become important in recent years is the Quarterly Census of Employment and Wages (QCEW), which "derives its data from quarterly tax reports submitted to State Employment Security Agencies by over 8 million employers subject to state Unemployment Insurance laws and from federal agencies subject to the Unemployment Compensation for Federal Employees program. This includes 99.7 percent of all wage and salary civilian employment. These reports provide information on the number of people employed and the wages paid to the employees each quarter."[5]

The types of data available are total number of jobs and total payroll, by SIC or NAICS industry, and aggregated to county or state. Because both the CES and the QCEW rely on payroll or tax records, they are considered to be of unusually high quality, but the number of variables measured is limited.

Another relatively new data source in the United States is the Quarterly Workforce Indicators, based on a partnership between states and the Census Bureau. Intended to provide data in which the unit of observation is the job, that is, the employer-employee pair, it combines data from multiple sources, including Unemployment Insurance data from the states, household data from the Census Bureau, and establishment data from the U.S. Department of Labor (Abowd et al. 2005). Because it is a voluntary partnership with states, few states were involved in the early years (the 1990s), and the number grew over time.

Other countries also have establishment surveys. Several studies of the United Kingdom examine the New Earnings Survey (NES), a very large-scale annual survey of employers about those of their employees who are currently in sample. Because the NES has evolved into a longitudinal survey, we delay further discussion to that section. Two articles covered in this volume use a Portuguese establishment survey, the *Quadros de Pessoal*. Based on personnel records, it has considerably more demographic detail then either the CES or the QCEW.

Longitudinal Surveys

Longitudinal surveys repeat measurements of the same subjects over a long period of time. In the United States, among the best known are the National Longitudinal Surveys (NLS), conducted by the Bureau of Labor Studies of the U.S. Department of Labor. They are a set of surveys designed to gather information at multiple points in time on the labor market activities and other significant life events of several groups of men and women. The most well-known are the surveys of Youth (NLSY79 and NLSY97), both of which began with about 10,000 people in their teens or early twenties at the time of the first interview. They are interviewed annually or, after a period of some years, biennially about many topics, including their schooling and labor market experience. For more than four decades, NLS data have served as an important tool for economists, sociologists, and other researchers.

The Survey of Income and Program Participation (SIPP) is a longitudinal household survey used in a few studies of the U.S. minimum wage. Its focus is the measurement of labor income and various government transfers, both cash and noncash, and includes questions that indicate labor force status. Begun in 1984, the sample size has varied over time, from 14,000 to more than 35,000 households. The length of time that households are in the sample has varied over time. Household members over the age of 14 are interviewed three times a year.[6] The size of the SIPP allows it to be used as a cross-sectional household survey for some purposes, but the linking of data across time, usually several years, allows the data to also be used as longitudinal data.

Longitudinal surveys such as the NLSY79, NLSY97, and the SIPP are useful for studying changes that occur over long periods of time, such as the number of job changes or unemployment spells that people experienced over some segment of their lives, the number of times they moved to a different county or state, or the number of years in which their family income was below the poverty threshold. They are also useful for examining cause-and-effect relationships. Cross-sectional surveys of the labor market have shown, for example, that workers who have been with their employers a longer period of time have higher earnings than workers who have shorter service with their employers. Cross-sectional surveys are not useful, however, for determining whether longer service leads to higher pay, whether higher pay leads to longer service, or whether there is a cause-and-effect relationship at all. Longitudinal surveys have been used to examine whether the statistical correlation between tenure and earnings exists because workers become more productive as they gain seniority and are paid more for that higher productivity or, conversely, because highly paid workers tend to stay with their employers for longer periods, rather than seeking employment elsewhere.

Several studies of the United Kingdom rely on the British Household Panel Survey (BHPS), a household survey conducted (mostly) every fall, in which the same households are followed for many years. From time to time, additional households are added to the panel. It was originally modeled after a long-running U.S. survey, the Panel Study of Income Dynamics.

The NES is a longitudinal establishment data set used in minimum wage studies for the United Kingdom. It is based on annual tax records from employers, and the sample includes every employee with the same last two digits in their National Insurance number, the British counterpart of a social security number. Although not originally intended to be longitudinal, because these two digits have been the same since the original survey in 1975, individuals remain in the sample indefinitely and can be tracked from one year to the next (Ada et al. 2006, p. 647). One consequence of the sampling design is that data on about 1 percent of employees are gathered each year. Because the data come from employers, they contain rich and accurate descriptive information about each employer and the position that an employee fills, but little demographic information beyond the age and sex of the employee. The questions of the survey refer to the first week of April, and the sample is constructed in February. Individuals whose earnings fall below the minimum required for this particular tax withholding (Pay as You Earn), in particular, part-time employees and low-earning women, are underrepresented in the data set.[7] Furthermore, individuals who are unemployed in February but not in April are also excluded.

VARIABLES

Several key variables reappear in many studies. Rather than describing them each time, or describing them only the first time they occur, we describe them below.

Measures of Employment

Employment is measured in several different ways. The degree of fineness turns on whether the measure refers to the total amount of paid (employed) labor, typically the number of hours, or a cruder measure. We will first look at the latter, because studies that use them are the most common.

In studies of demographic groups, the most widely used measure is the *employment ratio*. This is the fraction of the group under study that is employed. The teenage employment ratio is the percentage of teenagers who report having a job.[8] If at some moment all teenagers reported that they had a job, the teen employment ratio would be one. If none reported having a job, it would be zero, and if half did, it would be 50 percent. It automatically corrects for changes in the size of the teenage population, and studies that use it implicitly assume that if there were no trends and nothing changed but the size of the teenage population, a constant fraction of teenagers would always be employed. Employment ratios can be calculated for any demographic group or for the entire population. In many studies that use aggregate panels, where an observation is, for instance, of a particular state and year aggregated from the CPS, the teenage employment ratio would be the fraction of teenagers in that state who report having a job during the year.[9]

Industry studies and others that use establishment data more commonly measure employment as the number of jobs (number of individuals employed) or the growth rate of the number of jobs. Quasi experiments in which the unit of observation is a business establishment, perhaps a fast food restaurant, would measure the number of jobs at each establishment before and after the change in the minimum wage. Regression analyses of the restaurant industry generally use either the total number of jobs in the industry or the growth rate of the number of jobs in the industry.

Measures of Hours

As mentioned, these employment measures are somewhat crude, distinguishing between neither full-time and part-time employment nor differences in the length of the workweek. Controversy about the response of employment to the minimum wage suggested to some that less-crude measures might provide resolution. These tend to be variations on the number of paid hours of employment. Total hours, for an individual, an establishment or firm, or an industry, are a common choice. Others include average hours over all individuals in an establishment or an industry, and full-time equivalents (FTEs), that is, total hours divided by the number of hours considered to be in a full-time workweek (40 or 35, for example).

"Hours of employment" drawn from establishment data are based on actual hours that were paid for during a specified period, often a specific week. It is not uncommon for studies of demographic groups, which most often depend on household surveys, to include several measures of hours worked. As an example, before 1994 the CPS asked about both total hours worked at all jobs in the previous week and usual weekly hours worked. Starting that year, and continuing through the present, it asks separately for the number of hours at the primary job and at all other jobs, if any, in the previous week. The question on usual hours was changed in a parallel but somewhat problematic fashion. While before 1994 this was a simple question about "usual hours worked per week," since then this question has not only also distinguished between usual hours at the primary and all other jobs, but people who respond "variable," that is, that they do not have a usual number of hour of work per week, are coded as −4.[10]

A few observations about this are pertinent. To begin with, studies that use usual hours will not be directly comparable to studies that use actual hours; they are measuring closely related but different phenomena. Second, studies that use usual hours from the CPS for the period since 1994 must exclude people who answered "variable" since they are coded −4, unless the variable for hourly wage earners is used. Even if the studies do not address hours directly, those that use a measure of hourly earnings will exclude individuals who indicate that they work variable hours and are not paid by the hour from their sample because it is not possible to calculate hourly earnings. It is not evident that those excluded are, in either instance, statistically identical to those who remain.[11]

Third, it is useful to understand how "total hours of work," "average hours of work, conditional on employment," and "average hours of work" differ. The first is calculated as the product of average monthly hours and total monthly jobs. It is the total number of hours worked each month (in their case, in a particular industry) and is the obvious analog to the number of jobs. The second, common in studies that use data derived from establishment surveys, is the total number of hours that those employed have worked, divided by the number of employed. It tells us more about the length of the workweek than the amount of labor employed or paid for. While useful for some purposes—for example, determining whether the employed are actually earning more following a change in the minimum wage—it is not appropriate for examining the effect of the minimum wage on employment measured as the amount of labor paid for. Changes in the minimum wage that lead to changes in the number of individuals employed will cause this measure to vary differently from total hours. However, if the minimum wage does not influence the number of jobs, then it is possible to infer change in total hours from this measure. This can be seen with a bit of algebra. Let H_t, h_t, and J_t be the total number of hours, the number of hours per job, and the total number of jobs, all in period t: $H_t = h_t J_t$. If the minimum wage increases between periods one and two, then the change in hours is

$$
\begin{aligned}
H_2 - H_1 \quad &= h_2 J_2 - h_1 J_1 \\
&= h_2 J_2 - (h_1 J_2 - h_1 J_2) - h_1 J_1 \\
&= (h_2 J_2 - h_1 J_2) + (h_1 J_2 - h_1 J_1) \\
&= (h_2 - h_1) J_2 + h_1 (J_2 - J_1)
\end{aligned}
$$

If there is no change in the conditional number of average hours, then $h_2 - h_1$ equals zero, and the first term in the last line of the expression above is zero. If there has also been no change in the number of jobs, then the very last term in the line is also zero, and total hours have not changed.

The third measure, average hours of work (sometimes referred to as the unconditional average), is the total number hours that those employed work, divided by everyone in the same category (i.e., teenagers, immigrants, etc.), whether or not they are employed or even in the labor force. For instance, the unconditional average hours of work of teenagers is the total hours that employed teenagers work divided by all teenagers. So long as the number of teen-agers does not vary in response to changes in the minimum wage (and there are no large changes in its value from period to period), then this figure correlates highly with total (usual) hours of work. Where the second measure is used, it is necessary to combine the findings for hours with those for employment where possible, but this is a bit ad hoc.

The Minimum Wage

The value of the legislated minimum wage at any moment is a nominal variable; that is, without consideration for the price of anything else, it is mea-sured in terms of dollars per unit of the item under consideration, here an hour of labor. We can say that the federal minimum wage was $5.85 (per hour) for the year beginning on July 24, 2007, and that the minimum wage in Washing-ton, D.C., was $8.07 in January 2008. This raises two issues about measuring the minimum wage. The simpler one is "What is the measured value of the minimum wage when the data are aggregated over time?" If the unit of obser-vation is aggregated from monthly data up to a calendar year, as is frequently the case with panels that rely on the CPS, what is the appropriate value of the federal minimum wage for 2007? The standard approach is to set it to the aver-age value not over the course of the year but over the dates of the CPS surveys, which are monthly and refer to the week that contains the 12th of the month. The value of the federal minimum wage was $5.15 for the first seven surveys (January through July) of 2007, and $5.85 for the last five (August through September), so the annual value would be $5.44.

In some jurisdictions, there is more than one minimum wage law: for ex-ample, in the United States, not only is there a federal minimum wage, but many states have their own minimum wage. Except in well-specified situa-tions wherein, for example, a firm is smaller than a certain size specified in the federal law, the higher of the two applies. The standard practice is to ignore this condition because it applies to relatively few employees, and to use the higher of the applicable levels. Rather than repeatedly use the phrase "higher of federal or state minimum wage," this is commonly indicated by the phrase "effective minimum wage."

A more complicated problem pertains to inflation and the price level more generally. A minimum wage of $5.85 has a different impact in 2007, when the mean wage for U.S. teenagers was $8.20 per hour and the Consumer Price Index (CPI) had a value of 207, than it has in 1981, when the teenage mean wage was $3.77, and the CPI was 91. The cost of living also varies between cities, states, and regions, but there is no accepted index comparing costs geographically.

To think about possible solutions, consider a panel data set where each observation refers to a specific state and year and the relevant variables are constructed from CPS data. One common way of correcting for cost differences among states and over years is to calculate the average wage (for all employees, perhaps, or for prime-age adult males or teenagers) for each state and year, and divide that into the minimum wage. This is the *relative minimum wage*. As Card, Katz, and Krueger (1994) observe, in times of prosperity, both employment and wages will rise, and the rise in wages will cause a decline in the calculated value of the relative minimum.[12] Similarly, in times of recession, employment and wages will fall, and the decline in wages generates a rise in the relative minimum wage. As a result, there will be a negative correlation between employment and the relative minimum wage due only to movements in wages, whether or not employers respond to a higher minimum wage with lower employment or hiring. An alternative is to calculate *the real minimum wage*, dividing the nominal one by a price index such as the CPI. The shortcoming with this approach (at least for the United States) is that the CPI is not available at the same level of geographic disaggregation as the minimum wage. An equivalent approach is the inclusion of a distinct constant term for each year (annual fixed effects).[13]

The Kaitz index—a coverage-adjusted, relative minimum wage—is a measure of the minimum wage that once was quite common but no longer is. The relative part of this term is clear enough; *coverage adjusted* refers to the fraction of individuals employed in industries to which the minimum wage applies, industries that are *covered*. At different times in the past, different levels of the minimum wage have been relevant for different groups of individuals, and for different businesses or industries. There have been lower minimum wages for teenagers than for older workers, and minimum wages for smaller establishments have often been less. Adjusting for coverage uses a messy formula that is a weighted average of minimum wages that reflects the distribution of employment across industries, establishments, and demographic groups with different values of the minimum wage.[14]

Two other ways of measuring the minimum wage are the *fraction affected* (also sometimes called *fraction at risk*) and the *wage gap*. Card (1992a) introduced the fraction affected measure early in the NMWR in his cross-sectional analysis of change in employment following the 1990 increase in the federal minimum wage. Its value is the percentage of workers who, prior to an increase in the minimum wage, earn between the old and new values of the minimum wage. The intuition is that observations where this value is large are more sensitive to the minimum wage increase because it will be necessary to raise wages for a large fraction of employees to remain in compliance with the new, higher minimum wage. In Card's (1992a) study, with states as the level of analysis, it accounts for differing levels of the minimum wage across states before the federal increase. Employees initially earning below the minimum wage are excluded from the measure under the assumption that their employers are either not required to pay the minimum wage or have chosen not to comply, and this is likely to continue following the increase.

The wage gap, introduced by Currie and Fallick (1996), can be calculated for an individual worker or for a larger aggregation. For an affected individual, one who was previously earning less than the new, higher, value of the minimum wage following an increase, the wage gap is the difference between the new level of the minimum wage and her wage before the increase. It can be measured as a monetary value (e.g., in dollars) or as a percentage. For all others, those whose wage prior to the increase was already above the new, higher value of the minimum wage, the wage gap is set to zero. For establishments or regions, the wage gap is measured as the share of total payroll necessary to bring the fraction affected up to the new minimum wage.

Unlike the measures that incorporate the value of the minimum wage, both of these measures reflect the size of the relevant section of the lower tail of the wage distribution, the part of the employed workforce that is potentially affected by an increase in the minimum wage. Consequently, both are more sensitive to the ex ante facts on the ground. The wage gap goes beyond fraction affected in considering not only the size of this part of the tail, but the wage levels of those within it.

Wages

The terms *wages* and *earnings* are used inconsistently across studies. For the purposes of this review, *wage rate* refers to the straight-time hourly wage an individual is paid. *Earnings* commonly indicates the pretax amount in an employee's paychecks over some period. For those paid weekly (or biweekly or monthly), hourly earnings are the amount they are paid per week (or fortnight or month) divided by the number of hours they worked that week (or fortnight or month). For those paid by the hour, hourly earnings might also be their wage rate, but if they worked overtime at time and one-half or better, hourly earnings might be greater than their wage rate. While earnings can be computed for all employees, wage rates are only available for those who are paid by the hour. In this review, we use *wages* as a general term referring to employee pay. It encompasses both wage rates and earnings, but, unlike wage rates or earnings, it is not a specific measure.

Notes

1. Only 10 of the roughly 70 studies covered in Chapter 2 use privately generated data: Böckerman and Uusitalo (2009); Card and Krueger (1994); Dube, Naidu, and Reich (2007); Giuliano (2013); Katz and Krueger (1992); Machin, Manning, and Rahman (2003); Machin and Wilson (2004); Neumark and Wascher (2000); Orazem and Mattila (2002); and Skedinger (2006).

2. As time passes since the last census, the list of residences grows out of date. The Census Bureau addresses this by collecting data on building permits on an ongoing basis and augments the list of residences to keep the list current. The formula used to determine whether to include a particular household is quite complicated and is not of particular interest for our purposes, but the likelihood is not equal across all households because with careful design, it is possible to construct more accurate statistics for surveys of the same size (and thus cost) by allowing this likelihood to vary in certain systematic ways.

3. Canadian studies could aggregate the data by quarter. The sample size is similar to the CPS, and there are only nine provinces, so there would be less of an issue with small samples in causing excessive variance in the measures.

4. This may seem a strange way of defining the reference period, but it differs across establishments, depending on whether they pay weekly, biweekly, semimonthly, or monthly.

5. From http://www.bls.gov/cew/cewfaq.htm (accessed April 28, 2011).

6. This information drawn from the SIPP Web site, http://www.census.gov/sipp/overview.html on July 28, 2013.

7. Ritchie (1995) contains a wealth of information on the NES.

8. Individuals who are institutionalized or in the armed forces are not defined as part of the potential labor force and are not asked labor force questions in household surveys. Similarly, only those aged 16 or older are asked labor force questions, as those under 16 are not currently considered part of the potential labor force. There is no age limit after which the labor force questions are no longer asked.

9. Other common measures of employment outcomes, such as unemployment, are only rarely used in minimum wage studies. The definition of an unemployed person is one who is not only neither self-employed nor employed by another but is also actively seeking a job. The unemployment rate is the ratio of the number of those who are unemployed to the sum of those employed and the unemployed. A problem with this measure for minimum wage studies is that the distinction between the unemployed and those without jobs who are not actively seeking work is sensitive to influences such as the current condition of the labor market, the availability of unemployment benefits, and whether respondents are in school (full-time students are not classified as unemployed). Teasing out the effect of the minimum wage from other factors affecting the unemployment rate is considerably more challenging than the already difficult task of measuring the effect on the employment ratio.

10. In addition, since the early 1980s and continuing through the present, the CPS has had a separate question for hourly wage earners that before 1994 recorded the usual weekly hours "at this job" and since 1994, "at this rate." Analysts who rely on "usual weekly hours" rarely specify whether they are using this variable or one of the others, but the large number of missing values for this indicates its rare use.

11. In 2006, those who answered "variable" compose about 8.5 percent of respondents and 14 percent actual working hours, but 14 percent of teenagers and 10.6 percent of their actual hours. Those answering "variable hours" are as likely to be male as female among both teens and adults. Teenagers are more likely to be 16 or 17 and less likely to be 19.

12. Card, Katz, and Krueger (1994) are here extending an observation that Freeman (1982) made with reference to studies that analyze cross-sectional data.

13. It appears that Neumark, Schweitzer, and Wascher (2004) first introduced this approach.

14. Amendments to the Fair Labor Standards Act in 1961 and 1966 extended full minimum wage coverage to all but the smallest firms, making adjusting the minimum wage for coverage far less important. As a result, the Kaitz index has largely disappeared from minimum wage research.

References

Aaronson, Daniel. 2001. "Price Pass-Through and the Minimum Wage." *Review of Economics and Statistics* 83(1): 158–169.

Aaronson, Daniel, Sumit Agarwal, and Eric French. 2007. "The Spending and Debt Response to Minimum Wage Hikes." Working Paper No. 23. Chicago: Federal Reserve Bank of Chicago.

Aaronson, Daniel, Sumit Agarwal, and Eric French. 2011. "The Spending and Debt Response to Minimum Wage Hikes." FRB of Chicago Working Paper No. 2007-23. Chicago: Federal Reserve Bank of Chicago.

Aaronson, Daniel, and Eric French. 2007. "Product Market Evidence on the Employment Effects of the Minimum Wage." *Journal of Labor Economics* 25(1): 167–200.

Aaronson, Daniel, Eric French, and James MacDonald. 2008. "The Minimum Wage, Restaurant Prices, and Labor Market Structure." *Journal of Human Resources* 43(3): 688–720.

Abadie, Alberto, Alexis Diamond, and Jens Hainmueller. 2010. "Synthetic Control Methods for Comparative Case Studies of Aggregate Interventions: Estimating the Effect of California's Tobacco Control Program." *Journal of the American Statistical Association* 105(490): 493–505.

Abowd, John M., Bryce E. Stephens, Lars Vilhuber, Fredrik Andersson, Kevin L. McKinney, Marc Roemer, and Simon Woodcock. 2005. "The LED Infrastructure Files and the Creation of the Quarterly Workforce Indicators." No. TP-2006-01. Suitland, MD: U.S. Census Bureau, LEHD Program.

Abowd, John M., and Lars Vilhuber. 2011a. "National Estimates of Gross Employment and Job Flows from the Quarterly Workforce Indicators with Demographic and Industry Detail." *Journal of Econometrics* 161(1): 82–99.

———. 2011b. "Gross Employment, Job Flows, and the Role of Education in the Great Recession." Working paper. Ithaca, NY: Cornell University, ILR School, Labor Dynamics Institute.

Acemoglu, Daron, and Jörn-Steffen Pischke. 1999. "Beyond Becker: Training in Imperfect Labor Markets." *Economic Journal* 109(453): F112–142.

———. 2003. "Minimum Wages and On-the-Job Training." *Research in Labor Economics* 22: 159–202.

Ada, H., Elizabeth Roberts, Robert F. Elliott, David Bell, and Anthony Scott. 2006. "Comparing the New Earnings Survey (NES) and the Labour Force Survey (LFS): An Analysis of the Differences between the Data Sets and Their Implications for the Pattern of Geographical Pay in the UK." *Regional Studies* 40(6): 645–665.

Addison, John T., and McKinley L. Blackburn. 1999. "Minimum Wages and Poverty." *Industrial and Labor Relations Review* 52(3): 393–409.

Addison, John T., McKinley L. Blackburn, and Chad D. Cotti. 2009. "Do Minimum Wages Raise Employment? Evidence from the U.S. Retail-Trade Sector." *Labour Economics* 16(4): 397–408.

———. 2012. "The Effect of Minimum Wages on Labour Market Outcomes: County-Level Estimates from the Restaurant-and-Bar Sector." *British Journal of Industrial Relations* 50(3): 412–435.

———. 2013. "Minimum Wage Increases in a Recessionary Environment." *Grupo de Estudos Monetários e Financeiros* Working Paper No. 8. Coimbra, Portugal: University of Coimbra. http://gemf.fe.uc.pt/workingpapers/pdf/2013/gemf_2013-08.pdf (accessed February 19, 2014).

Addison, John T., and Orgul Demet Ozturk. 2012. "Minimum Wages, Labor Market Institutions, and Female Employment: A Cross-Country Analysis." *Industrial and Labor Relations Review* 65(4): 779–809.

Ahn, Tom, Peter Arcidiacono, and Walter Wessels. 2011. "The Distributional Impacts of Minimum Wage Increases when Both Labor Supply and Labor Demand Are Endogenous." *Journal of Business and Economic Statistics* 29(1): 12–23.

Akerlof, George A. 1970. "The Market for 'Lemons': Quality Uncertainty and the Market Mechanism." *Quarterly Journal of Economics* 84(3): 488–500.

Allegretto, Sylvia A., Arindrajit Dube, and Michael Reich. 2009. "Spatial Heterogeneity and Minimum Wages: Employment Estimates for Teens Using Cross-State Commuting Zones." IRLE Working Paper No. 181-09. Berkeley: University of California, Berkeley, Institute for Research on Labor and Employment.

———. 2011. "Do Minimum Wages Really Reduce Teen Employment? Accounting for Heterogeneity and Selectivity in State Panel Data." *Industrial Relations* 50(2): 205–240.

Alpert, William T. 1986. *The Minimum Wage in the Restaurant Industry.* New York: Praeger.

Anderson, John, and Orn Bodvarsson. 2005. "Do Higher Tipped Minimum Wages Boost Server Pay?" *Applied Economics Letters* 12(7): 391–393.

Angrist, Joshua D., and Jörn-Steffen Pischke. 2009. *Mostly Harmless Econometrics: An Empiricist's Companion.* Princeton, NJ: Princeton University Press.

Arulampalm, Wiji, Alison L. Booth, and Mark L. Bryan. 2004. "Training and the New Minimum Wage." *Economic Journal* 114(494): C87–C94.

Autor, David H., Lawrence F. Katz, and Melissa S. Kearney. 2008. "Trends in U.S. Wage Inequality: Revising the Revisionists." *Review of Economics and Statistics* 90(2): 300–323.

Autor, David H., Alan Manning, and Christopher L. Smith. 2010. "The Contribution of the Minimum Wage to U.S. Wage Inequality over Three Decades:

A Reassessment." NBER Working Paper No. 16533. Cambridge, MA: National Bureau of Economic Research.

Baker, Michael. 2005. "Minimum Wages and Human Capital Investments of Young Workers: Work Related Training and School Enrollment." Working Paper No. 2005 B-04. Ottawa, Ontario: Social Sciences and Humanities Research Council.

Baker, Michael, Dwayne Benjamin, and Shuchita Stanger. 1999. "The Highs and Lows of the Minimum Wage Effect: A Time-Series Cross-Section Study of the Canadian Law." *Journal of Labor Economics* 17(2): 318–350.

Bazen, Stephen, and Julie Le Gallo. 2009. "The State–Federal Dichotomy in the Effects of Minimum Wages on Teenage Employment in the United States." *Economics Letters* 105(3): 267–269.

Bazen, Stephen, and Velayoudon Marimoutou. 2002. "Looking for a Needle in a Haystack? A Reexamination of the Time Series Relationship between Teenage Employment and Minimum Wages in the United States." *Oxford Bulletin of Economics and Statistics* 64(Supplement): 699–725.

Belman, Dale, and Erika Groshen. 1998. "Is Small Beautiful for Employees?" In *Small Comfort: Small Business, Job Creation and Wages*. Washington, DC: Economic Policy Institute, pp. 1–60.

Belman, Dale, and Paul Wolfson. 2010. "The Effect of Legislated Minimum Wage Increases on Employment and Hours: A Dynamic Analysis." *Labour* 24(1): 1–25.

Bernstein, Jared, and James Lin. 2008. "What We Need to Get By." Briefing Paper No. 224. Washington, DC: Economic Policy Institute.

Bertrand, Marianne, Ester Duflo, and Sendhil Mullainathan. 2004. "How Much Should We Trust Differences-in-Differences Estimates?" *Quarterly Journal of Economics* 119(1): 249–275.

Bhaskar, V., and Ted To. 1999. "Minimum Wages for Ronald McDonald Monopsonies: A Theory of Monopsonistic Competition." *Economic Journal* 109(455): 190–203.

Bivens, Josh. 2011. "Three-Fifths of All Income Growth from 1979–2007 Went to the Top 1%." Washington, DC: Economic Policy Institute. http://www.epi.org/publication/fifths-income-growth-1979-2007-top-1 (accessed October 21, 2012).

Bjelland, M., B. Fallick, J. Haltiwanger, and E. McEntarfer. 2007. "Employer-to-Employer Flows in the United States: Estimates Using Linked Employer-Employee Data." Finance and Economics Discussion Series Working Paper 2007–30. Washington, DC: Federal Reserve Board.

Böckerman, Petri, and Roope Uusitalo. 2009. "Minimum Wages and Youth Employment: Evidence from the Finnish Retail Trade Sector." *British Journal of Industrial Relations* 47(2): 388–405.

Bouvet, Florence. 2009. "The Beveridge Curve in Europe: New Evidence Using National and Regional Data." Photocopy. Rohnert Park, CA: Sonoma State University.

Brown, Charles. 1999. "Minimum Wages, Employment, and the Distribution of Income." In *Handbook of Labor Economics.* Vol. 3, Orley Ashenfelter and David Card, eds. Philadelphia: Elsevier, pp. 2101–2163.

Brown, Charles, Curtis Gilroy, and Andrew Kohen. 1982. "The Effect of the Minimum Wage on Employment and Unemployment." *Journal of Economic Literature* 20(2): 487–528.

Burdett, Kenneth, and Dale T. Mortensen. 1998. "Wage Differentials, Employer Size, and Unemployment." *International Economic Review* 39(2): 257–273.

Burkhauser, Richard V., Kenneth A. Couch, and A. J. Glenn. 1995. "Public Policies for the Working Poor: The Earned Income Tax Credit versus Minimum Wage Legislation." Discussion Paper No. 1074-95. Madison, WI: Institute for Research on Poverty.

Burkhauser, Richard V., Kenneth A. Couch, and David C. Wittenburg. 2000. "A Reassessment of the New Economics of the Minimum Wage Literature with Monthly Data from the Current Population Survey." *Journal of Labor Economics* 18(4): 653–680.

Burkhauser, Richard V., and Joseph J. Sabia. 2007. "The Effectiveness of Minimum Wage Increases in Reducing Poverty: Past, Present, and Future." Contemporary Economic Policy 25(2): 262–281.

Burton, Michael, and Richard Patrick Dorsett. 2001. "The Degree of Monopsony Power in Agricultural Labour Markets, and the Impact of the Agricultural Minimum Wage: An Application to Craft Workers in England and Wales." *Applied Economics* 33(14): 1776–1784.

Butcher, Tim. 2005. "Special Feature: The Hourly Earnings Distribution before and after the National Minimum Wage." *Labour Market Trends* 113(10): 427–435.

Cameron, A. Colin, Jonah B. Gelbach, and Douglas L. Miller. 2008. "Bootstrap-Based Improvements for Inference with Clustered Errors." *Review of Economics and Statistics* 90(3): 414–427.

Campolieti, Michele, Tony Fang, and Morley Gunderson. 2005a. "Minimum Wage Impacts on Youth Employment Transitions, 1993–1999." *Canadian Journal of Economics* 38(1): 81–104.

———. 2005b. "How Minimum Wages Affect Schooling-Employment Outcomes in Canada, 1993–1999." *Journal of Labor Research* 26(3): 534–545.

Campolieti, Michele, Morley Gunderson, and Byron Lee. 2012. "The (Non) Impact of Minimum Wages on Poverty: Regression and Simulation Evidence for Canada." *Journal of Labor Research* 33(3): 287–302.

Campolieti, Michele, Morley Gunderson, and Chris Riddell. 2006. "Minimum Wage Impacts from a Prespecified Research Design: Canada 1981–1997." *Industrial Relations* 45(2): 195–216.

Card, David. 1992a. "Using Regional Variation in Wages to Measure the Effects of the Federal Minimum Wage." *Industrial and Labor Relations Review* 46(1): 22–37.

———. 1992b. "Do Minimum Wages Reduce Employment? A Case Study of California, 1987–89." *Industrial and Labor Relations Review* 46(1): 38–54.

Card, David, and John E. DiNardo. 2002. "Skill-Biased Technological Change and Rising Wage Inequality: Some Problems and Puzzles." *Journal of Labor Economics* 20(4): 733–783.

Card, David, Lawrence F. Katz, and Alan B. Krueger. 1994. "Comment on David Neumark and William Wascher, 'Employment Effects of Minimum and Subminimum Wages: Panel Data on State Minimum Wage Laws'." *Industrial and Labor Relations Review* 47(3): 487–497.

Card, David, and Alan B. Krueger. 1994. "Minimum Wages and Employment: A Case Study of the Fast-Food Industry in New Jersey and Pennsylvania." *American Economic Review* 84(4): 772–793.

———. 1995. *Myth and Measurement: The New Economics of the Minimum Wage.* Princeton, NJ: Princeton University Press.

———. 1999. "Reanalysis of the Effect of the New Jersey Minimum Wage Increase on the Fast Food Industry with Representative Payroll Data." Princeton University Industrial Relations Working Paper No. 393. Princeton, NJ: Princeton University.

———. 2000. "Minimum Wages and Employment: A Case Study of the Fast-Food Industry in New Jersey and Pennsylvania: Reply." *American Economic Review* 90(5): 1397–1420.

Carmeci, Gaetano, and Luciano Mauro. 2002. "The Convergence of the Italian Regions and Unemployment: Theory and Evidence." *Journal of Regional Science* 42(3): 509–532.

Carrington, William J., and Bruce C. Fallick. 2001. "Do Some Workers Have Minimum Wage Careers?" *Monthly Labor Review* 124(5): 17–27.

Chaplin, Duncan, Mark D. Turner, and Andreus D. Pape. 2003. "Minimum Wage and School Enrollment of Teenagers: A look at the 1990s." *Economics of Education Review* 22(1): 11–21.

Chen, Xiao, Philip B. Ender, Michael Mitchell, and Christine Wells. 2003. *Regression with Stata.* Los Angeles, CA: University of California–Los Angeles, Academic Technology Services, Statistical Consulting Group. http://www.ats.ucla.edu/stat/stata/webbooks/reg/default.htm (accessed February 22, 2011).

Clark, Tom S., and Drew A. Linzer. 2013. "Should I Use Fixed or Random

Effects?" Working paper. Atlanta, GA: Emory University. http://userwww.tomclarkphd.com/workingpapers/randomeffects.pdf (accessed December 17, 2013).

Clauson, Annette. 2008. "Despite Higher Food Prices, Percent of U.S. Income Spent on Food Remains Constant." *Amber Waves*, Sept. 1.

Cohen, Jacob. 1988. *Statistical Power Analysis for the Behavioral Sciences*. 2nd ed. New York: Academic Press.

Commons, John R., and John B. Andrews. 1916. *Principles of Labor Legislation*. New York and London: Harper & Brothers.

Connolly, Sara, and Mary Gregory. 2002. "The National Minimum Wage and Hours of Work: Implications for Low-Paid Women." *Oxford Bulletin of Economics and Statistics* 64(Supplement): 607–631.

Couch, Kenneth A., and David C. Wittenburg. 2001. "The Response of Hours of Work to Increases in the Minimum Wage." *Southern Economic Journal* 68(1): 171–177.

Crofton, Stephanie O., William L. Anderson, and Emily C. Rawe. 2009. "Do Higher Real Minimum Wages Lead to More High School Dropouts? Evidence from Maryland across Races, 1993–2004." *American Journal of Economics and Sociology* 68(2): 445–464.

Cunningham, James. 1981. "The Impact of Minimum Wages on Youth Employment, Hours of Work and School Attendance: Cross-Sectional Evidence from the 1960 and 1970 Censuses." In *The Economics of Legal Minimum Wages*, Simon Rottenberg, ed. Washington, DC: American Enterprise Institute, pp. 88–123.

Currie, Janet, and Bruce Fallick. 1996. "The Minimum Wage and the Employment of Youth: Evidence from the NLSY." *Journal of Human Resources* 31(2): 404–428.

Davis, Steven J., and John Haltiwanger. 1998. "Measuring Gross Worker and Job Flows." In *Labor Statistics Measurement Issues*, John Haltiwanger, Marilyn E. Manser, and Robert Topel, eds. Cambridge, MA: National Bureau of Economic Research, pp. 77–122.

DeFina, Robert H. 2008. "The Impact of State Minimum Wages on Child Poverty in Female-Headed Families." *Journal of Poverty* 12(2): 155–174.

De Fraja, Gianni. 1999. "Minimum Wage Legislation, Productivity and Employment." *Economica* 66(264): 473–488.

de Linde Leonard, M., T. D. Stanley, and H. Doucouliagos. 2013. "Does the UK Minimum Wage Reduce Employment? A Meta-Regression Analysis." *Bristish Journal of Industrial Relations*. doi: 10.1111/bjir.12031 (accessed March 5, 2014). First published online July 17, 2013.

Dickens, Richard, Stephen Machin, Alan Manning, David Metcalf, Jonathan

Wadsworth, and Stephen Woodland. 1995. "The Effect of Minimum Wages on UK Agriculture." *Journal of Agriculture* 46(1): 1–19.

Dickens, Richard, and Alan Manning. 2004a. "Has the National Minimum Wage Reduced UK Wage Inequality?" *Journal of the Royal Statistical Association* 167(4): 613–626.

———. 2004b. "Spikes and Spill-Overs: The Impact of the National Minimum Wage on the Wage Distribution in a Low-Wage Sector." *Economic Journal* 114(494): 95–101.

DiNardo, John, Nicole M. Fortin, and Thomas Lemieux. 1996. "Labor Market Institutions and the Distribution of Wages: 1973–1992." *Econometrica* 64(5): 1001–1044.

Dodson, Marvin E. III. 2002. "The Impact of the Minimum Wage in West Virginia: A Test of the Low-Wage-Area Theory." *Journal of Labor Research* 23(1): 25–40.

Dolton, Peter, Chiara Rosazza-Bondibene, and Jonathan Wadsworth. 2010. "The UK National Minimum Wage in Retrospect." *Fiscal Studies* 31(4): 509–534.

———. "Employment, Inequality and the UK National Minimum Wage over the Medium-Term" *Oxford Bulletin of Economics and Statistics* 74(1): 74–106.

Donald, Stephen G., and Kevin Lang. 2007. "Inference with Difference-in-Differences and Other Panel Data." *Review of Economics and Statistics* 89(2): 221–233.

Doucouliagos, Hristos, and T. D. Stanley. 2009. "Publication Selection Bias in Minimum-Wage Research? A Meta-Regression Analysis." *British Journal of Industrial Relations* 47(2): 406–428.

Draca, Mirko, Stephen Machin, and John Van Reenen. 2011. "Minimum Wages and Firm Profitability." *American Economic Journal: Applied Economics* 3(1): 129–151.

Drazen, Allan. 1986. "Optimal Minimum Wage Legislation." *Economic Journal* 96(383): 774–784.

Dube, Arindrajit, T. William Lester, and Michael Reich. 2010. "Minimum Wage Effects across State Borders: Estimates Using Contiguous Counties." *Review of Economics and Statistics* 92(4): 945–964.

———. 2011. "Do Frictions Matter in the Labor Market? Accessions, Separations and Minimum Wage Effects." IZA Discussion Paper No. 5811. Bonn: Institute for the Study of Labor.

———. 2012. "Minimum Wage Shocks, Employment Flows and Labor Market Frictions." Working paper. Berkeley: University of California, Institute for Research on Labor and Employment.

Dube, Arindrajit, Suresh Naidu, and Michael Reich. 2007. "The Economic Effects of a Citywide Minimum Wage." *Industrial and Labor Relations Review* 60(4): 522–543.

Dunlop, John T. 1950. *Wage Determination under Trade Unions*. New York: Macmillan.

Easton, Todd. 2006. "Metropolitan Wage Levels of Less-Educated Workers: 1986 to 1999." *Industrial Relations* 45(2): 119–147.

Eckstein, Zvi, Suqin Ge, and Barbara Petrongolo. 2011. "Job and Wage Mobility with Minimum Wages and Imperfect Compliance." *Journal of Applied Econometrics* 26(4): 580–612.

Edsall, Thomas B. 2013. "Does Rising Inequality Make Us Hardhearted?" *New York Times*, Dec. 10. http://www.nytimes.com/2013/12/11/opinion/does-rising-inequality-make-us-hardhearted.html (accessed April 16, 2014).

Ehrenberg, Ronald G. 1992. "Symposium Introduction." *Industrial and Labor Relations Review* 46(1): 3–5.

Ehrenberg, Ronald G., and Alan J. Marcus. 1982. "Minimum Wages and Teenagers' Enrollment-Employment Outcomes: A Multinomial Logit Model." *Journal of Human Resources* 17(1): 39–58.

Ehrenberg, Ronald G., and Robert S. Smith. 2012. *Modern Labor Economics: Theory and Public Policy*. 11th ed. Upper Saddle River, NJ: Prentice Hall.

Even, William Edward, and David A. Macpherson. 2003. "The Wage and Employment Dynamics of Minimum Wage Workers." *Southern Economic Journal* 69(3): 676–690.

———. 2014. "The Effect of the Tipped Minimum Wage on Employees in the U.S. Restaurant Industry." *Southern Economic Journal* 80(3): 633–655.

Evans, William, and Mark D. Turner. 1995. "Minimum Wage Effects on Employment and School Enrollment: Comment." Photocopy. College Park, MD: University of Maryland.

Fairris, David, and Roberto Pedace. 2004. "The Impact of Minimum Wages on Job Training: An Empirical Exploration with Establishment Data." *Southern Economic Journal* 70(3): 566–583.

Falk, Armin, Ernst Fehr, and Christian Zehnder. 2006. "Fairness Perceptions and Reservation Wages—The Behavioral Effects of Minimum Wage Laws." *Quarterly Journal of Economics* 121(4): 1347–1381.

Falk, Armin, and David Huffman. 2007. "Studying Labor Market Institutions in the Lab: Minimum Wages, Employment Protection and Workfare." *Journal of Institutional and Theoretical Economics* 163(1): 30–45.

Fallick, Bruce, and Charles A. Fleischman. 2004. "Employer-to-Employer Flows in the U.S. Labor Market: The Complete Picture of Gross Worker Flows." Finance and Economics Discussion Series Working Paper No.

2001-18. Washington, DC: Board of Governors of the Federal Reserve System.

Fang, Tony, and Morley Gunderson. 2009. "Minimum Wage Impacts on Older Workers: Longitudinal Estimates from Canada." *British Journal of Industrial Relations* 47(2): 371–387.

Fisher, Gordon M. 1992. "The Development and History of the Poverty Thresholds." *Social Security Bulletin* 55(4): 3–14.

Flinn, Christopher J. 2006. "Minimum Wage Effects on Labor Market Outcomes under Search, Matching, and Endogenous Contact Rates." *Econometrica* 74(4): 1013–1062.

Formby, John P., John A. Bishop, and Hoseong Kim. 2010. "The Redistributive Effects and Cost-Effectiveness of Increasing the Federal Minimum Wage." *Public Finance Review* 38(5): 585–618.

Fortin, Pierre, Manfred Keil, and James Symons. 2001. "The Sources of Unemployment in Canada, 1967–91: Evidence from a Panel of Regions and Demographic Groups." *Oxford Economic Papers-New Series* 53(1): 67–93.

Fougère, Denis, Erwan Gautier, and Hervé Le Bihan. 2010. "Restaurant Prices and the Minimum Wage." *Journal of Money, Credit and Banking* 42(7): 1199–1234.

Frazis, Harley J., Edwin L. Robison, Thomas D. Evans, and Martha A. Duff. 2005. "Estimating Gross Flows Consistent with Stocks in the CPS." *Monthly Labor Review* 128(9): 3–9.

Freeman, Richard B. 1982. "Economic Determinants of Geographic and Individual Variation in the Labor Market Position of Young Persons." In *The Youth Labor Market Problem: Its Nature, Causes, and Consequences*, Richard B. Freeman and David A. Wise, eds. Chicago: University of Chicago Press, pp. 115–154.

———. 1996. "The Minimum Wage as a Redistributive Tool." *Economic Journal: The Quarterly Journal of the Royal Economic Society* 106(436): 639–649.

Galbraith, John Kenneth. 1972. *The New Industrial State*. London: Deutsch.

Galindo-Rueda, Fernando, and Sonia Pereira. 2004. *The Impact of the National Minimum Wage on British Firms*. Final Reports to the Low Pay Commission on the Econometric Evidence from the Annual Respondents Database. London: Low Pay Commission. http://www.lowpay.gov.uk/lowpay/research/pdf/t0Z2NTSH.pdf (accessed August 7, 2012).

Gelman, Andrew, and Jennifer Hill. 2007. *Data Analysis Using Regression and Multilevel/Hierarchical Models*. New York: Cambridge University Press.

Georgiadis, Andreus. 2006. "Is the Minimum Wage Efficient? Evidence of the Effects of the UK National Minimum Wage in the Residential Care Homes

Sector." Centre for Market and Public Organisation Working Paper No. 06/160. Bristol, UK: Centre for Market and Public Organisation.

————. 2008. "Efficiency Wages and Economic Effects of the Minimum Wage: Evidence from a Low-Wage Labour Market." Centre of Economic Performance Discussion Paper No. 857. London: Centre for Economic Performance.

————. 2013. "Efficiency Wages and the Economic Effects of the Minimum Wage: Evidence from a Low-Wage Labour Market." *Oxford Bulletin of Economics and Statistics* 75(6): 962–979.

Giuliano, Laura. 2013. "Minimum Wage Effects on Employment, Substitution, and teenage Labor Supply: Evidence from Personnel Data." *Journal of Labor Economics* 31(1): 155–194.

Greene, William H. 2011. *Econometric Analysis*. 7th ed. Upper Saddle River, NJ: Prentice Hall.

Grimshaw, Damian, and Marilyn Carroll. 2006. "Adjusting to the National Minimum Wage: Constraints and Incentives to Change in Six Low-Paying Sectors." *Industrial Relations Journal* 37(1): 22–47.

Grogger, Jeffrey T. 2003. "The Effects of Time Limits, the EITC, and Other Policy Changes on Welfare Use, Work, and Income among Female-Headed Families." *Review of Economics and Statistics* 85(2): 394–408.

————. 2004. "Time Limits and Welfare Use." *Journal of Human Resources* 34(2): 405–424.

Grossberg, Adam J., and Paul Sicilian. 1999. "Minimum Wages, On-the-Job Training, and Wage Growth." *Southern Economic Journal* 65(3): 539–556.

————. 2004. "Legal Minimum Wages and Employment Duration." *Southern Economic Journal* 70(3): 631–645.

Grossman, Jean Baldwin. 1983. "The Impact of the Minimum Wage on Other Wages." *Journal of Human Resources* 18(3): 359–378.

Gundersen, Craig. 2006. "Are the Effects of the Macroeconomy and Social Policies on Poverty Different in Nonmetro Areas in the United States?" *Rural Sociology* 71(4): 545–572.

Gundersen, Craig, and James P. Ziliak. 2004. "Poverty and Macroeconomic Performance across Space, Race, and Family Structure." *Demography* 41(1): 61–86.

Hammerton, John Alexander, ed. 2011. "Mr. Punch on the Warpath: Humours of the Army, the Navy and the Reserve Forces." Project Gutenberg, Caption to the cartoon, "Military Education." http://www.gutenberg.org/files/38146/38146-h/38146-h.htm (accessed June 13, 2013).

Hansen, Christian B. 2007a. "Generalized Least Squares Inference in Panel and Multilevel Models with Serial Correlation and Fixed Effects." *Journal of Econometrics* 140(2): 670–694.

————. 2007b. "Asymptotic Properties of a Robust Variance Matrix Estimator for Panel Data When T Is Large." *Journal of Econometrics* 141(2): 597–620.

Harvey, Andrew, and Jared Bernstein. 2003. "Measurement and Testing of Inequality from Time Series of Deciles with an Application to U.S. Wages." *Review of Economics and Statistics* 85(1): 141–152.

Hashimoto, Masanori. 1982. "Minimum Wage Effects on Training on the Job."*American Economic Review* 72(5): 1070–1087.

Hirsch, Barry T., Bruce E. Kaufman, Tetyana Zelenska. 2011. "Minimum Wage Channels of Adjustment." IZA Discussion Paper No. 6132. Bonn: Institute for the Study of Labor.

Hoffman, Saul D., and C. Ke. 2012. "Employment Effects of the 2009 Minimum Wage Increase: New Evidence from State-Based Comparisons of Workers by Skill Level." Photocopy. Newark, DE: University of Delaware.

Hoffman, Saul D., and D. M. Trace. 2009. "NJ and PA Once Again: What Happened to Employment When the PA–NJ Minimum Wage Differential Disappeared?" *Eastern Economic Journal* 35(1): 115–128.

Holzer, Harry J., Lawrence F. Katz, and Alan B. Krueger. 1991. "Job Queues and Wages." *Quarterly Journal of Economics* 106(3): 739–768.

Horrigan, Michael W., and Ronald B. Mincy. 1993. "The Minimum Wage and Earnings and Income Inequality." In *Uneven Tides: Rising Inequality in America*, Sheldon Danziger and Peter Gottshalk, eds. New York: Russell Sage Foundation, pp. 251–275.

Hyatt, Henry R., and James R. Spletzer. 2013. "The Recent Decline in Employment Dynamics." IZA Discussion Paper No. 7231. Bonn: Institute for the Study of Labor.

Hyslop, Dean, and Steven Stillman. 2007. "Youth Minimum Wage Reform and the Labour Market in New Zealand." *Labour Economics* 14(2): 201–230.

Imbens, Guido W., and Jeffrey M. Wooldridge. 2009. "Recent Developments in the Econometrics of Program Evaluation." *Journal of Economic Literature* 47(1): 5–86.

Johnson, David S., John M. Rogers, and Lucilla Tan. 2001. "A Century of Family Budgets in the United States." *Monthly Labor Review* 124(5): 28–45.

Jones, Melanie K., Richard J. Jones, Philip D. Murphy, and Peter J. Sloane. 2007. "A Persistence Model of the National Minimum Wage." IZA Discussion Paper No. 2595. Bonn: Institute for the Study of Labor.

Kalenkoski, Charlene M., and Donald J. Lacombe. 2008. "Effects of Minimum Wages on Youth Employment: The Importance for Accounting for Spatial Correlation." *Journal of Labor Research* 29(4): 303–317.

Katz, Lawrence F., and Alan B. Krueger. 1992. "The Effect of the Minimum Wage on the Fast-Food Industry." *Industrial and Labor Relations Review* 46(1): 6–21.

Kaufman, Bruce. 2007. "The Impossibility of a Perfectly Competitive Labor Market." *Cambridge Journal of Economics* 31(5): 775–787.

Keil, Manfred, Donald Robertson, and James Symons. 2009. "Univariate Regressions of Employment on Minimum Wages in the Panel of U.S. States." Robert Day School Working Paper No. 2009-03. Claremont, CA: Claremont McKenna College.

Kloek, Teun. 1981. "OLS Estimation in a Model Where a Microvariable Is Explained by Aggregates and Contemporaneous Disturbances Are Equicorrelated." *Econometrica* 49(1): 205–207.

Knabe, Andreas, and Ronnie Schöb. 2008. "Minimum Wage Incidence: The Case for Germany." CESifo Working Paper Series No. 2432. Munich: CESifo.

Kramarz, Francis, and Thomas Philippon. 2001. "The Impact of Differential Payroll Tax Subsidies on Minimum Wage Employment." *Journal of Public Economics* 82(1): 115–146.

Krashinsky, Harry. 2008. "The Effect of Labor Market Institutions on Salaried and Self-Employed Less-Educated Men in the 1980s." *Industrial and Labor Relations Review* 62(1): 73–91.

Lam, Katherine, Catrin Ormerod, Felix Ritchie, and Prabhat Vaze. 2006. "National Statistics Feature: Do Company Wage Policies Persist in the Face of Minimum Wages? An Analysis of Earnings Data for Low-Paid Individuals, Linked with the Characteristics of Their Employer." *Labour Market Trends* 114(3): 69.

Landon, Stuart. 1997. "High School Enrollment, Minimum Wages and Education Spending." *Canadian Public Policy* 23(2): 141–163.

Laroque, Guy, and Bernard Salanie. 2002. "Female Part-Time Work and Financial Incentives." *Economique* 53(6): 1127–1147.

Lee, Chinkook, Gerald Schluter, and Brian O'Roark. 2000. "Minimum Wage and Food Prices: An Analysis of Price Pass-Through Effects." *International Food and Agribusiness Management Review* 3(1): 111–128.

Lee, David S. 1999. "Wage Inequality in the United States during the 1980s: Rising Dispersion or Falling Minimum Wage?" *Quarterly Journal of Economics* 114(3): 977–1023.

Lee, Wang-Sheng, and Sandy Suardi. 2011. "Minimum Wages and Employment: Reconsidering the Use of a Time Series Approach as an Evaluation Tool." *British Journal of Industrial Relations* 49(Supplement): s376–s401.

Leighton, Linda, and Jacob Mincer. 1981. "The Effects of Minimum Wages on Human Capital Formation." In *The Economics of Legal Minimum Wages*, Simon Rottenberg, ed. Washington, DC: American Enterprise Institute, pp. 155–173.

Lemieux, Thomas. 2002. "Decomposing Changes in Wage Distributions: A Unified Approach." *Canadian Journal of Economics* 35(4): 646–688.

————. 2006. "Increasing Residual Wage Inequality: Composition Effects, Noisy Data or Rising Demand for Skill?" *American Economic Review* 96(3): 461–498.

Levitt, Steven D., and Stephen J. Dubner. 2005. *Freakonomics: A Rogue Economist Explores the Hidden Side of Everything.* New York: William Morrow.

Long, James. 1999. "Updated Estimates of the Wage Mobility of Minimum Wage Workers." *Journal of Labor Research* 20(4): 493–503.

Luttmer, Erzo F. P. 2007. "Does the Minimum Wage Cause Inefficient Rationing?" *Berkeley Electronic Journal of Economic Analysis and Policy* 7(1): 49.

MacDonald, James, and Daniel Aaronson. 2006. "How Firms Construct Price Changes: Evidence from Restaurant Responses to Increased Minimum Wages." *American Journal of Agricultural Economics* 88(2): 292–307.

Machin, Stephen, Alan Manning, and Lupin Rahman. 2003. "Where the Minimum Wage Bites Hard: Introduction of Minimum Wages to a Low-Wage Sector." *Journal of the European Economic Association* 1(1): 154–180.

Machin, Stephen, and J. Wilson. 2004. "Minimum Wages in a Low-Wage Labour Market: Care Homes in the UK." *Economic Journal* 114(494): C102–C109.

MaCurdy, Thomas, and Frank McIntyre. 2001. *Winners and Losers of Federal and State Minimum Wages.* Washington, DC: Employment Policies Institute.

Maloney, Tim, and Gail Pacheco. 2012. "Assessing the Possible Antipoverty Effects of Recent Rises in Age-Specific Minimum Wages in New Zealand." *Review of Income and Wealth* 58(4): 648–674.

Marks, Mindy S. 2011. "Minimum Wages, Employer-Provided Health Insurance, and the Non-Discrimination Law." *Industrial Relations Review: A Journal of Economy and Society* 50(2): 241–262.

Mascella, Allison, Shahzia Teja, and Brennan S. Thompson. 2009. "Minimum Wage Increases as an Anti-Poverty Policy in Ontario." *Canadian Public Policy* 35(3): 373–379.

Mason, Colin M., Sara Carter, and Stephen K. Tagg. 2006. "The Effect of the National Minimum Wage on the UK Small Business Sector: A Geographical Analysis." *Environment and Planning C: Government and Policy* 24(1): 99–116.

Mastracci, Sharon H., and Joseph Persky. 2008. "Effects of State Minimum Wage Increases on Employment, Hours, and Earnings of Low-Wage Workers in Illinois." *Journal of Regional Analysis and Policy* 38(3): 268–278.

Mattila, J. Peter. 1981. "The Impact of Minimum Wages on Teenage Schooling and on the Part-Time/Full-Time Employment of Youths." In *The Economics of Legal Minimum Wages,* Simon Rottenberg, ed. Washington, DC: American Enterprise Institute, pp. 61–87.

McLaughlin, Colm. 2009. "The Productivity-Enhancing Impacts of the Minimum Wage: Lessons from Denmark and New Zealand." *British Journal of Industrial Relations* 47(2): 327–348.

Mincer, Jacob. 1976. "Unemployment Effects of Minimum Wages." *Journal of Political Economy* 84(4): S87–S104.

Mixon, J. Wilson. 1978. "The Minimum Wage and Voluntary Labor Mobility." *Industrial and Labor Relations Review* 32(1): 67–73.

Morgan, David R., and Kenneth Kickham. 2001. "Children in Poverty: Do State Policies Matter?" *Social Science Quarterly* 82(3): 478–493.

Morgan, Julian, and Annabelle Mourougane. 2005. "What Can Changes in Structural Factors Tell Us about Unemployment in Europe?" *Scottish Journal of Political Economy* 52(1): 75–104.

Mortensen, Dale T., and Christopher A. Pissarides. 1994. "Job Creation and Job Destruction in the Theory of Unemployment." *Review of Economic Studies* 61(3): 397–415.

Moulton, Brent R. 1986. "Random Group Effects and the Precision of Regression Estimates." *Review of Economics and Statistics* 72(2): 334–338.

———. 1990. "An Illustration of a Pitfall in Estimating the Effects of Aggregate Variables in Micro Units." *Journal of Econometrics* 32(3): 385–397.

Mulheirn, Ian. 2008. "The Impact of the 2006 National Minimum Wage Rise on Employment." *Economic and Labour Market Review* 2(9): 30–36.

Müller, Kai-Uwe, and Viktor Steiner. 2008. "Would a Legal Minimum Wage Reduce Poverty? A Microsimulation Study for Germany." IZA Discussion Paper No. 34-91. Bonn: Institute for the Study of Labor.

National Association of Child Care Resource and Referral Agencies. 2011. *Parents and the High Cost of Child Care*. Arlington, VA: National Association of Child Care Resource and Referral Agencies.

Neumark, David. 2001. "The Employment Effects of Minimum Wages: Evidence from a Prespecified Research Design." *Industrial Relations* 40(1): 121–144.

Neumark, David, and Olena Nizalova. 2007. "Minimum Wage Effects in the Longer Run." *Journal of Human Resources* 42(2): 435–452.

Neumark, David, Mark Schweitzer, and William Wascher. 2004. "Minimum Wage Effects throughout the Wage Distribution." *Journal of Human Resources* 39(2): 425–450.

———. 2005. "The Effect of Minimum Wages on the Distribution of Family Incomes: A Nonparametric Analysis." *Journal of Human Resources* 40(4): 867–894.

Neumark, David, and William Wascher. 1992. "Employment Effects of Minimum and Subminimum Wages—Panel Data on State Minimum Wage Laws." *Industrial and Labor Relations Review* 46(1): 55–81.

———. 1994. "Employment Effects of Minimum and Subminimum Wages—Reply." *Industrial and Labor Relations Review* 47(3): 497–512.

———. 1995a. "Minimum Wage Effects on Employment and School Enrollment." *Journal of Business and Economic Statistics* 13(2): 199–206.

———. 1995b. "Minimum Wage Effects on School and Work Transitions of Teenagers." *American Economic Review Papers and Proceedings* 85(2): 244–249.

———. 1996. "The Effects of Minimum Wages on Teenage Employment and Enrollment: Evidence from Matched CPS Surveys." *Research in Labor Economics* 15: 25–63.

———. 2000. "Minimum Wages and Employment: A Case Study of the Fast Food Industry in New Jersey and Pennsylvania: Comment." *American Economic Review* 90(5): 1362–1396.

———. 2001. "Minimum Wages and Training Revisited." *Journal of Labor Economics* 19(3): 563–595.

———. 2002. "State-Level Estimates of Minimum Wage Effects—New Evidence and Interpretations from Disequilibrium Methods." *Journal of Human Resources* 37(1): 35–62.

———. 2003. "Minimum Wages and Skill Acquisition: Another Look at Schooling Effect." *Economics of Education Review* 22(1): 1–10.

———. 2004. "Minimum Wages, Labor Market Institutions, and Youth Employment: A Cross-National Analysis." *Industrial and Labor Relations Review* 57(2): 223–248.

———. 2007. "Minimum Wages and Employment." IZA Discussion Paper No. 2570. Bonn: Institute for the Study of Labor.

———. 2008. *Minimum Wages.* Boston: MIP Press.

———. 2011. "Does a Higher Minimum Wage Enhance the Effectiveness of the Earned Income Tax Credit?" *Industrial and Labor Relations Review* 64(4): 712–746.

Orazem, Peter F., and J. Peter Mattila. 2002. "Minimum Wage Effects on Hours, Employment, and Number of Firms: The Iowa Case." *Journal of Labor Research* 23(1): 3–23.

Orrenius, Pia M., and Madeline Zavodny. 2008. "The Effect of Minimum Wages on Immigrants' Employment and Earnings." *Industrial and Labor Relations Review* 61(4): 544–563.

Orshansky, Mollie. 1963. "Children of the Poor." *Social Security Bulletin* 26(7): 3–13.

———. 1965. "Who's Who among the Poor: A Demographic View of Poverty." *Security Bulletin* 28(7): 3–32.

Pacheco, Gail A. 2011. "Estimating Employment Impacts with Binding Minimum Wage Constraints." *Economic Record* 87(279): 587–602.

Pacheco, Gail A., and Amy A. Cruickshank. 2007. "Minimum Wage Effects on Educational Enrollments in New Zealand." *Economics of Education Review* 26(5): 576–577.

Pacheco, Gail A., and V. Naiker. 2006. "Impact of the Minimum Wage on Expected Profits." *International Review of Applied Economics* 20(4): 469–490.

Page, Marianne E., Joanne Spetz, and Jane Millar. 2005. "Does the Minimum Wage Affect Welfare Caseloads?" *Journal of Policy Analysis and Management* 24(2): 273–295.

Partridge, Mark D., and Jamie S. Partridge. 1998. "Are Teen Unemployment Rates Influenced by State Minimum Wage Laws?" *Growth and Change* 29(4): 359–382.

———. 1999. "Do Minimum Wage Hikes Raise U.S. Long-Term Unemployment? Evidence Using State Minimum Wage Rates." *Regional Studies* 33(8): 713–726.

Pedace, Roberto, and Stephanie Rohn. 2011. "The Impact of Minimum Wages on Unemployment Duration—Estimating the Effects Using the Displaced Worker Survey." *Industrial Relations* 50(1): 57–75.

Pereira, Sonia C. 2003. "The Impact of Minimum Wages on Youth Employment in Portugal." *European Economic Review* 47(2): 229–244.

Persky, Joseph, and Ron Baiman. 2010. "Do State Minimum Wage Laws Reduce Employment? Mixed Messages from Fast Food Outlets in Illinois and Indiana." *Journal of Regional Analysis and Policy* 40(2): 132–142.

Phimister, Euan, and Ioannis Theodossiou. 2009. "Gender Differences in Low Pay Labour Mobility and the National Minimum Wage." *Oxford Economic Papers* 61(S1): i122–i146.

Pinoli, Sara. 2010. "Rational Expectations and the Puzzling No-Effect of the Minimum Wage." IZA Discussion Paper No. 4933. Bonn: Institute for the Study of Labor.

Portugal, Pedro, and Ana Rute Cardoso. 2006. "Disentangling the Minimum Wage Puzzle: An Analysis of Worker Accessions and Separations." *Journal of the European Economic Association* 4(5): 988–1013.

Potter, Nicholas. 2006. "Measuring the Employment Impacts of the Living Wage Ordinance in Santa Fe, New Mexico." Albuquerque, NM: University of New Mexico, Bureau of Business and Economic Research.

Powers, Elizabeth T. 2009. "The Impact of Minimum-Wage Increases: Evidence from Fast-Food Establishments in Illinois and Indiana." *Journal of Labor Research* 30(4): 365–394.

Powers, Elizabeth T., Joseph Persky, and Ron Baiman. 2007. *Impacts of the Illinois Minimum Wage on the Fast Food Industry: A Report to the Russell Sage Foundation.* New York: Russell Sage Foundation.

Ravn, Morten, and Jan R. Sorensen. 1997. "Minimum Wages: Curse or Blessing?" *Research in Labor Economics* 16: 343–368.

Reich, Michael, and Peter Hall. 2001. "A Small Raise for the Bottom." In *The State of California Labor, 2001.* Berkeley, CA: University of California Institute for Labor and Employment, University of California–Berkeley. http://repositories.cdlib.org/ile/scl2001/Section8 (accessed August 2, 2012).

Ritchie, F. 1995. "Accessing the New Earnings Survey Panel: Efficient Techniques and Applications." PhD thesis, University of Stirling, UK.

Robinson, Jonathan, and Helen Wadsworth. 2007. "Impact of the Minimum Wage on the Incidence of Second Job Holding in Britain." *Scottish Journal of Political Economy* 54(4): 553–574.

Ropponen, Olli. 2011. "Reconciling the Evidence of Card and Krueger (1994) and Neumark and Wascher (2000)." *Journal of Applied Econometrics* 26(6): 1051–1057.

Rosen, Sherwin. 1972. "Learning and Experience in the Labor Market." *Journal of Human Resources* 7(3): 326–342.

———. 1974. "Hedonic Prices and Implicit Markets: Product Differentiation in Pure Competition." *Journal of Political Economy* 82(1): 34–55.

Ross, Arthur Max. 1948. *Trade Union Wage Policy.* Berkeley, CA: University of California Press.

Rottenberg, Simon. 1981. *The Economics of Legal Minimum Wages.* Washington, DC: American Enterprise Institute.

Royalty, Anne Beeson. 2001. "Do Minimum Wage Increases Lower the Probability That Low-Skilled Workers Will Receive Fringe Benefits?" JCPR Working Paper No. 222. Chicago: Northwestern University and University of Chicago Joint Center for Poverty Research.

Sabia, Joseph J. 2008. "Minimum Wages and the Economic Well Being of Single Mothers." *Journal of Policy Analysis and Management* 27(4): 848–866.

———. 2009a. "Identifying Minimum Wage Effects: New Evidence from the Monthly CPS Data." *Industrial Relations* 48(2): 311–328.

———. 2009b. "The Effects of Minimum Wage Increases on Retail Employment and Hours: New Evidence from the Monthly CPS Data." *Journal of Labor Research* 30(1): 75–97.

Sabia, Joseph J., and Richard V. Burkhauser. 2010. "Minimum Wages and Poverty: Will a $9.50 Federal Minimum Wage Really Help the Working Poor?" *Southern Economic Journal* 76(3): 592–623.

Sabia, Joseph J., Richard V. Burkhauser, and Benjamin Hansen. 2012. "Are the Effects of Minimum Wage Increases Always Small? New Evidence from a Case Study of New York State." *Industrial and Labor Relations Review* 65(2): 350–376.

Sabia, Joseph J., and Robert B. Nielsen. 2013. "Minimum Wages, Poverty, and

Material Hardship: New Evidence from the SIPP." *Review of Economics of the Household* 1–40. doi: 10.1007/s11150-012-9171-8 (accessed December 17, 2013).

Samson, Lucie. 1994. "The Beveridge Curve and Regional Disparities in Canada." *Applied Economics* 26(10): 936–947.

Sargent, Thomas J. 1987. *Macroeconomic Theory*. 2nd ed. Boston: Academic Press.

Schiller, Bradley R. 1994. "Moving Up: The Training and Wage Gains of Minimum Wage Entrants." *Social Science Quarterly* 75(3): 622–636.

Sen, Anindya, Kathleen Rybczynski, and Corey Van de Waal. 2011. "Teen Employment, Poverty, and the Minimum Wage: Evidence from Canada." *Labour Economics* 18(1): 36–47.

Shannon, Michael. 2011. "The Employment Effects of Lower Minimum Wage Rates for Young Workers: Canadian Evidence." *Industrial Relations* 50(4): 629–655.

Short, Kathleen. 2010. "Who Is Poor? A New Look with the Supplemental Poverty Measure." SEHSD Working Paper No. 2010-15. Washington, DC: U.S. Census Bureau.

Sicilian, Paul, and Adam J. Grossberg. 1993. "Do Legal Minimum Wages Create Rents? A Re-Examination of the Evidence." *Southern Economic Journal* 60(1): 201–209.

Simon, Kosali I., and Robert Kaestner. 2004. "Do Minimum Wages Affect Non-Wage Job Attributes? Evidence on Fringe Benefits." *Industrial and Labor Relations Review* 58(1): 52–70.

Singell, Larry D., Jr., and James R. Terborg. 2007. "Employment Effects of Two Northwest Minimum Wage Initiatives." *Economic Inquiry* 45(1): 40–55.

Skedinger, Per. 2006. "Minimum Wages and Employment in Swedish Hotels and Restaurants." *Labour Economics* 13(2): 259–290.

Smith, Ralph E., and Bruce Vavrichek. 1992. "The Wage Mobility of Minimum Wage Workers." *Industrial and Labor Relations Review* 46(1): 82–88.

Spriggs, William E. 1994. "Changes in the Federal Minimum Wage: A Test of Wage Norms." *Journal of Post Keynesian Economics* 16(2): 221–239.

Stanley, T. D. 2001. "Wheat from Chaff: Meta-Analysis as Quantitative Literature Review." *Journal of Economic Perspectives* 15(3): 131–150.

———. 2005. "Beyond Publication Bias." *Journal of Economic Surveys* 19(3): 309–354.

———. 2008. "Meta-Regression Methods for Detecting and Estimating Empirical Effects in the Presence of Publication Selection." *Oxford Bulletin of Economics and Statistics* 70(1): 102–127.

Stanley, T. D., and Hristos Doucouliagos. 2012. *Meta-Regression Analysis in Economics and Business*. New York: Routledge.

Stanley, T. D., and Stephen B. Jarrell. 1989. "Meta-Regression Analysis: A Quantitative Method of Literature Surveys." *Journal of Economic Surveys* 19(3): 299–308.

Stevans, Lonnie K., and David N. Sessions. 2001. "Minimum Wage Policy and Poverty in the United States." *International Review of Applied Economics* 15(1): 65–75.

Stewart, Mark B. 2002. "Estimating the Impact of the Minimum Wage Using Geographical Wage Variation." *Oxford Bulletin of Economics and Statistics* 64(Supplement): 583–605.

———. 2004a. "The Employment Effects of the National Minimum Wage." *Economic Journal* 114(494): C110–C116.

———. 2004b. "The Impact of the Introduction of the UK Minimum Wage on the Employment Probabilities of Low-Wage Workers." *Journal of the European Economic Association* 2(1): 67–97.

Stewart, Mark B., and Joanna K. Swaffield. 2008. "The Other Margin: Do Minimum Wages Cause Working Hours Adjustments for Low-Wage Workers?" *Economica* 75(297): 148–167.

Stigler, George. 1946. "The Economics of Minimum Wage Legislation." *American Economic Review* 36(3): 358–365.

Summers, Lawrence H. 1985. "Papers and Proceedings of the Forty-Third Annual Meeting American Finance Association, Dallas, Texas, December 28–30, 1984." *Journal of Finance* 40(3): 633–635.

Sutherland, Holly. 2001. "The National Minimum Wage and In-Work Poverty." DAE Working Paper No. MU0102. Cambridge: University of Cambridge.

Taylor, Beck A., and Jonathan K. Arnold. 1999. "Another Look at Minimum Wages and Business Failure Rates." *Journal of Economic Issues* 33(4): 1005–1010.

Thompson, Jeffrey P. 2009. "Using Local Labor Market Data to Reexamine the Employment Effects of the Minimum Wage." *Industrial and Labor Relations Review* 62(3): 343–366.

Tulip, Peter. 2004. "Do Minimum Wages Raise the NAIRU?" *Topics in Macroeconomics* 4(1): 1163.

Turner, Mark D., and Berna Demiralp. 2001. "Do Higher Minimum Wages Harm Minority and Inner-City Teens?" *Review of Black Political Economy* 28(4): 95–121.

U.S. Bureau of Labor Statistics. 1973. "Employment and Earnings for the United States, 1909–1972." Bulletin 131 Z-9. Washington, DC: U.S. Government Printing Office.

U.S. Census Bureau. 2006. "Poverty Thresholds." Washington, DC: Census Bureau. http://www.census.gov/hhes/www/poverty/data/threshld/thresh06 .html (accessed July 12, 2012).

Van den Berg, Gerard J., and Geert Ridder. 1998. "An Empirical Equilibrium Search Model of the Labor Market." *Econometrica* 66(5): 1183–1221.

Vella, Francis. 1998. "Estimating Models with Sample Selection Bias: A Survey." *Journal of Human Resources* 33(1): 127–169.

Vedder, Richard, and Lowell Gallaway. 2002. "The Minimum Wage and Poverty among Full-Time Workers." *Journal of Labor Research* 23(1): 41–49.

Wadsworth, Jonathan. 2010. "Did the National Minimum Wage Affect UK Prices?" *Fiscal Studies* 31(1): 81–120.

Waltman, J., Allan B. McBride, and N. Camhout. 1998. "Minimum Wage Increases and the Business Failure Rate." *Journal of Economic Issues* 32(1): 219–223.

Warren, John Robert. 2003. "State-Level High School Completion Rates: Concepts, Measures and Trends." *Educational Policy Analysis Archives* 13(51): 1–35.

Warren, John Robert, and Andrew Halpern-Manners. 2007. "Is the Glass Emptying or Filling Up? Reconciling Divergent Trends in High School Completion and Dropout." *Educational Researcher* 36(6): 335–343.

Warren, John Robert, and Caitlin Hamrock. 2010. "The Effect of Minimum Wage Rates on High School Completion." *Social Forces* 88(3): 1379–1392.

Webb, Sidney, and Beatrice Webb. 1897. *Industrial Democracy.* London: Longmans.

Wessels, Walter. 1980. *Minimum Wages, Fringe Benefits, and Working Conditions.* Washington, DC: American Enterprise Institute for Public Policy Research.

———. 2005. "Does the Minimum Wage Drive Teenagers Out of the Labor Force?" *Journal of Labor Research* 26(1): 169–176.

———. 2007. "A Reexamination of Card and Krueger's State-Level Study of the Minimum Wage." *Journal of Labor Research* 28(1): 135–146.

Williams, Nicolas, and Jeffrey A. Mills. 2001. "The Minimum Wage and Teenage Employment: Evidence from Time Series." *Applied Economics* 33(3): 285–300.

Wolfson, Paul. 2011. "Phantom Results from Panel Regressions." SSRN Working Paper. Social Science Research Network. http://ssrn.com/ abstract=1839718 (accessed November 12, 2013).

Wolfson, Paul, and Dale Belman. 2001. "The Minimum Wage, Employment, and the AS-IF Methodology: A Forecasting Approach to Evaluating the Minimum Wage." *Empirical Economics* 26(3): 487–514.

————. 2004. "The Minimum Wage: Consequences for Prices and Quantities in Low-Wage Labor Markets." *Journal of Business and Economic Statistics* 22(3): 296–311.

Yuen, Terence. 2003. "The Effect of Minimum Wages on Youth Employment in Canada: A Panel Study." *Journal of Human Resources* 38(3): 647–672.

Zavodny, Madeline. 2000. "The Effect of the Minimum Wage on Employment and Hours." *Labour Economics* 7(6): 729–750.

Authors

Dale Belman is a professor in the School of Human Resources and Labor Relations at Michigan State University. He conducts research on unions and labor market regulation. His prior work on the minimum wage has focused on the application of time-series methods to estimate the effect of the minimum wage on earnings, employment, and hours in low-wage industries. Belman has also written about the construction industry, truckers and the trucking industry, public-sector employment, and low-wage work. He received his master's and doctoral degrees at the University of Wisconsin, Madison, and his bachelor's degree from Bowdoin College. He is president of the Institute for Construction Economics Research.

Paul J. Wolfson is on the research faculty at the Tuck School of Business at Dartmouth, where he has been involved in a wide variety of research projects, including studies of the effects of the minimum wage. He was previously the assistant director of the Retail Food Industry Center at the University of Minnesota, and before that he taught at the Carlson School of Management at the University of Minnesota; the Kellogg Graduate School of Management at Northwestern University; and the economics department at the University of Wisconsin, Milwaukee. He received his master's and doctoral degrees from Yale University and his bachelor's degree from the University of Chicago.

Author Index

Note: Italic letters *f, t, n* following a page number indicate a figure, table, or note. Double italics refer to more than one such item on that page.

Aaronson, Daniel, 62*t,* 70–71, 76, 243*t,* 246, 249, 257*nn*54–55, 384*t,* 385–386, 387–388, 389, 399*n*2, 425, 437
Abadie, Alberto, 46, 425
Abowd, John M., 345, 415, 425
Acemoglu, Daron, 283, 285*t,* 286–287, 288, 298*n*30, 425
Ada, H., 417, 425
Addison, John T., 37, 50, 51, 62*t,* 64, 69, 70, 71–72, 73*t,* 74, 77, 93, 95*t,* 111*n*27, 113–114*n*46, 152*t,* 213–216, 214*t,* 217, 218*t,* 222, 251, 316, 318*t,* 373*t,* 380*n*7, 425–426
Agarwal, Sumit, 243*t,* 246, 249, 257*nn*54–55, 425
Ahn, Tom, 15, 38, 40*t,* 42–43, 51, 75, 91, 108, 380*n*7, 426
Akerlof, George A., 75, 410, 426
Allegretto, Sylvia A., 30, 38, 40*t,* 44–45, 50–51, 54, 61, 74, 101, 105, 107, 108, 110–111*n*16, 111*n*27, 112*n*35, 114*n*51, 120, 121*t,* 122–123, 130, 141, 143*n*14, 152*t,* 201, 202*t,* 217, 426
Alpert, William T., 289, 292*t,* 294, 426
Anderson, John, 215*t,* 216, 254*n*30, 426
Anderson, William L., 267*t,* 276, 279, 430
Andersson, Fredrik, 415, 425
Andrews, John B., 237, 430
Angrist, Joshua D., 110*n*12, 426
Arcidiacono, Peter, 15, 38, 40*t,* 42–43, 51, 75, 91, 108, 380*n*7, 426
Arnold, Jonathan K., 399*n*12, 443
Arulampalam, Wiji, 283, 285*t,* 286, 288, 426
Autor, David H., 305*t,* 307, 337*n*3, 426–427

Baiman, Ron, 63*t,* 64–65, 124, 126*t,* 127–128, 131, 440
Baker, Michael, 2, 103, 104, 106, 266*t,* 269, 274, 275, 276, 277–278, 283, 285*t,* 286, 288, 402, 427
Bazen, Stephen, 33, 34*t,* 36, 47, 48*t,* 49, 50–51, 110–111*n*16, 152*t,* 427
Bell, David, 425
Belman, Dale, 3, 72, 73*t,* 76–77, 105–106, 126*t,* 127, 129–130, 131, 141, 152*t,* 209*t,* 211, 251, 299*n*41, 402, 427, 444
Benjamin, Dwayne, 2, 103, 104, 106, 402, 427
Bernstein, Jared, 7, 8*t,* 242*t,* 245, 249, 427, 435
Bertrand, Marianne, 28, 29–30, 104, 107, 110*n*11, 115*n*60, 119, 155, 165, 179*n*8, 263, 271, 277, 316–317, 320*t,* 372*t*–373*t,* 380*n*7, 381*n*8, 402, 427
Bhaskar, V., 75, 428
Bishop, John A., 322*t,* 433
Bivens, Josh, 301, 427
Bjelland, Melissa, 345, 427
Blackburn, McKinley L., 37, 50, 51, 62*t,* 64, 69, 70, 71–72, 73*t,* 74, 77, 111*n*27, 113–114*n*46, 152*t,* 213–216, 214*t,* 217, 218*t,* 222, 251, 316, 318*t,* 425–426
Böckerman, Petri, 81*t,* 114–115*n*54, 132*t,* 253*n*15, 363*n*19, 423*n*1, 427
Bodvarsson, Orn, 215*t,* 216, 254*n*30, 426
Booth, Alison L., 283, 285*t,* 286, 288, 426
Bouvet, Florence, 381*n*8, 428
Brown, Charles, 1, 102, 109*n*1, 109*n*5, 176, 428
Bryan, Mark L., 283, 285*t,* 286, 288, 426
Burdett, Kenneth, 75, 348, 351, 360, 373*t,* 428

Burkhauser, Richard V., 38, 39, 40*t*, 46, 47, 50–51, 54, 84, 142*n*3, 254*n*25, 312, 318*t*–319*t*, 428, 441
Burton, Michael, 224*t*, 227, 255–256*n*40, 428
Butcher, Tim, 225*t*, 227–228, 229, 243*t*, 247, 249, 428

Cameron, A. Colin, 30, 110*n*13, 317, 428
Camhout, N., 394*t*, 396, 399*n*12, 444
Campolieti, Michele, 77, 79, 81*t*, 82–84, 92–93, 108, 112*n*35, 114*nn*51–52, 152*t*, 254*n*25, 266*t*, 274, 275, 316, 319*t*, 428–429
Card, David, 3, 22–29, 33, 36, 50, 61, 64–65, 66, 67, 89, 103, 107, 110*nn*9–10, 116–117*n*78, 116*nn*74–75, 124, 142*n*2, 147, 212, 290, 304*t*, 306, 385, 393–395, 394*t*, 421, 423*n*1, 424*n*12, 429
Cardoso, Ana Rute, 78, 80*t*, 86–88, 111*n*18, 114*n*53, 115*n*65, 132*t*, 201, 202*t*, 204, 344, 346*t*, 348, 351–352, 352*t*, 353*t*, 355, 357, 360, 362*n*10, 363*n*14–15, 363*n*17, 376, 440
Carmei, Gaetano, 372*t*, 381*n*14, 429
Carrington, William J., 327–330, 328*t*, 330*f*, 331, 336, 429
Carroll, Marilyn, 390, 434
Carter, Sara, 394*t*, 395–396, 437
Chaplin, Duncan, 267*t*, 269, 276, 277, 429
Chen, Xiao, 179*n*3, 429
Clark, Tom S., 180*n*11, 430
Clauson, Annette, 310, 430
Commons, John R., 237
Connolly, Sara, 133–134, 135*t*, 139, 144*n*21, 145*n*26, 430
Cotti, Chad D., 37, 50–51, 62*t*, 64, 69, 70, 71–72, 73*t*, 74, 77, 111*n*27, 113–114*n*46, 152*t*, 213–216, 214*t*, 217, 218*t*, 222, 251, 426
Couch, Kenneth A., 121*t*, 142*n*3, 254*n*25, 312, 428, 430
Crofton, Stephanie O., 267*t*, 276, 279, 430

Cruickshank, Amy A., 266*t*, 269, 275–276, 440
Cunningham, James, 264*t*, 269–271, 279, 295–296*n*6, 430
Currie, Janet, 185, 232–235, 233*t*, 256*nn*43–44, 430, 442

Davis, Steven J., 345, 430
De Fraja, Gianni, 358, 360, 430
de Linde Leonard, M., 147, 150–151, 430
DeFina, Robert H., 316, 318*t*
Demiralp, Berna, 40*t*, 443
Diamond, Alexis, 425
Dickens, Richard, 209*t*, 224*t*, 227, 239, 241*t*, 245, 249, 251, 431
DiNardo, John, 303, 304*t*, 306, 337*n*2, 431
Dodson, Marvin E., III, 73*t*, 152*t*, 431
Dolton, Peter, 78, 94*t*, 97, 115*n*57, 116*n*67, 305*t*, 308, 431
Donald, Stephen G., 29–30, 46–47, 61, 65, 71, 107, 110*n*14, 124, 127, 155, 165, 179*n*8, 385, 402, 431
Dorsett, Richard Patrick, 224*t*, 227, 255–256*n*40, 428
Doucouliagos, Hristos, 147, 149–151, 178, 179*n*4, 430, 431, 442
Draca, Mirko, 255*n*36, 394*t*, 397–398
Drazen, Allan, 75, 431
Dube, Arindrajit, 30, 38, 40*t*, 44–45, 50–51, 54, 61, 62*t*, 64, 65–69, 74, 101, 105, 107–108, 110–111*n*16, 111*nn*18–19, 111*n*25, 111*n*27, 112*n*35, 113*nn*42–43, 113–114*n*46, 114*n*51, 114*n*53, 120, 121*t*, 122–124, 126*t*, 127, 130–131, 141, 143*n*14, 153*t*, 201, 202*t*, 212–213, 214*t*, 217, 293*t*, 294, 344, 346*t*, 348, 351, 353–355, 354*t*, 356–357, 360, 362*n*10, 363*nn*17–18, 377, 384*t*, 385, 423*n*1, 426, 431–432
Dubner, Stephen J., 410, 437
Duff, Martha A., 362*n*2, 433
Duflo, Ester, 28–30, 104, 107, 110*n*11, 115*n*60, 119, 155, 165, 179*n*8, 263,

Duflo, Ester, *cont.*
    271, 277, 316, 317, 320*t*, 372*t*–373*t*,
    380*n*7, 381*n*8, 402, 427
Dunlop, John T., 237, 432

Easton, Todd, 204–205, 206*t*, 432
Eckstein, Zvi, 38, 40*t*, 43–44, 51, 52*t*, 60,
    111*n*24, 432
Edsall, Thomas B., 337*n*1, 432
Ehrenberg, Ronald G., 1, 115*n*56, 264*t*,
    268, 270–271, 279, 295*n*1, 432
Elliott, Robert F., 425
Ender, Philip B., 179*n*3, 429
Evans, Thomas D., 362*n*2, 433
Even, William Edward, 62*t*, 68–69,
    113*n*45, 113–114*n*46, 126*t*, 127–129,
    131, 152*t*, 215*t*, 216–217, 329*t*, 331–
    333, 332*t*, 336–337, 432

Fairris, David, 283, 285*t*, 286, 288, 432
Falk, Armin, 196, 237, 240*t*, 250, 432
Fallick, Bruce, 185, 232–235, 233*t*,
    256*nn*43–44, 327–331, 328*t*, 330*f*,
    336, 345, 362*n*2, 422, 427, 429, 430,
    432–433
Fang, Tony, 77, 79, 81*t*, 82–84, 92–93,
    94*t*, 101, 108, 112*n*35, 114*nn*51–52,
    115*n*63, 266*t*, 274–275, 428, 433
Fehr, Ernst, 196, 237, 240*t*, 250, 432
Fisher, Gordon M., 309, 338*n*7, 433
Fleischman, Charles A., 345, 362*n*2,
    432–433
Flinn, Christopher J., 15, 38–39, 40*t*, 42,
    51, 75, 91, 111*n*23, 371, 372*t*, 379,
    380*nn*6–7, 433
Formby, John P., 322*t*, 433
Fortin, Nicole M., 303, 304*t*, 337*n*2,
    373*t*, 431
Fortin, Pierre, 373*t*, 433
Fougére, Denis, 383, 384*t*, 386–390, 433
Frazis, Harley J., 362*n*2, 433
Freeman, Richard B., 2, 433
French, Eric, 62*t*, 70–71, 76, 243*t*, 246,
    249, 257*nn*54–55, 399*n*2, 425

Galbraith, John Kenneth, 198, 263, 433
Galindo-Rueda, Fernando, 78, 100*t*,
    116*n*72, 433
Gallaway, Lowell, 126*t*, 127, 130–131,
    142, 144*n*17, 316–317, 319*t*, 444
Gautier, Erwan, 383, 384*t*, 386–390, 433
Ge, Suqin, 38, 40*t*, 43–44, 51, 52*t*, 60,
    111*n*24, 432
Gelbach, Jonah B., 30, 110*n*13, 317, 428
Gelman, Andrew, 180*n*11, 430
Georgiadis, Andreus, 220–222, 221*t*,
    344, 346*t*, 348–349, 355, 433–434
Gilroy, Curtis, 102, 109*n*1, 109*n*5, 176,
    428
Giuliano, Laura, 72, 73*t*, 75, 77, 91, 108,
    142*n*2, 218*t*, 219, 344, 346*t*, 348,
    356–357, 363*n*20, 423*n*1, 434
Glenn, A. J., 312, 428
Greene, William H., 179*n*5, 434
Gregory, Mary, 133–134, 135*t*, 139,
    144*n*21, 145*n*26, 430
Grimshaw, Damian, 390, 434
Grogger, Jeffrey T., 52*t*, 316, 318*t*, 434
Groshen, Erika, 299*n*41, 427
Grossberg, Adam J., 282–283, 287,
    297*n*24, 298*n*27, 298*n*33, 333, 335*t*,
    337, 346*t*–347*t*, 348, 358, 359–360,
    360–361, 363–364*n*23, 377, 434, 442
Grossman, Jean Baldwin, 237, 239, 241*t*,
    249, 256*n*50, 434
Gundersen, Craig, 316, 318*t*
Gunderson, Morley, 77, 79, 81*t*, 82–84,
    92–93, 94*t*, 101, 108, 112*n*35,
    114*nn*51–52, 115*n*63, 152*t*, 254*n*25,
    266*t*, 274–275, 316, 319*t*, 428–429,
    433

Hainmueller, Jens, 46, 425
Hall, Peter, 223–226, 224*t*, 226*f*, 243*t*,
    245–246, 255*n*38, 256*n*51, 441
Halpern-Manners, Andrew, 112*n*31, 444
Haltiwanger, John, 345, 427, 430
Hammerton, John Alexander, 17, 434
Hamrock, Caitlin, 267*t*, 276, 278, 444
Hansen, Benjamin, 38–39, 40*t*, 46–47,
    50–51, 54, 84, 441

Hansen, Christian B., 28, 30, 317, 434–435
Harvey, Andrew, 242*t*, 245, 249, 435
Hashimoto, Masanori, 281–282, 284*t*, 297*n*24, 435
Hill, Jennifer, 180*n*11, 430
Hirsch, Barry T., 62*t*, 71, 143*n*11, 237, 239, 240*t*–241*t*, 256*n*49, 435
Hoffman, Saul D., 52*t*–53*t*, 435
Holzer, Harry J., 358–359, 435
Horrigan, Michael W., 322*t*, 435
Huffman, David, 237, 432
Hyatt, Henry R., 345, 435
Hyslop, Dean, 78, 80*t*, 90, 91, 115*n*60, 131–133, 132*t*, 152*t*, 266*t*, 268, 274–275, 279, 371, 372*t*, 380*n*7, 399*n*11, 440, 446

Imbens, Guido W., 110*n*12, 435

Jarrell, Stephen B., 147, 443
Johnson, David S., 9, 435
Jones, Melanie K., 334, 335*t*, 337, 435
Jones, Richard J., 334, 335*t*, 337, 435

Kaestner, Robert, 290–291, 292*t*, 294–295, 298–299*n*36, 442
Kalenkoski, Charlene M., 47, 48*t*, 49–50, 108, 435
Katz, Lawrence F., 21–24, 116*nn*74–75, 116–117*n*78, 212, 305*t*, 307, 337*n*3, 358–359, 421, 423*n*1, 424*n*12, 426, 429, 435
Kaufman, Bruce, E., 62*t*, 71, 143*n*11, 237, 239, 240*t*–241*t*, 256*n*46, 256*n*49, 407, 412*n*2, 435, 436,
Ke, C., 52*t*, 435
Kearney, Melissa S., 305*t*, 307, 337*n*3, 426
Keil, Manfred, 33, 34*t*, 153*t*, 373*t*, 433, 436
Kickham, Kenneth, 316, 319*t*, 438
Kim, Hoseong, 322*t*, 433
Kloek, Teun, 28, 436
Knabe, Andreas, 322*t*, 436

Kohen, Andrew, 102, 109*n*1, 109*n*5, 176, 428
Kramarz, Francis, 78, 94*t*, 98, 116*nn*68–69, 323, 324*t*, 436
Krashinsky, Harry, 204–205, 206*t*, 208, 436
Krueger, Alan B., 3, 22, 23–29, 33, 36, 50, 61, 64–67, 89, 103, 107, 110*nn*9–10, 116*nn*74–75, 116–117*n*78, 124, 142*n*2, 147, 212, 290, 358, 359, 385, 393–395, 394*t*, 421, 423*n*1, 424*n*12, 429, 435

Lacombe, Donald J., 47, 48*t*, 49–50, 108, 435
Lam, Katherine, 225*t*, 227–229, 228*f*, 230*ff*, 231*ff*, 244*t*, 248–249, 436
Landon, Stuart, 267*t*, 269, 276–277, 436
Lang, Kevin, 29–30, 46–47, 61, 65, 71, 107, 110*n*14, 124, 127, 155, 165, 179*n*8, 385, 402, 431
Laroque, Guy, 78, 94*t*, 97–98, 324*t*, 436
Le Bihan, Hervé, 383, 384*t*, 386–390, 433
Le Gallo, Julie, 33, 34*t*, 36, 47, 48*t*, 49, 50–51, 110–111*n*16, 427
Lee, Byron, 316, 319*t*, 428
Lee, Chinkook, 383, 384*t*, 389–390, 436
Lee, David S., 304*t*, 306–308, 337*n*3, 436
Lee, Wang-Sheng, 78, 80*t*, 89–90, 115*n*59, 446
Leighton, Linda, 282, 284*t*–285*t*, 287, 297*n*24, 298*n*26, 346*t*, 348, 358, 436
Lemieux, Thomas, 303, 304*t*–305*t*, 306–307, 337*n*2, 431, 436–437
Lester, T. William, 30, 62*t*, 65–68, 69, 74, 101, 105, 107, 108, 111*n*25, 111*nn*18–19, 113–114*n*46, 113*nn*42–43, 114*n*53, 152*t*, 201, 202*t*, 212–213, 214*t*, 344, 346*t*, 348, 351, 353–355, 354*t*, 357, 360, 362*n*10, 363*n*17, 377, 431–432
Levitt, Steven D., 410, 437
Lin, James, 7, 8*t*, 427

Linzer, Drew A., 180*n*11, 430
Long, James, 328*t*, 331, 332*t*, 337, 437
Luttmer, Erzo F. P., 51, 52*t*, 58–60,
   112*n*38, 242*t*, 245, 249, 437

MacDonald, James, 70–71, 384*t*, 386–
   388, 389, 399*n*2, 425, 437
Machin, Stephen, 78, 99–101, 100*t*,
   116*n*70, 127, 139, 140*t*, 141–142,
   209*t*, 220, 221*t*, 255*nn*35–36, 348–
   349, 392, 394*t*, 397–398, 423*n*1, 431,
   437
Macpherson, David A., 62*t*, 68–69,
   113*n*45, 113–114*n*46, 126*t*, 127–129,
   131, 152*t*, 215*t*, 216–217, 329*t*, 331–
   333, 332*t*, 336–337, 432
MaCurdy, Thomas, 383, 384*t*, 390, 437
Maloney, Tim, 320*t*, 325–326, 338*n*14,
   437
Manning, Alan, 78, 99–101, 100*t*,
   116*n*70, 127, 139, 140*t*, 141–142,
   209*t*, 220, 221*t*, 224*t*, 227, 239, 241*t*,
   245, 249, 251, 255*n*35, 305*t*, 307,
   348–349, 392, 423*n*1, 426–427, 431,
   437
Marcus, Alan J., 264*t*, 268, 270, 271,
   279, 432
Marimoutou, Velayoudon, 47, 48*t*, 49,
   152*t*, 427
Marks, Mindy S., 290–291, 292*t*,
   294–295, 298–299*n*36, 299*nn*42–43,
   299*n*45, 437
Mascella, Allison, 322*t*, 437
Mason, Colin M., 394*t*, 395–396, 437
Mastracci, Sharon H., 53*t*, 110*n*14, 125*t*,
   437
Mattila, J. Peter, 72, 73*t*, 74, 77, 126*t*,
   127, 129, 131, 142, 153*t*, 218*t*, 219,
   264*t*, 269–271, 279, 295–296*n*6, 394*t*,
   396–397, 398, 423*n*1, 437, 439
Mauro, Luciano, 372*t*, 381*n*14, 429
McBride, Allan B., 394*t*, 396, 399*n*12,
   444
McEntarfer, E., 345, 427
McIntyre, Frank, 383, 384*t*, 390, 437
McKinney, Kevin L., 415, 425

Metcalf, David, 209*t*, 431
Millar, Jane, 316, 319*t*, 440
Miller, Douglas L., 30, 110*n*13, 317, 428
Mills, Jeffrey A., 47–49, 48*t*, 105, 444
Mincer, Jacob, 282, 284*t*–285*t*, 287,
   297*n*24, 298*n*26, 346*t*, 348, 358, 365,
   436, 438
Mincy, Ronald B., 322*t*, 435
Mitchell, Michael, 179*n*3, 429
Mixon, J. Wilson, 358, 363*n*21, 438
Morgan, David R., 316, 319*t*, 438
Morgan, Julian, 381*n*8, 428
Mortensen, Dale T., 75, 88, 348–349,
   351, 360, 428, 438
Moulton, Brent R., 28, 84, 107, 363–
   364*n*23, 373*t*, 402, 438
Mourougane, Annabelle, 381*n*8, 428
Mulheirn, Ian, 78, 94*t*, 96, 438
Mullainathan, Sendhil, 28–30, 104,
   107, 110*n*11, 115*n*60, 119, 155, 165,
   179*n*8, 263, 271, 277, 316–317, 320*t*,
   372*t*–373*t*, 380*n*7, 381*n*8, 402, 427
Müller, Kai-Uwe, 322*t*, 438
Murphy, Philip D., 334, 335*t*, 337, 435

Naidu, Suresh, 61, 62*t*, 64, 113–114*n*46,
   124, 126*t*, 127, 131, 152*t*, 212, 214*t*,
   293*t*, 294, 344, 346*t*, 348, 355,
   363*n*18, 384*t*, 385, 423*n*1, 432
Naiker, V., 394*t*, 395, 440
National Association of Child Care
   Resource and Referral Agencies, 310,
   438
Neumark, David, 3, 21–29, 32–33, 34*t*,
   36, 38–39, 40*t*, 45, 50–51, 52*t*–53*t*,
   55–56, 59–61, 78, 81*t*, 97, 103–104,
   106, 108, 109*n*5, 110*n*9, 110*n*15,
   111*n*27, 112*n*34, 112*nn*29–30,
   113*n*39, 116*n*73, 116*nn*75–76,
   122–124, 125*t*, 127–128, 141, 143*n*9,
   153*t*, 201, 203*t*, 204, 207*t*, 208, 210,
   252*n*12, 253*n*15, 254*n*27, 265*t*–266*t*,
   268–269, 271–274, 277, 316,
   318*t*–319*t*, 321, 323, 324*t*, 333–334,
   339*n*18, 372*t*, 380*n*7, 423*n*1, 424*n*13,
   438–439

Nizalova, Olena, 34*t*, 38, 51, 52*t*, 59–60, 113*n*39, 116*n*73, 124, 125*t*, 143*n*9, 253*n*15, 333–334, 438

Orazem, Peter F., 72, 73*t*, 74, 77, 126*t*, 127, 129, 131, 142, 153*t*, 218*t*, 219, 394*t*, 396–398, 423*n*1, 439
Ormerod, Catrin, 225*t*, 227–229, 228*f*, 230*ff*, 231*ff*, 244*t*, 248, 249, 436
O'Roark, Brian, 383, 384*t*, 389–390, 436
Orrenius, Pia M., 38, 50–51, 52*t*, 54–55, 60, 120, 121*t*, 124, 125*t*, 130–131, 141, 153*t*, 201, 202*t*, 204, 439
Orshansky, Mollie, 309, 439
Ozturk, Orgul Demet, 93, 95*t*, 152*t*, 373*t*, 380*n*7, 426

Pacheco, Gail, 78, 80*t*, 90–92, 115*n*61, 132*t*, 133, 144*n*19, 266*t*, 269, 275–276, 320*t*, 325–326, 338*n*14, 394*t*, 395, 437, 439–440
Page, Marianne E., 316, 319*t*, 440
Pape, Andreus D., 267*t*, 269, 276–277, 429
Partridge, Jamie S., 368, 370, 372*t*, 379*n*1, 381*n*9, 440
Partridge, Mark D., 368, 370, 372*t*, 379*n*1, 381*n*9, 440
Pedace, Roberto, 283, 285*t*, 286, 288, 372*t*, 375–376, 379, 382*n*16, 432, 440
Pereira, Sonia, 78, 80*t*, 86–87, 100*t*, 116*n*72, 132*t*, 153*t*, 253*n*15, 440, 433
Persky, Joseph, 53*t*, 63*t*, 64–65, 110*n*14, 124, 125*t*, 126*t*, 127–128, 131, 437, 440
Petrongolo, Barbara, 38, 40*t*, 43–44, 51, 52*t*, 60, 111*n*24, 432
Philippon, Thomas, 78, 94*t*, 98, 116*nn*68–69, 323, 324*t*, 436
Phimister, Euan, 329*t*, 334, 336, 440
Pinoli, Sara, 78, 80*t*, 88–89, 93, 102, 105, 107, 123, 344, 346*t*, 348, 349, 350–351, 355, 357, 362*nn*6–9, 402, 440
Pischke, Jörn-Steffen, 110*n*12, 283, 285*t*, 286–288, 298*n*30, 425, 426

Pissarides, Christopher A., 88, 348, 351, 438
Portugal, Pedro, 78, 80*t*, 86–88, 111*n*18, 114*n*53, 115*n*65, 132*t*, 201, 202*t*, 204, 344, 346*t*, 348, 351–352, 352*t*, 353*t*, 355, 357, 360, 362*n*10, 363*n*14–15, 363*n*17, 376, 440
Potter, Nicholas, 73*t*, 153*t*, 431
Powers, Elizabeth T., 63*t*, 64–65, 124, 126*t*, 127–128, 131, 143*n*13, 440

Rahman, Lupin, 78, 99–101, 100*t*, 116*n*70, 127, 139, 140*t*, 141–142, 220, 221*t*, 255*n*35, 348–349, 392, 423*n*1, 437
Ravn, Morten, 295*n*3, 441
Rawe, Emily C., 267*t*, 276, 279, 430
Reich, Michael, 30, 38, 40*t*, 44–45, 50–51, 54, 61, 74, 101, 105, 107, 108, 110–111*n*16, 111*n*25, 111*n*27, 111*nn*18–19, 112*n*35, 113–114*n*46, 113*nn*42–43, 114*n*51, 114*n*53, 120, 121*t*, 122–123, 124, 126*t*, 127, 130, 131, 141, 143*n*14, 152*t*, 201, 202*t*, 212–213, 214*t*, 223–226, 224*t*, 226*f*, 243*t*, 245–246, 255*n*38, 256*n*51, 293*t*, 294, 344, 346*t*, 348, 351, 353, 354–355, 354*t*, 356, 357, 360, 362*n*10, 363*nn*17–18, 377, 384*t*, 385, 423*n*1, 426, 431–432, 441
Richie, F., 423*n*1, 441
Riddell, Chris, 152*t*, 254*n*25, 429
Ridder, Geert, 373*t*, 374, 375, 444
Ritchie, Felix, 225*t*, 227–229, 228*f*, 230*ff*, 231*ff*, 244*t*, 248, 249, 436
Roberts, Elizabeth, 425
Robertson, Donald, 33, 34*t*, 153*t*, 436
Robison, Edwin L., 362*n*2, 433
Robison, Jonathan, 133–134, 135*t*, 138, 139, 141, 443
Roemer, Marc, 415, 425
Rogers, John M., 9, 435
Rohn, Stephanie, 372*t*, 375–376, 379, 382*n*16, 440
Ropponen, Olli, 63*t*, 441

Rosazza-Bondibene, Chiara, 78, 94*t*, 97, 115*n*57, 116*n*67, 305*t*, 308, 431
Rosen, Sherwin, 295*n*1, 412*n*2, 441
Ross, Arthur Max, 237, 441
Rottenberg, Simon, 297*n*23, 441
Royalty, Anne Beeson, 299*n*38, 441
Rybczynski, Kathleen, 316, 317, 319*t*, 442

Sabia, Joseph J., 38–39, 40*t*, 46–47, 50–51, 52*t*, 54, 60–61, 72, 73*t*, 74, 77, 84, 98, 111*n*19, 111*n*21, 111*n*27, 112*n*36, 113*n*40, 113*n*43, 120–122, 121*t*, 123–124, 125*t*, 126*t*, 127, 129–131, 141–142, 142–143*n*5, 143*n*8, 143*n*14, 153*t*, 201, 206*t*–207*t*, 210, 218*t*, 219, 222, 254*n*27, 316–317, 318*t*–320*t*, 321, 441–442
Salanie, Bernard, 78, 94*t*, 97–98, 324*t*, 436
Samson, Lucie, 377, 378*t*, 382*n*18, 442
Sargent, Thomas J., 116*n*77, 442
Schiller, Bradley R., 282, 338*n*15, 442
Schluter, Gerald, 383, 384*t*, 389–390, 436
Schöb, Ronnie, 322*t*, 436
Schweitzer, Mark, 53*t*, 153*t*, 252*n*12, 253*n*15, 316, 319*t*, 339*n*18, 424*n*13, 438
Scott, Anthony, 425
Sen, Anindya, 316–317, 319*t*, 442
Sessions, David N., 316, 319*t*, 443
Shannon, Michael, 81*t*, 132*t*, 442
Short, Kathleen, 338*n*8, 442
Sicilian, Paul, 282–283, 287, 297*n*24, 298*n*27, 298*n*33, 333, 335*t*, 337, 346*t*–347*t*, 348, 358–361, 363–364*n*23, 377, 434, 442
Simon, Kosali I., 290–291, 292*t*, 294–295, 298–299*n*36, 442
Singell, Larry D., Jr., 63*t*, 68, 69–70, 153*t*, 377, 378*t*, 442
Skedinger, Per, 100*t*, 114*n*53, 344, 347*t*, 348, 355–356, 363*n*19, 423*n*1, 442
Sloane, Peter J., 334, 335*t*, 337, 435

Smith, Christopher L., 305*t*, 307, 426–427
Smith, Ralph E., 328*t*, 331, 332*t*, 337, 442
Smith, Robert S., 115*n*56, 295*n*1, 432
Sorensen, Jan R., 295*n*3, 441
Spetz, Joanne, 316, 319*t*, 440
Spletzer, James R., 345, 435
Spriggs, William E., 237–239, 240*t*, 249, 251, 256*n*48, 442
Stanger, Shuchita, 2, 103–104, 106, 402, 427
Stanley, T. D., 147–151, 157, 178, 179*n*1, 179*n*4, 430–432, 442–443
Steiner, Viktor, 322*t*, 438
Stephens, Bryce E., 415, 425
Stevans, Lonnie K., 316, 319*t*, 443
Stewart, Mark B., 78–80, 85–86, 94*t*, 96–97, 115*n*58, 133–138, 135*t*, 139, 141, 142*n*3, 144–145*n*22, 144*n*21, 145*nn*23–24, 232, 233*t*, 234–235, 243*t*, 247, 249, 443
Stigler, George, 3, 443
Stillman, Steven, 78, 80*t*, 90–91, 115*n*60, 131–133, 132*t*, 152*t*, 266*t*, 268, 274–275, 279, 371, 372*t*, 380*n*7, 399*n*11, 446
Suardi, Sandy, 78, 80*t*, 89–90, 115*n*59, 446
Summers, Lawrence H., 407, 443
Sutherland, Holly, 322*t*, 443
Swaffield, Joanna K., 133–139, 135*t*, 141, 142*n*3, 144–145*n*22, 144*n*21, 145*nn*23–24, 443
Symons, James, 33, 34*t*, 153*t*, 373*t*, 433, 436

Tagg, Stephen K., 394*t*, 395–396, 437
Tan, Lucille, 9, 435
Taylor, Beck A., 399*n*12, 443
Teja, Shahzia, 322*t*, 437
Terborg, James R., 63*t*, 68–70, 153*t*, 377, 378*t*, 442
Theodossiou, Ioannis, 329*t*, 334, 336, 440
Thompson, Brennan S., 322*t*, 437

Thompson, Jeffrey P., 36, 50, 111n18, 201, 344, 347t, 355–356, 363n18, 443
To, Ted, 75, 428
Trace, D. M., 53t, 435
Tulip, Peter, 371, 373t, 374, 381nn11–12, 443
Turner, Mark D., 40t, 267t, 269, 276–277, 429

U.S. Bureau of Labor Statistics, 346t–347t, 362n2, 443
U.S. Census Bureau, 311t, 313, 338n8, 443
Uusitalo, Roope, 81t, 114–115n54, 132t, 253n15, 363n19, 423n1, 427

Van de Waal, Corey, 316–317, 319t, 442
Van den Berg, Gerard J., 373t, 374–375, 444
Van Reenen, John, 255n36, 394t, 397–398
Vavrichek, Bruce, 328t, 331, 332t, 337, 442
Vaze, Prabhat, 225t, 227–229, 228f, 230ff, 231ff, 244t, 248–249, 436
Vedder, Richard, 126t, 127, 130–131, 142, 144n17, 316–317, 319t, 444
Vella, Francis, 92, 444
Vilhuber, Lars, 345, 415, 425

Wadsworth, Helen, 133–134, 135t, 138–139, 141, 443
Wadsworth, Jonathan, 78, 94t, 97, 115n57, 116n67, 209t, 305t, 308, 384t, 391–392, 431, 444
Waltman, J., 394t, 396, 399n12, 444
Warren, John Robert, 112n31, 267t, 276, 278, 444
Wascher, William, 3, 21–29, 32–33, 34t, 36, 38, 40t, 45, 50–51, 52t–53t, 55–56, 61, 78, 81t, 97, 103–104, 106, 108, 109n5, 110n9, 111n27, 112n34, 112nn29–30, 116nn75–76, 122, 123, 125t, 127–128, 141, 153t, 201, 203t, 204, 207t, 208, 210, 252n12, 253n15, 254n27, 265t–266t, 268–269, 271–

274, 277, 316, 318t–319t, 321, 323, 324t, 339n18, 380n7, 423n1, 424n13, 438–439
Webb, Beatrice, 237, 444
Webb, Sidney, 237, 444
Wells, Christine, 179n3, 429
Wessels, Walter, 15, 38, 40t, 42–43, 51, 75, 91, 108, 380n7, 348, 358–360, 402, 426, 444
Williams, Nicolas, 47–49, 48t, 105, 444
Wilson, J., 78, 99, 100t, 101, 220, 221t, 394t, 397–398, 423n1, 437
Wittenburg, David C., 121t, 142n3, 254n25, 428, 430
Wolfson, Paul, 3, 28, 72, 73t, 76–77, 104–106, 126t, 127, 129–131, 141, 152t, 209t, 211, 251, 402, 427, 444
Woodcock, Simon, 415, 425
Woodland, Stephen, 209t, 431
Wooldridge, Jeffrey M., 110n12, 435

Yuen, Terrence, 77, 79, 81t, 82, 84, 101, 108, 112n35, 114n50, 115n55, 445

Zavodny, Madeline, 38, 50–51, 52t, 54–55, 60, 119–120, 121t, 124, 125t, 130–131, 141, 153t, 201, 202t, 204, 234–235, 439, 445
Zehnder, Christian, 196, 237, 240t, 250, 432
Zelenska, Tetyana, 62t, 71, 143n11, 237, 239, 240t–241t, 256n49, 435
Ziliak, James P., 316, 318t, 434

Subject Index

The italic letters *f, n,* or *t* following a page number indicate a figure, note, or table on that page. Double letters mean more than one such item on a single page.

Adult Education and Training Survey, 283
African Americans in labor force
  earnings and minimum wage effect on, 208, 254*n*26
  earnings of youth as, 201, 253–254*n*23, 317
  employment of youth as, 51, 112*n*29, 123
  gross labor flows for, and job tenure, 346*t*
  schooling and, 270, 273
Age of workers, 89, 94*t*
  middle-, as adults, 87, 97
  older adults, 93–97, 114*n*51
  teenage *vs.* young adult, varies by country, 34*t*–35*t*, 81*t*, 86, 90–91, 111*n*17, 115*n*57, 363*n*16
  young adults, 125*t*, 224*t*, 333
Aggregate panel data, 128, 130
  county-level, and hours worked, 126*t*, 129
  national, in older studies, 21–23
  studies using, on youth in labor force, 32–38, 34*t*–35*t*, 50
Agricultural workers
  less than minimum wage and, 227, 252*n*10
  minimum wage effect on, 209*t*, 224*t*–225*t*
Alabama, fast food and minimum wage in, 62*t*, 71, 239, 240*t*–241*t*
Alaska, federal *vs.* state minimum wage in, 109*n*4, 253*n*13
Australia, NMWR studies in, 1, 78, 80*t*–81*t*, 89–93, 115*n*59, 115*nn*61–62

Benchmark, minimum wage as, 6, 17*n*3, 250–251

Beveridge curve, definition of, 377
Black youth. *See under* African Americans in labor force
Blue-collar workers, wages for, *vs.* white-collar, 239, 256*n*50
Bound workers, 302
  definitions of, 22, 99, 109*n*2
  layoff of, 200, 253*n*18
  longitudinal studies of, and minimum wage, 232–236, 233*t*, 256*nn*43–45, 274
  as minimum wage variable, 21–22, 77–78, 85, 94*t*, 96–97
  recent studies of, and minimum wage, 223–236, 224*t*–225*t*, 250
  youth as, 80*t*–81*t*
British Columbia, Canada, wage inequality in, 304*t*, 306–307

California, 109*n*4
  bound workers in, 223–226, 224*t*, 226*t*, 246, 255*n*38
  minimum wage increase in, as employment opportunity, 22, 109*n*3
  restaurant studies in, 61–64, 62*t*, 65–66, 113*nn*41–43, 126*t*, 127, 212, 214*t*, 346*t*
Canada
  firm-provided training in, 285*t*, 286, 298*n*31
  minimum wage data since 2000 analyzed from, 1, 2, 384*t*
  NMWR studies in, 77, 79–84, 80*t*–81*t*, 114*nn*51–52, 115*nn*55–56, 132*t*, 152*t*, 266*t*
  provinces in, 30, 110*n*13, 267*t*, 274–277, 296*n*11, 296*n*15, 317
  restaurant prices in, 383, 384*t*, 385–386, 389, 399*n*2

Canada, *cont.*
  studies of minimum wage and poverty
    in, 313, 317, 319*t*, 321, 322*t*
  unemployment and vacancies in,
    373*t*, 377, 378*t*
  wage inequality in, 304*t*, 306–307
Card, David, as influential coauthor, 22,
    24–28, 110*n*9
Careers, minimum wage and, 336–337
Carnegie unit, definition of, 278, 296*n*17
Child care, cost of, 310, 338*n*9
Competitive labor market, 14
  alternatives to, 344, 356, 363*n*20
  as minimum wage research model, 3,
    10–12, 10*f*, 405, 406
  supply and demand in, 109*n*5, 110*n*7,
    116*n*68, 185, 302, 374, 407–409
Connecticut, federal *vs.* state minimum
    wage, 109*n*4
Connecticut, federal *vs.* state minimum
    wage, 253*n*13
Cornell University, minimum wage
    research and, 1
County-level data, 36–37, 74, 126*t*, 129,
    152*t*, 212–213, 216
  Maryland dropout rates and racial
    differences as, 267*t*, 278–279
  Iowa, and low-wage firms, 394*t*, 396–
    397

Demographic groups studies. *See*
    Immigrants; Single mothers;
    Youth in labor force

Earned Income Tax Credit (EITC)
  as antipoverty measure, 112*n*34, 321,
    323, 324*t*, 338*n*10, 401
  childless individuals and, 55–57, 60
  employment response of single
    mothers to, and minimum wage
    increases, 39, 40*t*
  interactions between, and minimum
    wage, 40*t*, 45–46, 55–60, 111–
    112*n*28, 112*n*37, 210, 253–
    254*n*23, 254*n*26
  race and, 55–56, 58, 60

Earnings
  definition of, 184, 251*n*1, 422
  hourly, and minimum wage, 3–10, 5*t*,
    119, 187*t*, 229–232, 230*ff*, 231*ff*,
    406
  low-wage, by immigrants, 2, 153*t*
  minimum wage effect on vulnerable
    groups and, 210–211, 222, 406
  minimum wage effects on, 183, 236–
    249, 256*nn*46–47, 332*t*
  ratios as inequality measurement,
    302–303
Eating and drinking establishments. *See*
    Restaurant industry
Economic inequality, 302, 308–326
  See also Income inequality; Wage
    inequality
Economic Policy Institute (EPI), basic
    family budget and, 7, 9
Education, 38
  college-level, 208, 269
  health insurance and, 291, 292*t*–293*t*,
    294, 299*n*46
  human capital formation and, 16,
    263–279
  income inequality and, 302, 303
  women in labor force and, 93, 203*t*,
    204, 206*t*–207*t*, 210
  See also High school
EITC. *See* Earned Income Tax Credit
Employers, 251*n*2
  benefits provided by, paying
    minimum wage, 280–294
    (*see also* Health care; Pensions;
    Training)
  contracts with, 407–408, 412*n*2
  cost of minimum wage to, 98–99
  firms as, 11–14, 16, 88, 116*n*72, 126*t*
  responses to minimum wage by, 119,
    250–251
  search models and wage distribution
    among, 14–15
Employment, 2
  accessions to and separations from
    (*see under* Labor market, gross
    flows in)

Employment, *cont.*
  elasticity of, and minimum wage, 1,
    3, 15, 17*n*2, 23, 43, 60, 98,
    111*n*24, 115*n*61, 200, 353–354,
    354*t*
    (*see also under* Teenage
    employment)
  full-time *vs.* part-time, and earnings,
    229, 231*ff*
  labor supply and demand curves in,
    407–408, 412*n*2
  measures of, 119, 142*n*1, 365, 417–
    418, 423*nn*8–9
  probability of, as expanded minimum
    wage issue, 2, 10*f,* 11–12, 13*f,* 15,
    17*n*6, 91, 99, 114*n*52
  responses in, to minimum wage
    increase, 22–24, 37–39, 50, 108–
    109, 152*t*–153*t,* 344, 356–357,
    401
  summary of findings on, 106–109,
    401–402
  timing of, responses to minimum
    wage increase, 51, 102–107,
    116*nn*73–77
  See also Industry studies of minimum
    wage
England
  agricultural workers in, 224*t,* 227,
    255–256*n*40
  average earnings elasticity in, 255*n*35
  small firms and minimum wage
    increase in, 394*t,* 395–396
EPI. *See* Economic Policy Institute
European Union (EU) countries, 381*n*8
  graded agricultural workers in, 227,
    252*n*10

Family income, 322*t*
  adequacy of, and minimum wage,
    7–10, 8*t,* 17*n*4
  estimate models of, 246, 256*n*52,
    257*nn*53–55
  low, in Utah, 8*t,* 9
  minimum wage effect on, 270, 296*n*7

poverty thresholds and, 310–313,
  311*t,* 336
U.S., and labor force status, 313,
  314*t*–315*t*
Fast food establishments. *See* Restaurant
  industry
Finland, 132*t,* 363*n*19
  NMWR studies in, 80*t*–81*t,* 114–
    115*n*54
Firms
  decisions by, and human capital
    investment, 261–262, 289,
    295*nn*1–2, 298–299*n*36, 298*n*35
  government surveys and, 414–415,
    423*nn*4–5
  intra-, wage structure and restaurant
    productivity, 238–239, 251,
    256*n*48
  job layoffs and, behavior, 16, 255*n*37
  life cycle for, 352*t,* 362*n*1, 394*t,* 396,
    398, 399*n*14
  single-establishment, in Iowa, 142,
    153*t*
  small, and minimum wage, 347*t,* 359,
    390, 394*t,* 399*n*8
  variable measures of, 283, 298*n*28
  wage distribution changes in, and
    spillover issues, 245, 375
  See also Employers
Food purchases, poverty and, 7, 8–9, 8*t,*
  17*n*5, 309–310, 401
France
  antipoverty policies in, 323, 324*t*
  NMWR studies in, 78, 90, 94*t,* 97–99,
    116*nn*68–69
  restaurant prices in, 383, 384*t,* 386–
    389
Fringe benefits
  effect of minimum wage on, and
    wages, 15, 358
  health care and pensions as, in
    research, 289–294, 292*t*–293*t,*
    299*nn*37–46, 300*n*47
  legally mandated and volunteer, 288–
    289, 298*n*35, 298–299*n*36, 299*n*37

Fringe benefits, *cont.*
   training as, and effect of minimum
      wage increase, 2, 280–281
Funnel plots, 153–157, 179*nn*6–7

Gender differences, 287, 379
   education and, 205–208, 206*t*–207*t*,
      270, 379
   effect of minimum wage on earnings
      and, 229, 230, 231*ff*, 250, 306, 406
   effect of minimum wage on wages
      and, 16, 50–51, 54, 245, 253–
      254*n*23, 303, 306–308, 333–334,
      336, 337*n*2
   EITC and employment with, 45–46
   gross labor flows and quits with, 346*t*,
      361
   hours worked in U.K. and, 136–138,
      139, 142, 145*nn*23–24
   teenage hours worked and, 120, 130,
      141, 143*nn*6–7
   unemployment duration and, 376,
      381*n*16
Georgia, fast food market in, 62*t*, 71,
   239, 240*t*–241*t*
Germany, simulation studies of minimum
   wage and poverty in, 321, 322*t*
Goldilocks value, definition of, 371
Greensboro, North Carolina, minimum
   wage restaurant survey in, 238–
   239, 256*n*48

Hazard functions, 361, 375
Health care
   firms and insurance for, 290–291,
      292*t*–293*t*, 294, 298–299*n*36,
      299*n*42, 299*n*46
   research on, as fringe benefit with
      minimum wage, 289–294,
      292*t*–293*t*, 299*n*38
High school
   college-, wage gap, 305*t*, 307
   dropout rates and, 278–279
   graduates of, 39, 40*t*, 43, 54, 60, 250,
      278, 296–297*n*18, 317, 382*n*15

   nongraduates of, 38, 39, 40*t*, 46–47,
      54–55, 112*n*31, 112*n*33, 124, 321
Hiring processes
   costs of, 119, 351, 362*n*12, 399*n*10
   job accessions among, 343, 344, 354*t*,
      356
Hispanics in labor force
   earnings and minimum wage effect,
      208, 254*n*26, 333
   earnings of youth as, 201, 253–254*n*23
   employment of youth as, 51, 112*n*29,
      123
   schooling and, 273, 279, 297*n*20
Home care industry
   British nursing homes as, 219–222,
      221*t*, 225*nn*35–37
   gross labor flows in, 346*t*, 349
   low-wages for job skills in, 2, 78
   in non-U.S. countries, 78, 99–102,
      139, 140*t*, 142, 150–151
   price response to minimum wage in,
      390, 394*t*, 399*n*8
Home-making, value of, and unpaid
   work, 14
Hospitality industry, 2
   in Sweden, 100*t*, 114*n*53
   in U.S., 61, 62*t*–63*t*, 68, 378*t*
Hotel sector. *See* Hospitality industry
Hours worked, 119–145
   consequence of minimum wage
      increase on, 2, 15, 153*t*, 401
   elasticity of, 120, 123–124, 129–130,
      141–142, 143*n*15
   as measures of employment, 119–120,
      142*nn*1–2, 418–420, 424*nn*10–11
   non-U.S. studies of, 131–142
      (*see also* e.g., *under* Low-wage
      workers; Teenage employment)
   types of, 142, 142*n*4, 142–143*n*5,
      143*nn*8–9, 144*n*16
   U.S. studies of, 120–131, 141–142
      (*see also* e.g., *under* Restaurant
      industry; Youth in the labor force)
Household income, 251*n*2, 301, 322*t*
   government surveys and, 413–414,
      423*nn*2–3

Household income, *cont.*
  low-, and minimum wage effect, 184,
    325–326, 387, 394*t,* 401
  See also Family income
Human capital investment and minimum
    wage, 16
  employee benefits research on, 288–
    294, 292*t*–293*t*
  firms' decisions for, in employees,
    261–262, 280–294, 284*t*–285*t,*
    292*t*–293*t,* 295*nn*1–2, 297*nn*21–
    22, 298*nn*33–34
  individual decisions for, in self, 260–
    262, 263
  NMWR studies on, 281–287,
    284*t*–285*t,* 297*nn*23–25,
    298*nn*26–32
  non-U.S. countries on, 274–276
  review of education literature and,
    276–279, 296*nn*14–17, 296–
    297*n*18, 297*nn*19–20
  school enrollment, 263, 268–269,
    279, 295*nn*3–5
  schooling and, 263–279, 264*t*–267*t,*
    295*n*5
  schooling research on, 269–274,
    281–288, 295–296*n*6, 296*nn*7–10,
    333

Illinois, fast food restaurants in, 63*t,*
    126*t,* 127–128
Immigrants, 34*t*
  hours worked by, 124, 125*t,* 131
  low-wage earnings, 2, 153*t*
  minimum wage and education of, 38,
    60, 124, 125*t,* 131
  public policies and, 51–54, 53*t*
Income adequacy
  measures of, 7–10, 8*t,* 17*n*4
  See also under Household income,
    low-
Income inequality
  effect of minimum wage on, 301, 303,
    337*n*2
  measures of, 302–303
  possible causes of, 302, 337*n*1

Indiana, fast food restaurants in, 127, 128
Individual-level data, 125*t*
  poverty and, 318*t*–319*t*
  youth employment studies with,
    38–47, 40*t*–41*t,* 50–51
  youth hours worked and, panels, 121*t,*
    123
Industry studies of minimum wage
  home care, 2, 78, 99–102
  hospitality, 2, 100*t*
  low-wage, 126*t,* 129–131, 209*t,*
    211–222, 218*t,* 251
  restaurant, 15, 22, 24–27, 78, 124,
    125*t*–126*t,* 127–129, 212–217,
    214*t*–215*t*
  specific occupation and, with
    spillover effect, 238–245,
    240*t*–244*t,* 256*nn*46–50
Inflation, unemployment and, 371, 373*t,*
    374, 381*n*12
Iowa
  federal *vs.* state minimum wage in,
    74, 129
  single-establishment firms *vs.* chains
    in, 142, 153*t*
Ireland, average earnings elasticity in,
    255*n*35
  See also Northern Ireland
Italy, unemployment and minimum
    wage, 372*t,* 381*n*14

Jackson, Mississippi, minimum wage
    restaurant survey in, 238–239,
    256*n*48
Job accessions
  definition of, 343–344, 357, 363*n*15
  elasticity estimates of, 353–354, 354*t*
  findings on, 356–357, 409
  studies including, 346*t*–347*t,* 352–
    356, 352*t,* 353*t*
Job disappearance, reasons for, 14, 185,
    250
Job layoffs
  employment elasticity of bound
    workers and, 200, 253*n*18,
    253*nn*20–21

Job layoffs, *cont.*
as employment separation, 350–351,
357, 402–403
firms' behavior *vs.*, 16, 119, 185
wage gap and, 82–84
Job searches, cost of, 14, 408
Job separations
adult *vs.* teen, 352–353, 363*n*15
definition of, 343–344, 357, 363*n*15
elasticity estimates of, 353–354, 354*t*
findings on, 356–361
studies including, 346*t*–347*t*, 352–
356, 352*t*, 353*t*
Job skills, 2, 302
unskilled workers and gross labor
flows, 347*t*, 355–356
Job tenure
gross labor flows and, 346*t*, 354–355
unemployment duration and, 376–
378, 381*n*17
Job turnover
consequence of minimum wage
increase on, 2, 145*n*25
gross labor flows and, 349–350, 354*t*,
361
Job vacancies, 2
as labor market measure, 365, 368,
377, 378*t*, 379, 380*n*3
use of search models for, 14, 349–351

Kaitz index, 109*n*1, 371
as traditional minimum wage
variable, 21, 23, 97, 110*n*7
Kalman filter, 49
Kernel density, 192, 193*f*, 195*f*, 197*f*,
252*n*12
Krueger, Alan B.
as influential coauthor, 22, 24–28,
110*n*9
publication bias issue and, 147, 179*n*4

Labor force
bound workers in, 22, 109*n*2
individuals in, and self-investment
decisions, 260–261

minimum wage and nonstudent
participants in, 4–7, 5*t*, 9–10
participation in, 2, 4, 14, 312, 362–
363*n*13, 365, 366*t*, 379, 403
(*see also specific groups, e.g.,*
Women in the labor force; Youth
in the labor force)
status in U.S., and family income,
313, 314*t*–315*t*, 336
Labor market, 302
agnostic gross flow models of, 355–
356
colloquial types of, 3, 37–38, 123,
152*t*, 256*n*45
gross flows in, 16, 343–364,
346*t*–347*t*, 355–356, 402–403,
406
(*see also* Job accessions; *under*
minimum wage research issues;
Job separations)
innovation and craftsmanship in,
410–411
measures of, 119, 142*n*1, 365, 367*t*
minimum wage increase effect on,
405–406
non-involvement in, and minimum
wage changes, 2, 301
traditional models of, 10–15, 10*f*,
13*ff*, 348–355, 405
transaction costs in, 407–409
Leisure, value of, and job searches, 14
Longitudinal studies
bound workers and minimum wage
in, 232–236, 233*t*, 256*nn*43–45,
274
in U.K., 416–417, 423*n*7
in U.S., 415–416, 423*n*6
Low-wage workers, 96
definition of, and wage-gap measure,
82–84
in demographic groups and industries,
2, 125*t*, 126*t*, 131
hours worked by, in U.K., 133–139,
135*t*, 142
hours worked by, in U.S., 124, 127–
130, 133–139, 135*t*

Low-wage workers, *cont.*
  length of time as, 16, 326–333,
    328*t*–329*t*, 330*t*, 332*t*, 336, 338–
    339*n*16, 339*n*17
  (*see also* Wage growth)
  in non-U.S, developed countries, 78,
    82, 93–99, 94*t*–95*t*, 115*nn*63–65,
    116*nn*66–69, 322*t*, 324*t*
  U.S. sectors of, 71–77, 73*t*, 152*t*
  See also under Household income,
    low-, and minimum wage effect

Manufacturing sector, 130
  price response to minimum wage in,
    390, 399*n*8
  quits in, 347*t*, 358–359
Maryland, dropout rates and racial
  differences in, 267*t*, 278–279
Men in labor force, 60, 96, 333
  education and, 205, 208, 403
  gross flows of, 346*t*, 361
  job training and minimum wage of,
    297*n*24
  unemployment duration of, 376,
    381*n*15, 403
  white, and minimum wage effect on
    average wage, 206*t*
Meta-analysis, 147–182
  employment effect data extraction
    and, 151–159, 152*t*–153*t*, 154*f*,
    155*f*, 156*f*, 157*f*, 158*t*, 179*t*
  equations leading to metaregression
    in, 148–149, 179*nn*1–3
  literature survey using, on teenage
    employment response, 149–151,
    179*nn*4–5
  metaregression quality estimates,
    159–165, 161*t*, 164*t*, 177, 179–
    180*n*10, 179*n*9, 180*n*11, 181*nn*12–
    14
  models of metaregression control
    equations in, 165–166, 181*nn*15–16
  overall models of meta-estimates in
    regression technique, 166–171,
    168*t*, 173*t*, 174*t*–175*t*, 177, 181–
    182*n*19, 181*nn*17–18

separate effects models for wait-staff
  youth and their workplaces, 171–
  172
separate estimates for effect of wait-
  staff youth and their workplaces,
  172–176, 173*t*, 174*t*–175*t*,
  182*nn*20–21
Mid-Atlantic states, time effects of
  economic factors in, 122
Minimum wage
  citywide, 61, 152*t*–153*t*, 212
  definition of, 6, 17*n*3
  distribution of hourly earnings and,
    3–10, 5*t*
  dollar values of, 42, 46, 111*n*23,
    115*n*55, 129, 187–189, 187*t*, 189*t*,
    192
  federal *vs.* state, 33–36, 74, 109*n*4,
    110–111*n*16, 112*n*38, 113*n*39,
    189–191, 190*t*, 196, 216–217,
    253*n*13, 283, 317, 380*n*5
  measuring effects of, 184–186,
    251*nn*1–2, 252*nn*3–6, 401
  more earnings but close to, 240*t*–244*t*,
    250
  responses to, 119, 390, 394*t*, 396–
    397, 399*n*8
  tipped *vs.* nontipped (*see under*
    Restaurant industry)
  variables and, 1, 21–22, 36, 80, 420–
    422, 424*nn*12–14
  ways to gauge, changes as common
    NMWR feature, 21
  See also Low-wage workers; Poverty
    and minimum wage; Spillover
    effect of minimum wage
Minimum wage research, 1–3, 16, 17
  data sources and variables for, 16,
    413–423, 423*n*1
  NMWR as post-2000 papers on, 1,
    15, 17*n*1, 142*n*1, 401
  simulations in, 76, 105–106, 117*n*79,
    321–322, 322*t*, 334
  See also Statistical analyses

Minimum wage research issues
    gross labor flows and data collection
        among, 345, 348, 362nn2–5
    helpfulness to low-income
        households, 325–326, 336
    size and timing of minimum wage
        effects among, 1, 2–3, 17n2
    what are outcomes of minimum wage
        increases among, 1, 2
    who is affected among, 1, 2, 21–22,
        109n2, 326, 385, 399n4
Minimum wage research models
    competitive labor market, 3, 10–12
    empirical studies as, in developed
        countries, 1, 17n1
    monopsony labor market, 3, 12–14,
        13ff
    search, of labor market, 3, 14–15
Mississippi
    child care cost in, 310, 338n9
    minimum wage restaurant survey in,
        238–239, 256n48
Monopsony labor market
    definition of, 12
    dynamic, vs. monopsonistic
        competition, 75–76, 385
    as minimum wage research model, 3,
        12–14, 13ff, 405–406
Moulton problem, 28, 84, 107, 110n11
Minimum wage. See Minimum wage

Netherlands, unemployment rate and
        minimum wage in, 373t, 374–375,
        381n14
Neumark, David
    critiques of others' work by, 25, 27
    as influential coauthor, 22–24, 109n5,
        110n9, 122, 127
New England states, 109n4, 122
New Jersey
    fast food restaurants in, 63t, 152t, 385
    minimum wage increase in, and quasi
        experiment construction, 22,
        24–27, 107, 110n10
New Mexico, living wage ordinance
        impacts in, 153t

New minimum wage research. See
    NMWR
New York (State), 40t
    synthetic control group based on,
        46–47, 112nn32–33
New Zealand
    NMWR studies in, 1, 78, 80t–81t, 90,
        115n60, 152t, 266t, 394t
    study of minimum wage and poverty
        in, 320t, 325–326, 338nn13–14
    teenage employment in, 131–133,
        132t, 144nn18–19, 274–276,
        296nn12–13, 395
    unemployment rate in, 371, 372t
NMWR (New minimum wage research)
    early 1992 papers with common
        features of, 21–30
    post-2000 papers as, 1, 15, 17n1,
        31–102
    (see also specific developed
        countries, e.g., Canada; United
        States)
    retrospective of 1990s studies, 28–30,
        110nn11–12
Nonagricultural sector, aggregate hours
        data in, 130
North Carolina, minimum wage
        restaurant survey in, 238–239,
        256n48
Northern Ireland, small firms and
        minimum wage increase in, 394t,
        395–396
Northwest states, employment effects of
        minimum wage in, 153t
Nursing home industry, 2, 219

Occupation studies of minimum
        wage, spillover effect in, 238–245,
        240t–244t, 256nn46–50
Oregon
    fast food restaurants in, 63t, 68, 378t
    higher minimum wage in, than
        federal, 109n4
Organisation for Economic Cooperation
        and Development (OECD)
    countries

OECD *cont.*
  labor participation of women in, 369*t*, 373*t*
  NMWR studies in, 80*t*–81*t*, 94*t*–95*t*

Pennsylvania
  counties in, as controls in quasi experiment, 22, 24–27, 107, 110*n*10
  fast food restaurants in, 63*t*, 152*t*, 385
Pensions, as fringe benefit with minimum wage, 289–291, 292*t*–293*t*, 299*n*38, 300*n*47
Politics, left-center, and minimum wage increases, 350, 362*nn*7–8
Portugal
  gross labor flows in, and teenagers, 346*t*–347*t*, 351–353, 352*t*, 353*t*, 354*t*
  NMWR studies in, 78, 80*t*–81*t*, 86–89
  teenage employment in, 132*t*, 153*t*
Positive economics methodology, 76
Poverty and minimum wage
  anti-, measures, 55–60, 112*n*34, 323, 324*t*, 338*n*8, 338*t*
  definitions of, 6, 17*n*3, 113*n*40, 309–310, 338*nn*5–6
  empirical studies of, 313, 316–321, 318*t*–320*t*, 326, 338*nn*10–11
  impacts of, 16, 124, 301, 308–326, 336
  simulation studies of, 321–322, 322*t*
Poverty line, 338*n*7
  below or near, population and minimum wage, 2, 16, 183–184, 336
  family, thresholds, 310–313, 311*t*
  as income adequacy measure, 7–8, 8*t*
Prices
  effect of minimum wage increase on, 2, 374, 383, 399*nn*1–9, 405
  effect on product market of, 383–392, 384*t*
Product market, 16
  effect of prices on, 383–392, 384*t*
  output of, 392
  profitability and, 392–398, 394*t*, 399*nn*10–14, 405

Productivity, 185
  rising minimum wage and, 280–281, 297*n*21
  wages and, 251, 255*n*39, 295*n*3
Profitability
  effect of minimum wage increase on, 2, 16, 255*n*36, 281, 399*n*6
  product market and, 392–398, 394*t*, 405
Public policy
  antipoverty, in France, 323, 324*t*
  antipoverty, in U.S., 55–60, 112*n*34, 323, 324*t*, 338*n*8
  immigrants and, 51–54, 53*t*
  intended consequences of, 411–412
  minimum wage as tool of, 401, 404, 406, 411–412
Publication bias, 147, 153, 157–159, 158*t*, 179*n*4

Quarterly Census of Employment and Wages (QCEW)
  as data source, 212–217, 254*n*28, 255*n*34
Quasi experiment construction, 22, 294
  data from, 77, 80*t*–81*t*
  regressions and, as common NMWR feature, 21, 34*t*–35*t*, 36–37, 40*t*, 52*t*–53*t*, 62*t*–65*t*, 80*t*–81*t*, 94*t*–95*t*, 100*t*, 121*t*, 126*t*
Quits, 346*t*–347*t*, 357–361, 402–403

Racial differences
  job training and minimum wage with, 297*n*24
  schooling and, 270, 273, 279
  teenage employment and, 42, 45, 51, 112*n*29, 123
Restaurant industry
  fringe benefits in, 292*t*, 294
  gross labor flows in, 344, 346*t*, 353–354, 362*n*10354*t*
  meta-analysis of wait-staff youth and their workplaces, 171–176, 173*t*, 174*t*–175*t*, 182*nn*20–21, 402

Restaurant industry, *cont.*
  national chains in, 71, 239, 256*n*49,
    386
  studies of minimum wage in, 15, 22,
    24–27, 61–71, 62*t*–63*t*, 78, 105,
    152*t*, 212–217, 214*t*–215*t*,
    254*nn*28–31, 255*n*32
  tipped *vs.* nontipped minimum wage
    in, 62*t*, 68–69, 113–114*n*46,
    113*n*45, 127–129, 216–217,
    252*n*10, 254*nn*29–31
  in U.S., 61–64, 62*t*, 65–66, 113*nn*41–
    43, 124, 126*t*, 127–129, 131, 384*t*,
    386–390, 399*nn*3–7
Retail sector, 22
  hours worked in, 126*t*, 127, 129, 131
  low wages in, 73*t*, 77, 114*nn*48–49
  minimum wage and employment in,
    152*t*–153*t*.
  minimum wage effect on, 217–219,
    218*t*, 255*nn*33–34
  price response to minimum wage in,
    390, 394*t*, 399*n*8
  teens or youth in, 34*t*, 38, 80*t*, 121*t*,
    123–124, 132*t*, 346*t*, 356
Right-to-work laws, 222, 251
  non-right-to-work *vs.*, and unions,
    219, 255*n*34

Salt Lake City, Utah, low-family incomes
    in, 8*t*, 9
San Francisco, California, restaurant
    studies in, area, 61–64, 62*t*, 126*t*,
    127, 212, 214*t*, 293*t*, 294, 346*t*,
    384*t*, 385
Santa Fe, New Mexico, living wage
    ordinance impacts in, 153*t*
School enrollment, 14
  human capital investment and
    minimum wage, 263, 268–269,
    279, 295*nn*3–5
  influenced by minimum wage, 1, 2,
    23–24, 110*n*6, 270, 404–406
  teen employment-, categories, 270–
    274, 296*nn*8–9

Schooling
  early research on, as human capital
    investment, 269–271, 281–288,
    295*n*4
  human capital investment and, 263–
    279, 264*t*–267*t*
  race and, 270, 273, 279
  recent research on, as human capital
    investment, 271–274
  wage path and, 326–327, 333, 337
Scotland, 255*n*35
  small firms and minimum wage
    increase in, 394*t*, 395–396
Search models
  contact rate and wage offers in, 14,
    43, 368, 370, 380*n*4
  gross labor flows and, 344, 348,
    349–355, 362–363*n*14, 362*nn*6–
    12, 363*nn*14–17
  in minimum wage labor market
    research, 3, 14–15, 18*n*7, 40*t*, 51,
    297*n*22
Service industry, 222
  price response to minimum wage in,
    390, 394*t*, 396–397, 399*n*8
Shock effect, definition of, 403
Simulation studies, 76
  minimum wage and poverty in, 321–
    322*t*
  teenage employment in, 105–106,
    117*n*79
Single mothers, 2
  EITC and minimum wage increases,
    39, 40*t*, 51, 55–60, 112*n*34,
    112*n*37
  hours worked by, 124, 125*t*, 131
  low-education, and minimum wage,
    54–55, 60–61, 113*n*40, 124, 125*t*
  poverty and, 319*t*, 323
  wage distribution and, 202*t*,
    206*t*–207*t*, 208, 210
Spain, NMWR studies in, 78, 80*t*–81*t*,
    86–89, 346*t*
Spillover effect of minimum wage,
    236–249
  definition of, 191

Spillover effect of minimum wage, *cont.*
measurement of, 246–247, 257*n*55
specific industry and occupation
studies, 238–245, 240*t*–244*t,*
256*nn*46–50
U.K. studies, 241*t*–244*t,* 247–249,
257*nn*56–57
U.S. studies, 240*t*–243*t,* 245–247,
256*n*52, 257*nn*51–54, 399*n*7
State panel data, 22–23
poverty and, 316, 318*t*–319*t*
youth employment and, 22–23,
34*t*–35*t,* 38, 152*t*
youth hours worked and, 120, 121*t,*
125*t,* 126*t*
Statistical analyses
bias as issue in, 147, 153, 179*n*4,
253*n*15, 296–297*n*18, 296*n*12,
298*n*34, 382*n*18
geographic differences in, 44–45, 48*t,*
49, 111*n*25, 111*n*27
limitations of and problems with,
28–30, 51, 90–92, 107–109,
110*n*13, 114*n*51, 116–117*n*78,
178, 216–217, 255*n*32, 263, 268–
269, 295, 316–317, 321, 338*nn*10–
11, 381*nn*8–11
proto- (difference-in-differences),
22, 45, 87, 90, 96, 109*n*3, 110*n*12,
136–138, 361
standard errors in, 155, 179*nn*7–8,
181*n*17, 363–364*n*23, 368, 370,
379, 380*n*7, 382*n*18
synthetic control groups in, 46–47,
112*nn*32–33
See also Meta-analysis
Supply and demand. *See under*
Competitive labor market
Sweden
gross labor flows in, 347*t,* 348, 355–
356
NMWR studies in, 100*t,* 114*n*53
Switzerland, spillover effect of minimum
wage in, 240*t,* 250

Taxes
firing, and firm behavior, 349–351,
362*n*4
pre-, treatment of employee benefits,
289, 298–299*n*36, 298*n*35
records from, as data with multiple
uses, 251*n*2, 362*n*4, 396
Teenage employment, 4, 368, 369*t,* 379*n*1
effect of minimum wage increase on,
1–3, 21–23, 80*t*–81*t*
elasticities in, 38, 111*n*21, 200,
253*nn*20–21
gross labor flows and, 346*t*–347*t,*
351–353, 352*t,* 353*t,* 354*t,* 355–
356, 362*n*10, 363*n*14
hours worked in, and U.S. studies,
120–124, 121*t,* 130–131, 142*n*4
hours worked with gender differences
in, 120, 143*nn*6–7
in non-U.S. developed countries,
82, 86–91, 93, 105, 131–133,
132*t,* 144*nn*18–19
race in, 42, 45, 112*n*29, 123, 201,
253–254*n*23
school enrollment and, categories,
270–274, 296*nn*8–9
schooling and minimum wage for,
264*t*–267*t,* 269–279
simulations of, 105–106, 117*n*79
U.S. and, 33–38, 34*t*–35*t,* 47–50, 48*t,*
111*nn*17–18
wage distribution and, 201–204,
202*t*–203*t,* 253–254*nn*23–25,
253*n*22
Texas, fast food industry in, and
minimum wage effect, 22
Time-series data
aggregates of, 126*t,* 127, 316
dynamics of, 76–77, 126*t,* 129–130
early minimum wage research with,
1, 21, 22
NMWR studies with, 105–106, 116–
117*n*78, 117*n*79, 126*t,* 144*n*17
now-dated, 357–358, 363*n*21
older, 23, 47–49, 48*t,* 109*n*5,
269–270, 295–296*n*6

Time-series data, *cont.*
  problems with, 377, 378*t*
Trade unions
  right-to-work *vs.* non-right-to-work
    states and unions, 219, 255*n*34
  wage gap and, 236, 256*n*45
  weakening, and income inequality,
    302, 303
Training, 119
  employer-provided, 280–288,
    284*t*–285*t*, 297*nn*21–25,
    298*nn*26–34, 404
  human capital formation and, 16,
    295*n*2

Unemployment, 14, 98
  duration of, 365, 368, 372*t*, 375–377,
    379–380*n*2, 382*nn*15–17, 403
  inflation and, 371, 373*t*, 374, 381*n*12
  minimum wage and, 2, 16, 70, 99,
    114*n*47, 267*t*, 278
  study data and, 254*n*27, 381*n*8, 403
Unemployment insurance, administrative
    data and, 26, 110*n*8, 362*n*4, 396
Unemployment rate
  business cycle and, 109*n*5, 110*n*7,
    371, 372*t*
  definition of, 365, 367*t*, 368
  as labor market measure, 370–375,
    372*t*–373*t*, 379, 381*nn*8–14
  poverty level and, 321, 338*n*10
  teenagers and, 368, 369*t*, 403
United Kingdom
  bound workers in, 223, 224*t*–225*t*,
    227–232, 230*ff*, 231*ff*, 232, 233*t*,
    235, 255–256*n*40, 255*n*39
  firm-provided training in, 285*t*, 286
  home care industry in, and minimum
    wage, 219–222, 221*t*, 225*nn*35–
    37, 394*t*, 397, 399*n*13
  hours worked by low-wage earners in,
    133–139, 135*t*, 141–142, 144*n*20
  lagged effect of National Minimum
    Wage in, 136, 144–145*n*22,
    144*n*21

meta-analysis on teenage employment
    response in, 150–151
minimum wage data since 2000
    analyzed from, 1, 15, 16, 329*t*,
    334, 335*t*
minimum wage established in, 227–
    229, 256*n*42, 390
NMWR studies in, 78, 80*t*–81*t*,
    85–86, 94*t*, 96–97, 99–102, 100*t*,
    115*nn*64–65, 116*nn*66–67,
    116*nn*70–72, 209*t*, 394*t*, 395–396
restaurant prices in, 384*t*, 391–392,
    399*n*9
spillover effect of minimum wage on
    specific industries and occupations
    in, 241*t*–244*t*, 247–249, 257*nn*56–
    57
wage distribution in, 228, 228*f*
United States
  labor laws in, 205, 290, 299*n*42, 411
  labor participation studies in, 369*t*,
    372*t*–373*t*, 378*t*
  meta-analysis on teenage employment
    response in, 149–151, 167, 170,
    172–173, 176, 178
  NMWR studies in, 32–77, 120–131,
    152*t*–153*t*, 202*t*–203*t*, 206*t*–207*t*,
    209*t*, 384*t*, 394*t*
  right-to-work states in, 219, 222, 251
  schooling and minimum wage studies
    in, 264*t*–266*t*, 267*t*, 333
  spillover effect of minimum wage in
    specific industries and occupations
    in, 240*t*–243*t*, 245–247, 256*n*52,
    257*nn*51–54
  as statistical variable in meta-
    analysis, 165, 166–167, 168*t*,
    170–173, 173*t*, 174–176, 174*t*–175*t*
  studies of minimum wage and poverty
    in, 313, 316–317, 318*t*–320*t*, 321,
    322*t*
  wage inequality in, 303, 304*t*–305*t* ,
    306–308
  See also specific states or regions,
    e.g., California; New England
    states

Utah, low-family incomes in, 8*t,* 9

Wage distribution, 186–211, 187*t,* 189*t,*
190*t,* 252*nn*7–10, 360–361,
363*n*22
2006–2010 period and, 192–211,
193*f,* 195*f,* 197*f,* 252*nn*11–12,
253*n*13
changes in firms', and spillover
issues, 245, 399*n*7
effect of minimum wage decline on,
303, 304*t*–305*t,* 306, 337*n*2, 370,
380*n*6
effect of minimum wage increase on,
2, 153*t,* 302, 387, 401, 404
inequality and, 301–308, 337*n*3,
381*n*12, 404
teenagers and, 201–204, 202*t,* 253–
254*nn*23–25, 253*n*22, 355
in U.K., 228, 228*f,* 305*t,* 308, 338*n*4,
404–405
Wage equations, productivity and, 227,
251, 255*n*39
Wage gap, 255*n*36, 256*n*45
college-high school and, 305*t,* 307
hours worked in U.K. and, 136–138,
139, 145*nn*23–24
measure of, as minimum wage
variable, 22, 75, 82–84, 86, 96,
233*t,* 234–236, 256*n*43, 304*t*–305*t*
Wage growth
factors affecting, 326–331, 330*t,*
333–337, 335*t*
training of women and, 282, 297*n*24
Wage inequality
Canada and, 304*t,* 306–307
minimum wage impact on, 16, 250,
320, 336
U.S. and, 303, 304*t*–305*t*, 306, 307–
308
Wage models, efficiency in, 344, 348–
349
Wage rate
definition of, 184, 256*n*41
poverty level and, 321, 338*n*10
use of, 252*n*7, 252*n*11

Wages, 295*n*3
average, 197–200, 250, 253*nn*14–16
definitions of, 184, 251*n*2, 374–375,
381*n*13, 422
effect of minimum wage increase
on average, 185–186, 199–201,
251, 252*nn*3–6, 253*nn*17–21
equations for, 74, 91–92, 115*n*62,
129, 227, 251, 255*n*39
minimum wage effect on, 1, 15–16,
183–185, 202*t*–203*t,* 206*t*–207*t,*
209*t,* 251
satisfactory, as benchmark, 6, 17*n*3
See also Low-wage workers; Wage
distribution
Wales, 255*n*35
agricultural workers in, 224*t,* 227,
255–256*n*40
small firms and minimum wage
increase, 394*t,* 395–396
Wascher, William
critiques of others' work by, 25, 27
as influential coauthor, 22–24, 109*n*5,
110*n*9, 122, 127
Washington (State), 109*n*4
hospitality industry jobs in, 63*t,* 68,
378*t*
Welfare benefits, minimum wage and,
316, 318*t*–319*t*
West Virginia, as low-wage area, 152*t*
White-collar workers, wages for, *vs.*
blue-collar, 239, 256*n*50
Whites in labor force, 206*t*
employment of youth as, 42, 45, 123
Wisconsin, service industry response to
minimum wage in, 394*t,* 397
Women in labor force
education and, 93, 203*t,* 204–205,
403
hours worked in U.K., 134–139, 135*t,*
142
low-wage, and job skills, 2, 94*t*–95*t,*
403
married, 78, 94*t,* 97–98, 324*t*
part-time, 85, 134–139, 135*t,* 145*n*26

Women in labor force, *cont.*
  recent studies of, 152*t,* 373*t,* 379,
    380*n*7
  wage growth of, 282, 297*n*24, 333
  wage inequality and, 16, 250
  See also Single mothers

Youth in labor force, 43
  as bound workers, 80*t*–81*t,* 115*n*64
  definitions and studies of, in non-U.S.
    developed countries, 80*t*–81*t*
  effect of minimum wage on, 15, 21,
    51, 79–93, 114–115*n*54, 115*nn*55–
    62
  hours worked by, 120–124, 131–133,
    142
  individual-level data studies, 38–47,
    40*t*–41*t*
  metaregression of wait-staff, and
    their workplaces, 156, 156*f,* 171–
    176, 173*t,* 174*t*–175*t,* 182*nn*20–21
  poverty and minimum wage of, 317,
    320*t,* 321
  schooling and minimum wage for,
    264*t*–266*t,* 270–272, 333
  studies using aggregate panel data,
    32–38, 34*t*–35*t*
  U.S. studies of, 32–51, 34*t*–35*t,*
    40*t*–41*t,* 48*t*–49*t,* 120–131, 369*t,*
    372*t,* 379
  See also Teenage employment

About the Institute

The W.E. Upjohn Institute for Employment Research is a nonprofit research organization devoted to finding and promoting solutions to employment-related problems at the national, state, and local levels. It is an activity of the W.E. Upjohn Unemployment Trustee Corporation, which was established in 1932 to administer a fund set aside by Dr. W.E. Upjohn, founder of The Upjohn Company, to seek ways to counteract the loss of employment income during economic downturns.

The Institute is funded largely by income from the W.E. Upjohn Unemployment Trust, supplemented by outside grants, contracts, and sales of publications. Activities of the Institute comprise the following elements: 1) a research program conducted by a resident staff of professional social scientists; 2) a competitive grant program, which expands and complements the internal research program by providing financial support to researchers outside the Institute; 3) a publications program, which provides the major vehicle for disseminating the research of staff and grantees, as well as other selected works in the field; and 4) an Employment Management Services division, which manages most of the publicly funded employment and training programs in the local area.

The broad objectives of the Institute's research, grant, and publication programs are to 1) promote scholarship and experimentation on issues of public and private employment and unemployment policy, and 2) make knowledge and scholarship relevant and useful to policymakers in their pursuit of solutions to employment and unemployment problems.

Current areas of concentration for these programs include causes, consequences, and measures to alleviate unemployment; social insurance and income maintenance programs; compensation; workforce quality; work arrangements; family labor issues; labor-management relations; and regional economic development and local labor markets.